THE GOVERNANCE OF PROBLEMS

Puzzling, powering, participation

Robert Hoppe

First published in Great Britain in 2011 by

Policy Press
University of Bristol
1-9 Old Park Hill
Bristol BS2 8BB
UK
t: +44 (0)117 954 5940
pp-info@bristol.ac.uk
www.policypress.co.uk

North America office:
Policy Press
c/o The University of Chicago Press
1427 East 60th Street
Chicago, IL 60637, USA
t: +1 773 702 7700
f: +1 773-702-9756
sales@press.uchicago.edu
www.press.uchicago.edu

© Policy Press 2011
Reprinted 2013, 2014, 2015

British Library Cataloguing in Publication Data
A catalogue record for this book is available from the British Library.

Library of Congress Cataloging-in-Publication Data
A catalog record for this book has been requested.

ISBN 978-1-84742-962-9 paperback

Cover design by Policy Press
Front cover: image kindly supplied by Eva Heinsbroek
Printed and bound in Great Britain by www.4edge.co.uk

I dedicate this book to my father, Frits Hoppe,
who devoted his life to understanding and, where possible,
alleviating the problems of many others.

Contents

List of boxes, figures and tables

Boxes

Figures

Tables

About the author

After affiliations to Radboud University Nijmegen (1972-74), the Free University Amsterdam (1974-86), the University of Amsterdam (1986-97), and Rutgers University (1992-93), Robert Hoppe presently is Professor of Knowledge and Policy at the University of Twente, where he also directs the Public Administration curriculum and Policy Studies courses for European Studies, Health Sciences and Civil Engineering, and the Governance of Knowledge and Innovation Graduate Programme.

Next to articles in journals such as *Knowledge & Policy*, *Science and Public Policy*, *Poièsis and Praxis*, *Administrative Theory & Praxis*, *Journal of Comparative Policy Analysis*, *Organisation & Environment*, *International Review of Public Administration*, *Policy & Politics*, *Creativity and Innovation Management*, *Acta Politica*, *Beleidswetenschap*, *Beleid en Maatschappij*, *Bestuurskunde* and *Bestuurswetenschappen*, his book publications (in English) include *Handling frozen fire. Political culture and risk management* (with Aat Peterse) (Westview Press, Boulder, 1993), *Technology assessment through interaction. A guide* (Rathenau Institute, The Hague, 1997), 'Pollution through traffic and transport: the praxis of cultural pluralism in parliamentarian technology assessment' (with John Grin) in Michael Thompson et al (eds) *Cultural theory as political science*, Routledge, London, 1999), and he is co-editor of *Knowledge, power, and participation in environmental policy analysis* (*Policy Studies Review Annual*, Volume 10, Transaction Publishers, New Brunswick, 2001), and *Working for policy* (submitted to Amsterdam University Press, 2010).

Hoppe's fields of interest are long-term policy dynamics and innovation, especially the role of technology; the methodological and institutional implications of deliberative and participatory policy analysis and technology assessment; the governance of expertise; and the applications of Q Method.

Preface

The idea for this book emerged gradually. In 1989, in my inaugural address at the University of Amsterdam, I made the case for a less solution-oriented and relatively more problem-oriented approach in the discipline of public administration. I introduced the problem typology, which also organises this book; and on this basis proposed a more problem-oriented heuristic for policy design by arguing from problem sensing through problem definition to problem solving.

Two decades and many publications later, these seminal ideas have worked their way into the discourse, and some of the practice for policy making in the Dutch public sector. For example, the problem typology and its implications for practical policy making were spelled out in guidelines for interactive technology assessment, published in 1997 by the Rathenau Institute (Grin, Van de Graaf and Hoppe, 1997). Later, the problem types were included as a tool for policy/risk analysis in the Dutch Institute for Public Health and the Environment (RIVM) and the (then) Environment and Nature Assessment Agency's (MNP) (2003) joint *Guidance for uncertainty assessment and communication* (van der Sluijs et al, 2003). More recently, the problem typology and the notion of more problem-oriented policy making organises and informs the Scientific Council for Government Policy's advice entitled *Learning government. The case for problem-oriented politics* (*Lerende overheid: Een pleidooi voor probleemgerichte politiek*) (WRR, 2006).

It was only logical, then, to think that it might be useful to put all my major, single- as well as co-authored, publications on this theme between the covers of one book. A research leave grant by the Dutch Organisation for Scientific Research (NWO) 'Shifts in Governance' research programme offered the opportunity to start writing; a subsequent sabbatical leave granted me the time to finish a first draft.[1] Although the title *The governance of problems* was in my mind from the very beginning, only while writing it did it dawn on me that doing the concept full justice implied much more than just updating earlier publications and writing some new connecting texts. Thus, from a mere rearrangement of previous publications, the book evolved into its present shape: a sustained reflection on the Lasswellian idea of a problem-oriented policy analysis adapted to governance for the 21st century; and a policy analysis adapted to today's vastly more complex practices of boundary work between science, society, policy and politics. Policy analysis just can no longer pretend to 'speak truth to power', yet, more modestly, may still facilitate policy making as 'making sense together'.

Thus, new chapters had to be written; and the rearrangement and updating of earlier work was to become much more encompassing than originally envisioned. I could never have done and completed this without explicit or tacit dialogues with many others: former teachers, inspiring peers, examples, opponents, alive or deceased; and colleagues and students who brought fresh insights, who thought along with, or resisted, my arguments; and some who had the generosity to read drafts of chapters and sometimes the whole book. I owe them all a great debt.

Here I mention only the most important and clearly remembered ones in alphabetical order: Marjolein van Asselt, Hal Colebatch, William Dunn, Frank Fischer, John Forester, Henk van de Graaf, John Grin, Willem Halffman, the late Oscar van Heffen, Matthijs Hisschemöller, Andries Hoogerwerf, Thomas Hoppe, Margarita Jeliazkova, Toon Kerkhoff, Pieter-Jan Klok, Arno Korsten, Stefan Kuhlmann, Gijs Kuypers, Anne Loeber, Kris Lulofs, Duncan MacRae Jr, Aat Peterse, Marty Rein, Jan Rotmans, Arie Rip, Paul Sabatier, the late Donald Schön, the late Petra Schreurs, Ig Snellen, Arco Timmermans, Michael Thompson, Arnošt Vesely, Anne Wesselink, Céleste Wilderom and the late Aaron Wildavsky.

Finally, the tangible aspects of book production would not have been realised so smoothly without the perseverance and other contributions of my editor at The Policy Press, Emily Watt; and the editorial precision and speed of my secretary, Evelien Rietberg. I thank them for their humble but essential services.

Rob Hoppe
Enschede
October 2009

Note

[1] Research for this book was financially supported by a research leave grant (number 814-42204) from the Dutch Organisation for Scientific Research (NWO), Social and Behavioral Sciences Section, the 'Shifts in Governance' programme; and a sabbatical leave from the University of Twente, Faculty of Management and Governance.

ONE

A problem-processing perspective on governance

Governance of problems

People as problem processors

People are problem-processing animals. Not that we are all worrywarts, of course. But people do tend to be concerned about conditions they feel uneasy about. They brood over situations they experience as uncomfortable or troublesome, especially if they see no obvious way out. One might call this the substantive logic of problem processing: experiencing an uncomfortable situation, diagnosing the nature of the problem and figuring out what to do to solve, or at least, alleviate the problem. Most problems have a personal character; they concern people as problem owners, their families, relatives, friends, colleagues, fellow members of sports clubs and the like. How people solve problems usually remains their own business. Why bother about others, as long as satisfactory solutions can be figured out and acted on by yourself and other known people in your own household, or social circles or communities? But some of these apparently small problems may come to be seen as problems of larger scope. If your occasional backache turns out to be a serious threat to your capacity to work and earn a decent income, it helps to have a public or private health insurance system and a well-organised healthcare system.

In mobilising assistance in problem processing beyond the scope of family, household and community, people have access to two such larger systems. One is the market system, which organises and coordinates assistance through the transactions between people as buyers and sellers. The other is politics and the state, which organises and coordinates assistance through the use of multiple forms of governance that mix voluntary and compulsory forms of mutual adjustment between citizens, proximate policy makers and political decision makers. This book focuses on the latter system. But the mere use of the term 'governance' implies that the other forms of social coordination are far from neglected. In other words, next to a substantive logic, problem processing also has an institutional logic. For us, ordinary people, usually the substantive or provision logic is more important than the institutional logic. Yet, as will become clear throughout the rest of this book, the governance of problems at the political level entails that '(d)etermining the domain for market, state, family, enterprise, and civil society

... is a serious task for every society, not to be disposed of by all-too-common dogma' (Lindblom, 2001: 107).

This is because some problems cannot be seriously tackled without forms of collective action. This means, for example, that people have to enter politics in the governance of their personal problems. If speeding cars in front of your house endanger your children, it helps to mobilise not just the neighbours to help you wave at cars to lower their speed. At least, you can make them sign a petition to your local government. Better still, you may enlist support from a local political party for a speed limit or some physical speed inhibitors or 'sleeping policemen' in your street.

People expect responsive governance

Turning to politics or government for help in solving citizens' problems is quite a step. For one, they are not sure whether their claims are acknowledged as serious enough to merit state action. Of course, politics is a competition for recognition of different problem claims. In one sense, politics provokes antagonism and competition for recognition of rivalling claims and proposals of responding to adversity. Yet, once there is some agreement and mutual adjustment of claims among people, politics also provokes synergy and collaboration: '[governments] are instruments for vast tasks of social cooperation' (Lindblom, 1968: 32; Dauenhauer, 1986: 64-5). In that sense, their help could be of decisive importance.

It is fashionable these days to argue that the pincer movement of privatisation and globalisation has diminished the powers of government. Indeed, downwards, through decentralisation, national government has voluntarily ceded power to local, regional and nongovernmental governance bodies; and, upwards, through globally increased market interdependencies, it has been forced to share power with international or transnational governance bodies and multinational corporations. Therefore, national governments no longer hold an undisputed monopoly as one-and-only site for defining the common interest. They are no longer the only site to turn to in the allocation of public values through policy preparation, implementation and service delivery (Bovens et al, 1995; Anderson, 2003: 4, 104ff).

Yet, in spite of their weakened monopoly, governments are still unique players in the public domain. The public powers vested in states remain indispensable resources for collective action for all other 'partners' in governance; especially legitimacy and authority, backed up by all sorts of constitutions, laws, taxation, and use of coercion through physical force. If people in their capacity as citizens can harness such state powers in their interests, their scope of collective action is substantially broadened and enhanced (Bogason, 2000: 5-6, 29ff). This applies as well to those highly influential citizens who normally decry and protest state influence most – the entrepreneurs (Lindblom, 1977, 2001). People therefore start pressing their public problems on governments as legitimate concerns or claims for public action. After all, they expect their governments and public sectors to respond to their real collective needs; and do so legitimately, timely, effectively and in a reasonably efficient way.

To use an expression of former UK Prime Minister Tony Blair, people expect government to be organised around *their* problems. The emergence and institutionalisation of the welfare state and its administrative apparatus, including the omnipresence of its continuing reforms, is testimony to both the persistence and the success of this claim. In an influential report entitled *Modernising government*, the British government declares:

> Modernisation ... must be for a purpose: to create better government to make life better for people ... modernisation of government (must) be a means to achieving better government, better policymaking, better responsiveness to what people want, better public services. People want government which meets their needs, which is available when they need it, and which delivers results for them. People want effective government, both where it responds directly to their needs, such as in healthcare, education and social services and where it acts for society as a whole, such as protecting the environment, promoting public health and maintaining our prison and immigration services and defense capability. (Cabinet Office, 1999: para 1.2)

Yet, the straightforward and apparently self-evident expectation of responsive governance is deeply problematic. One may even claim that the very demand for 'organising government around citizens' problems' at the same time elicits all the 'problems around government'. American political scientist Schattschneider (1960 [1988]: 134-5, emphasis added), speaking about the US in the 1950s, already signalled the problem:

> People are able to survive in the modern world by learning to distinguish between what they must know and what they do not need to know.... Our survival depends on our ability to judge things by their results and our ability to establish relations of confidence and responsibility so that we can take advantage of what other people know.... *Democracy is like nearly everything else we do; it is a form of collaboration of ignorant people and experts.* The problem is not how 180 million Aristotles can run a democracy, but how we can organize a political community of 180 million ordinary people *so that it remains sensitive to their needs.*

Democratic politics as governance of problems

Responsive governance appeals to our elementary notion of democratic politics. The political system is like a chain connecting the needs, desires and political demands of citizens to public policies that (1) allocate valuable goods, services or performances in society; and (2) manage to induce most members of society to accept such allocations as binding (Easton, 1965: 22-24; Thomassen, 1991: 26). The chain is made up of many intermediary links. Social movements, interest groups and even journalists interpret and articulate citizens' worries as issues for public debate and political decisions. Political parties attempt to reflect such issues in party platforms designed to attract as many citizens/voters as possible. Voted into power and supported by majorities of elected politicians in Parliament, governments take policy decisions; bureaucratic policy staff and science-based experts help governments translate problems into actionable policies and programmes, ready for implementation in the networks of public, nongovernmental and private organisations responsible for the delivery of goods, services and performances to citizens.

Responsive democratic governance vitally depends on practices of debate, interrogation and dialogue. In democratic politics, the ruled or citizens as 'distant' policy makers have definite rights and possibilities to question the rulers or proximate policy makers and political authorities. Vice versa, rulers have rights, but also privileges and plenty of opportunities to influence the questions posed by the ruled. They open up debate around certain questions or keep such problems off the agenda. Similarly, they open up debate around particular answers as problem solutions or close down such debates. Governance of problems is not only about problems or topics to be discussed; it also concerns quality controls and the allowance or disallowance of information, procedural and competence rules for who can and cannot participate in the question-and-answer game. In short, rulers and ruled in interaction and political struggle implicitly or explicitly decide on who, on behalf of whom, may question/answer what, when and how. Rulers and ruled make use of an 'ensemble' of institutions, beliefs, practices and rules around the question–answer game of democratic politics. Jointly, I propose to call their engagement with this ensemble, the way it is used by rulers and ruled, the *governance of problems.*

The system is democratic and responsive if a majority of citizens feels satisfied with the problem-processing chain's final link – policy outputs. Or, if they are not happy, at least they can live with them as legitimate outputs of the question-and-answer process. But satisfaction and legitimacy are far from self-evident, for two reasons. First, from a cognitive or rational point of view, questioning or problem finding, posing the right questions, does not nearly get the attention devoted to providing the right answers, or problem solving. (This is the major theme of Chapter Two.) Second, from the point of view of a political division of labour, the cognitive rift between answering and questioning is exacerbated by the inevitable cleavage between rulers and ruled. The intermediaries between citizens as questioners and public authorities or decision makers as answer-givers are not neutral messengers. They inevitably frame citizen needs and demands according to interests, frames of reference, and role conceptions of their own. (This is the major theme of Chapters Three and Four.)

Jointly these two reasons give rise to the possibility, if not the frequent experience and common expectation, of a structural mismatch between problem perception and definition by larger segments of the citizenry and their proximate policy makers and administrators. Perhaps worse, democratic governance systems may lose viability due to insufficient attention to quality maintenance of the question-and-answer game between rulers and ruled. (This will be more extensively argued in Chapter Two.) There are many examples: the US government's false 'intelligence' about weapons of mass destruction in Iraq as a pretext to sending troops into the Middle-East; the Australian government's equally untrue election story about children thrown overboard by asylum seekers to force a naval ship to rescue them and thereby enter Australia; the Dutch electorate's failure until very recently to force their government to give reasons for involvement in the Iraq war; let alone the public's own role in the financial and economic crisis since 2007. With Nick Turnbull one may observe:

> [O]ur problem today is perhaps that there is not enough questioning. This applies to all sides of policy debates.... In many cases, political elites continue to suppress questioning, direct it in ways that serve entrenched interests, or dissuade others from introducing new problems. And while policy regimes have failed to respond to some public demands, the public itself continues to look the other way in the face of important questions. (Turnbull, 2005: 222; also 389, note 59)

The need for more reflexive[1] problem structuring

The threat of a structural mismatch between problem finding and problem solving in our governance systems should be taken seriously. It may lead to an infarct of the question-and-answer game, which is the heart of democratic governance. Many examples will be adduced in the rest of this book. Its major thesis and message is that in order to maintain a sufficiently responsive system for the governance of problems, contemporary democracies ought to develop more reflexive institutions and practices of substantive, or *policy*-oriented and institutional, or *polity-* or, more broadly, *governance*-oriented problem structuring. Problem structuring refers to the search, debate, evaluation and political struggle about competing problem representations and framings. Problem structuring, whether as analytic or political process, is an intermediary but vital step on the way to authoritative policy problem definition and political choice of policy designs. Citizens have come to dislike the imposition of the welfare-cum-administrative state's well-ordered, but professionally and bureaucratically pre-structured problem frames and top-down rule, however effective and efficient in their own terms. They rather want their governments to develop the skills and institutions to prudently and democratically transform their experiences of problematic situations and their ways of framing problem representations in truly intersubjective but authoritative public definitions of policy problems. Simultaneously, citizens ought to become better, more critical questioners themselves (Lindblom, 1990; Turnbull, 2005). *Better governance implies political sensitivity to different types of problems; and more and better reflexive problem structuring through better institutional, interactive and deliberative designs for public debate and political choice.*

Approach

This book takes a multidisciplinary, interdisciplinary and conceptual as well as pragmatic approach. It is multidisciplinary in that it approaches its subject – *problem processing in governance systems* – from a political science (powering, participation), a policy analytic (puzzling) and a generic social science (governance) perspective. It is interdisciplinary in that puzzling, powering and participation are consistently analysed from a unifying social-constructivist perspective on problem structuring in political task environments. This brings together and organises many insights from political science, public administration, the sociology of problems, decision sciences, organisation studies and policy studies in novel ways. Particularly for policy studies and policy analysis, the governance of problems approach is a necessary update and revitalisation of the discipline's problem orientation (also Turnbull, 2005). Proposed as the hallmark of policy analysis in an age of high modernism by Lerner and Lasswell in the 1950s (Lerner and Lasswell, 1951), a problem-oriented policy analysis badly needs redefinition for 21st-century governance. The governance of problems approach transcends the traditional stages- or phase-model; and adds new dynamics as well as the idea of meta-governance to the widely accepted network models of policy making. (This is the topic of Chapters Six and Nine.) The governance of problems approach avoids the high expectations of (social) science as problem solver *par excellence* so typical for policy analysis and policy science under the high modernism of the 1950s and 1960s. Under the 21st-century conditions of a Mode-2, or post-normal, science, the relationship between policy and science has changed, too. (This topic is addressed in Chapter Seven.) The governance of problems approach to policy analysis is pragmatic in that it shows how major conceptual and theoretical issues can be applied to the pragmatics of policy design and to the running of experiments in mini-public deliberative policy analysis (in Chapter Nine). The idea that political life can be studied as a strategic undertaking around the governance of problems, as problem framing and solving, also picks up (in Chapters Five, Eight and Ten) the original themes of empirical decision-making theory, that is, how to take better account of the small brain/complex environment situation, the relation between puzzling (cognition) and powering (interaction), and how to better exploit the intelligence of democracy for policy-oriented and social learning.

This introduction to the governance of problems as the topic of this book is, of course, just a set of preliminary statements and judgments, which needs persuasiveness through evidence and argument. Providing these will be my task in the other chapters. The rest of this chapter is devoted to explicating some key

assumptions and concepts underlying the structure of my argument. At the end
of the chapter, the plan of the book is set out.

Puzzling and powering

Man as 'homo respondens' and politics as puzzling

One may not expect to understand politics and governance without any
understanding of individual man. Hence, an author should explicate his image
of man (Moon, 1975: 192). This is all the more important where in the social
sciences rational choice has become the dominant perspective; and even where
claims of comprehensive rationality are rejected in favour of bounded rationality,
the image of man is limited to cognitive or rational aspects. Instead of reducing
the image of man to variations of 'homo cogitans', we need more holistic images
of man, which include, for example, emotions, sociality, and attitude to the human
condition as such.

I believe that the best short expression of the nature of man in this broader
sense is to be found in the philosophical anthropology of an international cast of
(political) philosophers like Karl Jaspers, Hannah Arendt, Maurice Merleau-Ponty,
Paul Ricoeur, Bertrand de Jouvenel, Peter Sederberg and Bernhard Dauenhauer.
They would all typify man as a speaker, as living in and through discourse, first;
but, given that, foremost as '*homo respondens*'. Let me quote German philosopher
Karl Jaspers (1981: 55):

> Among all life forms only man is aware of his finitude. As undefinitive
> and imperfectable being ('Unvollendbarkeit') this finitude means more
> than a mere awareness of his condition. Man has a sense of loss, from
> which spring both a moral duty and a possibility. Man finds himself
> in a completely hopeless situation, but in such a way that, through his
> freedom, there is the strongest possible appeal to (self)development
> ('Aufschwung'). [translation by RH]

Awareness of his own finitude condemns man to *freedom*, as it were. Having been
thrown into this life, man is forced to find an answer to the exigencies, challenges
and possibilities of the human condition. But his freedom in choice of answer
simultaneously constitutes his *responsibility*. Each answer, however personal and
unique, goes beyond his individual self as act with consequences for the Other –
be it the objective Other of things in the world, or the subjective Other of fellow
human beings. Thus, man is free; but it is a freedom-in-responsibility. That is why
man is a 'homo respondens': free to answer, but also answerable to the objective
and subjective Other (also Dauenhauer, 1986: 80).

In this image of man, politics comes naturally to human beings. It is the social
space where man's words and deeds are shared, and where his actions gain durability
and responsibility by being remembered (Arendt, 1958: 177). In the political

sphere, man gives accounts of his thinking and acting; he becomes accountable to others, answers their questions about his acts, and thereby discovers and continually shapes and reshapes his own identity. In this precise sense, politics is grounded in questioning and answering:

> Political activity is responsible precisely to the extent that it fosters and maintains an open dialectic among men. ... man's speaking, and indeed his entire way of being, is interrogatory. (Dauenhauer, 1986: 43)

As I will argue in Chapter Two, to the extent that policy making is a political activity, it is a dialectical and interrogative process of making sense and giving meaning to the adversities and opportunities in the situation of a political collectivity.

Man as unity-in-disharmony and politics as powering

On the one hand, man is a respondent; on the other, he is also *unity-in-disharmony*. Jaspers (1960: 147) expresses the idea in the following way:

> Man is always more than he knows of himself. He is not what he is at a particular juncture in time or what he aims for; he is *'en route'*.... That is why man is essentially a broken creature. Whatever he thinks about himself, in thinking he contrasts himself to himself and others. Everything appears to him as difference. This is equally true when he distinguishes between his being and his appearance, between his thinking and his acting, or between his actions and his intentions.... The decisive fact is that man is forced to contrast himself to others and other things. Being human means being torn between opposites. But he cannot remain in this alienated state. How he conquers his internal disharmony is what makes him as a person. [translation by RH]

Being unity-in-disharmony is what condemns man to be a problem processor. After all, problems are disharmonies that people try to conquer – disharmonies in his own experience of a discomforting present and images of more desirable future conditions; disharmonies between his problems and those of others; disharmonies between his ways of solving problems and those of others. The disharmony penetrates politics and policy making as the struggle over truly 'wicked' problems. Political and policy-making processes are fraught with conflicting interests, radically divergent problem framings, competing alternative problem solutions, and highly uncertain outcomes. Problems are 'wicked' 'in a meaning akin to that of "malignant" (in contrast to "benign") or "vicious" (like a circle) or "tricky" (like a leprechaun) or "aggressive" (like a lion, in contrast to the docility of a lamb)' (Rittel and Webber, 1973: 160). They are 'wicked' because:

[T]he problems that planners must deal with are … incorrigible ones, for they defy efforts to delineate their boundaries and to identify their causes, and thus to expose their problematic nature. The planner who works with open systems is caught up in the ambiguity of their causal webs. Moreover, his would-be solutions are confounded by a still further set of dilemmas posed by the growing pluralism of the contemporary publics, whose valuations of his proposals are judged against an array of different and contradicting scales. (Rittel and Webber, 1973: 167)

'Domesticating' wicked problems means structuring them, by leaving out of consideration certain aspects or dimensions of the problem as originally manifesting itself. It means that 'wicked' problems are never solved in the sense of satisfactorily dealing with and meeting every term of the problem. In 'wicked' problems some terms are only partially met; some not at all. That is why wicked problems can only be settled, never solved. And because they are only settled, some people sooner or later may want to open debate or re-engage in contestation about the unsolved or only partially solved problem parts. This makes wicked problems returning 'monsters' for politics and policy making.

The disharmony even penetrates to the image of politics itself. Politics' beautiful face is puzzling on collective's behalf. Yet, it does not always manifest itself as peaceful dialogue, debate and mutual consultation about essentially shared projects in some idyllic city-state or 'polis'. Politics has its ugly face, too. It is about powering; a contest of contradictory wills and visions, a race for power and influence; it may stop short of outright violence, but legitimate and not-so-legitimate use of instigation and coercion is all in the political game. In analysing politics and policy making as governance of problems, the tension between puzzling and powering, between reason and will, between argumentation and instigation is a major theme. Reason tries to find discursive closure in debates over policy problems on the sole basis of the strength of the best argument; therefore, it grants science and scientific policy analysis a strong voice in the governance of problems. In contrast, political will strives for nondiscursive closure, either through amicable or forcible instigation, that is, 'sparking off contributory actions' (De Jouvenel, 1963: 8), or through the complicated arithmetic of interests and volitions in voting and negotiation, or through the use of legal authority and legitimate coercion. In the governance of problems as powering, ruling proximate and authoritative policy makers use problem framings and definitions to mobilise political support. Science and policy analysis deliver the argumentative ammunition for them and their political opponents.

Puzzling and powering, then, are different, even diverging logics in the governance of problems. The distinction is an important theme in the composition of the book. Chapters Four through Six discuss how policy makers use the governance of problems to define the scope and composition of policy networks as the political theatre or arena for policy making. Also, they create a division of labour between audience and players, and a cast of different sorts of players with differential powers and competencies.

Chapters Two and Three are devoted to policy analysis as puzzling. Chapter Seven is about scientific epistemologies' influence on academic policy analysis; and its contrast to policy analysis doable in the world of politics and administration.

The governance of problems, though, has a third pillar next to puzzling and powering. One cannot puzzle or power without participation in the game of question-and-answer that is policy making.

Governance as a quest for political participation and institutional alignment

Just a fashion-word?

'Governance' is the fashion-word in politics and the social sciences. Its etymological roots date back to the Greek verb *kubernein* (in at least the beginning of the first millennium BC): steering a vessel or chariot. Plato was the first to use it in a metaphorical sense for the steering or government of people. From the Greek, the verb found its way into Latin, and from there to French, English, Spanish and Portuguese as a generic label for 'government of people'. Thus, it is perhaps the oldest and most generic word for any activity or process of deliberately using power in order to coordinate sizeable groups of people's performances to bring about desirable aggregate results and avoidance of risk and undesirable outcomes.[2]

Thus, strictly speaking, 'governance' designates almost any effort to deliberately influence one group of people on behalf of some other group. One may legitimately wonder what analytical purchase there is in turning to such a hypergeneric concept. The answer is that in the course of history, 'governance' acquired specific, time, place and actor bound connotations that were decisive for its use or disuse: 'Governance is constructed by the questions asked' (Rhodes, 2000: 67). For example, in some of the countries mentioned, the term lost popularity in the 17th to 18th centuries because it was tainted too much by the *Anciens Régimes* of absolute monarchy. 'Governing', for the process or activity, or 'government', for the institutions or set of political and administrative apparatus of the state, became the almost universally preferred term in the 19th century and most of the 20th century. Yet, in the 1990s, 'governance' was to make a glorious and international comeback. So, if 'governance' was the answer, what were the questions?

State penetration of life-worlds

'Governance' once was dismissed because of its too close links with an oppressive absolute monarchy. Paradoxically, in our days the rejection of 'government' in favour of 'governance' is to be found in questions about the overwhelming power of the modern state. In his *The history of government*, Sam Finer observes how only during the past two centuries of its 5,200 years of known history, government became unremittingly intrusive into the homes, occupations and daily lives of citizens (Finer, 1999: 1624, 1610–11). Extension of the franchise and the partition of the state into three more or less independent but overlapping legislative, judicial and executive powers did nothing to hamper the growth of government's ability to act directly, by its own agents, upon the population and its behaviour through surveillance, control and direction. Jürgen Habermas (1981) analysed the power of the state as one important manifestation of the colonisation of the citizen's life-world. Even when in the age of welfarism (in domestic politics) and development aid (abroad) the political intention was to improve the human condition, states increased their central control, imposed their own standards on citizens' lives and, generally, tried to make the lives of citizens as legible and transparent as possible to state surveillance (Scott, 1998). Anthony Giddens (1985: 309, emphasis added), too, observes:

> Administrative power now increasingly enters into the minutiae of daily life and the most intimate of personal actions and relationships. … the possibilities of accumulating information relevant to the practice of government are almost endless. Control of information … can be directly integrated with the supervision of conduct in such a way as to produce a high concentration of state power. Surveillance is a necessary condition of the administration of states, whatever end this power be turned to. It is not only connected with polyarchy but more specifically with the actualization of citizen rights. *The provision of welfare cannot be organized or funded unless there is a close and detailed monitoring of the life of the population, regardless of whether they are actually welfare recipients or not….*

So, the first question that drives the quest for 'governance' is the state's intrusiveness. This question has a logical counterpart: is a 'state-less' society possible?

Retreat to the market, and the idea of a self-regulatory society

Where ever-increasing state discipline was questioned, the freedom and autonomy of citizens were celebrated as ideals. All the more so since a democratic state was said to emerge from some sort of 'social contract' between free citizens, which in the form of a state would subsequently further the interests of citizens as free and emancipated individuals. Politically, this idea was operationalised as the ever-widening expansion of the franchise, eventually effected through mass political parties. For the rest, the idea of the state as springing from a 'social pact' was pretty silent about how such a state would operate after the conclusion of the pact. Literally, the king as embodied 'head of state' was replaced by an idea, the artificial political construct of popular sovereignty, embodied in the elected members of a representative Parliament (legislative power). And because the Parliament was supposed to somehow represent all citizens, and the executive was controlled by Parliament, Parliaments were believed to express a unified, 'general will' of the people, as a kind of *deus ex machina* of democracy. In other words, democratic governments governed over a body of citizens constructed to be a unified, abstract and generalised mass: 'Generality can lead to a representation of society as a unified will because it is based on the possibility of abstracting from particular man' (Rosanvallon, 2006: 222). The only weak constraint on this generalised and abstract ruling was the judiciary branch. It was equally concerned with a generalisable idea of citizenship in designing a system of civil rights applicable to any individual citizen without exception. Yet, within this framework of generalisable legal constraints, it sometimes forced the state to take into account some particularities and differences between individual citizens – primarily in terms of property rights.

From the perspective of production and consumption of goods and services, the same idea of free and emancipated people appeared to be embodied in the emergence and fierce expansion of the market system as separate institutional domain for the coordination of the particular needs of individual men, however different among themselves. As convincingly argued by Pierre Rosanvallon (2006: 147-59), the political advocates of the free market system immediately attacked the social contract foundation of the state. Economic liberalism pictured the market system as politically superior to all other forms of social coordination. It constructed the market system as the ideal of the autonomy of individuals by depersonalising the social relationship; it is the archetype of an anti-hierarchical society, in which relations of passion, kin, violence or power no longer play a decisive role:

> The price system is the mechanism that fulfils this task [self-interested action that makes everyone better off, RH] without central direction, *without requiring people to speak to one another or to like one another....* Economic order can emerge as the *unintended* consequence of the actions of many people, each seeking his self interest. The price system works so well, so efficiently, that we are *not aware of it* most of the time (Friedman, quoted in Rosanvallon, 2006: 151-2, emphasis added)

In precisely this sense, economic liberalism gives expression to a profound aspiration of civil society as opposed to the state: the ideal of an entirely self-regulated or self-guided society.

In reality, of course, the market system was not just an inclusionary movement for all people as voluntary sellers and buyers. Rapid introduction of the market system in fact created the sharp social cleavage between the masses of the industrial proletariat and entrepreneurial or capitalist elite, ruling the masses in their corporations, characterised by Lindblom (2001) as 'islands of command in a sea of market'. This led, first, to the emergence of stronger and stronger workers' protective associations and political parties. Their ideal became the replacement of capitalism by socialism. The Marxist ideal of unhampered individual self-development and the withering away of the state, that is, the harmonious anarchy of communism as a substitution of the reign of men with the administration of things, clearly is the second historically important expression of the idea of a self-guiding society. So strong became this ideal, and this is the second historical development of importance, that during the First World War in Russia, and after the Second World War in large parts of Central and Eastern Europe, and in China and other parts of South-East Asia, states were founded that were devoted to the realisation of communism. Except for China, since the demise 'real socialist' states in the 1980s, we know that this experiment failed, leading some to declare the ultimate victory of the market system. In 2009, with a rampant crisis of financial capitalism spilling over to what is called the 'real economy', and in the face of an imminent ecological crisis, it is equally clear that the market system's superiority was announced too soon. This leads to a third set of questions making for the revival of 'governance'.

'Governance' as a response to complexity, variety and the threat of fragmentation

No doubt, a third theme in the revival of 'governance' is the sheer complexity and variety or fragmentation in governing a hypercomplex society facing economic and ecological crises. After the Second World War, at least in the nation states of Western Europe, and to a less extent the US, Canada, Australia and New Zealand, a different experiment took place: designing a welfare state that balanced workers' protection against the benefits of capitalism. After some five decades of experience, the result is a highly complex, variegated and intertwined system of 'governance'. The institutional orders of households, corporations, markets, civil society and the state appear to criss-cross each other in chaotic, hardly understandable but troublesome ways.

The power of corporations has grown to the extent that almost everybody now acknowledges that the privileged position of business interests in the political system downgrades its claim to be democratic; but this is accepted as the price for making the market system work as the generator of wealth for many people in these societies (Lindblom, 2001: 249). Under welfarism, the state has become a vast administrative apparatus, where the executive – and no longer Parliament – is the main source of social regulation or policy making; and with lots of delegated powers and competencies to non-elected bureaucrats (as the 'fourth branch' of government), in their turn assisted and advised by lots of equally non-elected experts (as the 'fifth branch').

Globalising markets have nevertheless nibbled away at the sovereignty of states to regulate their societies. The European Union in Europe, but also worldwide international regulatory bodies like the International Monetary Fund and the World Bank, to mention just these, are constraints on the sovereignty of states. Simultaneously, numerous governance arrangements, from well-known corporatist forms to more recent practices like negotiated rule-making with many civil society associations and organisations, also restrict state sovereignty. Pierre Rosanvallon (2006: 193-4) observes:

> [T]he growth of the self-organizing capacity of civil society stands out as the truly remarkable phenomenon. A complex system of interests and wills substituted for the former ideal type of *the* political will, a model that presupposes a unified actor.... The regulations did not disappear, but they lost their comprehensive scope and, above all, their legibility. Society has not stopped 'willing', but it has come to express its wishes in muted tones.... Civil society indeed has a 'politics', but a discreet and silent one, the result of a multitude of deliberations in low voices and discreet choices that are never openly tallied.

Thus, in debates on 'governance' the bewildering variety of ways in which governing occurs is a major theme. The focus is on the differential set of authorities, different from case to case, which seek to make people's behaviour governable; the very diverse strategies, technologies and instruments of governmentality that they use; and the conflicts between them and the way these conflicts are played out (Rose, 1990: 21). Historically, this process from government towards governance may be summarily sketched as a process away from hierarchy and elitism; moving towards more and more inclusive forms of individual interest-driven and social or solidarity-driven *participation in social coordination*.

If it is, nevertheless, useful to find a broadbrush, holistic term for designating change in these heterogeneous and potentially rivalling modes of mutual adjustment and deliberate coordination of human activities for collective purpose, '*governance*' (in keeping with its etymological roots) can be *defined* as a *hypercomplex socio-cybernetic system* (Kooiman, quoted in Pierre, 2000: 252):

In contrast to the state or the market, socio-political governance is directed at the creation of patterns of interaction in which political and traditional hierarchical governing and social self-organisation are complementary, in which responsibility and accountability for interventions are spread over public and private actors.

In other words, *governance is about efforts to align or bring about concerted action across multiple, competing institutional modes of social coordination for public purpose* (O'Toole, 2000: 278).

In a governance approach to policy making, two quests are visible and join each other. The first quest is for institutional alignment. It is a complementarity not predefined through ideology or policy paradigms. Rather, it is a complementarity discovered in and through policy practice, in social and policy-oriented experimental and learning processes (Helderman, 2007: 103-4; 254). In Chapters Two, Six and Nine, this thought will be elaborated in notions like institutional entrepreneurship, venue creation and interpolable balancing as institutional 'tinkering' from within the context of existing opportunities and constraints.

The second quest is about civic engagement or political participation by ordinary citizens and functionaries. Inspired by Charles Lindblom, another adherent of the self-guiding society (Lindblom, 1990: 213-30), the turn to governance may be considered the intellectual reflection of a general trend towards problem-specific, practical arrangements for social and political decision making as improved 'probing'. Improved probing means the continuous process of involving more citizens and lay persons or non-authorities and non-professionals in societal guidance. It means reaching beyond the state, the market and science as standing institutional arrangements for societal probing. Institutionally, governance means the mixing of different institutional arrangements (like state, markets, civil society and science) for the delegated probing of people's volitions in more optimal participatory and deliberative shapes or spaces of democratic governance. Ultimately, it rests on the recognition that wants, needs or preferences are webs of socially and politically created and recreated, never just 'discovered', volitions.

The issue is: who participates in this creation of volitions? Thus, the question of governance strongly implies the question: who participates in governance? In Chapters Four, Nine and Ten, questions of participation will figure prominently.

Implications for policy analysis

Governance of problems means problem structuring

Taking my cues from philosophical anthropological assumptions about the nature of man, I have depicted politics and policy making as puzzling and powering in efforts to domesticate problems of social coordination; problems that are, in principle, always 'wicked'. Domesticating a wicked problem means structuring it in such a way that it becomes fit for (partial) solutions, or settlements. I have also argued that such efforts may be fruitfully analysed as political question-and-answer games that require different modes of the *governance of problems*. Reflection on the meaning of governance in political and social science debates revealed deep-seated worries about institutional alignment among very different, potentially competing and clashing, but practically entwined modes of social coordination. This is an issue that ultimately boils down to questions of who participates, how elites control masses and, vice versa, how masses control elites.

In order to show the implications of a governance of problems and problem-structuring perspective for policy analysis, we need a conceptual map that contains 'problem structure' as a core variable. After all, it is imperative to show who poses what kinds of questions in policy discourse; and who came up with what kinds of answers; and how this question-and-answer process, this dialogue between problem finding and problem solving, moved policy debate on (or not) towards an authoritatively structured problem, as a basis for further efforts in policy design and implementation. In fact, it means a reconsideration of the Lasswellian problem orientation to policy analysis in terms of a primacy of problem finding over problem solving in policy debates. As I will show in Chapter Two, all too frequently the priority is the other way round (see Turnbull, 2005: 131). Another advantage of this approach is to escape from the limits of 'adjectival' policy analysis, that is, policy analysis that starts from subject areas or policy domains as usually labelled in the media or by government officials. Policy analysts should not let political or media authorities define problems for them. Rather, policy analysts ought to find the standard for their own work in its relevancy for the governance of problems in public debate. They should begin by respecting the many problem frames, definitions and structures aired in public debate by all those who care to participate; and not give priority to those of some subset of actors, however politically important.

To that end, a well-known typology of problem structures will be the core variable of a map of the governance of problems. Anticipating the detailed argument in Chapters Two, Three and Four, a simple definition of a problem says that it is a deviation between an existing state ('is') and a desirable one ('ought'). The 'is' is represented in the stock of available and relevant knowledge that can be used in understanding the problem; especially in moving away from the problematic situation, perhaps but not necessarily towards the more desirable situation. There can be more or less certainty on this stock of knowledge. The 'ought' is represented in the set of norms, values, principles, ideals and interests at stake in defining the problem. There can be more or less ambivalence or ambiguity of normative issues at stake. Crossing the certainty of knowledge and the ambivalence of values dimensions, one gets a simple fourfold typology of problem structures as in Figure 1.1.

Figure: 1.1 Simple typology of problem structures

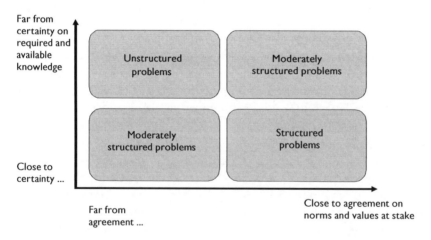

The simple point is that participants in policy debates, especially proximate policy makers and authoritative decision makers, try to steer public debates in any of these four directions; and thereby create quite different political task fields for themselves and others. People discussing a structured problem's technicalities and the efficiency of finetuning means to context or each other will have a very different kind of debate than those discussing unstructured, 'wicked' policy problems in open networks with fluid participation of multiple players. Moderately structured problems with shared principles and goals lead to debate on the set of means; particularly about their effectiveness in view of foreseeable outcomes on agreed evaluation dimensions. But how to handle debate on unstructured or wicked problems where lack of knowledge makes it impossible to foresee which course of action will generate which outcomes; and where evaluation standards are so ambiguous and/or contested that it is impossible to reason in terms of a shared or general interest? The claim of this book essentially is that, depending on policy players' preferences, selection of problem structure triggers implicit selective affinities with a number of other dimensions of the political task field, namely affinity with citizens' cultures (Chapter Four), policy network type (Chapters Five and Six), style of doing policy analysis (Chapter Seven), type of democracy (Chapter Eight) and type of political participation by citizens and other policy players (Chapter Nine).

Puzzling, powering and participation

These selective affinities show up once the governance of problems is studied from the three different perspectives of puzzling, powering and participation. In a highly simplified, first-cut model (to be explained, elaborated and refined later), the argument is depicted in Figure 1.2.

Figure 1.2: The governance of problems as puzzling, powering and participation

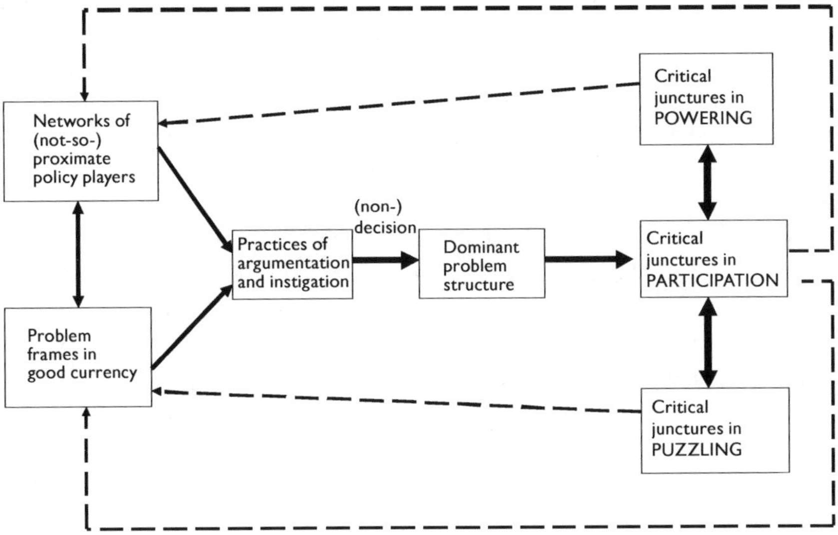

First, problem structure depends on *puzzling* or analysis as cognitive support for authoritative policy choice (Colebatch, 2006b: 319) on behalf of the collective (Heclo, 1974: 305); that is, on how well founded or convincing the problem claims are, and a judgement as to whether government really is in a position to make a difference. Returning to the case of backaches used in the very beginning of this chapter, scores of medical specialists, health insurance economists, policy analysts at the Department of Health, and perhaps some experts in occupational health and safety working for a trade union or nationwide patient platforms, have already performed a lot of puzzle work. Based on rules of evidence-based medicine, they have established what sorts of backaches are treatable; and decided which treatments deserve coverage in health insurance plans. Their puzzling or policy-analytic work may have as an outcome a state policy that does not cover your particular sort of backache; thus, you should pay for medical assistance out of your own pocket.

Problem structure depends, second, on *powering*; that is, on sufficient pressure and influence mobilised for a problem claim in the political process of aggregation, priority setting and choice among the many demands on the state's problem-solving capacity. Problem structuring also is about the power differentials between the variety of players in a particular policy network; players that have to be instigated into cooperative, collective action through persuasion and partisan analysis, or not-so-benign political tactics and strategies of mutual adjustment. Suppose you really are convinced that your type of backache should be covered by health insurance, for example because it is shared by a majority or sizeable minority of all backache sufferers. You might try to establish local and national interest groups of fellow backache patients and organise a lobby. Since your political lobby work will create only a weak signal and its problem claims are likely to be construed as the self-interested whining of work-shy employees, you seek allies with political clout and credibility. There may be reputed medical professionals willing to back up your complaints as real and treatable; or influential employers' associations in support of insurance coverage, because additional costs, even in the shape of placebo treatment, are more than compensated for in gains of Gross Domestic Product and tax revenues due to the expected reductions in sick leave. After some more intense lobby work directed at strategically selected Members of Parliament (MPs), the political support of these influential players may well result in putting the issue back on the agenda of the Department of Health.

Third, problem structure depends on *participation*; that is, on who is included or excluded from having a voice in the puzzling; and whose resources and connections create what weight and influence in the powering. It is clear that well-developed policy-analytic skills and an audible voice in puzzling, and sufficient clout and diplomatic skills in powering, largely depend on participation. After all, decisions are made by those who show up. Only recognised medical expertise makes your backache problem a topic in consultations on coverage between health department officials and health insurance economists. Only well-targeted informal lobbying and permanent presence and visibility in public debate may guarantee that your problem is part of the political negotiations potentially leading to concrete policy proposals. Participation, puzzling and powering are three interdependent conditions in the governance of problems, with participation as the central, but also potentially wobbly, pillar. This is because participation may not only decisively influence puzzling and powering, it may also be influenced by problem structure (as explained in Chapters Three and Five).

Plan of the book

To repeat, the major thesis of this book is that contemporary democracies, in order to maintain a sufficiently responsive system for the governance of problems, ought to develop more reflexive institutions and practices of policy-oriented and polity-oriented problem structuring. A structural mismatch between problem perception and structuring by larger segments, if not a majority, of the citizenry and their proximate policy makers, is a real possibility; and thus a threat. Equally threatening is the risk that the entire question-and-answer game between rulers and ruled at the heart of democratic governance comes to a standstill. Citizens have come to dislike the imposition of a government's well-ordered, but professionally and bureaucratically pre-structured, problem frames and top-down rule, no matter how effective and efficient in their own terms. They rather want their governments to develop the skills and institutions to prudently and democratically transform citizens' experiences of problematic situations, and their ways of framing problem representations, in truly intersubjective but authoritative public definitions of policy problems. Better governance implies political sensitivity to different types of problems; and more and better reflexive problem structuring through better institutional, interactive and deliberative designs for public debate and political choice. This message will be fleshed out in the rest of the book.

Chapter Two, 'The governance of problems: a map', serves a number of functions. First, it defines key concepts and conceptual distinctions used throughout the book. Second, it underlines the theoretical, political and societal relevance of the distinction between problem finding and problem solving. Finally, it formulates the specific research questions to be answered, and the conceptual model of the governance of problems that organises the book.

In Chapter Three, 'Analysing policy problems: a problem-structuring approach', I address the socio-cognitive aspects of problem structuring in defining political environments or task fields from the viewpoint of policy players. From this perspective, I show it to be useful to distinguish between four types of problem structures: structured, unstructured and two types of moderately structured problems (see Figure 1.1, above).

In Chapter Four, 'Cultures of public policy problems', the politico-cognitive aspects of problem structuring are embedded in their cultural-institutional ecology and dynamics. I show how each of the four problem structures has strong selective affinities or congruencies with only one type of cultural-institutional environment: hierarchy, individualism, groupism or enclavism, and isolationism or fatalism.

In Chapter Five, 'Problem types and types of policy politics', I move one step closer to policy practice by showing how policy constrains the politics of policy making in different types of policy networks: rule in closed professional networks, negotiation-and-search in oligopolistic networks with two or more competing advocacy coalitions, accommodation in designed networks of strong ethical and worldview antagonism, and learning and/or agonistic politics in open issue networks. This chapter may be read as a sustained reflection on and amendment of Lowi's thesis that policy determines politics.

In Chapter Six, 'Problem-structuring dynamics and meta-governance', the types of policy networks and policy politics distinguished in the previous chapter are illustrated through case examples. It is shown that types of problem structures and policy politics change through time. Therefore, using concepts like policy or institutional entrepreneurship, and meta-governance, I show that policy players actually have some leverage in shaping policy networks and problem structures.

Narrowing the perspective to the puzzle aspect of problem framing and structuring, Chapter Seven, 'Making policy analysis doable and reflexive', addresses the historical development of policy analysis. It shows how policy analysis had to radically revise its epistemological and methodological assumptions. From decision support to leaders and their top-level staff or 'speaking truth to power', policy analysis had to revamp itself as 'making sense together'. Meanwhile, leaving epistemological differences aside, in practice several doable styles of policy analysis have developed. The chapter ends with an overview of doable styles in policy analysis as instruments for reflexive practitioners.

Chapters Eight and Nine address the macro-level question of how to move the political system as a whole towards a more reflexive level of the governance of problems. Chapter Eight, 'The plural democracies of problems: a meta-theory', exploits and elaborates the notion of the intelligence of democracy by showing how each of the problem structures has selective affinities with different, but standard, theories of political democracy: Schumpeterian procedural democracy, liberal-pluralist democracy, accommodationist elite-cartel democracy and deliberative and/or participatory democracy. The day-by-day practice of democracy requires us to tinker with different modes of democratic governance to successfully deal with different problem structures. Chapter Nine, 'Public engagement and deliberative designs', focuses on shifts in governance as gently nudging the governance system towards more deliberative and participatory modes of problem structuring. The notion of meta-governance, introduced in Chapter Six, is elaborated as deliberate interpolable balancing through the alignment and transformation of institutions in policy networks. The chapter also analyses and evaluates modes of civic engagement and discusses the challenges and possibilities of running experiments in mini-public deliberative policy analysis.

But one should not turn a blind eye to the ironies of the inevitable and perennial tension between instigation or powering, and deliberation as a mode of puzzling. Therefore, Chapter Ten, 'Responsible and hopeful governance of problems', discusses how such tensions can be managed, instead of slipping into non-negotiable contradictions. I advocate a governance of problems as fruitful oscillation and alternation between puzzling and powering. This requires politicians to foster a politics of responsibility, reflexiveness and hope, which believes in the correction of powering by prudential puzzling; and the approximation of the regulative ideal of a self-guiding society through participation of more and more people in the question-and-answer game of democratic governance.

Notes

[1] It is important to point out that, following common contemporary social science parlance, I use the term 'reflexive' to mean 'conscious', 'intended' or 'controlled'. Think of looking at yourself in a mirror. It usually refers to self-critical reflection on one's behaviour, leading to learning and sometimes real change. This is the exact opposite of everyday usage of 'reflexive' in the meaning of 'reflex-like', 'automatic', 'uncontrolled' or not self-conscious. Think of the knee reflex. In everyday parlance social science 'reflexivity' would be 'reflectiveness'.

[2] Although there is a clear overlap between 'governance' as a concept in politics and the social sciences and 'cybernetics' as an interdisciplinary academic field, to my knowledge there is no direct theoretical link, in the sense that 'governance'-thinkers heavily or exclusively draw on the body of knowledge of 'cybernetics' as a scientific discipline. The most recent definition of cybernetics actually narrows 'governance' to instrumental rationality in goal-directed, efficient behaviour 'to understand and define the functions and processes of systems that have goals, and that participate in circular, causal chains that move from action to sensing to comparison with desired goal, and again to action. Studies in cybernetics provide a means for examining the design and function of any system, including social systems such as business management and organizational learning, including for the purpose of making them more *efficient* and *effective*' (Wikipedia, consulted 16 January 2009). Instead, governance theorising frequently uses notions derived from complexity and chaos theory.

TWO

The governance of problems: a map

Government organised around problems, not problems around Government. (Tony Blair, speech on civil service reform, 24 February, 2004)

Introduction

Much has already been written on responsive governance. This book brings together issues that are traditionally treated separately: the analysis of problems (puzzling), the politics of problem framing and network management (powering) and the politics of political participation. The conceptual 'umbrella' to be used for integrating these different themes is *problem structuring*. It is a powerful analytic concept, which manages to integrate a lot of political and policy science insights in an easily grasped way.

First, this chapter deals conceptually with the question: what is problem structuring? Second, using the development of the welfare state and, particularly, the events of 'Paris 1968' as historical illustrations, it will show the political relevance of problem structuring. The question underlying this part is: what do we know about how much influence citizens do actually exert on the structuring of public policy problems? The chapter ends with the articulation of research questions dealt with in the rest of the book; and with a conceptual map of the governance of problems, which explains the organisation of the book.

Problem structuring and responsive governance[1]

Problem finding versus problem solving

What do I mean by problem structuring? First, problem structuring refers to the cognitive, puzzle aspect of processes of problematisation in politics and public policy. It emerges from an experience and reflection on the practical tension between *problem finding* and *problem solving*.[2] Very generally, a problem is a gap between a current situation and a more desirable future one. Problem processing is usually considered to be about problem solving. It means that people start looking for ways of bridging or diminishing the gap between an 'is' and an 'ought'. Problem solving assumes that people have consent on values at stake and have identified policy ends; thus, they can afford to focus attention on finding the most effective and efficient means. By applying those means, they develop expertise, a division of labour, collaboration, organisation and other coordination mechanisms. In short, problem-solving efforts usually start a process of institutionalisation around the shared problem; a social recognition that there exists a set of organisations that provide a 'permanent' solution to a 'permanent' problem of a collectivity (Berger and Luckmann, 1967: 69-70); one may also speak of politics as 'issue machines' (Braybrooke, 1974: ix) that result in the collective normalisation of a problem. One speaks, for example, about 'housing policy', or 'healthcare policy' or 'criminal youth policy':

> It is as though there were a political gateway through which all issues pass. Disputed from the moment they are in sight of it – and more hotly as they approach – they pass (if they pass) through, and drop out of controversy for a time. Managing the procession are certain 'gatekeepers' – not just the Cabinet of the day, but bureaucrats, journalists, association heads and independent specialists camped permanently around each source of problems. To talk of a political process is to recognize some hint of a pattern in the way in many different fields the controversial is transformed into routine. (Davies, quoted in Colebatch, 2005: 15)

Clearly, to the extent that a government has already been organised around problems, it is the result of institutionalised problem-solving practices. Along with the set of policy players involved, the problem frame and definition itself gets stabilised and fixed.

However, what is often neglected is that problem processing actually starts from problem finding: 'governing depends on the identification of situations as problems, the recognition of expertise in relation to these problems and the discovery of "technologies" of governing which are seen as an appropriate response' (Colebatch, 2006b:313; also 2002b: 431-2). In a philosophical or 'problematological' redemption of questioning-about-questions as the basis of thought, politics, democracy and policy making, Turnbull (2005: 96) argues that:

> [T]he problem solving concept shifts the focus from debating the meaning of the problem to confirming the solution.... In fact, defining politics as dissolution of problems leads to authoritarianism because it condemns the agency of human beings and is consistent with attacks on the rights of citizens to ask questions. Going back to the origins of Western philosophy, Plato's authoritarianism resulted from his own rejection of Socrates' questioning method in favor of an essentialism that eliminated the problematic *a priori*. (Turnbull, 2005: 91)

William Dunn (2007: 53, emphasis added), too, has pointed out that next to the instrumental rationality of problem solving there is in policy analysis another, more foundational form of rationality:

Erotetic rationality refers to a process of questioning and answering.…
In many of the most important cases, analysts simply do not know
the relationships between policies, policy outcomes and the values in
terms of which those outcomes should be assessed. Here, the frank
acknowledgement of ignorance is a prerequisite of engaging in a
process of questioning and answering, a process that yields rationally
optimal answers to questions that 'transcend accreted experience and
outrun the reach of knowledge already at our disposal.' (Rescher, 1980:
6). Erotetic rationality is closely related to problem structuring as the
central guidance system of policy analysis.

In contrast to problem solving, then, *problem finding* presupposes openness to new
information on facts and values, so that policy ends may be either reconsidered
or newly formed; an activity that may entail a new search for alternative means.
Problem finding resists institutionalisation of problem solving – at least, overly
strict forms of organisation around fixed problems. Nevertheless, in both practice
and theory, solving problems attracts more attention than problem finding. Hence,
a problem often is presented as an objective given. Finding problems is hardly
considered an issue in itself. Political theory and political struggle alike focus
more on alternative solutions than the nature and content of the problem itself.
Chisholm (1995: 472) has convincingly argued that political struggle and political
theory both pay attention only to the tip of the iceberg and ignore what is below
the water surface (see Figure 2.1).

Figure 2.1: The decision as an iceberg

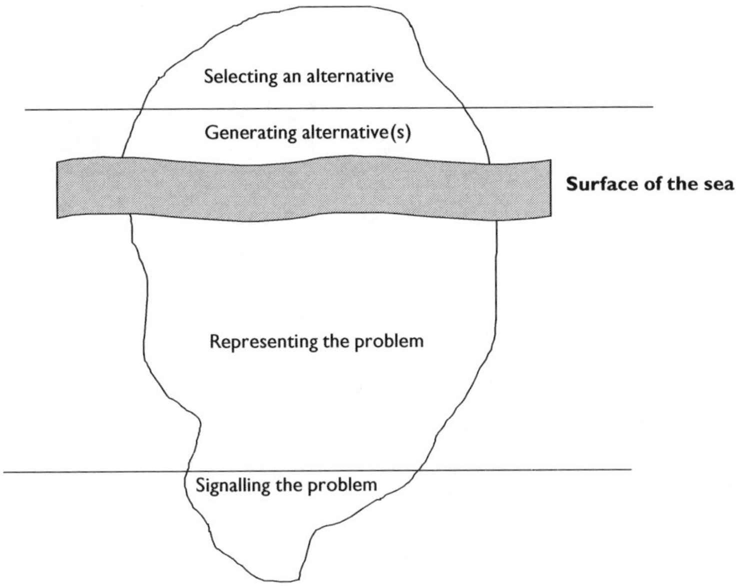

Selecting an alternative

Generating alternative(s)

Surface of the sea

Representing the problem

Signalling the problem

Source: Adapted from Chisholm (1995: 472)

Problem-solving bias in politics and administration

The focus on solutions rather than problem identification and representation is well documented. Leo Klinkers (2002: 23), former professor of public administration and later policy consultant, concludes from ample experience:

> [C]ivil servants are weak in analysis. They rather start working on solutions immediately, and corrupt quality thinking by falling in the trap of solution-thinking. Analysis costs too much time …, thinking hard hurts your brain, and especially your heart, because a lot of issues emerge that you would rather leave in the dark and not-discussed. Efforts at analysis are frequently smothered in the slogan 'We should not get lost in doomsday scenarios'. Or, equally damning: 'There are a lot of successes too, aren't there?' [translation RH]

At best, governments tend to be ambivalent about investing in problem-finding capacity. They have great difficulty in refocusing capacity building for better governance from problem solving to problem finding. The UK government, in its White Paper entitled *Modernising government* (Cabinet Office, 1999: para 2.3) admits that the 'emphasis on management reforms [= problem solving, RH] has brought improved productivity, better value for money and in many cases better quality services… On the other hand, little attention was paid to the policy process and the way it affects government's ability to meet the needs of people.' Yet, the same White Paper devotes but little attention to devising new policy-making procedures and institutions to improve government's ability for problem analysis and responsive problem structuring. Instead, its focus is on professionalising policy making through special purpose organisations for so-called 'joined-up' policy making around allegedly shared political goals and the government's overall strategic purpose (Cabinet Office, 1999: para 2.7). The issue of responsive governance is in fact 'downsized' to better-managed, more flexible policy implementation as service delivery (Cabinet Office, 1999: chapter 3).

As another example of the practice of governmental policy making, consider Boom and Metze's (1997) report entitled *De slag om de Betuweroute* (The battle over the Betuwe-line). The Betuwe-line Project in the Netherlands was concerned with the problem of keeping an expanding Rotterdam harbour well connected to the rest of Europe. The project started, not with a thorough problem analysis, but with how one potential solution, a new trajectory for a freight-only railway between Rotterdam and the German border, could be squeezed into the densely populated and river-rich Dutch landscape. Nobody thought about alternative means of freight transportation until too late in the political decision-making process. Solution-focused policy design is far from a Dutch peculiarity, though. Consider, for example, Flyvbjerg's (1998: 11ff) *Rationality and power.* Flyvbjerg meticulously describes how the Aalborg Project in Jutland, Denmark, aspired to integrate environmental and social concerns in inner-city planning, including how to deal with car mobility. But the project started out from and stuck to the solution of creating a supersized bus terminal right in the middle of the historical city centre.

The concept of problem structuring

Both problem finding and problem solving are indispensable moments in high-quality policy making. However, countering the normal tendency, in this book I will stress problem finding. *Problem structuring* is the connecting or overarching concept necessary for a balanced view of problem processing as the 'whole iceberg' of both problem finding and problem solving. In moving from inchoate signs of stress on the system to one or more solvable policy problems, policy analysts and other 'puzzlers' normally

> face a large, tangled network of competing problem formulations that are dynamic, socially constructed, and distributed throughout the policy-making process. In effect, analysts are faced with a meta-problem – a problem-of-problems that is ill-structured because the domain of problem representations held by stakeholders is unmanageably large. (Dunn, 2007: 83)

Problem structuring, then, is about the search and evaluation – with a view to potential integration – of competing problem representations. It produces information on what problem(s) to solve (Dunn, 2007: 6).

This implies that the 'puzzler' takes an active part in the problem-structuring process; consciously or not, he imposes structure on tangled problematic situations and multiple problem representations or framings. Seen from a puzzling perspective, problem setting or problem finding, therefore, is a creative process (Turnbull, 2005: 103). Interpretive frames provide the link between worrisome clues experienced or observed in a situation, and the later clear articulation and formulation of *the* problem. 'Frames' are interpretive schemas or groups of ideas or 'paradigms', which generate broad attitudes and orientations towards a problematic situation. They highlight certain worries over others, select out irrelevant ones and bind the remaining concerns in a coherent pattern. The key to understanding frames is to see them as questioning processes 'that structure the world by delimiting the field of possible answers' (Turnbull, 2005: 102).

This is more than just a technical argument in a methodology of policy analysis as cognitive activity. Bridging problem finding and problem solving through problem structuring inevitably also is an 'essentially political activity to produce new insights on what the problem is about' (Hisschemöller and Hoppe, 2001: 51). Problem framing is part of the way citizens, intermediaries between citizens and decision makers, and public authorities in government allocate attention and prioritise problems on the public, the political and the decision-making and implementation agenda; all in the context of the practical workings of democracy in a given polity. Therefore, the politics of problem framing implies several modes of political interaction, involving such roles as citizens, representatives of economic and non-commercial interest groups and associations, party leaders, politicians elected in Parliaments, administrative functionaries and experts. This means that both problem framing and problem solving are related to the exercise of power. Problem framing may be the less publicly visible part of problem processing. However, to the extent that the opaque choice of a problem frame actually triggers the inclusion of some and exclusion of other alternatives, it is of equal political importance:

> Political conflict is not like an intercollegiate debate in which opponents agree in advance on the definition of the issues. As a matter of fact, the definition of alternatives is the supreme instrument of power.... He who determines what politics is about runs the country, because the definition of alternatives is the choice of conflicts, and the choice of conflicts allocates power. (Schattschneider, 1960 [1988]: 66)

Problem structuring and participation

If the two moments in problem processing are part of powering in politics, the analysis and politics of problem finding and framing is inextricably tied to *a politics of participation*: 'Whoever decides what the game is about decides also who can get into the game' (Schattschneider, 1960 [1988]: 102). Immediately the issue is raised of the citizen's role vis-à-vis other political players in political arenas: what is the citizen's proper role in problem structuring as an essential part of policy making as problem processing? Usually, citizens are cast in the role of 'distant', sometimes informed and monitorial (Schudson, 1998), but mostly ignorant policy makers. Other players, like interest group representatives, advice-giving experts, policy-advising and implementing civil servants, and politicians, are seen as 'naturally' involved, more 'proximate' policy makers. My analysis will focus on the dangerous tensions between political participation in problem structuring by citizens and more proximate policy makers (see also Dery, 2000).

In standard political theory, longstanding views on the capacity for informed, rational political judgement by the average voter or typical citizen are rather pessimistic. Such pessimism flows from two sources. Some, most famously Schumpeter (1942), are convinced that 'ordinary' citizens just lack the skills for responsible political judgement. Alternatively, others, like Schattschneider (1960 [1988]) and Lindblom (1968), believe that in our hypercomplex societies, citizens have no choice but to outsource political judgement to specialists that can spend all their working hours as more 'proximate' policy makers. Therefore, many politicians, administrators and political scientists still believe that ordinary citizens are to be kept out of policy making as much as possible.

In political and administrative practice, however, the 'old', modernist politics of traditional government through representative democracy, the welfare-cum-administrative state and the scientific estate is more and more contested. It is complemented, if not claimed to be replaced, by a 'new', postmodern politics that promises to tap societal needs and knowledge better, and improve both the input and the delivery end of policy making through social- and policy-oriented learning. It is widely believed that this may be achieved through more political involvement or giving more voice to civil society or ordinary citizens compared to proximate policy makers and other experts. This is not only true for nation states; it applies to international and transnational governance structures as well. The 2001 White Paper on European governance (European Union, 2001: 11, 12, 14-15, 33, [emphasis in original]) states:

> *Making the Union operate more openly*: Democracy depends on people being able to take part in public debate. To do this, they must have access to reliable information on European issues and be able to scrutinize the policy process in its various stages.... *Reaching out to citizens through regional and local democracy*: ... The process of EU-policymaking ... should allow Member States to listen and learn from regional and local experiences.... *Involving civil society*: Civil society plays an important role in giving voice to the concerns of citizens and delivering services that meet people's needs.... It (provides) a chance to get citizens more actively involved in achieving the Union's objectives and to offer them a structured channel for feedback, criticism and protest.... *Build public confidence in the way policy makers use expert advice*: The EU's multidisciplinary expert system will be opened up to greater public scrutiny and debate.... It must boost confidence in the way expert advice influences policy decisions.

In other words, wider political participation and empowerment of citizens is back in the public debate and public agendas of many countries. Yet, it remains ambiguous as to what extent a 'reinvented' politics actually allows more citizen involvement or empowerment through participatory or deliberative or other new forms of democracy.

Summary

In this section, I have outlined the approach that permeates this book. It is a problem-processing view of governance, or *the governance of problems*. Technically, it uses some key conceptual distinctions that have been listed in Box 2.1 for the reader's convenience. I have stressed the process of problem structuring as vital for a responsive governance of problems. The importance of problem structuring was discovered and originates in the study of how policy analysts cognitively move from inchoate signs of problematic situations, through the unravelling of multiple stakeholders' problem representations, to doable, solvable problems for public policy. I have also explained why problem structuring is not just an issue in the epistemology and methodology of policy analysis, but is also inextricably tied into issues of political power games and participation. Thus, *puzzling*, *powering* and *participation* are indispensable moments in public problem processing. They are usually dealt with in separate parts of the literature. The *basic question* of a problem-structuring approach to the governance of problems is: by taking a problem-structuring perspective, what may we learn about the possibilities and impossibilities, the enabling and constraining driving forces behind responsive democratic governance in our technologically, socially and economically hypercomplex societies?

Box 2.1: Key terminology used in this book:

Problem
Problems are experienced as non-acceptable discrepancies between real situations and desired future situations; between a socially constructed 'is' and 'ought'. However, from a political as well as cognitive point of view, they vary in terms of degree of consent on relevant, valid knowledge on what is and will or can be; as well as in terms of degree of consent on values, norms and standards at stake in defining a desirable future situation. This insight is the basis for a fundamental typology of different kinds of public problems: structured, unstructured and two types of moderately structured problems (see Chapters One and Three).

Problem processing
Refers to all cognitive and non-cognitive, explicit or tacit, social or individual, political or non-political activities, especially all sorts of claims people make on other people, to do something about a 'problem'; the concept includes all the other concepts listed in this box.

Problem finding (problem sensing, problem identification)
Refers to claims that some set of conditions in the real or virtual future world ought to be considered a 'problem', that is, ought to be seen by others as an undesirable situation, as compared to some conception or other of a more desirable, future situation.

Problem framing (problem representation, problem categorisation)
Refers to different, frequently contradictory or clashing ways of representing or categorising conditions found to be 'problematic' by citizens, stakeholders and other, more proximate policy makers in finding and identifying a particular problem. 'Frames' are interpretive schemas or groups of ideas or 'paradigms', which generate broad attitudes and orientations towards a problematic situation. They highlight certain worries over others, select out irrelevant ones, and bind the remaining concerns in a coherent pattern. For example, drug use can be framed as a public order or as a public health problem.

Problem structuring (analytically: problem diagnosis)
Refers to the search, debate, evaluation and political struggle about competing problem representations or framings. Problem structuring, whether as an analytic or a political process,

is a necessary intermediate step on the way to problem definition or authoritative choice in policy designs. Problem structuring may aim at some 'integration' of different problem frames or representations, with a view to creating feasible, doable problems for public modes of governance. Formally, problem structuring is defined as the self-conscious search, analysis and evaluation of competing problem representations and problem framings, with a view to their possible integration. In a more political twist, one could also define problem structuring as the political activity to produce information on divergent views of what the problem is about, with a view to a synthetic, or at least politically plausible, choice of authoritative problem definition.

Problem definition (problem choice)
Refers to an authoritative problem definition as the temporarily fixed outcome of processes of problem finding, framing and structuring; always a cognitive-cum-political selection or choice from a larger set of politically or intellectually mobilised problem framings, expressed in formal policy designs.

Problem solving
A concept referring to all that people may or can do to actually bridge the formally acknowledged or taken-for-granted gap between current undesirable and future, desirable situations; problem solving means finding, elaborating and selecting alternative courses of action for successful goal achievement, that is, to diminish or actually eliminate the gap.

Problems around government

The horns of the dilemma

The need for a problem–structuring approach may be argued from the claim implied by Tony Blair's aphorism: that we should and can have a 'government organised around (citizens') problems', *without* all the 'problems around Government' that have become manifest since, roughly, the 1970s.

But what if the very ways in which governments have been organised around citizens' problems generate all the problems around government? What if we are dealing with a real dilemma? After all, in the final decades of the last century, politics, the welfare state and public policies were repainted in public opinion, the news industry and even by politicians themselves, from a problem solver to a major cause of problems for citizens. In terms of economic science, market failures to be corrected by states have been far superseded in priority by an urgent sense of across-the-board government failure. Many have diagnosed a crisis of state legitimacy, or a serious rupture, a yawning 'abyss' between the state and its citizens, to be remedied only by a 'new' politics.

In Dutch politics, nothing illustrates the shift from an 'old' to a 'new' politics better than the last weeks of August 2001. On 30 August 2001, Prime Minister Wim Kok (Labor), respected leader of an almost eight-year-old 'purple' coalition government by Labour (PvdA), conservative liberals (VVD) and progressive liberals (D'66), announced his decision not to run for office again, and to end his political career. Nine days before, Pim Fortuyn, the flamboyant, populist *enfant terrible* of Dutch politics, and charismatic proponent of a 'new' politics in a more 'livable Holland', announced his decision to establish a new political party. His political platform was a constant accusation of Dutch democracy as ruled by elites that co-opt each other but neglect authentic citizen interests:

> Due to this lack of democratic quality, we, citizens, have been saddled with a public sector increasingly emptied from its original intention, i.e. the delivery to citizens and firms of services perfectly reflecting their needs. On the contrary, services delivered frequently do not correspond to any needs, or show poor to abominable quality. (Fortuyn, 2002: 12) [translation RH]

A masterful media performer, Fortuyn charmed almost the entire electorate by ending his first campaign speech with the military salute: 'At your service!'.

Fortuyn was shot on 6 May 2002. That same evening only prudent police action nipped public rioting in the immediate surroundings of the Dutch Parliament and the Prime Minister's department in the bud (De Vries and Van der Lubben, 2005: 22-31). In the polls the hastily established political party, 'Lijst Pim Fortuyn' (LPF), was predicted to enter a 150-seat Parliament with a landslide 36 seats. Electoral campaigns for all political parties came to a halt. In the national elections of 15 May 2002, the LPF won 23 seats; subsequently, joining Christian Democrats (CDA) and Conservative Liberals (VVD), the LPF became the third party in a new centre-right coalition Cabinet. Since then, Fortuyn's political party has turned out to be a dismal failure, although not without profound influence on the issues of public debate, the platforms and agendas of most Dutch political parties, and Cabinet decision making. Beyond doubt, *Fortuyn demonstrated the possibility and political threat of gross mismatches between problem perception and framing among large segments of the electorate, and those of a political and administrative elite in power, unchallenged for too long* (De Vries and Van der Lubben, 2005; Keman, 2008: 150).

For all Fortuyn's claims to incarnate a 'new' politics, his 'At your service!' merely repeats politics' and the welfare state's most important claim to legitimacy. Politicians, in return for being voted into power over the welfare state apparatus, promise to use that power to solve public problems put on the agenda by citizens. Public policies are supposed to be rational answers to public problems. However, often the contrary is true; Fortuyn himself magisterially exploited that theme – problems do not decrease, but intensify; they do not vanish, but turn out to be complex and persistent. This is not just due to some citizens' behaviours creating problems for other citizens; higher-level governments generate problems for lower-level governments, and vice versa.

Referring to the US context of the 1990s, Schneider and Ingram (1997: 5) also note that policy failure has become a sort of to-be-expected, 'normal accident':

The policy design problems are not the normal product of a rapidly changing world that will be met by reasonable collective solutions. Instead, they have taken on the character of long-term policy failures. Rather than provide institutions and symbols to ensure that the self-correcting mechanisms of pluralist democracy will be operative, the policies deceive, confuse, and in other ways discourage active citizenship, minimize the possibilities of self-corrections, and perpetuate and exacerbate the very tendencies that produced dysfunctional public policies in the first place.

In other words, governments create as many problems or more than they pretend to solve; and this is not accidental, but systemic failure. Was Milton Friedman right that government solutions are usually as bad as or worse than the problem itself? Why?

The welfare state: intended solutions and unintended problems

Contemporary welfare states, in their manifold manifestations in Europe, the US and Canada, are products of the later phases of modernity (Wagner, 1994). Modernity is social-science shorthand for the historical project to inscribe and translate the principles of Enlightenment and individual freedom into society's social, economic, political and cultural practices. This modernisation process has become increasingly riddled with conflicts and crises rooted in dilemmas between autonomy and discipline. Dreams of rationality and individual autonomy have clashed with the realities of their unavoidable boundaries, the practical constraints of increased interdependencies in time and space between people (Elias, 1991), and the realities of an ever-more penetrative state bent on standardisation, central control and making society legible to the centre (Scott, 1998).

A first protracted crisis of modernity is the period from 1848 until around 1900. By the turn of the 18th into the 19th century, the permeation of society by modern legal and economic institutions had increased considerably. Large parts of the population were disembedded, often traumatically, from their *Gemeinschaft*-like life-worlds and thrown into larger systems and processes of *Vergesellschaftung*. Mid-19th century, this entailed a strong sense of loss of intelligibility and manageability of modernising societies among political and administrative elites. Simultaneously, at least in Europe, there was a first wave of moderate social security legislation and measures to mitigate for workers the risks of industrial labour. Scholars such as Marx, Tönnies, Weber and Durkheim developed their *grands critiques* of modernity. Especially the rationalisation of industry and state bureaucracy were analysed as a double-edged process of enlarging and speeding up the modernity project, while simultaneously disciplining, instead of liberating, individuals.

From 1900 until roughly the beginning of the Second World War, social scientists observe an increasing formalisation, conventionalisation and homogenisation of practices in the institutionalised, semi-autonomous spheres of the economy, politics and science. In economics, new boundaries were set on permissible activities: building of technical-organisational systems on a society-wide scale, conventionalisation of work practices and standardisation of consumption. In politics, the mass party and its channelled political participation emerged. Also, the beginnings of the welfare and administrative state were discernible, as well as disciplining methods extending into family life. Finally, we see the blossoming of the modern conception of the natural sciences and technology as a basis for military and industrial complexes; and the social sciences as new conventionalised modes of representation of social realities and as decision aids.

From the end of the Second World War until '1968', this new order is carried into perfection. In this age of *organised modernity*, politics is about politicising the social (Arendt, 1958); the welfare state is perfected in the sense of a new compromise between freedom and discipline: life's uncertainty is reduced for 'social citizens', but the price for free 'political citizens' is to have their lives monitored and normalised. An ever-higher proportion of an increasing Gross National Product is distributed through state channels; social security legislation socialises risks and minimises uncertainty, but standardises the biographies and identities of citizens; distributive justice is somehow realised in a world of individual freedom, inequality and difference, but the number of those entitled to social benefits is bounded. The social and political world is not populated by 'persons', but by 'functionaries' in the service of large organisations in an 'organisational state' (Denhardt, 1981; Lauman and Knoke, 1987). On this 'closure' of modernity in a thoroughly organised modern welfare state and bureaucracy, Wagner (1994: 100) comments:

> [I]t is easy to see that a welfare state ... has very little in common with the liberal state as envisaged in the mid-19th century. It almost shows more affinities with the 'police state' of the *ancien regime*. What distinguishes it from the latter, though, is its commitment to the idea that the sovereign people are the ultimate arbiter of how, and how intensively, their own activities should be safeguarded and surveilled. But both the society of late absolutism and the 20th century welfare state showed 'a kind of political a priori' that allowed the emergence and operation of authorities whose task was 'the calculated supervision, administration, and maximization of the forces of each and all'.... Governmentality (Foucault) refers to technologies that are employed for structuring the space of the practices of domination. It assumes that they can be structured, it is 'programmatic' in that it is characterized by an eternal optimism that a domain of society can be administered better or more effectively, that reality is, in some way or other, programmable.

The over-organised nature of a closed modernity leads to a new major crisis in '1968' and beyond. Segments of the citizenry experience a severe loss of personal autonomy, and start breaking up this organised modernity. People experience globalisation, de-conventionalisation of work and consumption patterns in economic practices. In politics and administration there is the loss of a legitimate domination centre (state power), knowledgeable and managerially powerful enough to 'steer' other spheres of society. In science, lay persons become fearful of large-scale technologies, and scientists and scholars face a crisis of representation of society, symbolised by the different evaluation of postmodernist epistemologies that reject grand narratives, objectivity and law-like regularities in favour of indeterminacy, difference, uniqueness and discontinuity. Living through the last decades of the 20th century, many people feel overwhelmed by uncertainties and risks, leading analysts to speak of 'an end to modernity' or postmodernism (Lyotard, 1984), and a 'risk society' (Beck, 1992) dominated by a 'politics of fear' (Bauman, 1992).

The breaking up of organised modernity certainly does not justify speaking about the 'end of modernity'. However, especially possibilities for the formation of social identities and political community and deliberation are in serious trouble in contemporary Western societies. The repercussions for responsive governance are serious. The problem-structuring conventions, habits and routines of the governance of problems by the welfare and administrative state are being questioned and criticised. Interestingly, these difficulties were anticipated already by the French scholar Michel Foucault. Most of his informed conjectures have been confirmed by later research on citizen attitudes and political behaviour (overview in Dalton, 2000, 2008).

The ramifications of Paris-1968

In an interview in May 1984 with US philosopher Rabinovitz on the 1968 student and workers' rebellion in Paris, Foucault sketches the discontinuity between an organised and a different kind of late modern politics in three developments.[3]

First, Foucault observes a *de-ideologised, personalised type of problematisation* put forward for public debate by citizens:

> As for the events of May 1968, it seems to me they depend on another problematic. I wasn't in France at that time; I only returned several months later. And it seemed to me one could recognize completely contradictory elements in it: on the one hand, an effort, which was very widely asserted, to ask politics a whole series of questions that were not traditionally a part of its statutory domain (questions about women, about relations between the sexes, about medicine, about mental illness, about environment, about minorities, about delinquency); and, on the other hand, a desire to rewrite all these problems in the vocabulary of a theory that was derived more or less directly from Marxism. But the process that was evident at that time led not to taking over the problems posed by the Marxist doctrine but, on the contrary, to a more and more manifest powerlessness on the part of Marxism to confront these problems. So that one found oneself faced with interrogations

that were addressed to politics but had not themselves sprung from a political doctrine. From this point of view, such a liberation of the act of questioning seemed to me to have played a positive role: now there was a plurality of questions posed to politics rather than the reinscription of the act of questioning in the framework of a political doctrine.

The 'politicising the personal', frequently claimed of feminist perspectives only, can be generalised to the de-ideologisation of problematisation discourses among citizens. It was the spirit of the times to shed one's ideological feathers. In the Netherlands, in 1966, a new pragmatic-progressivist[4] political party, Democrats '66, was established; it proclaimed to be totally pragmatic, free from any ideological constraints on thinking about problems of public or political concern, and solutions provided by collective state action. A recent op-ed in the new Dutch daily *NRC.next* (6 April 2006: 19), launched in March 2006 to attract young adult subscribers who no longer read 'normal' daily newspapers, demonstrates how deeply entrenched among the younger generations is this de-ideologisation and individualisation of political thinking, preference formation and demand formulation (Stolle and Hooghe, 2004: 159; Bang, 2003):

> People drop out of politics not because they are disinterested or indifferent to the general interest; they drop out of the system because it no longer links up to their needs.... Individualization and autonomy are the mantras on which we were educated. That's why we want to effectively take action on our own.... This is the new participation of the young generation. [translation RH]

This does not entail the complete disappearance of established political ideologies from political relevance. Rather, such belief systems have to compete with alternative, less articulated and more fragmented frames, beliefs, attitudes and emotions. Authors like Giddens (1991) and Castells (1997) use the label 'life politics' for the syndrome of small narratives, group identities, religious or ethnic convictions and lifestyles that are somehow linked to the life projects of their adherents. Beck (1997) speaks about a 'subpolitics' in which daily life decisions made on the basis of personal or professional identities acquire strong political meanings. Spheres traditionally considered professional and private, for example nutrition advice and food consumption, become issues of political debate and political power games. Foucault correctly designated this as a liberation of the act of questioning from the standard political framings offered by the old elites. Back in 1968, personalisation and de-ideologisation of political discourses began as a revolt of a highly educated *avant garde*. In the beginning of the 21st century, in societies with more advanced levels of educational achievement for larger segments of their populations, it has become the basic political attitude of critical and monitorial citizens that make up a large part of the adult, younger electorate.

Retreat on public goals, and of government

Second, in the same 1984 interview, Foucault already pointed out the difficulties for public problem processing that this individualistic political thinking and experiencing would entail:

> For example, I don't think that in regard to madness and mental illness there is any 'politics' that can contain the just and definitive solution. But I think that in madness, in derangement, in behavior problems, there are reasons for questioning politics; and politics must answer these questions, but it never answers them completely. The same is true for crime and punishment: naturally, it would be wrong to imagine that politics have nothing to do with the prevention and punishment of crime, and therefore nothing to do with a certain number of elements that modify its form, its meaning, its frequency; but it would be just as wrong to think that there is a political formula likely to resolve the question of crime and put an end to it. The same is true of sexuality: it doesn't exist apart from a relationship to political structures, requirements, laws, and regulations that have a primary importance for it; and yet one can't expect politics to provide the forms in which sexuality would cease to be a problem.

To put personal experience first in public problem processing, confronts politics with insoluble or only partially solvable problems. In the long run, and compared to the immediate solutions offered by a fully developed welfare state, would this not imply more moderate expectations about the capacity to govern; and perhaps a *retreat on objectives* (Wildavsky, 1980 [1979]) of state policy making? It is fair to say that from the mid-1970s onwards, most nation states did indeed experience an erosion of governing capacity (Peters, 1996). Most proximate policy makers felt that they were no longer as capable of formulating, implementing and evaluating policy as they were during the heyday of government during the 1960s and 1970s. Especially national strategic policy, which requires the horizontal coordination of policies and programmes across different domains, was a reason for concern.

For an explanation, some analysts pointed to technological and economic drivers of globalisation. Particularly after the fall of communism, globalisation meant that states had to enter an international competition for comparative advantage in economic regulation. For the larger international corporations it meant an opportunity for 'nation shopping': acquiring more favourable fiscal, environmental and labour regulation through playing off one state against another. But for national policy elites it meant a loss of national autonomy. This was exacerbated by an increasingly difficult fiscal position for government. Political and administrative elites felt that they had to 'do more with less'. With the disappearance of 'really existing socialism' as a disliked, undemocratic alternative, they expected their citizens to become more critical about the performance of their own states.

Hence, diffuse support for democratic governance would no longer be enough to stay in power. Henceforward, output-related performance would loom larger in citizens' minds. This triggered numerous efforts of 'reinventing government' (Osborne and Gaebler, 1992) and 'New Public Management' (e.g. Hood, 1991). It appeared that the state had only two alternatives: to transform itself either into a *'supermarket state'* (Olsen, 1988), that is, its functions would become those of mere service delivery to citizens-as-consumers; or into a *'partnering state'*, that is, its functions would be to enable and empower citizens, in their own ways and on their own terms, to practice the freedom of personal growth and identity building (Bang, 2003, 2004).

Other analysts attributed the loss of governing capacity to a more polarised and politicised style of policy making over issues and cleavages in public opinion that no longer reflected standard liberal–conservative or left–right schemata. Materialist issues competed for public attention and public agenda status with post-material issues (Inglehart, 1977, 1990); traditional issues of social status or class competed with or were superseded by issues of gender, religion, ethics, risks, social impacts of technological innovation, quality of life and many more.

Democracy in an age of distrust

Returning to the ramification of Paris-1968, if political ideology and citizen needs and demands become uncoupled, Foucault anticipated *problems of collective will formation, deliberation and aggregation, authority and representation*:

> But it is also necessary to determine what 'posing a problem' to politics really means. … in these analyses I do not appeal to any 'we' – to any of those 'wes' whose consensus, whose values, whose traditions constitute the framework for a thought and define the conditions in which it can be validated. But the problem is, precisely, to decide if it is actually suitable to place oneself within a 'we' in order to assert the principles one recognizes and the values one accepts; or if it is not, rather, necessary to make the future formation of a 'we' possible by elaborating the question. Because it seems to me that 'we' must not be previous to the question; it can only be the result – and the necessary temporary result – of the question as it is posed in the new terms in which one formulates it.

De-ideologisation and individualisation of problem-processing discourse among citizens implies not only a rethinking of state functions and capacities; it also affects political interactions between citizens, and between citizens and state authority as well. For example, Hajer (in Hajer and Wagenaar, 2003: 95-6) describes how, in the Dutch province of Friesland, the policy shift from nature conservation to nature development is 'constitutive' of the region and its political community. He attributes this precisely to the fact that it is only through and after confrontation with a disliked policy programme that the many different types of people in that region discover a shared interest and develop a counter-discourse to the national policy.

If problems posed to politics by citizens are no longer pre-structured ideologically, they obviously escape from traditions, collective memories, shared symbols and other markers of collective identity that constitute polity, political decision and action, representative democracy and even citizenship itself. How then to continue to reason and work through problems together, to trust meaningful representation structures and to arrive at public judgement and responsible collective decisions and actions? This politicisation of the personal in a political structure dominated by the welfare-cum-administrative state breeds *distrust in representation and authority*. It creates the problem of democracy in an era of distrust (Rosanvallon, 2006: 235 ff). Rules of authority (by political and administrative elites), representation (through elected politicians) and delegation (to civil servants, assisted by expert advisers) that formed the basis of its functioning (Catlaw, 2006), have lost their taken-for-granted character. Observes one Belgian political analyst for the 1990s:

> Political innovation has created a new type of citizen-subject. People now believe that democratic representation is hearing the echo of one's own weak voice in public policy. Representation assumed groups and categories of citizens and meant to render their collective voice ('the general interest'), but this is no longer true. (Blommaert, 2001) [translation RH]

This echoes for Belgium in the 1990s what Schattschneider (1960 [1988]: 113-4) observed for Americans 30 years earlier:

> Americans now think that their title covers the whole government, lock, stock, and barrel, not merely a piece (the House of Representatives) of it. Like all great proprietors they are not interested in details or excuses; they want *results*. In other words, they believe that they have a general power over the government as a whole and not merely some power within the government.

Who influences problem structuring?

Of course, ordinary citizens never had much say over actual policy making (Lindblom, 1968: 43ff). In fact, to classic political philosophers, politics is not thinkable without the ruler–ruled relationship among participants in a political community (Dauenhauer, 1986). But empirical political science shows the ruler–ruled dichotomy to be permeable and differentiated in its modern guise. Deferential citizens (Almond and Verba, 1963) were used to the natural authority of political and administrative elites that actually governed the nation. As distant policy makers, they did not mind 'outsourcing' their responsibilities for political judgement to more proximate policy makers – legislators, executive leaders, party leaders, interest group leaders, especially economic interest group representatives (Lindblom, 1977, 2001: 61ff, 236ff), bureaucrats, expert advisers or journalists (Lindblom, 1968: 30, note 3). In a system of representative democracy, these proximate policy makers are to some extent motivated to *reconstruct* citizens' policy preferences because political parties compete for votes to win elections and temporarily govern the country (Lindblom, 1968: 101ff).

Party leadership is motivated to seek out information on citizens' preferred policy positions (on major issues) over and beyond the insufficient information provided by the ballot itself. How else to arrive at a party platform that may attract a majority of voters? For this very reason, opinion polling and running focus groups have become profitable political industries. Using these apparently neutral tools as communication channels, the political and interest group-based proximate policy makers simultaneously respond to and mould citizen demands. The questions asked in political surveys and focus groups, and the composition of the groups themselves, give proximate policy makers plenty of opportunity to structure and channel the so-called free and spontaneous public debate by ordinary citizens in their independent civic associations. Thus:

> [A]ny policymaking system has a prodigious effect on the very preferences, opinions, and attitudes to which it itself also responds. It is not, therefore, a kind of machine into which are fed the exogenous wishes, preferences, or needs of those for whom the machine is designed and out of which come policy decisions to meet these wishes, preferences, or needs. The machine actually manufactures both policies *and* preferences. (Lindblom, 1968: 101–2)

It is no exaggeration to claim that this Janus-faced character of public policy making and the entailed division of tasks in public policy making largely leaves problem structuring in the hands and minds of the proximate policy makers.[5] Thus, one should not confuse convergence between expressions of citizens' policy and spending preferences and government policy as a sure sign that democracy works (Dalton, 2008: 232). Through forms of political participation in institutionalised, normal intermediary arrangements and associations – voting, party and labour union membership, support of interest groups – active citizens exercise some minimal influence on how proximate policy makers structure, and subsequently solve, their problems. However, problem structuring was and is the proximate policy maker's task – and prerogative. As long as citizens were satisfied with the compromise between autonomy and discipline provided by the welfare state, the system of representative democracy and bureaucratic administration sufficed. All this was thrown into turmoil and doubt when large segments of the electorate lost their respect for authority, participated less and less in electoral politics, but remained firm believers in democracy (Inglehart, 1999). In an overview article, Russell Dalton (2000: 926) concludes:

Advanced industrial democracies are experiencing an evolution in the
patterns of electoral choice that flow from the breakdown of longstanding alignments and party attachments, the development of a more
sophisticated electorate, and efforts to move beyond the restrictions
of representative democracy.

These changes in citizens' political attitudes and behaviour may partly be
interpreted as a rejection of older styles of politics and policy making; and as a
yearning for new forms that expand the democratic process and broaden public
involvement in the decisions affecting their lives (Dalton, 2000: 934, 2008: 237ff).
There is no denying that the action repertoire of critical and monitorial citizens
has increased. However, it appears to have taken a rather eclectic, short-term, ego-
focused, inwardly looking turn. Stolle and Hooghe (2004: 160-2) summarise the
newer forms of political participation in four key characteristics:

- First, modern citizens reject working in institutionalised umbrella associations;
  instead, they prefer more flexible, clearly non-hierarchical network-like forms
  of cooperation.
- Second, traditional public–private boundaries are questioned; for example,
  political consumerism, consumer boycotts and other forms of lifestyle politics
  mix private and public motivations in often opaque ways (Spaargaren and
  Mol, 2008).
- Third, political mobilisation patterns are spontaneous, irregular and permit
  easy exits.
- Fourth, they are potentially less collective and group-oriented in character; for
  example, virtual participation through internet-based petitioning, or credit-
  card membership of interest groups, have an ego-centred character atypical
  of traditional political participation in union meetings, mass rallies, or voice
  in public hearings.

Being involved and engaged in politics through the newer modes of participation,
ironically, has not taken the deliberative turn towards more direct participatory
styles of politics, predicted or wished for by many political theorists (Barber,
1984, 1990; Dryzek, 1990). Regarding citizen influence on problem structuring,
the present situation may be characterised as follows. Traditional forms of
political participation conducive to at least minimal citizen influence on problem
structuring by proximate policy makers have seriously weakened. Voting turnout
has consistently declined in many Western democracies. Single-issue voting,
candidate-centred political campaigning and increased partisan volatility, effectively
diminish this minimal influence. Although it is too early to have a definitive
picture of the problem-structuring impacts of newer modes of participation,
they appear less conducive to serious opinion formation and interest aggregation
of citizens through deliberation and mutual adjustment needed for long-term

institutionalised decision-making processes. American political scientist Russell Dalton (2008: 257) warns that:

> [C]itizen interest groups, social movements, individual citizens, and various political groups are now more vocal about their political interests and have greater access to the democratic process. At the same time, the ability of political institutions to balance contending interests – and to make interest groups sensitive to the collective needs of society – has diminished.

French political historian and philosopher Pierre Rosanvallon (2006: 242-3) speaks of 'negative democracy' in which the powers of rejection or veto have become the dominant form of political intervention. For proximate policy makers and citizens alike, the spreading but fluid forms of new political participation may be blurring the visibility and legibility of citizens' real, collective needs and wants. Essentially negative and reactive, the newer forms of participation may be unable to serve to structure or bear a positively defined collective project (Rosanvallon, 2006: 247).

In other words, notwithstanding a broadening of participation possibilities, it is as yet unclear how the newer political participation contributes to a rebalancing of citizens' and proximate policy makers' influence in the political dialogue on effective problem structuring for public policy making. Regarding this vital issue of democratic governance, political and policy analysts ought to ask the question: to what extent do citizens depend on the efforts of benign or not-so-benign proximate policy makers to reconstruct, aggregate and integrate their problem representations and framings in authoritative problem definitions and choice? To what extent does this entail the possibility or threat of gross mismatches between problem sensing and framing by large segments, maybe a majority of the population, and the professionalised or still ideology-driven problem structuring and problem selection by political and administrative elites and proximate policy makers?

Need for a problem-structuring approach

Recapitulation and conclusion

It is time to recapitulate and draw a normative conclusion. The conclusion is that we need a problem-structuring approach to the governance of problems in order to maintain, or perhaps restore, sufficient congruence between problems experienced, perceived and framed by ordinary citizens, and the ways these problems are reconstructed by proximate policy makers. More formally, *contemporary democracies, in order to maintain a sufficiently responsive system for the governance of problems, ought to develop more reflexive institutions and practices of policy-oriented and polity-oriented problem structuring.*

This conclusion, or the practical goal for this book, is premised upon the informed political estimate that at this juncture of the democratic journey a structural mismatch between problem perception and structuring by larger segments, if not a majority of the citizenry, and their proximate policy makers, is a real possibility; and therefore a threat to democratic governance. To move broad issues from the public agenda to political and decision agendas of public bodies, and from there to feasible implementation programmes, undoubtedly requires more precise problem definitions. This is the specialised task of authorities and expert proximate policy makers. But citizens have come to dislike the imposition of their governments' well-ordered, but professionally and bureaucratically pre-structured problem frames and top-down rule, no matter how effective and efficient in their own terms. They rather want their governments to develop the skills and institutions to prudently and democratically transform citizens' experiences of problematic situations and their ways of framing problem representations in truly intersubjective but authoritative public definitions of policy problems. *Better governance implies political sensitivity to different types of problem structures; and more and better reflexive problem structuring through better institutional, interactive and deliberative designs for public debate.*

The serious possibility for a structural mismatch between lay and expert problem processing is derived from a number of observations and scientifically warranted beliefs. Most important among them is that problem structuring is the vital link in problem processing. Problem processing is usually divided in two chunks: problem finding and problem solving. The more visible part, *problem solving* through alternative creation and choice, naturally has drawn the most empirical and analytic attention – both in theory and in political and administrative practice. Consequently, the less visible, submerged part of problem processing, that is, *problem finding* through problem sensing, problem identification, and problem representation through problem framing has received far less attention. Nevertheless, invisible problem representation through problem framing arguably determines or triggers the alternatives considered in visible problem solving and decision making. Thus, if we want to develop a less opaque view of problem processing we need to (re)connect the visible to the invisible parts. I propose that this is a feasible task if we focus on *problem structuring*. This part of problem processing I define, following Dunn (2007: 6), as the *self-conscious search, analysis and evaluation of competing problem representations and problem framings, with a view to their possible integration and definition.* In a more political twist, one could also define problem structuring as *the political activity to produce information on divergent views of what the problem is about, with a view to a synthetic, or at least a politically plausible choice of authoritative problem definition* (Hisschemöller and Hoppe, 2001).

In order to focus on problem-structuring aspects of public problem processing, I coin the concept of *governance of problems*. By this concept I mean the ensemble of *all those institutions, beliefs, rules and practices that are used by citizens and other policy players in public problem processing in a political system.* The concept of governance, of course, is supposed to carry all the qualifications usually meant by most authors when they warn against focusing on the state or the government as an allegedly monopolistic player in defining the common good and public policy. I agree with all connotations of institutional complementarity and more inclusive participation implied by the semantic switch from government to 'governance' (as argued in Chapter One); as long as it is acknowledged that the state has a number of interdependent political and administrative resources – legislation, taxation, use of legitimate physical force – which other players in society need in order to better solve problems with a collective, public or solidarity character.

A governance of problems approach both reasserts and supersedes the current policy-analytic or puzzling approach to problem structuring. Problem structuring, *as a property of a political system and process*, is as much about powering and participation as it is about puzzling. This is *a fortiori* the case in a normative approach informed by the possibility of a structural mismatch between problem structuring by ordinary citizens and proximate policy makers. In other words, the normative, practical task of this book – to ensure sufficient congruence or responsiveness between problem structuring by citizens and by proximate policy makers, in a more reflexive policy- and polity-oriented governance of problems – has definite implications for its *scientific goal: to explore and to develop a problem-structuring approach to the governance of problems; and to do so in a way that pays balanced attention to puzzling, powering, and participation.*

Research themes for a problem-structuring approach

Looking at citizens' potential impacts on problem structuring, the starting point is that in the governance system of representative democracy coupled with the welfare-cum-administrative state complex, ordinary citizens largely 'outsourced' problem structuring tasks to proximate policy makers. Proximate policy makers resided in institutionalised intermediary organisations like political parties, umbrella organisations like labour unions and employers' associations, and the vested interest groups. Because they had incentives to pay attention to or reconstruct citizen wants, needs, desires and policy positions, citizens kept some sort of minimal control; yet, this control was largely exercised within the boundaries provided by political, administrative, business and scientific elites in their ideology- or profession-driven, standardised policy problem framings. Roughly since Paris-1968, citizen behaviour and political participation is transforming in two directions. First, there is a consistent *downward trend in participation in electoral politics and the intermediary institutions.* Politicians and other proximate policy makers increasingly have serious problems in standing up to their conventional roles as intermediaries between government and citizens in civil society. In other words, neither the outside-in initiative model of democracy, nor the inside-access and mobilisation model of the corporatist state, which uses selected interest groups as intermediaries, performs as well as it did before. Certainly, ordinary citizens have become more aware of the dividing line in democratic politics between elites and ordinary people. This probably is a major motive for the younger, better-educated, more critical and monitorial cohorts of citizens to develop *alternative forms of political participation* – which is the second trend.

Through social movements, informal and sometimes virtual networks, more sophisticated and critical citizens have opened up political communication channels for strong, short-term responses to experienced policy failures. However, it is far from clear to what extent these newer modes of political participation are functionally equivalent mechanisms for exerting some control on proximate policy makers' problem-structuring and problem-solving activities.

How is the governance of problems, especially responsive governance, affected by such changes? How do they affect previously normal processes of problem structuring in public policy making? Are citizens really forfeiting chances for a responsive governance of their problems? Or are we overlooking alternative, less visible perhaps, structures and dynamics for aligning problem processing by citizens and proximate policy makers?

Given this overall *problématique*, in this book I will ask and answer a number of implied questions. A *first set of questions* tackles the socio-political contexts of *policy*-oriented puzzling and powering in the governance of problems:

- How may one *usefully* conceptualise problem structures? Is it possible to distinguish between types of differently structured problems? More particularly, can this be done for political task environments, that is, for politically dominant or hegemonic, and authoritatively chosen problem definitions and their translation into implementation routines and doctrines?
- Given the increased cultural fragmentation among political audiences, do different political cultures align with differently structured types of problems? What does this mean for cultural congruence between citizens and proximate policy makers?
- Given the trend in policy making to decompose the governance task into more and more functionally separate policy domains, in which policy-making tasks are accomplished by recognised players in network structures, do different types of networks recursively reproduce certain types of problem-structuring processes? Or do problem structures vary independently of types of institutionalised policy networks?

A *second set of questions* particularly addresses the puzzling or policy-analytic aspect of *policy*-oriented problem structuring:

- How did epistemological and methodological justifications of professional policy analysis develop over time; and how did they adapt to the changing political landscapes for problem structuring and solving? Especially, how did the turn to a more argumentative, problem-sensitive and frame-reflective type of policy analysis come about?

- What does this turn mean in practice? Is it possible to distinguish between several doable styles in the practice of policy analysis? Is there a link between these styles and the epistemological battles of academic policy analysts?

So far, research questions have addressed *policy*-oriented aspects of problems structuring. They concern aspects of problem structuring that are relevant from the point of view of the design, implementation and evaluation of specific policies. However, there are other aspects of problem structuring that have a broader context, in that they affect the polity as a whole or the entire set of non-policy-specific aspects of the governance of problems for a political system. Therefore, I address a *third set of questions* focusing on the *polity*-oriented, democratic and participatory aspects of a governance of problems:

- Given the divergent nature and different structures of public policy problems, can contemporary democracies successfully deal with all problem types? Or, alternatively, do different types of democracies have a bias in favour of some and at the disadvantage of other differently structured problems?
- Given the practical, political aim of a problem-structuring approach to democratic and responsive governance of problems, is it possible, and if yes, how, to nudge democracy towards more reflexive, deliberative and participatory modes of policy- and polity-oriented problem structuring?

Having formulated an overall research theme and more specific questions, I will set out a conceptual framework that elucidates the idea of the governance of problems. It will bring out the theoretical meanings and notions behind the questions asked. It will also clarify the composition of this book as a whole.

A conceptual model of the governance of problems

Multiple accounts of policy and policy making

On the face of it, the idea of the governance of problems could simply draw on the dominant paradigm of policy and conventional map of the policy-making process. This is, of course, the stages and cycle model of instrumentally rational problem solving. Wayne Parsons (1995: 77) gives a depiction of this hegemonic mapping as presented in Figure 2.2.

The inadequacy of this model is that 'problem (situation)' and 'problem definition' are just the opening moves or stages in the cycle. This ushers in all the conceptual limitations and inadequacies of the iceberg model of problem processing. What is needed is a model that understands the policy-making process without implicit or explicit comparison to the normative, linear and instrumental model. Also, we need a model that pictures policy making as a continuous questioning process, without implicitly starting from a hypothetically resolved problem; and then, in justifying the solution, proceeds to a series of logically related, but 'discrete' thought steps.

Figure 2.2: Stages and cycle model of the policy-making process

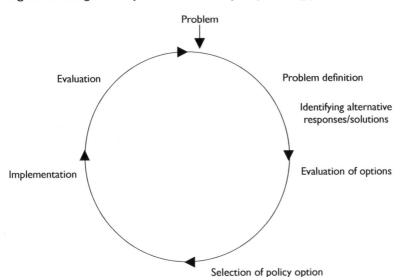

Source: Parsons (1995: 77)

If problem structuring is the continuous interpretive process that permeates and drives the entire multiframe and multiplayer policy-making process, the model ought to be amended. Dunn's (2007: 4) version renders the notion of a governance of problems through problem structuring much better (see Figure 2.3).

Figure 2.3: Dunn's model of a process of integrated policy analysis

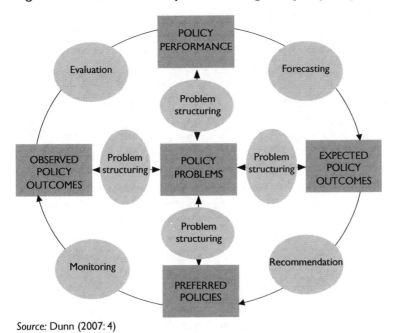

Source: Dunn (2007: 4)

However, this mapping still conceptualises problem structuring as a central intellectual activity in the set of activities making up policy design. Dunn locates problem structuring only in the puzzle or policy-analytic aspect of policy making. Also, he tends to see policy analysis primarily as decision support by proximate policy makers for political authorities. It is not clear how his model would include the powering and participation aspects of problem structuring by the total array of players differently involved in policy making, citizens included.

On closer examination of the state of the art in policy studies, the dominant paradigm and model is contested by at least two alternatives (Colebatch, 2002a, 2005, 2006b): *policy as structured interaction*, or play of power constrained by formal and informal rules on political strategies and tactics of partisan mutual adjustment among stakeholders and proximate policy makers; and *policy as social construction of meaning*, conferred on concepts used in (competing) political and administrative discourses on social problems, policy programmes and projects, but also discourse on political leadership and political obstacles or opposition. It is important here to clarify my response to this situation. *Whether or not one sees the existence of multiple accounts as problematic or not – and if not, how one sees the relationships between them – ultimately determines how one conceptualises policy and policy making.*

The sacred model

Colebatch (2006b: 318) calls the accounts of 'policy as authoritative choice' and 'policy analysis as advice or decision support' the official or *sacred* account. It is used by politicians, proximate policy makers and experts as front-office talk because it offers excellent rhetorical means to rationalise and sell the outputs of policy making to voters and citizens. After all, citizens expect government to respond to their problems; so the apparently rational movement from problem through decision to solution is common sense. It easily justifies the outsourcing of responsibilities for political judgement by ordinary citizens as lay persons; and vice versa, legitimises the prerogatives and specialised tasks of proximate policy makers, expert advisers and political authorities.

However, the sacred account is used, both in theory and practice, not because of its empirical accuracy. Actually, the puzzle is rather why, in the face of mounting evidence for alternative models (e.g. Sabatier, 1991), it is still the dominant account. Even more so, because in policy practice too there is 'a disconnect between the analysts' perception of self-worth (often drawn from the rational-actor model) and the real contribution that the individual makes in the nooks and crannies of the policy process' (Radin, 2000: 183).

In essence, the dominant model serves as a social myth; it is a Platonic 'noble lie' without which practice is alleged to fall apart. It validates the outcome of policy-making processes as a rational account of how politicians make a difference. By itself this shows that the problem-solving account has strategic power implications for the practice of policy work. For example, by saying 'We are talking just ideas now, not decisions', policy makers implicitly distinguish between policy analysis or design, and policy adoption or decision making. Drawing such a boundary implicitly reinforces status and power differences between proximate policy makers or analysts, and authorities and elected politicians who, in the regulated play of power, defend their monopoly on authoritative decisions against other policy players. Similarly, stressing 'This is mere implementation!' implicitly commands street-level bureaucrats and non-state organisations in a policy network around some issue not to challenge the dominant problem definition or adapt policy objectives inherent in adopted policy designs. Yet, such challenges and adaptations might well merit the label 'rational' if they are reflexive responses to changing circumstances on the ground. These examples alone suffice to show how puzzling and powering are inextricably tied in policy-making processes.

The profane model

The challenger, called the *'profane'* or experiential account, is policy as structured interaction and rule-constrained power play. In such an account the advice or decision support by policy 'analysts' is embodied in policy 'workers' as political auxiliaries, as networkers, boundary spanners or policy diplomats, or as policy entrepreneurs (Colebatch et al, 2010: in press). Not analytical competencies, but negotiation, 'soft' coordination, maintenance of good contacts with other key players, and instigation or 'sparking-off' of supportive or at least non-veto stances, become key social skills for trained policy workers. In these types of back-office account for policy it makes no sense to speak of the rational solution, based on unshakable evidence and the persuasive power of the better arguments. The adopted course of action rather appears epiphenomenally as victorious alternative because it just happened to get more political support from stakeholders in processes of mutual adjustment based on calculated interests and political deals. Policy is not a rational solution to some problem; to the extent that it is a cognitive or cultural phenomenon, it results from partisan analyses (Lindblom, 1968) inspired by fixed commitments of important resources by vested interests and known stakeholders in issue machines. And here too, policy is part of shaping the political action itself. Saying 'We need a gun control, anti-abortion or climate change policy' is a political claim for attention on other policy makers; it is a politically inspired attempt at problem framing or even for exclusive control over problem definition; it seeks commitment of (some of) *their* resources for achieving *your* policy objectives.

A social-constructivist double perspective

It bears stressing that the sacred and profane, official and experiential, front- and back-office accounts of policy and policy making are being actively used both in academic theory and political-administrative practice. These are plausible facts in the social construction account of policy. If policy is viewed as being part of political sense making, as claims to control and fix the meaning of concepts used in political debates and struggles, it is only logical to apply this insight to the policy-making process itself. It means we may *subsume the sacred and profane accounts of policy under the social construction account.* The implication is that policy making may be constructed or viewed as, indeed, encompassing puzzling (sacred, rational problem-solving account), powering (profane, structured interaction and power-play account) and participation (because policy players are all engaged in exercises of sense making and meaning giving).

However, more important even, from a social constructivist point of view, *policy making becomes the governance of problems.* Participants in policy making all do so from different positions in space–time, with different experiences, stakes, values, norms and beliefs. The possibility of collective action may become a reality only if they manage to create some common or shared understandings on why they seek cooperation and collective action at all. The essential process therefore is the joint construction of problems as a condition for joint responses. This can only be achieved by insisting that one's understanding of a situation as problematic, and of some joint actions as better than other responses, ought to be recognised by other participants as valid. In other words, *problem claims processing* is the way in which situations come to be seen as 'shared problems' to which collective projects, actions and plans are the proper 'shared response'. Analysis or instigation, rationality or power, puzzling or powering – from a social constructivist position they appear as alternative or entwined modes of claiming (and making sure) that certain problems come to be shared so as to be processed for joint responses. That is why I propose to view policy making as the governance of problems.

Mapping the governance of problems.

The purpose of the map to be presented here (see Figure 2.4) is to help understand why problem definitions are, or are not, or only partially, accepted in public, collective action. The perspective is a social-constructivist interpretation of problem processing by political and policy players, in which there is due attention to puzzling, powering and participation in mostly sub-surface problem finding and problem structuring, and directly visible problem solving. Figure 2.4 depicts how, in this view, transition, framing and design dynamics of problem structuring connect socio-political and knowledge contexts to each other and to policy designs.[6] They are the 'transmission belts' of problem structuring in a governance of problems. The theoretical claim, to be illustrated in the rest of the book, is that these translation, framing and design dynamics correspond to politically dominant problem frames and problem structures.

Designs as strategic problem-solution couplings

Above, it was argued that citizens outsource their policy-making tasks to more proximate policy makers and authorities. These policy players have moderate incentives to reconstruct citizens' preferences in order to maintain their roles

Figure 2.4: Map of mechanisms in problem structuring and a governance of problems

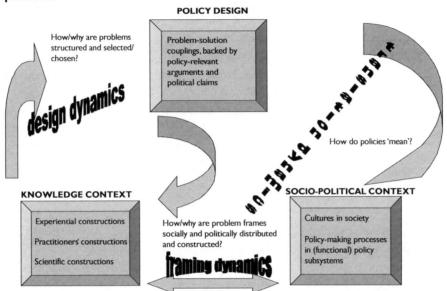

and functions. Whether justified or not, they will certainly claim that their policy designs address citizens' concerns and issues. Such authoritative claims will always be there; policy designs and decisions are never *tabula rasa*, emerging from the heads of individual policy makers trying to solve problems. Therefore, quite different from the stages and cycle model, analysis departs from the upper box representing adopted policy designs and standing implementation regimes. Policy design is inextricably interlaced with processes of structured interaction between politicians and other proximate policy makers, resulting in authoritative decision making or policy adoption, and structured commitments of resources in implementation regimes. Quite simply, it means that, once politically decided, adopted and officially proclaimed by government, policy designs cannot be changed or ignored as easily as other types of political preferences or decisions. Shore and Wright (1997) argue that policy designs establish order by structuring discourse on problems, goals and means through framings that bolster the authority of rulers by limiting and neutralising potentially opposing views. Majone and Wildavsky (1979: 165) observe that policy designs, once politically adopted, tend to become doctrines, publicly justifying governmental intervention programmes and routines. True, during implementation, policies are continuously subjected to multiple influences of individuals, interests and institutions. Hence, only after political argumentation, debate and decision taking in some representative or other properly authorised body, political protagonists of a policy design have a chance (but no guarantee) to infuse a policy design with sufficient political power and support so as to acquire its disciplining and justificatory function during implementation (Majone, 1978: 211).

The justificatory function of official policy texts is essentially in its promise to achieve certain goals in a public effort to meet citizens' needs and solve or keep a problem under control. Thus, in a problem-processing approach, analysts need not be interested in all elements of policy designs. Instead, the focus will be on claims about problem-solution couplings[7] and their argumentative backing in policy documents reflecting the beliefs of their designers. It is imperative to carefully analyse from a cognitive-political perspective the types of problems posed to government by its citizens. Logically speaking, all problems are experienced as non-acceptable discrepancies between real situations and desired future situations; between a socially constructed 'is' and 'ought'. However, from a political as well as cognitive point of view, *they vary in terms of degree of consent on relevant, valid knowledge on what is and will or can be; as well as in terms of degree of consent on values, norms and standards at stake in defining a desirable future situation.* This insight is the basis for a fundamental typology of different kinds of public problems: structured, unstructured and two types of moderately structured problems (see Chapters One and Three). It means to start to unravel the twists and turns of policy processes by empirical, interpretive reconstructions of policy belief systems; in particular, what they tell us about politically dominating problem definitions, and the social and political distribution of alternative problem framings (Van de Graaf and Hoppe, 1989: 100-29; Hisschemöller, 1993: 39-41; Fischer, 2003: 191-8). This book is built on the thesis that the differently structured types of problems, through translation, framing and design dynamics, have selective affinities or congruencies with different cultures as ways of life, different types of policy networks, different types of doing policy analysis and even different types of democracy and citizen participation. Ultimately, the successful dealing with different types of problems requires different styles of governance. This is the normative and political, pragmatic implication for the *good governance of problems*.

Translation dynamics

Policy designs and their hegemonic problem definition impact on wider social contexts through *translation dynamics* (Schneider and Ingram, 1997: 79). They are about 'how policies mean' (Yanow, 1996). Given the nature of policy making as a question-and-answer game, it is imperative to pay attention to the public's role as an active audience. The model distinguishes (only) between two types of socio-political contexts (depicted in the lower right-hand box in Figure 2.4). First, the meaning of policy designs and implementation regimes is constructed through interpretive processes by groups, or target populations in society at large; they are conceptualised as *cultures and ways of life in society* (see Chapter Four). Second, translation dynamics also involve the more immediate policy domains through interpretive processes in *policy politics*, that is, types of politics and mutual adjustment between proximate policy makers working in networks of specific policy domains (see Chapters Five and Six).

Using grid-group cultural theory, congruencies will be revealed between preferred ways of problem structuring by proximate policy makers and certain ways of life or cultures as coherent configurations of institutions, beliefs and behavioural strategies (see Chapter Four). Firms, civil society associations and individual citizens will experience a policy design's impact on their action strategies and options. This happens mostly in their interpretation of policy messages (of which official policy texts will be only a small segment); and in their encounters with policy instruments wielded by policy implementers. Both interpretations and encounters are routinely informed by their own cultures or ways of life, with their typical day-by-day problem-solving practices. Depending on how policy designs impact on their cultures, citizens will construct their own favourable or not-so-favourable interpretation of the meaning of the policy for them. In such translation processes, citizens' long-term, stable conceptions of the role of government, of implementing agencies, of interest groups and of citizenship itself are shaped and reshaped. Patterns of political power, interaction and participation are reinforced or weakened as well (Schneider and Ingram, 1997). This is how policy implementation practices are always a communicative and interpretive process between policy players and ordinary citizens (Grin and Van de Graaf, 1996).

The translation dynamics of policy framings and designs may also impact on how political authorities and specialised proximate policy makers themselves, formally and informally, cooperate and compete in the play of power around policy problems. In the 'cacophony' of societal debate and preference formation in civil society and the media, authorities and proximate policy makers turn to (and actively facilitate the crystallisation of) more conveniently arranged functional networks of policy-relevant players (Lauman and Knoke, 1987). They mostly consist of bureaucratic agencies, business organisations, civil society associations and other nongovernmental single-issue organisations, around policy issues defined by themselves: 'The practice in almost all governments is for policies to emerge from the "stovepipes" that link functional experts at all levels of government with interest groups and with other advocates within the policy area' (Peters, 1996: 2).

Thus, politicians and policy makers have come to rely more on systems of functional, neo-corporatist interest representation, next to the traditional nationwide systems of representative democracy. In these functional policy domains or subsystems, networks of proximate policy makers are involved in a policy issue on a continuous basis. Bureaucratic agencies and other types of public sector organisations involved in implementation of the policy 'read' the official policy design; and subsequently adapt or redirect their standard operating routines, personnel policies, budget strategies and strategic plans. Like in the translation dynamics for culture, for these policy domains the question arises as to whether or not types of problem structuring correspond to particular types of policy networks; particularly, the ways they structure rules of interaction, inclusion and exclusion from the 'corridors of power'.

Framing dynamics

Moving on from the translation dynamics of powering and participation in the socio-political context, the map focuses next on the puzzle aspect of framing dynamics. In politics, problem representations and framings are always contested; but the contest is not random or open. One may observe that policy designs and the socio-political contexts co-construct, as it were, a knowledge context (depicted in the lower left-hand box of Figure 2.4). There is a kind of co-evolution of a direct translation dynamics between design and knowledge context; and a mutual *framing dynamics* between socio-political and knowledge contexts. The major issue here is *how different types of knowledge on how to frame problems are socially and politically distributed*.

The concept of 'knowledge' is a problematic and multifaceted one (see Rooney et al, 2003b; Rooney and Schneider, 2005: 1936). Knowledge is different from data and information. Data are loose 'bits' like numbers, words, sounds and pictures. When organised one way or another, they are the building blocks of information, for example as texts, statistics, tapes or movies. Knowledge comes about when intellects process, make sense of and give meaning to information. This is a complex social activity that situates knowers in relation to larger interpretive contexts. When talking of politics, policy making and problem processing, these larger *interpretive-relational contexts* are policy designs, policy (implementation) regimes in networks, and the cultural, socio-political context. Culture, and cultural differences, provide individuals and groups with the basic templates or intellectual, attitudinal, emotional and institutional 'compass' directions with which to bring coherence and system to their interpretation of policy-relevant information. Regarding specific problems, policy texts, verbal communications and other information about policy designs provide a more focused interpretive context for their responses.

But there is a *social-relational context* to knowledge as well. This is why some analysts think we should not talk about 'knowledge' as a noun for a static phenomenon, but about 'knowing' as a verb for giving meaning and developing understanding (Rooney et al, 2003b: 3). These processes transcend solitary minds. They depend on social interactions and structures by intellects that occupy different cultural orientations and domains, and belong to different policy networks, or play out different roles in the same network, but do communicate with each other in some structured ways. There is an important difference in how people socially construct meaning. As cultural 'animals' belonging to particular ways of life, knowledge construction has a high 'beer mat' scent; it will be largely *experiential*, that is intuitive, sometimes unarticulated, or even tacit and non-verbal. As policy network actors, proximate policy makers construct meaning and knowledge in much more conscious, deliberate and articulated ways. However, as *practitioners' knowledge*, their constructions still display considerable elements of unarticulated know-who, know-what and know-how, and tacit learning from (sometimes) trendy 'best practice'. It is only as members of *professional or scientific* communities that knowledge construction takes on full-blown forms of articulation, codification and hence publicly transparent knowledge, emphasising know-why and evidence-based learning.

In this book, the focus is not on the experiential and practitioners' knowledge constructions; or on the role of the media in the social constructions of problems and knowledge. Instead, attention is trained on scientific and professional knowledge, especially on the art and craft of policy analysis and giving policy advice or being a good policy worker (in Chapters Five through Seven). Of course, the important insight that professional and scientific knowledge never stands alone is acknowledged. Policy analysis can no longer be conceptualised as putting 'theory' into 'practice'. Policy analysis is a dense and frequently opaque interplay of lay, practitioners' and professional or academic knowledge. In a very real sense, it is co-constructed by the other manifestations of knowledge. Co-construction of different types of knowledge is the central tenet in contemporary theories on the changing role of science in society, like post–normal science (Funtowicz and Ravetz, 1992; Ravetz, 1999), Mode 2 science (Nowotny et al, 2001), new relationships between universities, industry and government (Etzkowitz and Leydesdorff, 1997), not to mention the many digitally supported knowledge networks that have sprung up during the last decade to connect experts such as academicians and professionals with practitioners (Halffman and Hoppe, 2005). In this new knowledge landscape, policy advice and policy analysis moved from neo-positivist and critical-rational modes of 'speaking truth to power' in the direction of interpretive and neo-pragmatist modes of 'making sense together' (Hoppe, 1999).

Design dynamics

If looked at from the perspective of usable knowledge for and in policy (Lindblom and Cohen, 1979; Lindblom, 1990), the knowledge context of policy design processes is frequently underdetermined and understructured. *Design dynamics* is the way in which political order is argumentatively extracted from and imposed on available stocks of knowledge with a view to coming to a political judgement and political decisions on how to act as a polity. *Design dynamics are about the political-cum-intellectual structuring and political choice of problem definitions.* Designs come about, alternatively, as quasi-rational use of the toolkit of methods of optimisation under constraints; or as satisficing by trained problem solvers like policy analysts (Simon, 1992; Dunn, 2004); or as boundedly rational processes of incremental borrowing, tinkering, lesson drawing, knowing-in-action and reflection-on-practice by reflective practitioners (Braybrooke and Lindblom, 1963; Schön, 1983; Rose, 1993). Design dynamics at their best feature what Dunn (2004: 1-2) considers the true calling of policy analysis: 'inquiry designed to create, critically assess, and communicate information that is useful in understanding and improving policies'.

In the real world of policy analysis, higher-order problem-structuring heuristics are the actual drivers behind design processes (Hoppe, 1983). Normatively, problem structuring would see to the 'congruence' of lower-order problem-solving methods (Dunn, 1988: 724): 'The appropriateness of a particular type of method is a function of its congruence with the type of problem under investigation'. Thus, from a prescriptive and methodological point of view, problem structuring is about putting intellectually defensible and politically authoritative closure on debates about constraints on problem definitions and solutions through responsible problem decomposition, and prudent constraint sequencing during the design process. Some problem decompositions and some forms of constraint sequencing do less violence to problem sensing and framing outside of proximate and authoritative policy-making circles; and, therefore, result in more effective, efficient and legitimate policies as attempted problem solutions. Chapter Seven explores what such a frame-reflective and problem-oriented method of policy structuring and design would look like. Policy analysis as 'making sense together' requires more reflexive problem structuring; which in its turn requires a rethinking of the toolkit for 'doable' policy analysis, policy advice, or policy work as a craft.

Perhaps needless to repeat that policy designs are not merely cognitive or rational processes. Political, institutional, organisational and other social and structural forces bring their constraining effects to bear on design processes. We know that politicians judge policy proposals from a knowledge interest in the risks and opportunities of power enlargement, maintenance or loss (Schneider and Ingram, 1997: 111ff; 't Hart et al, 2002). The admissibility and weight of policy information about effectiveness, efficiency and organisational and financial feasibility more often than not also depends on answers to questions such as 'How many believe this?', 'Who are they?', and 'With what intensity do they believe it?'; or 'How will this policy proposal affect electoral chances and coalition strategy?' (Webber, 1992).

Bureaucratic agencies too have their own interests in political visibility, maintaining a policy culture and decision-making style, and standard operating procedures. All of these are potential sources of constraints on problem framings and definitions. The same is true for institutionalised boundary work by science advisers in independent think tanks and government-sponsored boundary organisations between science and politics (Jasanoff, 1990; Guston, 2001; Hoppe, 2005). Besides that, the line between framing and design dynamics sometimes is blurred and permeable. Politicians, interest groups, policy analysts and sometimes even science advisers act as policy entrepreneurs (Kingdon, 1984; Roberts and King, 1991; Zahariadis, 2003) working both sides of the line: influencing public opinion on problem definitions or favoured problem solutions, and simultaneously working hard to get problem definitions and solutions accepted in authoritative policy texts.

Political and bureaupolitical realities ought to be accounted for in a view of design dynamics. Charles Lindblom (1968: 32-33) already taught that the puzzling of policy analysis is not a substitute for the play of power; as partisan analysis it 'does not avoid fighting over policy; it is a method of fighting'. And Aaron Wildavsky (1980 [1979]: 17) used to say that policy making is both cogitation and interaction, where clever and creative cogitation is in the service of improved political interaction. Political interaction improves when there are less ill-structured problems or structural mismatches between problem definitions and policy designs by authoritative decision makers and problem framings by other relevant political, societal and economic actors in the system.

Normative implications for the polity

So far, translation, framing and design dynamics have been discussed as policy-specific mechanisms of problem-structuring processes. Jointly, they can be said to make up a polity's drivers in the governance of problems. It means that, next to a *policy*-oriented approach, one should also pay attention to a *polity*-oriented approach to the governance of problems. Institutions matter, and should be brought back into policy analysis. This is where a governance of problems addresses what Paul Diesing (1962: 171-2) calls political rationality: the concern about the preservation of a sufficiently well-developed, long-term and productive problem-processing capacity for the political system or polity as a whole. This can be done through linking up the conception of problem structuring and problem processing to normative political theory.

From such a perspective, the problem typology and notions of responsible problem structuring and reasoned political choice of problems have considerable implications. They can be summarised as the development of a normative theory of the governance and democracy of problems. Any political regime or system ought to have sufficiently flexible and robust governance structures and policy-making repertoires to deal in appropriate ways with all types of problems. The final three chapters of this book explore such implications. Chapter Eight takes steps in the direction of a democratic meta-theory for the governance of problems. Chapter Nine reflects on the possibilities of a meta-governance of problems; that is, nudging the political system to more reflexive, deliberative and participatory modes of problem structuring. In this framework, different forms of citizen participation are studied from the angle of different types of problem structuring. Special attention is given to ironies and perplexities of running deliberative and participatory democratic experiments in policy analysis.

A final theme in a polity-oriented normative view on the governance of problems, addressed in Chapter Ten, concerns the relationship between powering and puzzling. In their handbooks and other writings, policy analysts too self-evidently and unreflexively attribute primacy to puzzling or analysis over powering or instigation. Normatively, this amounts to a preference for a politics of vision. Yet, in practice, more often than not one experiences the primacy of instigation practices over design quality. Shapiro, a one-time political appointee heading the Office of Information and Regulatory Affairs (OIRA), as part of the US President's Office of Management and Budget (OMB), summarises his experience by the observation that when politics and analysis openly conflict, politics always trumps analysis (quoted in West, 2005). When this is condoned, one may speak of a politics of will. More frequently, the asymmetrical relation between power and reason is regretfully acknowledged, an attitude characteristic for a politics of realism or resignation. These are all views that I reject in favour of a politics of hope and prudence. Applied to the governance of problems this means that puzzling and powering, in designed alternation or oscillation, and under steadily increasing participation and probing by involved people, can work in tandem for wise societal guidance.

Notes

[1] Readers who are unfamiliar with or who are keen on clarity of conceptual distinctions before they are introduced and explained in this section, are advised to turn to Box 2.1 on pages 30-31, where major concepts in a governance of problems approach are listed.

[2] A philosophical reflection on and elaboration of this tension is to be found, under the label of problematology, in Turnbull (2005).

[3] Michel Foucault, interview: Polemics, Politics and Problematizations, source: http://foucault.info/foucault/interview.html

[4] This double label deliberately evokes the American historical connotations of 'pragmatism' and 'progressivism'. Positioning themselves as 'outsiders' whose intention was a reform of the Dutch political system of pillarised, consensus democracy, D'66 embraced non-ideological pragmatism as its political philosophy, and as frequent concrete political stance it adopted outright pro-technocratic and pro-professionalisation positions. In the 1980s and 1990s, they evolved into a kind of discourse coalition builder between Conservatives (VVD) and Liberals (Labour).

[5] Problem-structuring heuristics and methods will keep us occupied in major parts of Chapters Three through Seven of this book. Here, the focus is more on the institutionalised and newer modes of political participation by citizens, and their potential impact on problem structuring in the democratic governance of problems.

[6] In presenting this map, I gratefully acknowledge inspiration from Schneider and Ingram (1997: 73ff).

[7] In Chapter Three it is explained why I speak of problem-solution *couplings*.

THREE

Analysing policy problems: a problem-structuring approach

We do not discover a problem 'out there'; we make a choice about
how we want to formulate a problem. (Lindblom and Cohen, 1979: 50)

Introduction

This chapter introduces the typology of policy problems that underlies the rest
of the book. This requires some preliminary conceptual work. Choosing a social-
constructivist approach, the first section develops the perspective of a politics of
meaning. It views politics as the collective attempt to control a polity's shared
response to the adversities and opportunities of the human condition. The second
section gives an overview of how others have approached the social and political
analysis of policy issues or problems. Here the proposal is to look at problem
structuring as socio-cognitive processes that frame political task environments.
From this perspective, four types of policy problems are posited: structured,
unstructured and two types of moderately structured problems. The third section
discusses properties of structured versus unstructured problems; and analyses how
unstructured problems get to be structured through problem decomposition
and constraint sequencing. These two processes do not always follow the gradual
increase in professional or scientific insight. Frequently, problem decomposition
and constraint sequencing follow from critical events, like political decisions, mood
swings in public opinion or changes in important markets. Different framings of
the HIV/AIDS issue in Europe, the US and South Africa illustrate the concepts
introduced in this chapter.

The politics of meaning

A social-constructivist approach

'What disturbs men's minds is not events but their judgements on events', wrote
Epictetus, a Stoic philosopher (c. 55 – c. 135 E.C.), in his *Discourses and Manual*
(5, trans. Matheson, 1916). This statement is an early precursor of what we now
call a constructivist interpretation of reality (for an overview, see Schwandt,
1994). Most of us would agree that knowing and thinking are not passive. Our
minds do not merely mirror reality but are actively engaged in creating images
of reality. This is amply demonstrated in disciplines as diverse as phenomenology,
humanistic hermeneutics, experimental cognitive psychology and neuroscience.

The insight takes on a special meaning for the social sciences, where it is also acknowledged that experiences of reality are in fact social constructions. Social actors attribute 'reality' to phenomena not only as individual minds and speakers; but also as exponents of shared systems of intelligibility – written or spoken language, and images or symbols, mostly. The conventions of language and its concepts and symbolisms generate a social process of meaning giving or interpretation. These processes are socially distributed, not of universal validity, but valid for special, albeit sometimes large, groups or categories of people.

One can hardly underestimate the importance of (social) constructivism in social science research and theory. In one discipline after another, interpretivism, symbolic interactionism, linguistics, speech act theory, ethics of communicative action, discourse analysis, conversation analysis, argumentation theory and the like, rose to popularity. In feminist theory, for example, the centrality of the concept of 'gender', meaning the social construction of 'male' and 'female' as distinct from the anatomical difference, is unthinkable without a social-constructivist approach (Outshoorn, 1989: 13ff). Much the same can be claimed for the significance of the gender concept in practical politics and anti-discrimination policy (Mansbridge, 1986).

In political science and the policy sciences, too, social constructivism has become an important strand of research and theory (for an overview, see Parsons, 1995: 94–109). Anticipating the trend in the early 1960s, French political philosopher and political scientist Bertrand de Jouvenel (1963:99) formulated as a first axiom of *The pure theory of politics*: 'The working of words upon action is the basic political action'. Pursuing this theme, other authors (Sederberg, 1984; Fischer and Forester, 1993; Hajer, 1995; Stone, 1997; Hoppe, 1999) developed a theory of the politics of meaning. Politics is conceptualised as an attempt to control shared meaning:

> [L]anguage itself is highly unstable and shifting because symbolization is always incomplete.... The role of the Law [and Public Policy, RH] is, therefore, to institute meaning by establishing an authoritative 'no!' that stops the sliding of meaning. This authoritative no allows for the creation of sense and viable contexts for human interaction by fixing meaning. (Catlaw, 2006: 267)

Thus, politics becomes an arena for conflict over the concepts used in framing political judgements on social problems, public policies, and political leaders and enemies (Unger, 1987: 10; Edelman, 1988; Rochefort and Cobb, 1994). In the case of democracies, this conflict is managed by a public debate and structured communication and interaction between political players. The temporary and always contestable result is a negotiated definition of meanings shared by a majority in the polity or the dominant advocacy coalition in a policy domain.

In such a view of politics, public policy making becomes the privilege and capacity to authoritatively define the nature of shared meanings (Sederberg, 1984: 67) in relevant policy language, texts, objects and artefacts (Yanow, 1999).

It is a never-ending series of communications and strategic moves by which various policy actors in all kinds of forums of public deliberation and coupled arenas of policy subsystems construct intersubjective meanings. These meanings are continually written into the 'authored documents' of collective projects and plans; and in the 'constructed texts' (Yanow, 1999) of implementers' routines and practices, and the ways ordinary citizens or target populations interpret their encounters with formal policy actors. All these ways of 'how policies mean' (Yanow, 1996), in conjunction with the interpretation of contingencies and surprises unrelated to policy, may generate the new issues in the next round or episode of political judgement and meaning constructions; and so on (see Figure 2.4, Chapter Two).

Social and political analysis of public policy problems

Social constructivism gained ascendancy in the sociological analysis of social problems (Spector and Kitsuse, 1977; Gusfield, 1981). The social constructivist view in policy and politics also gained much popularity in political science as the politics of problem definition and agenda setting (Elder and Cobb, 1983; Kingdon, 1984; Baumgartner and Jones, 1993; Rochefort and Cobb, 1994; Cobb and Ross, 1997b; Zahariadis, 2003). Sociologists and political scientists are both interested in 'what we choose to identify as public issues and how we think and talk about these concerns' (Rochefort and Cobb, 1994). Political scientists, particularly, add an agenda–setting perspective to this general interest: how to get issues, talked about in public opinion and public debate, on or off the political and institutional agendas of political parties and Parliaments; and how to move on to the policy or decision agendas of, say, departments or other administrative agencies.

The former problem was Schattschneider's (1960 [1988]) main theme in his classic work entitled *The semi-sovereign people*. His basic hypothesis is that the politics of problem framing is about privatising or expanding the scope of political conflict. Political parties and interest groups manipulate problem frames in order to decrease or increase chances for mobilising political support. This political knowledge interest has dominated much research and writing on the politics of problem framing to this very day. At first, researchers were interested in how new issues are framed and put on the agenda successfully by political strategies for expansion of conflict (Cobb and Elder, 1972). Later they developed an interest in strategies of agenda denial through problem avoidance, attack or redefinition (Cobb and Ross, 1997b). Because problem framings are examined mainly for their (in)capacity to mobilise large audiences for political support, the connection between problem finding and solving (through institutions, agencies, or in implementation structures and policy networks) is not a well-articulated theme in this strand of the literature.

The relation between problem framing, agenda setting and policy development or design is representative of another branch in the study of political problems: the development of *issue typologies*. This type of theorising and research attempts to connect policy substance to policy process. The basic idea in political science is Lowi's (1995 [1972]) famous thesis that policy determines politics, in the sense that 'perceived attributes of the policy determine the attributes of the political process that makes that policy' (McCool, 1995: 175). Each type of policy creates and institutionalises its own type of distinct political subsystem and 'policy politics' in the political architecture of the whole.

For Lowi, a citizen's proximity to state coercion is the most important characteristic of politics. Therefore, his typology focuses on coercive impacts of policy and policy instruments on citizens and society. In *regulative* policies (like rules against fraudulent advertising, or unfair competition), governments have the highest and immediate coercive impact on citizens' lives or corporate conduct. Since regulative policies define the relationship between politics and citizen in direct hierarchical terms, and because they affect every citizen equally, Lowi hypothesises that it brings about an open and truly public and pluralist-competitive kind of politics. This is how the properties of policy define state–society and state–citizen relations (Stone, 1997: 259-62). Because they also shape political arenas and types of power relations around issues, policies define types of political processes or policy politics. Coercive impact is lowest in so-called *constituent* or system maintenance policies (like organisational reforms or propaganda on birth control), because here government coercion is remote, and works only through changing the environment of individual conduct, not the conduct itself.

Distributive policies (like tariffs and subsidies for particular industries) are of an in-between type: coercion is low but works directly on individual firms. In Lowi's eyes, distributive policies mostly lead to a 'privatised', pork barrel, closed and clientelist or patronage kind of politics. They distribute benefits to small, well-defined constituencies at public cost. The other in-between type of policy is *redistributive*, like progressive income taxes, social security and many other welfare state programmes. Here coercion is immediate, but pertains to classes of people, not individuals. These kinds of policies lead to a conflictual kind of politics between peak associations of business and labour, mobilising groups along lines of class. Overall, used normatively by political scientists as guardians of democratic quality, Lowi's typology suggests a preference for regulatory policies because they lead to political processes in which interest groups and citizen participation most closely approximate pluralist democratic ideals.[1]

Others have also devised typologies using other traits of policies, but with the same aim of improving democratic governance. For example, Wilson (1989: 72-89) devised a typology around the confrontation between government agencies and interest groups, depending on a policy's anticipated or perceived pattern of allocation of benefits and costs. When most or all of a policy's benefits go to a small, identifiable interest (business sector, profession, locality), but most or all costs are borne by all taxpayers, the policy will institutionalise a political arena where an agency is confronted with one dominant interest group, which favours its goals in an atmosphere of *client politics*. Civil aviation regulation before the big deregulation of the 1980s had this character. The opposite type is an *entrepreneurial*

---

politics, in which the implementing agency has to fight a dominant interest group hostile to its official goals. This type of policy politics is created by a policy that concentrates costs (on an industry, locality, region or a profession), but spreads benefits over a large number of people. National highway traffic safety under the spur of scandals and a clever policy entrepreneur like Ralph Nader is a good example.

The third case occurs when a policy generates both high per capita concentrated costs and per capita concentrated benefits, like in occupational health and safety regulation. Here, the implementing agency can hold its own in a system of *interest group politics*, exactly because it is 'sandwiched' between rival interest groups strongly motivated to organise in the conflict over its goals. Finally, Wilson's typology acknowledges a political situation of *majoritarian politics*, where implementing agencies do not meet overt and permanent opponents or proponents. This occurs in cases such as national defence, where the policy appears to distribute widely dispersed benefits and impose widely distributed costs.

Wilson believes that most policies enact clientelist and entrepreneurial political environments, leading to 'big government' and overproduction of goods and services through the public sector. Paradoxically, Wilson's political and administrative science-based issue typology shows the same knowledge interest as those of political economists and public choice scholars. The latter look at the public (collective) or private (market) quality of goods and services provided to citizens (Olson, 1965; Moe, 1980; Weimer and Vining, 1999). Wilson (1989: 369ff) and the public choice theorists have argued for policies that create markets, or introduce and institutionalise market-like elements, or at least deregulation in the public sector.

Neo-positivist and social-constructivist criticism of issue typologies

Issue typologies like Lowi's and Wilson's have been criticised on both neo-positivist and social-constructivist counts. From a neo-positivist position Greenberg et al (1977) and Smith (2002) have pointed out that issue typologies are hardly testable due to the complicated nature and theoretical underspecification of concepts like policy, policy processes, policy contexts and policy outputs or outcomes. One major problem is the multiplicity of aspects to take into consideration. Does Wilson take into account all types of a policy's costs and benefits? Do these costs and benefits and their pattern of concentration and dispersal not change over time? In classifying a policy issue, should we give more weight to participants' ('subjective') perceptions or to analysts' ('objective') judgements or measurements?[2] And how to deal with the problem of multiple participants with diverging views on the matter?

Also, using these typologies it turns out that most policies are mixes of more or less coercive instruments; the dispersed or concentrated character of costs and benefits is very difficult to establish. Unambiguous classification of existing policies is near impossible or a very rare case.[3] Then, there are problems in specifying the timeframe for differences between policy intentions and policy outputs or real impacts on societies, or in specifying relevant interactions between the many influences or independent variables impinging on stages in policy processes, outputs and outcomes.[4] While Lowi seems to limit the empirical domain of his typology to the agenda-setting and policy formulation-plus-adoption stages of policy making, Wilson clearly expands it into the policy implementation stage and its outcomes.

It has also been pointed out that problem framing is not just political strategy and tactics, but also has strong institutional traits. Policies may change and bring about a new politics after radical change during the punctuation period in long-term policy dynamics (Baumgartner and Jones, 1993). As solutions become institutionalised, during the long-term equilibrium or incremental policy adaptation normally following radical change, the type of policy politics also recursively and routinely recreates particular types of problems. Thus, Lowi's iconoclastic turnaround of political science wisdom of the 1960s – not politics determines policy, but policy determines politics – must be viewed by contemporary insight as an arbitrary breaking into the causal loop of mutual constitution of politics and policy: 'as politics creates policy, policies also remake politics' (Skocpol, 1992: 58). Or, as Schneider and Ingram (1997: 6) put it: 'policy designs are a product of their historical context, but they also create a subsequent context with its own form of politics from which the next round of public policy will ensue'.

The most thorough criticism of the issue typology literature actually has come from a social-constructivist point of view. Steinberger's basic claim is that the meaning attributed to a policy is inherently ambiguous; and thus itself becomes the focus for political struggle:

> [Policy controversies] generally involve two (or more) entirely different and competing understandings and definitions of the very same policy, of its purpose, its substance and its potential impact....The implications are that each policy is likely to have different *meanings* for different participants; that the exact meaning of a policy, then, is by no means self-evident, but, rather, is ambiguous and manipulable; and that the policy process is – at least in part – a struggle to get one or another meaning established as the accepted one. (Steinberger, 1980, in McCool, 1995: 223)

Therefore, a typology of policy issues would have to discover and order what meanings are relevant to those involved in defining the policy.

To our knowledge, there have been two efforts to apply these suggestions for new theory building. Anderson (1997) has argued that 'suasion' should be included in the Lowi typology. Suasion denotes language- and communication-based, manipulatory or educational techniques of governing, or the deliberate creation of 'governmentality'. Anderson mentions the genesis of public health policies by the hygienist movement in the US and Europe as the perfect example. According to Anderson, suasion fits in the Lowi typology as a milder form of coercion. Lowi (1997) himself rejected the use of 'suasion' as a separate category; if anything, language, communication, persuasion and education are underlying all other policy types. Lowi himself might not agree, but this is the typically social-constructivist and interpretivist response in line with Steinberger's suggestions.

Schneider and Ingram (1997) advanced a theoretically much more sophisticated social-constructivist policy-making theory. In their view, policy is made in processes of social knowledge construction about the identities of target populations, in contexts of power and institutional relationships. They focus on two types of contexts that have a socially divisive and therefore degenerative effect on democratic politics.

In one context, politicians strategically manipulate the social construction of issues and target populations for political gain. They stereotype a policy's target population into 'deserving' and 'undeserving' groups. In policy designs, they confer benefits (subsidies, tax breaks, one-stop service provision) on the 'deserving', and burden the 'undeserving' with punishments, high costs or neglect. Through the advocacy of some groups considered as 'deserving' (for example the entrepreneurial middle-class citizen), politicians create a constituency that will re-elect them, and simultaneously create an image of policy success for a broader political audience. Through stigmatising other groups as 'undeserving' (for example 'economic' as opposed to 'political' refugees) or 'deviants' (for example drug addicts, young criminals, potential terrorists), politicians in fact strengthen their positive public image, but at the price of alienating substantive parts of the citizenry from politics and democratic participation.

The other policy context is sometimes advocated as the proper antidote to the former, 'populist' way of engaging in politics and policy making. Instead of exploiting the stereotypes and stigmas in the social construction of knowledge by the masses, politicians and policy makers should stick to the sober and evidence-based processes of scientific and professional knowledge production for policy. If politicians see more risks than opportunities in a particular policy issue, and if science manages to speak with one voice, problem framing, definition and policy design are left to experts and professionals. However, these 'technocratic' policy contexts also degenerate democratic politics by turning citizens and voters into passive spectators and mere consumers of programme delivery.

Schneider's and Ingram's theory is a real step forward in a social-constructivist programme of theory development in political science, public administration and policy science. They correctly emphasise the relatively understudied role of the social construction of knowledge in contexts of policy design and formulation. However, their dichotomised picture of populist versus technocratic political contexts for public policy making is too simplistic. The role of the social construction of knowledge in policy design and formulation is probably more complex, rich, multifaceted and diverse. For example, in the literature on knowledge utilisation (for good overviews, see Weiss, 1980, 1991; Webber, 1992; Landry et al, 2003; Nutley et al, 2007), a more fine-grained picture of the role of knowledge in policy analysis and design emerges. This is confirmed if one looks at work on problem finding and problem solving in such diverse fields as operations research and systems analysis (Ackoff, 1978; Mason and Mitroff, 1981; Midgley, 2000), design and decision sciences (Kleindorfer et al, 1993; Dorst, 2004), artificial intelligence (Simon, 1973), policy analysis (Rittel and Webber, 1973; Dery, 1984; Chisholm, 1995; Dunn, 2007), the social study of science and technology (Hoppe, 2005) and cognitive psychology (Hammond, 1996).

This literature will figure prominently in the next section, which enquires into the cognitive activities of human beings in their attempts, as problem finders and solvers, to structure problems. Notions from cognitive psychology and bounded rationalities are used as a baseline for linking up types of structuring policy problems to design processes in politically shaped task environments.

The social and political construction of public problems

Problems as social constructions and claims

Let us start from a simple and common-sense definition of the concept of a 'problem': one has a problem when one experiences a gap or disparity between a moral standard and an image of a present or future state of the world. Someone who claims to be plagued by a problem, implicitly or explicitly passes a moral judgement. One uses a standard involving value or worthlessness, desirability or undesirability, to pass judgement on present or expected acts or situations (e.g. Frankena, 1973; Rokeach, 1973). Some call moral standards strictly phenomenological, subjective facts of our inner, personal lives (Hodgkinson, 1983: 31-2). Life presents itself to us as a series of moments-facts-events. To these phenomena we attribute value; it is what we appreciate. Values are, to put it inelegantly but unambiguously, 'in ourselves', not 'in things out there'. People attribute or ascribe value to things. In principle, this is a voluntary act.

However, in political or administrative practice, value attribution is part of social conventions, social status, upbringing and educational background, political ideology, group interest and, ultimately, expressions of political influence and power (Safranski, 1999).[5] Values are confronted not just as inner feelings with a strictly private character. They are also confronted as externally imposed constraints, limits or claims. For example, a public health officer involved in preventing HIV/AIDS is drawn into difficult political and ethical dilemmas:

> Attempts to curtail epidemics raise – in the guise of public health – the most enduring political dilemma: how to reconcile the individual's claim to autonomy and liberty with the community's concern with safety? How does the polity treat the patient who is both citizen and disease carrier? How are individual rights and the public good pursued simultaneously? (Baldwin, 2005: 3)

In this political dilemma, where moral claims for both sides can be traced to constitutional clauses and public law, policy actors confront the ethical as objectified social constructions, as group claims and as political power.

Presented as numbers and tables in statistical reports and government documents written by scientists or officials, problems and problem descriptions sometimes take on the garb of objective, merely factual statements about a situation. However, especially public problems are always claims of groups of people about the way they experience a situation:

> [H]aving a problem is a claim on others, on how they ought to think about our situation and how they ought to act…. I, as an outside advisor, may claim that a society or an organization has a problem…. But the problem is posed by me, and unless others feel it or can be made to feel it, it will not be a problem for them. They may concur in my definition or choose another one. But my saying that a society has a problem … is an act that limits the set of possibilities that can be designated by the members of the society. I have attempted to take over the problem-defining process, and the society's politics. (Krieger, 1981: 39-43)

This makes any attempt to frame public problems essentially contested, and thus part of the political process and political conflict – as Schattschneider (1960 [1988]) taught us so convincingly. What he (and many other political scientists interested in agenda setting) overlooked in his account of problem finding and framing, is that understanding the situation and coming to agreement about it necessarily changes our understandings – sometimes the understanding of ourselves; not as political manipulation in the strategy and tactics of politics, but as an unavoidable part of the process of coming to agreement on the nature of a public issue or problem. In forging agreement on public problems, politicians create stories of a group's problem that help them and others, who originally do not belong to that group, to structure their experiences. They concoct from the stories of problematic situations experienced by some, a more overarching, more collective story, capable of mobilising more people behind a problem formulation. In doing so, the story about the problem changes from the purely local, in some way contingent story of some group of people, to a more 'cosmopolitan' or at least more decontextualised, and in that sense more 'rational' account for a majority.

Transformation of original problem experiences of a particular group of claimants into a more overarching, collective problem formulation for a political majority, then, is more than clever political manipulation. It is inherent in coming to some agreed version of the problematic situation in a democratic way. Some alienation or distance between individual citizens' or a particular group's problem experience and a politically viable and acceptable problem framing is an unavoidable socio–cognitive fact of democratic life. It is not necessarily, as many political scientists have claimed, self- or group–interest–driven 'bias'. In principle, this cognitive dimension is independent from processes of political representation and aggregation. The transformation of a problem formulation, and the subsequent distance or potential alienation felt by some of the original problem owners, would also occur under the most participatory and deliberative forms of politics and collective decision making.

Let us now shift from the normative to the factual or empirical aspect in problematisation. The fact–value distinction is still frequently justified by invoking the idea that the world of 'values' is created by our own fiat, whereas the world of 'facts' is an indubitable, external given . But epistemologists meanwhile agree that the idea of immediately 'given' sense data as rock-bottom baseline for human knowledge is a misconception. Every form of human observation and every 'fact' discovered through observation, is inevitably coloured or pre-structured by frequently implicit, hidden theoretical notions (Diesing, 1991; Ziman, 2000). Thus, in an indelible way, events and situations that we 'see' and 'experience' are influenced by concepts and mindframes acquired in the course of our life. In the political, administrative and policy sciences, such insights have generated a flood of research into the ontological, causal and finalistic (means–goals) assumptions in policy paradigms, heuristics, mindframes, cognitive maps, cultural scripts and the like (Hoppe, 1999; Fischer, 2003).

Although we should relativise the fact–value distinction from an epistemological point of view, we cannot do away with it in practice. When we justify our values, we do appeal to the consent of others in terms of arguments of 'goodness' or 'justice' or 'utility'. When we make claims about facts, we appeal to the consent of others in terms of 'truth', 'verisimilitude' and 'honesty'. On top of that, in spite of many differences, there exists a fair amount of agreement on the rationality of procedures and methods for convincing an academic or professional community of experts on the truth-value of individual propositions and theories. Similar methods or procedures for arguing the superiority of ethical claims or theories, like in ethics, theology and law, are more contested (Fischer, 1980; Dunn, 1983).

More importantly, however suspect the fact–value distinction has become from an epistemological point of view, it is historically entrenched in many institutions of modernity. Particularly, the boundaries between the institutions of science and politics, and between politics and administration, have exactly the fact–value distinction as one of their pillars. In the practical boundary work between representatives of these institutional spheres, the fact–value distinction is continuously appealed to as a basis for demarcation and coordination of activities (Jasanoff, 1990; Halffman, 2003). For example, people working for independent think tanks and policy analysts working in state bureaucracies both refer to science as being experimental, empirical, independent, certified, measured, reliable, consistent, careful, meticulous, peer reviewed, published, factual and so on; whereas policy and politics are labelled as a matter of values, decisions, implementation of political decisions, choice, wisdom, practical knowledge, management and so on.

Ezrahi (1990) has convincingly argued that methods of 'objective' science were complementary to – and actually strengthened – the depersonalised authority of democratically elected political leaders and bureaucratically organised civil servants. In other words, the fact–value distinction may be epistemologically suspect and contested; in political, administrative and scientific practice the boundary line is continuously constructed on the basis of the fact–value organisation of activities, tasks, projects, policy programmes and the like. This does not mean that the boundary is clear, pre-given and conflict free. On the contrary, boundary work entails almost day-to-day negotiations between representatives of the different institutional spheres to draw the line situationally and contingently (Halffman, 2003). The point is that, in doing so, policy-relevant actors appeal to fact–value-laden institutional narratives. 'Bureaucracy' is shorthand for the front-office narrative that bureaucrats serve and obey democratically accountable politicians, and everything entailed in the division of labour between instrumental and substantive rationality in day-to-day policy work. 'Decisionism' conveys a similar narrative that truth-telling science bows to the primacy of value-proclaiming politics. Put more precisely, in the back-office negotiations and consultative mutual cooperation of their day-to-day boundary work, civil servants and experts act 'in the shadow' of institutional rules of bureaucracy and decisionism (Hoppe and Huijs, 2003).

This is exactly the reason why, as a first step in following Steinberger's (1995 [1980]) suggestions, the fact–value distinction provides the analyst with two socially and politically grounded dimensions for a typology of policy problems. Every effort to pin down a problem is a double social construct. And this is not all. In problem framing and definition, fact-constructions are linked to norm-constructions through comparison; and this comparison is also a social construction in itself. Here too, the comparison, in political or administrative practice, is not just an individual act of free will. Politicians, administrators, and policy and science advisers cannot just arbitrarily compare values and facts and on that basis attribute the label 'problem' to the judgement that the facts of a situation do not meet some standard. In order to do this successfully, they have to take into account the distribution of agreement and disagreement and power relations in different forums (see Watzlawick et al, 1974):

- the degree of consent on (prognosticated) facts in all kinds of political, administrative and scientific or professional forums, the media and public opinion;
- the degree of consent on values at stake;
- the degree of consent on the problem formulation itself, that is, the comparison of fact- and value-sets.

For example, in Amsterdam city government during the latter half of the 1980s, the norm of equal treatment irrespective of gender, and facts about preferential treatment for women, were linked as a goal to a means. In the political climate of those days, there was strong agreement on the factual need and normative desirability of this instrumental link. Whoever would politically criticise this construction between a value and a fact as in reality ineffective, or as an unjustified gap between the practice of a policy programme and an ethical standard of non-discrimination, would not only fight a lost political cause; even the courts would rule against them.

In summary, the elegant simplicity of the concept of a 'problem' as a gap between a moral or ethical standard and some existing or expected situation cannot conceal its deeply problematic structure. Anyone formulating a problem constructs an easily contestable connection between ontologically disparate elements: moral standards or ethical guidelines (norms, values, principles, ideals), on the one hand, and facts, 'data' or empirical elements, on the other. Straddling the fact–value distinction, the concept of a 'problem' expresses the inextricable entwining of fact-values or value-facts in politics and administrative practice (Forester, 1989: 240–1). Exacerbating the epistemological hybridity of the concept, one should add the second property of public policy problems: they are social constructs in every respect. Thus, when a politician or policy maker, on behalf of some authoritative political institution or public agency, formulates a problem, and this formulation gets accepted by a majority, a very complex and delicate social 'composition' has been created. It is both complex and delicate because as a political and social fabric it may be torn apart in three ways:

- the social construction of the facts may be denied, or judged to be incomplete, biased, misleading or even a set of outright lies, and so forth;
- the social construction of values may be judged as incomplete, one-sided, wrong or unjust in principle, and so on;
- the comparative link between facts and values may be rejected as illogical, irrelevant, not plausible, nonsensical, and so on.

At the same time, having contributed to the bringing about of such a delicate fabric as a politically accepted problem definition, why should one be modest about one's achievement? And why not resist any effort at deconstruction and reframing as wrong-headed, even malicious? After all, the universal and rational notion of problem processing claims that problem-solving efforts require stable problem definitions lest they become 'moving targets'.

Four types of policy problems

The simple definition of a 'problem' hides a complex social construction. In this section, the heuristically productive and theoretically plausible reduction of that complexity for purposes of political judgement, policy analysis and policy design is at stake. It means that one should be able to distinguish between types of problems in the public sector. What is needed is a typology of policy problems, as a kind of model of the task environments that politicians and other policy makers face in the analysis, design and evaluation of public policies. But first we need some minimal assumptions about the problem-processing behaviour of politicians and proximate policy makers (see Dorst, 2004).

Like all human beings, politicians and proximate policy makers are cognitive misers – perhaps even more so than other people, due to the information overload of the hypercomplex social-institutional contexts in which they usually operate. In their task environments, they have good reasons to want maximum intellectual results from minimal cognitive efforts. For them, processing problem claims in a more or less rational way involves three distinct, but connected demands (see Gigerenzer et al, 1999):

- *Bounded rationality* (Simon, 1947, 1957): dealing with problems – from experiencing a problematic situation, to problem framing and defining, through to applying search-and-stop rules for alternative creation and selection, or problem solving – is intendedly, but boundedly rational. As an information-processing system, the human brain runs into cognitive limits determined by our neurophysiologic make-up, like the processing capacity of short- and long-term memory. The human capacity for information processing is less than fully adapted to the complexity of our environment. Dealing rationally with problems should make realistic demands on time, speed and computational skills of ordinary people. The implication is that human beings, politicians and policy makers among them, unavoidably use strategies and heuristics of complexity reduction. Practically, it means that that there will always be a tension between analysis and intuition; analysis as a 'step-by-step, conscious, logically defensible (cognitive) process', and more intuitive ways of problem coping that somehow produce a solution, but through unarticulated, tacit ways, without the transparency and consistency of more analytic methods (Hammond, 1996: 60ff).
- *Ecological rationality* (Hammond, 1996: 111ff; Goldstein and Hogarth, 1997): rational problem processing is always a performance in a real-world environment or task environment. From an evolutionary point of view, the human capacity to survive and adapt to changing environments implies that rationality works successfully only through some kind of correspondence between the inner and outer life-world. Like many other animals, humans use multiple fallible indicators to judge this correspondence between problem-processing efforts and the task environment. Monitoring policy fields by elaborate sets of economic, social, cultural and ecological indicators, of course, is a well-known device for policy makers (e.g. MacRae, 1985; MacRae and Whittington, 1997). Practically, ecological rationality introduces a tension between generality and specificity, the cosmopolitan and the local, situational, or contextual elements in problem processing.
- *Social rationality* (Janis and Mann, 1977; Tetlock, 1997): this is a special form of ecological rationality, as people making claims on other people (see above) socially construct most of a human problem-processing context. Psychologist Philip E. Tetlock (1997: 660-1) gives an excellent description of the socially

constructed task environment of political and public life in his two core assumptions on humans as 'would-be' politicians: (a) 'accountability of conduct as a universal feature of the natural decision environment', as the most important link between individual policy makers and the social-political environments in which they typically act; and (b) people act as approval-and-status seekers, keen on protecting and enhancing their self-esteem, social image and identity, while acquiring power and wealth. Practically, these assumptions give rise to two interdependent tensions. First, a tension between a correspondence theory of truth, based on criteria of accuracy in representing a 'real-life' world; and coherence theories of truth based on criteria of logical and attitudinal consistency with prior beliefs and positions (Hammond, 1996). Second, a tension between judgements arrived at through one's personal feelings, intuitions, observations and analyses; and judgements generated by social pressures or instigation by others-as-group-members (Hoppe, 1983). The de-ideologisation and individualisation processes in coming to political judgement, discussed in Chapter Two, clearly exacerbate both. Individualisation of political judgement erodes trust of socially instigated judgements; de-ideologisation attributes a less prominent place to a coherence theory of political truth, and boosts a correspondence theory of political truth. The rising number of performance indicators and league tables in policy making evidences the trend.

Acting boundedly, ecologically, and socially rational, policy actors will be prone to use an acceptability heuristic (Tetlock, 1997; confirming Braybrooke and Lindblom, 1963): in accounting for their decisions they will first and foremost look at acceptability in the eyes of those who have to support, represent or otherwise publicly cover them. Projecting this on the dimensions of accountability for the framing and definition of public problems, policy makers and politicians confront different potential situations.

Regarding moral or ethical standards, they will distinguish between policy problems whose standards, norms, values and objectives are more or less agreed to. Similarly, concerning perceptions of present and future situations or conditions, and the deliberate transformation of problematic present into improved future, they will distinguish between policy problems in which there is more or less certainty on available and usable knowledge. Using these two dimensions – degree of agreement on normative claims at stake, degree of certainty on relevant and available knowledge – one may construct the following typology of the socio-cognitive status of problems for policy makers in political task environments (see Figure 3.1).[6]

The heart of the typology is the opposed pair of structured versus unstructured problems. One can speak of *structured problems*, when policy designers perceive unanimity or near consensus on the normative issues at stake, and are very certain about the validity and applicability of claims to relevant knowledge. They simply know how to turn a problematic present situation into the improved, or desirable, unproblematic future situation. A structured problem is like a puzzle. However

Figure 3.1: Four types of problem structures

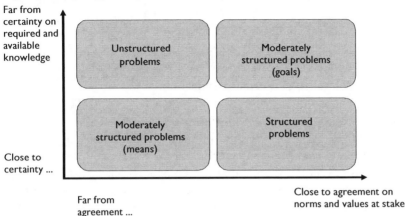

Far from
certainty on
required and
available
knowledge

Unstructured
problems

Moderately
structured problems
(goals)

Moderately
structured problems
(means)

Structured
problems

Close to
certainty ...

Far from
agreement ...

Close to agreement on
norms and values at stake

complex, the pieces of the puzzle are given, and for each puzzle there is just one configuration of pieces representing an adequate solution (Mason and Mitroff, 1981; Dery, 1984). There exists a solution for the problem that, for all practical purposes, is complete and fully guaranteed; usually by means of standardised methods of applied science or professional practice. Rittel and Webber (1973) give as examples 'domesticated' problems of low complexity from the early days of statehood, like building and paving roads, designing and building housing (but see Simon, 1973), eradicating dread diseases (but see Baldwin, 2005) and providing clean water and sanitary sewers. Many, not all[7], problems of a medical nature fall into this category. Scientific, technical, evidence-based treatment and therapy make for high levels of certainty on relevant knowledge. Also, there appears to be near unanimous consent on the goals of medicine: prevention of disease and injury, promotion and maintenance of good health, relief of pain and suffering caused by maladies, care and cure of the sick, care for those who cannot be cured, and avoidance of premature death and pursuit of peaceful death (Callahan, 2003: 88-92). It is because of these two properties that the problem definition of structured problems can be kept out of the sphere of subjectivity, politics and overt interest struggle (De Jouvenel, 1963: 206-7). Thus, structured problems are usually matters of administrative implementation and professional routine.

One may speak of *unstructured problems* when policy makers observe widespread discomfort with the status quo, yet perceive persistent high uncertainty about relevant knowledge claims, and high preference volatility in mass and elite opinion, or strong, divisive, even community-threatening conflict over the values at stake. Rittel and Webber call such unstructured problems 'wicked',[8] because any solution effort immediately spawns new dissent and more intense conflict. Unstructured problems are difficult to disentangle 'webs' of interrelated problems; they resist decomposition in (quasi)independent clusters of problems. There is dissent and conflict over which pieces belong to the 'puzzle', and over which arrangement of the pieces means 'solving' the puzzle. In the risk societies of late modernity, where the distribution of risks has succeeded the welfare state's distribution of goods as the focus of public debate (Beck, 1992), the volume and intensity of unstructured problems appear to be on the rise. Sometimes the negative side effects of entrenched technologies cause a U-turn from structured to unstructured problem. Issues like the car mobility problem (Hendriks, 1999; Hoppe and Grin, 2000), the building of nuclear power plants in the Netherlands in the 1980s (Hisschemöller, 1993: 71–8), contemporary planning for a nuclear phase-out in Belgium (Laes et al, 2004) and anthropogenic global warming (Peterse, 2006) belong in this category. Sometimes it is the unbridled research and innovation drive, which leads to new, unstructured problems. This may manifest itself in new medical technologies like (therapeutic) cloning and xenotransplantation or breakthroughs in preventive screening by genomics (Callahan, 2003; Hoppe, 2008a). Contrary to structured problems, unstructured problems occasionally are in the political spotlight, and may even generate sustained, intractable political controversies (Schön and Rein, 1994).

Moderately structured problems (ends) occur when policy makers observe a great deal of agreement on the norms, principles, ends and goals of defining a desirable future state; but simultaneously considerable levels of uncertainty about the relevance and/or reliability of knowledge claims about how to bring it about. This kind of problem typically leads to disputes over what kind of research might deliver more certain knowledge for solving the problem. Given uncertain knowledge, and thus uncertain effectiveness and efficiency of interventions, moderately structured problems (ends) also frequently raise issues of bargaining about who will be responsible for expenditures in financing or otherwise enabling certain interventions; and for risks in the case of ineffectiveness or negative side effects. Issues like traffic safety (Hoppe and Grin, 2000), ambient particulate matter (Peterse, 2006), fighting obesity and many issues of policies for routinely agreed-upon socio-economic goals like maximising Gross Domestic Product and minimising inflation (Halffman and Hoppe, 2005) belong to this problem type.

Moderately structured problems (means) exist when relevant and required knowledge leads to high levels of certainty, but there is ongoing dissent over the normative claims at stake. The key characteristic of this type of policy problem is not knowledge certainty, but the valuative ambiguity, and frequently the contested and divisive nature of the ethics of the problem. The Dutch debate on abortion provides an excellent example. When the issue arrived at the political agenda, a new, fully safe abortion technique had been introduced. The early debate focused on the in-principle moral permissibility of abortion; later phases concentrated on the conditions under which abortion might be permissible; and on alternative procedures of consultation for establishing such conditions (Outshoorn, 1986). In US political and policy studies, the concept of 'morality policy' (Mooney, 1999; Smith, 2002) or even 'sin policy' (Meier, 1999) has been coined to cover a cluster of moderately structured (means) problems that are generally high on the conservative political agenda, and characterised by an emphasis on fundamental notions of right and wrong, high political salience and low information costs. Abortion, euthanasia or physician-assisted suicide, racism and anti-discrimination policies in general, same-sex marriage, capital punishment, gun control, smoking, family and (criminal) youth policy would all belong to this class of problem constructions.

In spite of the illustrations given for clarity's sake, the four problem types are ideal types in the Weberian sense: simplifying and to some extent screening out some problem properties in order to bring other aspects (in this case, cognitive and design facets in a political task environment) into sharper relief. For one thing, the typology's dimensions are not inherently dichotomous; consequently, not every policy problem will be unambiguously classifiable as one of the four types. In real-life cases, one encounters hybrid pairings, as will become clear from later examples and case narratives. For another, it will frequently be the case that different policy actors will classify the 'same' problematic situation differently; and even for the same policy actor, problem types are stable only for certain periods of time. In the next section, it will become clear how to deal with these familiar analytic problems of multiple policy actors and the temporality and transformation of problem frames. Here only the heuristic value of the typology is claimed for the analysis of politically authoritative policy design – be it from a formally political, bureaucratic or scientific position. Given the assumptions about the bounded, ecological and social rationality of politicians and policy makers, we cannot expect them to define problems 'objectively'. Policy problems are by definition socio-political constructs and presuppose political (inter)subjectivity. However, this subjectivity does not operate randomly. People may display certain judgemental and behavioural patterns in defining problems. (Chapter Four will treat this hypothesis in depth from a cultural perspective, Chapter Five from the angle of types of policy networks and policy-making processes.)

From the basic assumptions the expectation is derived that governmental policy makers and decision makers prefer to define 'their' problems as structured. Doing so minimises their uncertainty, limits the need for search activities and constrains the range of alternative solutions to existing repertoires. Furthermore, it is hypothesised that when there is too much complexity or social conflict, they will continue trying to minimise 'trouble'. Therefore, they will prefer to identify these politically more sensitive situations as one of the two classes of moderately structured problems. They would rather not admit to themselves and others that they have fully unstructured problems on their hands. This implies that governmental policy makers will show a marked tendency to ignore, sometimes to actively screen out, information that may complicate the policy problem under scrutiny. This tendency need not be deliberate, or even acknowledged. Policy makers may be completely unaware of their screening relevant information away from the policy arena since they may not consciously grasp the biases that are inherent in their own belief systems and policy frames (see Chapter Four).

Another reason for problem-framing bias or sheer neglect is that policy makers when finding and choosing a problem frame immediately find themselves bound by a 'legitimate' problem space and a political discourse to discuss it. That is, they determine what can, cannot, may and may not be said about the problem without being labelled as transgressing politically 'correct' boundaries or rules of the political language game. In respecting rules of political correctness, they implicitly decide on which values are at stake and pre-structure which (type of) knowledge is relevant and required for problem solving. In the case of gaps between problem understanding by official policy makers and other influential proximate policy makers and stakeholders or the public at large, they run the risk of tackling what is called the 'wrong problem'. They may treat as 'structured' a problem that other stakeholders – be they peak associations, pressure groups, target populations, or even their own executive managers and street-level bureaucrats – experience and define as much more complex and controversial than they are willing to admit. It is exactly at this point where, if they go unacknowledged, unattended to or denied for too long, intractable policy struggles occur.

But before taking up these points, the distinction between structured and unstructured problems is to be elaborated. For a full understanding of the nature and function of the problem typology, the question of how problems acquire some sort of structure should be dealt with.

On structuring unstructured problems

Properties of structured and unstructured problems

Think of a textbook-level mathematical problem, or a typical chess problem in your daily newspaper – white moves and checkmates in four. These are examples of structured problems. Not all structured problems are trite and simple. Some structured problems are extremely complex, like offshore oil drilling or putting a man on the moon. The point is that structured problems have a track record of 'doability'. We know for sure that a feasible, well-understood method, strategy, mostly an algorithm, exists that satisfies all criteria for an adequate, successful solution. In a sense, the problem has become non-existent now that its solution is known and available to all who care to learn the 'trick'.

On a somewhat higher level of sophistication, we may think of problems of disorganised or organised technical and social complexity as continuously solved by experts or professionals who have routinised or black-boxed scientific discoveries and methods (Schön, 1983). Those experts are for hire for those with sufficient resources, who can thus make experts' knowledge work for their purposes. In a sense, relatively well-structured problems are the basis of the intricate divisions of labour between occupations in our industrial, service and knowledge economies. Large-scale functional organisations in business, the public sector and civil society are considered to be the repositories of the knowledge and skills to solve all kinds of structured problems (Chisholm, 1995). Contemporary ideas about governance are about 'weaving' ever-different webs or networking arrangements between such organisations by linking up their standard operating procedures in order to solve ever-changing societal problems. Note the implicit assumption in this type of administrative thinking: most 'new' problems are solvable through innovative mixes of and tinkering with existing (partial) solutions or standard operating procedures.

This explains the attractiveness of solutions to supposedly well-structured problems to politicians and policy makers. Even if they realise that most politically salient problems are not quite fully structured, they would want to move problems into the quadrant of structured problems rather sooner than later (Schön, 1983; March and Simon, 1993 [1958]). The problem with this idealised image of scientific and professional problem solving is that between structured and unstructured problems there is the huge class of moderately structured problems. For these kinds of problems it is not or not yet clear whether they will make it from unstructured to structured. For many public policy problems, one has to acknowledge that the understanding of the causes of social ills for which improvement is sought is weak, as is knowledge about the effectiveness, efficiency and possible side effects of available or new policy instruments. In addition, improvement of a problematic situation may mean very different things to different people. Sometimes even one group's improvement of the situation is another group's loss. There is more than a kernel of truth in the idea that government and public administration are a receptacle or 'garbage can' for problems that private-sector or civil-society types of organisations consider as unsolvable, or too risky to try.

The transformation of an unstructured into a structured problem has been conceptualised as a process of closing open constraints. Constraints refer to any or all elements that go into the definition of a problem; they are either 'given' and 'closed', or 'open' and amenable to choice. To mention only some of the most salient ones in ideal-typical form (complete lists in Simon, 1973: 183; Mason and Mitroff, 1981: 10-11) see Table 3.1.

Table 3.1: Structured versus unstructured problems

	Structured problem	Unstructured problem
Testability	Definite criteria for testing proposed solutions; errors can be clearly pinpointed.	No single criteria system or solution rule exists; solutions are better or worse relative to one another.
Explanation	Clear explanation for gaps between 'is' and 'ought'; all knowledge is accurate and codified.	Many possible explanations for for same discrepancy; different explanations fit different solutions; not all knowledge articulable.
Tractability	One well-representable problem space, with exhaustive list of imaginable and permissible operations to transform initial state, through intermediate, to goal states.	Ambiguous and uncertain problem spaces; exhaustive, enumerable list of permissible operations not possible.
Finality	Clear solution and ending point; closure possible and observable.	No stopping rules (apart from practicable amounts of time for search and information processing); permanent vigilance required.
Reproducability and replicability	Can be made to repeat itself many times; trial and error under controlled conditions possible.	Essentially one-shot operation; limited possibilities for trial-and-error learning.

Yet, as argued above, in real–life situations, constraints on the definition of problems and problem spaces are elusive, and socially and historically constructed. Simon (1973) himself already relativised the distinction by showing that any so–called structured problem (chess, designing a house, ship building) can be deconstructed as, stripped to its essentials, unstructured. Problems presenting themselves to problem solvers in the real world are best considered 'ill–structured'; 'well–structured' problems actually are 'ill–structured' problems formalised for and codified by previous problem solvers (Simon, 1973: 186).[9]

Simon went on to show how unstructured problems acquire their structure in the ways in which designers, using their personal, professional, organisational or institutional long–term memories during design processes, *decompose* an unstructured problem–in–the–large into more and more structured partial problems–in–the–small. Given the historical and serial nature of problem processing, the *sequence of bringing constraints to bear on a problem* in large part determines the properties of the problem definition; and hence its influence on the delineation of a problem space for generating and testing alternatives, and eventually, the choice of a solution (Chisholm, 1995: 478).

The historical and serial nature of problem processing brings out another property of moderately or under–structured problems. In rational, front-office accounts of problem solving where designers explain or justify what they have done and why they have done it to principals or other outsiders, they treat problems as structured: they formulate and describe the nature of the problem first; they present alternatives generated and solutions chosen later. More importantly, problem description and solution are presented as separate and logically independent. Put differently, the hallmark of rationality is that the *solution fits the problem* – and not the other way round. However, in the case of moderately structured or unstructured problems, any formulation and description of 'the problem' is implicitly or explicitly dependent on some accepted solution. Rationality and rationalising become blurred. *The problem fits the solution* – and not the other way round: 'problem understanding and problem resolution are concomitant to each other ... the problem can't be defined until the solution has been found' (Rittel and Webber, 1973: 161; compare Mason and Mitroff, 1981: 10; and March and Olsen, 1976: 26-7). In other words, rather than speaking of problems and solutions separately, in case of moderately and unstructured problems we should be speaking about *problem-solution couplings*.

This is even more true if we realise that, in politics and administration, problem decomposition and constraint sequencing are not merely or even mainly professional issues. Frequently, they follow from critical moments in political decision making, mood swings in public opinion or developments in relevant markets. The critical incident model depicted in Figure 3.2 is a good account of how problem decomposition and constraint sequencing in politics and administration result in temporary spaces or niches where authoritative or dominant problem definitions flourish – until critical incidents intervene and a new dominant problem definition emerges.

Figure 3.2: How dominant problem definitions come about and change

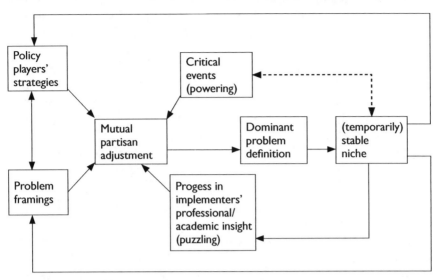

Source: Adapted from Vergragt (1988)

The model posits the presence of several policy players with different strategies and framings of the problematic situation. Through persuasion, bargaining and others types of partisan mutual adjustment they attempt to gain authoritative acceptance for their claims. This usually results in one problem framing becoming the hegemonic or dominant problem definition. The dominant problem definition creates a niche, that is, a more or less stable constellation of constraints on problem-solving efforts. This means that policy implementers may puzzle about alternative solution ideas within the bounds of the set of constraints; and professional or academic evaluators make all kinds of discoveries about the pros and cons of the constraints implied by the dominant problem definition. These learning processes or important external political events may or may not have anything to do with the policy concerned (hence the dotted double arrow running from the niche box to the critical event box as powering in Figure 3.2). They may lead up to novel critical moments or events that may lift (some) older constraints or introduce new ones. The historical sequence of such processes creates path dependencies in problem definitions or constraint sequencing. Such path dependencies themselves constitute a kind of meta-constraint in the sense that they either facilitate or work against the adoption of novel problem–solution couplings.

An illustration: coping with AIDS

The difference between structured, moderately structured and unstructured problems in real life can perhaps be grasped best from the way scientists construct 'doable' problems by way of controlled experimentation (Fujimura, 1987).

A problem is considered structured when, however complex, the chances of successfully solving it through methods of experimental laboratory and applied research are judged plausible (see also Hammond, 1996: 233-93). In this sense, all contributors to the AIDS special issue of *Scientific American* in October 1987 considered the AIDS epidemic a *structured problem*:

> To sum up, AIDS is a scientific research problem, to be solved only by basic investigation in good laboratories. The research done in the past few years has been elegant and highly productive, with results that tell us one sure thing: AIDS is a soluble problem, albeit an especially complex and difficult one. (Gallo and Montagnier, 1988: 31)

To them the retrovirus called human immunodeficiency virus (HIV) was the one and only cause of AIDS. Thus, public debate on the goals of AIDS policy was meaningless. The goal then was to cure AIDS and prevent its dissemination. This required generous research funding.

If scientific methods are judged less applicable, either in principle, or in practice, the less structured the problem. In principle, such methods fall short[10] in cases where the problem is due to controversies on the moral standards to be used in judging 'improvement' of the problematic situation. Sometimes objections to scientific methods are more practical, yet decisive. There may be good reasons not to subject human or animal subjects to rigorous scientific experiments. Alternatively, the problem may turn out to be trans-scientific (Weinberg, 1972). It may well lend itself to scientific formulation and method, but the number of statistically required research subjects is unmanageably large; or the duration and costs of experimentation are prohibitive. In the late 1980s, some feared that trans-scientific constraints might seriously hamper progress in finding a curative or preventive vaccine against the cause of AIDS – HIV:

> Yet AIDS vaccine researchers are still working in the dark compared with their predecessors at least in one respect: (1) they have no good animal model for the disease…. In the meantime, there is no way to establish criteria for the efficacy of (vaccines) before injecting them in humans…. (2) Clinicians also expect to be confronted with a shortage of trial volunteers…. (3) … Leaders of corporate research … have warned that the uncertainty surrounding the risks of vaccine-related injuries and compensation for them could ultimately hinder development. (Matthews and Bolognesi, 1988: 105)

These fears would lead to classification of the AIDS problem as *moderately structured (ends)*. Strong research funding was still seen to be a necessary part of the solution. But, depending on one's estimate of the pace of scientific progress, either an individualist, voluntaristic public health policy aimed at changing risky behaviour, or a control-and-containment strategy for breaking transmission routes, were deemed necessary complementary routes to a solution.

Surprisingly perhaps, there were some who defined the AIDS problem as *moderately structured (means)*, thus stressing its ethical and normative side. So-called AIDS dissidents or denialists, South–African President Thabo Mbeki being the best known and politically most influential, framed the problem in this mode. In a pragmatic guise, this problem definition saw HIV as one among many social cofactors like poverty, malnutrition, bad sanitation and other environmental risk factors. It was certainly not necessarily the most important or sufficient cause of the AIDS epidemic. In its purest form, it

> sprang from a long-standing belief in disease as a sign of imbalance between humans and nature, a cosmic and moral indication that things were out of joint.... [T]he fight against AIDS [is] seen as inseparable from a major reform of the status quo. In a world without AIDS, all people would be taught about sexuality, drugs, and health; all drug addicts would be treated; everyone would have access to basic health care; no one would maltreat gays or ethnic minorities; and there would be no homeless. (Baldwin, 2005: 22, 24; compare Douglas, 1996a)

Testimony to the interpretive plurality of any particular issue, one US sociologist and policy analyst went on record in 1988 arguing that, from a policy or administrative perspective, the AIDS issue is in fact *unstructured*:

> [G]enerating policies for AIDS is at best a vague and general activity, one that comes hard against the granite wall of constitutional law no less than medical and chemical inadequacies.... For the moment, and many moments to come, there is very little agreement on the need for information, hardly any consensus on the implications of the medical aspects of the AIDS issues, and virtually no agreement on the moral basis of behavior.... In the meantime, the demand for policy serves to exacerbate rather than alleviate partisan concerns. (Irving Horowitz, 1988: 57, 63)

Although clearly overstating the case, from the point of view of policy analysis and policy design it may be useful to consider a public issue or policy problem 'from scratch', so to say. It means taking seriously the possibility of deconstructing any politically adopted problem definition into an unstructured problem – as Simon (1973) actually demonstrated in discussing the 'structure' of ill-structured problems.

In a carefully written historical and comparative analysis of how democratic Western states dealt with the HIV/AIDS problem, Baldwin (2005) shows in detail how and why different sets of policy actors chose different problem definitions and different solutions. Baldwin provides valuable insights into how problem structuring works – both in the large and the small, and in the short and the long term. He shows why problem claims processing actors with standing at the public policy table who face seemingly identical challenges may end up with quite different problem-solution couplings. More precisely, Baldwin traces dissimilar problem framings and definitions to differences in the implicit or explicit organisation or 'infrastructure' of their problem decomposition, and differences in the sequencing of constraints on overall problem solutions (Chisholm, 1995: 477).

In all democratic Western states, there was a more or less identical social and political cast of actors involved in framing the AIDS problem – first, politicians and governmental officials and policy analysts; second, the (public) health professionals, with medical researchers as an important sub-community; third, the public at large; and among them, fourth, social categories, interest groups, or target populations holding special stakes. In the US, for example, such special groups were labelled the four 'H group' of Haitians, hookers, heroin addicts and haemophiliacs. Although governing politicians and their policy staffs were in the political lead, they were primarily looking at the health professionals for feasible and acceptable problem framings.

Basically, health professionals advocated two alternative framings of the issue. Like all professional problem solving, their typical way of structuring the AIDS problem was to break it down into relatively independent sub-problems. The AIDS problem was essentially broken down into three sub-problems: finding a cure, caring for the already infected and preventing the still healthy from being infected. Depending in part on group bias and in part on public debate, health professionals arrived at different beliefs on how much progress could be made, how fast and at what cost. With no cure on the horizon, prevention would be the only effective *collective public health* approach to controlling a potential AIDS epidemic. As a solution strategy this meant falling back on well-known control-and-containment strategies against transmissible diseases and potential epidemics, dating back as far as the early 19th century. The collective approach to public health was informed by contagionist beliefs, which focused on excluding the infectious, banning transmissive human behaviour, and sanitationist engineering of large parts of the human environment. It required a top-down approach that subjugated individual interests to those of the collective. Policy instruments involved identification and reporting of sero-positives, contact screening, isolation and quarantining, and enforcement of legal sanctions against those unwilling to comply. Although not widely practised anymore in the 1980s, the collectivist policy approach was frequently still inscribed into public health law and organisational routine; and in that sense it was still in the toolkit of public health officials and health professionals.

However, medical research scientists (quoted above) and other public health professionals, originally supported by civil libertarians and gay activists, favoured an *individualised public health* policy frame. This approach was ushered in by the bacteriological paradigm shift that rocked the medical world in the late 19th and early 20th centuries. The individualised approach located the cause of diseases in micro-organisms, thereby ethically 'neutralising' disease carriers. It focused on the education and persuasion of people to adopt a scientifically informed kind of personal hygiene. In this view, an individualist governmentality and voluntaristic approach to the AIDS epidemic were advocated: let science quickly develop a preventive or curative vaccine; meanwhile, persuade the healthy to avoid risky behaviour; discourage sero-positives from transmissive behaviour; educate the public at large about the benefits of latex; provide what treatment and care are available and financially acceptable; but do not impose, even less enforce, sanctions. After all, individuals are responsible for their own behaviour; and sexual governmentality, or the 'self-imposed quarantine of the condomed', was to take over from state regulation and repression (Baldwin, 2005: 261, 263, 266-7).

Although confronted with the same biological problem, developed Western states adopted different strategies. Only the Netherlands, Britain and non-Bavarian Germany consistently adopted and implemented the 'modern', individualist strategy. Most other states, among them countries with venerable civil liberty traditions such as Sweden (Baldwin, 2005: 153-4, 227-8, 279-80) and the US (Baldwin, 2005: 230-40), adopted the restrictive, traditional collectivist approach:

> The unprecedentedly rapid growth of medical knowledge naturally affected the measures implemented to counteract the spread of AIDS. At the onset, with the disease believed to afflict especially the outcast and marginal, the precautions broached included traditional sanctions.… When the disease was later thought to threaten the population at large, … tactics changed to a more voluntary and consensual approach … (originally) developed for chronic diseases. Still later, the wheel came full circle as a new approach, taken because of the growing promise of treatment, partly rehabilitated traditional precautions.… Coupled to epidemiological reasons for a revised approach came a sociological and political one: the wider spread of the disease among powerless minorities.… Resistance to measures that subordinated individuals to the group weakened accordingly. (Baldwin, 2005: 31-2)

In the gut response of states on how to deal with AIDS, adopting the traditional or modernist strategy, the hand of history or path dependence made itself felt through the sequencing of constraints on problem definitions. Path dependence theory holds that only bounded innovation is possible. What happened at critical junctures in the past affects possible outcomes of processes occurring later, sometimes much later, in time. They set in motion mechanisms of continuity or reproduction that keep channelling outcomes in a particular way; but without completely precluding change in other directions (Thelen, 2003: 217-22). In politics and administration, the slow wheels of legislation and bureaucracy generate policies that have a high legacy or inheritance (Rose, 1990) or off-the-shelf or incremental character. With the legal provisions and organisational repertoires of fighting epidemics like cholera still available, the choice for politics and the health profession presented itself as: follow the tried-and-tested old ways, or relinquish them as outmoded and try a new approach. How this framing choice was made partly depended on what Baldwin calls a historical deep-structure of stable geographic, topographic and demographic factors, or 'geo-epidemiology'.

For example, because of their geographical position as an outlier in Northern Europe, beleaguered from all sides, and with a lack of economic necessity for an open borders strategy, the Swedes stuck to a contain-and-control strategy. The English, to the contrary, were 'innovating' the voluntaristic-consensual approach for the same, but different-focused, historical causes:

> Into the AIDS era, Sweden remained among the harshest interveners.... Its state elites were firmly convinced that, though Sweden's approach might be drastic, it was also effective and equitable in treating all citizens as equally dangerous and culpable.... Swedish officials congratulated themselves on already having their procedures in place. With a venerable system for venereal diseases ready to go, it would have been ridiculous not to apply it to HIV. The British ... had their system of venereal disease education and treatment in place by the First World War. Their sanitationist and voluntarist bent continued into the AIDS epidemic.... Lessons were consciously drawn from the past to cement support for a liberal, consensual strategy. (Baldwin, 2005: 4, 227ff, 280-6)

Thus, historical deep structures and change mechanisms like institutional inertia and lock-ins, hidden in the long-term memories of public health institutions and professional communities, tilted the original structuring of the AIDS public policy problem in two alternative directions.

In the problem typology, both AIDS policy problem frames fall in the moderately structured (ends) quadrant. There was substantial agreement between relevant sets of policy actors on the policy's goals; but considerable dissent on appropriate, effective and efficient means and risks of failure. Later policy adaptations appear to be a matter of modulations on these originally selected major themes, depending on additional constraints on the problem space. Such constraints originated from the interaction between puzzling and powering: new scientific insights (puzzling), and the political constellation of forces driving policy-making dynamics (powering). Next to long-term structural causes effective through institutional memories of the health profession, agencies' short-term strategic political behaviour in historical and local contingencies enters the explanatory scene.

Medical researchers quickly found out that AIDS was not (only) a sexually transmissible disease. Other transmission routes through blood contacts (needle exchange, blood transfusion, pregnancy of infected mothers) existed and were equally important. The resulting idea that AIDS represented the return of classic, acute epidemic transmissible disease, 'the plague', was short-lived. Laboratory research resulted, not in fully effective cures, but in hybrid partial-cure-and-care technologies that turned AIDS into a chronic disease like some forms of cancer.

Although these scientific developments certainly affected the problem's tractability, and made elements of a control-and-contain strategy more plausible again, it left intact AIDS's framing as a moderately structured (ends) problem.

The same goes for changes in the social incidence and political dynamics of AIDS. The political-administrative elites took various policy initiatives depending on their perception of the deserving or undeserving character of threatened or afflicted groups. 'Good' citizens in general, haemophiliacs and white gay people were deserving; others like drug addicts, prostitutes, the homeless and black immigrants from former colonies in European countries were considered less or undeserving. For the deserving groups, policy initiatives followed the individualist-voluntaristic approach; the undeserving groups were frequently confronted with efforts to introduce or tighten more elements of the control-and-containment strategy. Policy success depended partly on the political influence and pressure these undeserving groups were nevertheless able to mobilise. In a delightful analytic twist, Baldwin demonstrates the moral ambiguity hidden in the political strategy of distinguishing between deserving and undeserving target populations in anti-AIDS policy:

> Holding individuals accountable for their actions and thus their health had two sides: the *individual responsibility* of democratic citizenship but also the *blaming of victims* for their own misfortunes ... when precautions were individualized, making all responsible for themselves, the implication was that, if infection nonetheless ensued, no one was to blame but oneself. Having apparently been thrown out the front door, fault and blame were escorted in again through the back one. (Baldwin, 2005: 263-4, emphasis added)

Next, Baldwin quotes a Swedish liberal politician arguing that legal restrictions are only compulsory for the small minority of recalcitrants and criminals who resist normal procedures – not for the bulk of honest, law-abiding, average citizens. The logically ensuing re-moralisation of individualised public health policies against AIDS is finally illustrated by a German politician, also a liberal one, who expresses his conviction that condoms are good, but fidelity is better (Baldwin, 2005: 268).

Wrong-problem problems

There is one final analytical point to be made. The social and political distribution of political and policy actors' problem frames normally results in the political selection of a temporarily stable, dominant problem frame for governmental policy through a combination of path-dependent institutionalisation processes and political strategising in various stages of policy making. This opens the possibility of serious mismatches between the effectively dominant governmental problem definition, and alternative problem framings alive among other groups in society. Using a mathematical and statistical metaphor, some authors call this a *Type III error.*

> One of the most popular paradigms in mathematics describes the case
> in which a researcher has either to accept or reject a null hypothesis.
> In a first course in statistics the student learns that he must constantly
> balance between making an error of the first kind (that is, rejecting the
> null hypothesis when it is true) and an error of the second kind (that is,
> accepting the null hypothesis when it is false) ... practitioners all too
> often make errors of a third kind: solving the wrong problem. (Raiffa,
> 1968: 264; compare Mason and Mitroff, 1981; and Dunn, 2004: 85-6)

This idea is important. After all, distinguishing between types of policy problems
by the way they are cognitively framed is meant to improve our political
understanding of structural mechanisms and agential strategies that either
contribute to or hamper the solution, resolution or control of particular societal
problems through collective action. In the case of AIDS, such a structural
mismatch might have emerged, had voluminous and politically strong parts of
the population insisted on defining AIDS, not as a moderately structured (ends),
but as a moderately structured (means) problem. On an international scale, the
outrage among Western politicians, health professionals and medical researchers
triggered by 'denialist' South–African anti-AIDS policies, is a good indicator of
the potentially disastrous political controversy that such a mismatch might cause in
national political systems. Yet, 'dissenting' groups may have good reasons for their
deviating but preferred problem framing. With no cheap medical treatment against
AIDS available due to R&D and marketing strategies of Western multinational
pharmaceutical corporations, nor any serious financial aid from rich donor
countries to buy their expensive medicines, defining North–South political and
economic discrepancies in the remit of AIDS policy makes political sense from a
South-African point of view. The political function and potential value of such
symbolic politics is to keep issues on the public and political agenda (Hoppe, 1989).

Here it suffices to acknowledge that due to strongly divergent problem
decompositions among groups of policy actors and hard to redirect path
dependencies and institutionally entrenched beliefs, attitudes and routine practices,
Type III errors or *wrong-problem problems* do occur in politics and public policy.
When they are present, they trigger or fuel controversy and deadlocks. The concept
of the wrong-problem problem will be used as a heuristically sensitising concept
for cases where political or administrative institutions with the authority and power
to define and delineate a problem space either (a) consider a problem structured
where it should instead have more plausibly been defined as moderately structured,
or (b) where it is defined as moderately structured when it actually is completely
unstructured, or should be more plausibly defined as a moderately structured
problem of a different kind. Policy designers and those who politically adopt such
designs as official policy erroneously assume sufficient agreement on the values
at stake, or sufficient amounts of certainty on relevant knowledge claims. This
definition is consistent with the criteria used to define the four problem types.

In politics, however, wrong-problem problems are frequently not 'mistakes' in the intellectual sense of the word. They occur due to what has been called the 'rationality of power' (Flyvbjerg, 1998: 225-36). More precisely, those in possession of control over the means of rationality – scientists, policy advisers, policy analysts, risk analysts and so on – may be able to describe, interpret and analyse the multiple ways in which other politically and policy relevant parties frame a problem. However, those who actually control the means of power, may unilaterally define 'reality', that is, they have the power to decide that a particular problem will be treated as if it were of a certain problem type; thereby ignoring alternative problem framings. In doing so, they also decide on the types of cognitive instruments or methods and the types of political and administrative interactions to be used in 'solving' the problem. In other words still, those in power, deliberately or in their own blindness, define what counts as 'rationality' and knowledge. The relationship between power and rationality in problem framing is asymmetrical: 'power has a rationality that rationality does not know. Rationality, on the other hand, does not have a power that that power does not know' (Flyvbjerg, 1998: 234).[11]

Notes

[1] In terms of Lowi (1997: 196, 198) himself: 'It is quite conceivable that political scientists can develop criteria for policy choice in terms of predicted and desired impacts on the political system, just as economists, biologists, and the like attempt to predict and guide policies according to their societal impacts.... [I]f two policies have about an equal chance of failure or success in the achievement of some social purpose the legislature has agreed upon, then the one should be preferred that has the most desirable impact on the political system'. Here I will not elaborate on this normative use of issue typologies. I will return to it in Chapter Eight.

[2] As far as hypothesised impacts of policies as statutes on the working of the political power arena are concerned, Lowi (1972, in McCool, 1995: 184) clearly states that it is the perception of top-most officials, for example presidents, that count. However, it remains true that he does not say how to deal with divergent views of different types of policy actors.

[3] In that sense, policy instrument typologies in the policy and administrative sciences, whether of the first substantive, or second procedural variety (Howlett, 2004), are the successors of the first Lowian typologies developed in the 1960s and 1970s.

[4] More recent theories like the advocacy coalition framework (Sabatier and Jenkins-Smith, 1993), punctuated equilibrium dynamics (Baumgartner and Jones, 1993) or evolutionary models of policy dynamics (John, 1998) perhaps do a better job in specifying the many independent and intermediary variables; but as far as integration effects are concerned, they hardly fare better.

[5] Safranski (2005 [1999]: 214-215 writes, 'Behind every value attribution hides the will to power'. This is equally true for the 'highest values': 'God, the ideas, the metaphysical....

However, even the will to power has misunderstood itself for a long time. People believed to discover independent essences, while, in fact, they invented them out of the force of the will to power.... They have denied their own value-creating energy.... Obviously, they would rather be victim and receiver than author and giver, perhaps out of fear for their own freedom' [translation RH].

[6] I do not claim any originality here. To my knowledge, the typology was first constructed and used by Thompson and Tuden (1959) in order to link decision styles to organisational structures. It has been used later by numerous authors in many different fields: business management (Nutt, 1989), policy studies (Douglas and Wildavsky, 1983; Dryzek and Ripley, 1988), science, technology and society studies (Ezrahi, 1980), organisation studies and organisational learning (Crossan et al, 1993; Stacey, 1996; Choo, 1998), and this list is far from exhaustive. Of course, the multiple uses by numerous authors strengthen my judgement that the typology is valid across many fields of application (see Chapter Five).

[7] Consult Callahan (2003) and Hoppe (2008a) for the presence of not-so-structured problems in medicine and healthcare.

[8] The 'wickedness' of unstructured problems, of course, is the opposite of 'domestication' in structured problems. Note how the use of the concept of 'wicked problems' in the governmental reform literature completely misses the political and cognitive aspects of unstructured problems by defining them as problems 'that cross departmental boundaries and resist the solutions that are readily available through the action of one agency' (representative example in 6 et al, 2002: 34). Focusing on the technical, administrative and organisational aspects of service delivery for particular problems turns almost any problem into a 'wicked' one. Putting a man on the moon, for instance, would be an extremely 'wicked' problem; so would offshore oil drilling for energy safety. Yet, we know that these are structured, quite 'doable' problems, albeit managerially and technically very complex ones. In the original meaning of the word, it is the inextricable mix of (cognitive) puzzlement and political conflict that makes tackling certain problems unstructured or 'wicked'.

[9] Following Hisschemöller (1993: 26-7), I reject the terminology of *'well-structuredness'* and *'ill-structuredness'* of problems. They are value-laden concepts, apparently accepting the desirability of moving away from unstructured problems as soon as possible towards technically controllable structured problems. As will become clearer in what follows, I prefer to speak of *un*structured problems when authoritative decision makers and their policy designers acknowledge the unstructured nature of a public policy problem. Problems are ill-structured when they deny or only partially acknowledge this.

[10] This is not to say that science cannot contribute to the control of moderately structured (means) problems. I will return to this theme in Chapter Five.

[11] A vivid example of how this works in practice is given by an American journalist reporting on a meeting with a Bush government aide (Ron Suskind, 'Without a doubt', *The New York Times Magazine*, 17 October 2004): 'In the summer of 2002, after I had written an article … that the White House didn't like … I had a meeting with a senior adviser to Bush. He expressed the White House's displeasure, and then he told me something that at the time I didn't fully comprehend – but which I now believe gets to the very heart of the Bush presidency. The aide said that guys like me were "in what we call the reality-based community," which he defined as people who "believe that solutions emerge from your judicious study of discernible reality." I nodded and murmured something about enlightenment principles and empiricism. He cut me off. "That's not the way the world really works anymore," he continued. "We're an empire now, and when we act, we create our own reality. And while you're studying that reality – judiciously, as you will – we'll act again, creating other new realities, which you can study too, and that's how things will sort out. We're history's actors … and you, all of you, will be left to just study what we do."

FOUR

Cultures of public policy problems

'[R]eceived culture' seems to have had a greater role in defining the range of legitimate alternatives than any policy elite or interest group. (Bosso, 1994: 199)

Introduction

Why do some proximate policy makers prefer to frame and define problems as (over)structured and not un(der)structured? May one predict that policy makers who adhere to different cultures or ways of life will be more inclined to construct and process some problem types rather than other types? How about the congruence between policy makers' preferred ways of problem framing and structuring, and the cultural inclinations of people in civil society?

This chapter constructs a culturalist theory of the socio-political contexts of problem framing and structuring in the public domain in Western welfare states. Proximate and authoritative policy makers mobilise cultural bias in their authoritative selection of problem definitions, expressed in official policy designs. This triggers and fuels processes of translation and framing dynamics; processes that, through political communications in the media and the practices of policy implementation, impinge on the debates over problem frames among citizens in civil society. In this way, ordinary people interpret official policy intentions and practices; and come to attribute positive or negative meanings to governmental policy performances (Schneider and Ingram, 1997).

Using grid-group cultural theory and the typology of policy problems, it is shown how, in such translation and framing dynamics, each culture or way of life corresponds to a particular problem-framing and problem-definition strategy. Hierarchists will impose a clear structure on any problem, no matter what. Isolates will see social reality as an unstable casino in which any privileged problem structure jeopardises chances for survival. Enclavists (or egalitarians) will frame any policy problem as an issue of fairness and distributive justice. Individualists will exploit any bit of usable knowledge to improve a problematic situation. These four focal or default strategies are part of larger repertoires of problem-framing and problem-definition strategies; each cultural solidarity type disposes of a differentially composed set of secondary, fall-back strategies. Finally, it is suggested that the links between grid-group cultural theory and policy problem types may serve the policy worker or practitioner as analytic tool for active and (self-)critical problem structuring and (re)framing.

Cultural roots of policy problem structuring

Framing civil aviation expansion

In the mid–1990s, the Dutch government was seriously pondering the future of civil aviation in its national economy. The focal point was what should happen to Schiphol Airport Amsterdam, at the time Europe's fourth largest airport in passengers and freight, and fiercely expanding at a projected 9% growth rate per year. To support Cabinet decision making, the government organised a public inquiry. It was designed as a 'societal dialogue' with some 80 participants, ranging from government departments, local governments in the area, the airport authorities, related industries and other business interests, vested interests like employers', trade unions' and environmental movements' representatives, and inhabitants of residential areas in Schiphol Airport's vicinity. From the end of 1996 until July 1997, this heterogeneous stakeholder forum was to discuss the policy problem, phrased by the Cabinet as 'should the government accommodate further growth of civil aviation; and if so, how?' (TNLI, 1997: 8)

During the dialogue, five problem frames emerged. Some framed the problem as one of international economic competition on a globalising market, and argued that expansion of civil aviation infrastructure was a sheer necessity. Others framed it as a public budget problem, and argued the opposite by claiming that expansion would be a squandering of public funds. Yet others viewed the problem as one of essentially regional accommodation of expanding airport facilities, or as ecological modernisation of the civil aviation sector, or as finding sustainable solutions to growing demands for mobility. From these perspectives, the 'yeah/nay' dilemma of the former two problem frames, logically implied in the government's phrasing of its policy problem, was superseded by more complex, qualified and innovative answers. When the chips came down, however, the Cabinet chose to continue policies of the previous 30 years to conditionally tolerate the airport's (infrastructure) expansion. It obviously ignored the richer problem definitions (Van Eeten, 2001) and failed to arrange a subsequent governance space for a creative confrontation of different levels and problematic aspects of the overall problem (RMNO, 2009).

Received culture

Like in this example, policy scholars frequently observe that 'at the regime or macro-level of discussion and analysis there are remarkably few alternatives actually under debate' (Bosso, 1994: 184). The explanation is hardly deliberate elite influence or interest group pressure, but 'received culture' (Bosso, 1994: 199). Sometimes a cultural regime implicitly suppresses many alternative problem definitions. At other times, when core values are no longer stable or self-evident, they trigger heated and protracted controversies and even outright political conflict and stalemate. This is perhaps most clearly shown in the anti- versus pro–gun control debate in the US. Guns are historically saturated with conflicting meanings:

> Used to wrest national independence and to tame the western frontier, guns are thought to resonate as symbols of 'honor', 'courage', 'chivalry', and 'individual self-sufficiency'.... As tools of the trade of both the military and the police, guns are also emblems of state authority ... others see it as expressing distrust of and indifference toward others.... For those who fear guns, the historical reference points are not the American Revolution or the settling of the frontier, but the post-bellum period, in which the privilege of owning guns in the South was reserved to whites, and the 1960s, when gun–wielding assassins killed ... John and Robert Kennedy, and Martin Luther King jr. To these citizens, guns are emblems not of state authority, but of racism and reaction. (Braman and Kahan 2003a: 10-11; also Vizzard, 1995)

In both cases, policy problems are seen as cultural and political constructions. Harry Eckstein (1997: 26) defines culture as 'the variable and cumulatively learned patterns of orientations to action in societies'. In line with the assumption of human beings as cognitive misers, such patterns of orientations economise action by relieving people of the impossible task of interpreting afresh every situation before acting. They also render interactions between people, who may be complete strangers, predictable through conventions, habits, rules, routines and institutions. Thus, a culturalist approach to problem definition claims that limits to rationality are primarily cultural; and so are the rules for imposing closure on problem framing and definition, the invention of alternatives, and the scope of costs and benefits considered.

Yet, policy scientists have hardly begun taking the next logical step: if a policy problem is a politico-cultural phenomenon, one should self-consciously construct a theory of problem framing and problem structuring in public policy making on a systematic culturalist approach to a politics of meaning. Granted, we have Joseph Gusfield's (1981) brilliant research essay *The culture of public problems: Drinking-driving and the symbolic order*. In this book, Gusfield uses anthropological and literary concepts like dramaturgy, ritual and rhetoric to interpret how the history of social and collective problematic situations gives rise to political definitions of problems of public policy. We owe to Gusfield the important insight that the structure of public problems is always made up of the interrelationships between three symbolic elements: problem ownership (or who claims a say in defining a problem?); causality (or which theory of causes and consequences of the problematic situation is publicly espoused?); and accountability (or who is praised or blamed for [failing to] solve the problem?) (Gusfield, 1981: 6ff).

However, even after almost 30 years since Gusfield's important publication, later developments remain disappointing. Rochefort and Cobb's (1994) and Cobb and Ross' (1997a) books offer good examples of this trend, in spite of their rich empirical illustrations. In addition, Gusfield's study is based on just one single case, in one part of the US, in the 1970s. Yet, the book's title speaks of 'the' culture of public problems, and about 'the' symbolic order. Such premature generalisation deserves challenging. Gusfield's merit is in his way of conceptualising the theoretical problem. Leaning on his work, this chapter will attempt to complement it by using empirical and theoretical work from the policy sciences on the typology of policy problems. It will demonstrate that not singularity, but plurality rules; that it is more useful to speak of several cultural styles in policy problem framing, with each style featuring its own typical problem structure in Gusfield's sense of the term.

What is grid-group cultural theory?

Types of cultural theory

In a culturalist approach, one may distinguish between the attitudinal and the inclusive approaches. The attitudinal approaches, like the civic culture (for example, in Almond and Verba, 1963) and the (post-)materialist culture studies in political science (Inglehart, 1990), use a restrictive definition of culture as a mental product of individuals, that is, meanings, values, norms and symbols. Culture is operationalised as the aggregate of individual attitudes, and individuals are seen as single units of analysis, free from social contexts. In policy analysis, this social-psychological approach leads to the assumption of possible congruence or harmony between policy and political culture, where differences in culture have to be bridged by an 'imposed', unifying governance culture (Van Gunsteren, nd). The inclusive approach defines culture more comprehensively. First, in a social-constructivist fashion, culture is seen as a way of world making, or as a way of creating conceptual order and intelligibility through labels, categories and other principles of vision and division. Second, culture is studied as part and parcel of a way of life; individuals are seen in the context of prior social solidarities and institutions. In research and policy analysis, the inclusive approach leads to 'an institutional theory of multiple equilibriums, in which different cultural contexts have opposing effects upon the thought and action of the individual' (Grendstad and Selle, 1999: 46).

Within the inclusive approach, there is a further split between the romantic and modernist vision of culture (Van Gunsteren, nd). In the romantic version, the study of culture is a lifelong undertaking; only 'going native' provides the feel for detail and the finegrained distinction necessary fur truly grasping the essence of another (sub)culture; and the set of cultures is infinite in complexity and variety. In policy studies and analysis, this leads to advocacy for one particular culture, or to becoming a specialist, like the area specialists in the analysis of international politics and foreign policy. In modernist, Marxist and technological visions, culture is a dependent variable of underlying economic and technological realities. For policy studies and analysis, quick analysis and practical understanding of culture is possible, but at the cost of seeing it as false consciousness in need of a reality correction. Grid–group cultural theory avoids both extremes. Being familiar with its four ideal-typical cultures – hierarchy, enclavism/egalitarianism, isolationism/fatalism and individualism – speeds up analysis and orientation because it is a continuous warning sign against assuming one homogeneous culture, or applying just one particular cultural lens to analyse a policy problem. The social-constructivism underlying cultural theory will prevent one from falling into the trap of reducing culture to false consciousness.

Cultural theory was first developed by Mary Douglas. She tried to remedy the failure of anthropologists to systematically compare cultures (Douglas, 1978). Consequently, Douglas herself elaborated the theory (especially, Douglas, 1986), but it was also quickly put to use in understanding policy debates on environmental problems and risks (Douglas and Wildavsky, 1983). In the 1980s and 1990s, the cultural theory bandwagon was joined by authors from many different social science disciplines, like Michael Thompson, Steve Rayner, Chris Lockhart, Richard Ellis and Christopher Hood. In 1990, Thompson, Ellis and Wildavsky produced what still stands as the most comprehensive statement and justification of cultural theory between the covers of one book (Thompson et al, 1990). In this way, cultural theory came to political science (Thompson et al, 1999) and policy studies and analysis (Hoppe, 2002, 2007).

Grid and group

Cultural theorists claim that the social world ticks the way it does due to selective affinity and mutual dependency between social relations, cultural biases and behavioural strategies. Therefore, adherents of grid–group cultural theory belong in the inclusive camp. The theory distinguishes between internal structures called 'grid' and external structures called 'group'. *Grid* refers to the types of rules that relate people to one another on an ego-centred basis. Grid is low when there are few binding rules, and when people negotiate rules among themselves. Therefore, if grid is low, you get symmetrical transactions. Grid is high when rules are numerous and complex, and when they are imposed without people having much of a say in accepting or rejecting them. Therefore, if grid is high, you get asymmetrical transactions. *Group* refers to the experience of belonging to a bounded social unit. High group means that people identify strongly with those they see as members. Thus, if group is high, you get restricted transactions. Low group means that people don't care for membership but for people who are intrinsically interesting for some reason or other. If group is low, you get less exclusive, unrestricted transactions.

The group and grid dimensions of human transactions are constructed as the ultimate causal drivers in ordering social relations. These give rise to cultural biases as justifications for particular social orders. As justifications and sets of available orientations to action, the cultural biases influence behaviour by making it patterned and coherent. The properties of social relations in grid–group cultural theory are about relational patterns, or stable types of transactions between people. Combining the group and grid dimensions gives you a social map with four *types of relationships*. Two of them – markets and hierarchy – are well known and thoroughly analysed in the social science literature (e.g. Lindblom, 1977, 2001). However, if the known types of social relationships are classified by two discriminators, a full typology should, in addition, pay attention to the other two possibilities: clans or enclaves, and systems of isolation or zero-networks (see Figure 4.1.)

Figure 4.1: Cultural theory's grid/group typology

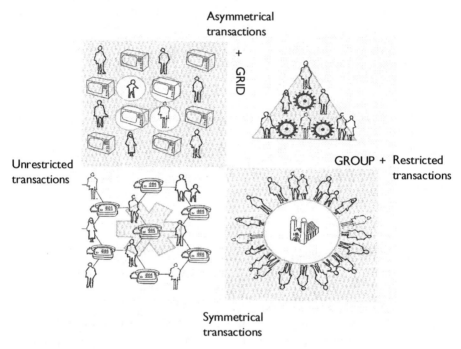

Sources: Thompson (1996); symbols taken from front page of Schmutzer (1994)

Grid-group cultural theory's fundamental claim is that corresponding to these four types of social relationships are *cultural biases.* These refer to sets of shared values and beliefs (Thompson et al, 1990: 1) or stable orientations to action (Eckstein: 1988: 790) or dispositions/habitus (Bourdieu, 1998: 6). They are thought of as judgements of value, which function as justifications of specific organisational structures. It is supposed that each develops its own typical set of beliefs, a cognitive and moral bias that contributes to reflexivity in the social organisation (Douglas, 1998). In the language of complexity theory, the cultural biases function as stable attractors in socio-cultural landscapes. Grid-group cultural theory posits four viable or long-term sustainable cultural biases. These are:

- active or competitive individualism (Thompson et al, 1990: 34–5);
- pattern–maintaining or conservative hierarchy (Douglas and Wildavsky, 1983: 90–2);
- egalitarian sects or dissident enclaves (Douglas, 1986: 38–40; Sivan, 1995: 16–18); and
- backwater isolates or fatalists (Schmutzer, 1994; Douglas, 1996**b**: 183–7).

Michael Thompson claims the existence of a fifth cultural bias: indifference to and active avoidance of the group and grid dimensions of life result in hermit-like autonomy.

The orientations or dispositions underlying cultural biases guide judgement and action in many ways. Cultural theorists have inquired into the interpretive and more practical correspondences between the cultural biases and *action strategies* in many social fields (for an overview, see Mamadouh, 1999). Perhaps the theory's most important claim here is its rigorous demonstration of the poverty of (individualist) 'homo economicus' as the model for all individual behaviour, and thus the existence of 'missing persons' in much of contemporary social science (Thompson et al, 1990: 40–7; Douglas and Ney, 1998). Complementary models like, for example, Simon's (1947) 'homo administrator' (for hierarchy), sectarian man and fatalist man would be necessary to fill in the gaps.

Cultural dynamics

To some, the group/grid scheme is basically a typology. If looked at as a construction of ideal types to which reality does not correspond in a one-to-one way, cultural theory as grid–group analysis offers considerable conceptual resources for comparative research and theory development. Real-life phenomena can be analysed as dyadic or triadic hybrids (Hood, 1998); the process of hybrid formation can take different time paths and have different critical junctures; and, therefore, some such hybrids may show more stability through time than others. Other theories conceptualise social change as faster or slower movement from one to another pole on a one-dimensional scale (modernism – postmodernism, materialism – postmaterialism). Grid–group analysis obliges one to perform the more demanding task to trace (simultaneous) changes between the four quadrants of its two–dimensional socio–cultural space (Thompson et al, 1990: 75ff).

One more element deserves elucidation, that is, grid–group cultural theory's account of social and political change. Culturalist approaches generally have often been rejected as too static, better geared to explaining social stability than transformation. Social stability is unlikely as grid–group cultural theory views the mutual engagement of the four cultures/solidarities as continuous social and political struggle. The gist of grid–group cultural theory has been captured by pointing out that:

[M]odes of social control are the focal point.... Individual choice ...
may be constricted either through requiring that a person be bound
by group decisions or by demanding that individuals follow the rules
accompanying their station in life. Social control is a form of power....
It is the form of power – who is or is not entitled to exercise power
over others – that differs [between the ways of life]. (Thompson et
al, 1990: 6)

Moreover, Douglas stresses the institution-based and constitution-making nature
of human choice:

In the social sciences, a choice is treated as ... arising out of the needs
inside the individual psyche.... [In t]he theory of culture ... a choice
is an act of allegiance and a protest against the undesired model of
society.... [E]ach type of culture is by its nature hostile to the other
three cultures.... [A]ll four coexist in a state of mutual antagonism in
any society at all times. (Douglas, 1986; 1996a: 43)

The continuous struggles for cultural hegemony in different social fields imply
agonistic interactions between people. Therefore, the theory hardly predicts the
social harmony characteristic of theories of social stability. Grid-group cultural
theory's model of social change as political and social struggle for cultural
hegemony and learning makes the theory eminently suitable as the core of the
translation and framing dynamics in the study of the politics of problem framing.

Cultural theory and spaces for public discourse

One way of thinking of a political culture is as a discursive space within which a
polity's public discourse may legitimately move. The legitimate discursive space
is 'inhabited' by a number of belief systems. Political scientists habitually narrow
the discursive space for Western democratic political discourse by modelling it as
a one-dimensional left – right or materialist – postmaterialist continuum. Cultural
theory breaks a social and political system down into at least four constituent
elements, and some more hybrid forms if necessary for adequate analysis.

In late-modern, capitalist and democratic welfare states one would expect to
find a preponderance of an individualist way of life, with all kinds of politically
active shades of the other solidarities. First, welfare states are based on a capitalist
order of production and consumption. An entrepreneurial class with relatively
easy access to public policy making dominates the organisation of economic life
(Lindblom, 1977, 2001). The culture of competitive individualism characterises this
entrepreneurial class. In a country like the Netherlands, an individualist cultural
bias and its concomitant governance style is estimated to resonate well with
almost one quarter (23%) of the electorate (Motivaction, 2001). Second, welfare
states depend on a strong state, which intervenes in capitalism in order to secure

stable economic, social and, if possible, ecologically sustainable development. State agencies and adjacent public sector organisations depend on professional and scientific expertise. People inhabiting such organisations, while constrained by the function of their institutions in a capitalist economic order, will also display a cultural blend of hierarchic collectivism and egalitarian distributive justice. There are claims by political scientists that the electorate has steadily increased in knowledgeability and critical, monitoring skills. Yet, almost one fifth (18%) of the Dutch electorate may be said to belong to the type of 'deferential citizens' (Almond and Verba, 1963), which feels strongly attracted to a hierarchical cultural bias in politics and public policy (Motivaction, 2001). Third, both capitalism and bureaucracy give rise to movements and trends that reflect, in their strongest manifestation, anti-statist and anti-bureaucratic idealism. A common feature is a call for more public and political participation in the name of 'small is beautiful' communitarian ideals. In a milder variation, people believe in a government and a bureaucracy that is more flexible, coordinating, joined-up or even 'holistic', in the sense of uniting public and private organisations in collaborative governance networks. Here, a mix of egalitarian and individualistic cultures is at work. Although no more than one tenth of the Dutch electorate can be labelled as strong egalitarians, the hybrid egalitarian-individualist bias is popular among approximately one third (30%) (Motivaction, 2001).

Finally, all three types of elites struggle for power over public policy making, as each desires its ideas to control the content, implementation and outcomes of public policies. This is where the 'grip' phenomenon comes in. Each of the different ways of life both organises its own adherents and simultaneously attempts to disorganise the others. Individualist entrepreneurs try to both organise bureaucracy in one-stop shops for their own convenience, but simultaneously disorganise it by minimising state rules that interfere with their preferred ideas of competition and 'a level playing field'. Counter-elites with an egalitarian bent will attempt to replace individualist interpretations of equality as equal starting conditions by their equality of results. And so on, and so forth. All three politically active, but more or less hybrid, ways of life – individualism, hierarchy and egalitarianism – attempt to mobilise the explicit or implicit support of an apparently apathetic or fatalistic mass of isolated spectators. Research by Motivaction (2001) shows that a surprising 30% of the Dutch electorate belongs to this category of 'outsiders'. They are:

> the cultural equivalent of compost: a rich, generalised and unstructured resource, formed from the detritus of the active biases, and upon which these active biases, each in its distinctive way, can then draw for its own sustenance.... Fatalists, therefore, are an essential component of the total system, even though (indeed, precisely because) they do not feature in the policy debates that so exercise the three active ways of life. (Thompson et al, 1990: 93-4)

In other words, and following Schattschneider (1960) who defined politics as the organisation of bias, the translation and framing dynamics around possibly authoritative problem definitions may be conceptualised as mobilisation strategies of the three active solidarities in capitalist welfare states to achieve cultural and political hegemony for their bias in political definitions of public problems and solutions. Such strategies may involve all sorts of advocacy (Sabatier and Jenkins-Smith, 1993) and discourse coalitions (Hajer, 1995) between management, expertise, bureaucracy and counter-elites, all trying to interpret, but also to influence and win over, public opinion to its side.

Towards a systematic culturalist theory of problem structuring

Do some proximate policy makers with voice in the political framing of policy issues prefer to structure a problem as Type A rather than Type B, and why? Can policy actors adhering to different ways of life or solidarities,[1] that is, hierarchy, enclavism, individualism and isolationism,[2] be predicted to have differential skills in dealing with different problem types? Can we predict different problem-framing and problem-structuring strategies from policy makers or analysts belonging to different cultural solidarities when confronted with problematic situations?

These larger questions will be ordered in sub-questions, which follow the logic of the problem typology presented in Chapter Three. First, can one predict the primary orientation of an adherent of a particular solidarity to frame a problematic situation as a particular type of problem? Second, what can we say about dispositions and skills in coping with the remaining other types? In answering these questions, the starkest contrasts will be treated first. The best-studied type is the hierarchist policy maker or analyst, who is an expert in framing and then solving structured problems. Then the least-studied and frequently overlooked one is presented: the isolate policy maker or analyst, who sees unstructured problems everywhere and identifies solving them with personal and organisational survival. Next comes the individualist type, who wants to move away from problems, if only a few inches. Finally, one arrives at the enclavist policy maker, who sees value conflicts as the root cause of every problem and their overcoming as a precondition to any solution.

Hierarchists: 'structure it!'

Policy makers and analysts working in large, complex bureaucracies of the public and corporate sectors are clearly exposed to strong hierarchical social relationships and interaction patterns.[3] These organisational structures themselves express a cultural bias or general disposition to world making characterised as paradigm protection (Thompson and Wildavsky, 1986: 280-1) or belief in 'strong' theories or methods – if possible, certified by science, or more traditionally, founded in religion. Although these two are often believed to be mutually exclusive, in a hierarchist world they are in fact compatible.[4] In a modern handbook on socio–cybernetic policy analysis, 'a systematic methodology for understanding and solving complex real world social problems' (Rastogi, 1992: 12), we do indeed find them both, side by side.[5] In the beginning of his book, Rastogi professes that any effort at problem solving begins with an ordered knowledge base, generated by a scientific methodology and an interdisciplinary theoretical language fit for complexity: 'The methodology is based on the cybernetic concepts of feedback cycles. The conceptual base … is extremely parsimonious. It abjures ad hoc assumptions; it is coherent and consistent in its approach, procedures and analytic capabilities; it permits assessment of the validity of analysis; and, its inferences are empirically testable' (Rastogi, 1992: 12).

Turning to the topic of long-term, lasting solutions, Rastogi (1992: 16) opines that the root causes of social problems are 'the abnormal or disturbed emotions/ motives of the social actors participating or involved in the problem situations'. To 'nullify' these, we need a belief system of 'super-rational values':

> The only basis on which the intrinsic nature of moral values may be posited and all human beings may naturally and harmoniously relate themselves together is their common identification with the Divine. (…) This framework of truth, love, inner serenity, and righteous action … is rational in an absolute and universal sense. It provides the basis for eliminating the polluting symptoms of horror in social problems. It makes possible a lasting and steady state solution to the malfunctioning of social systems. (Rastogi, 1992: 114, 117)

Given these world-making orientations, the hierarchist's rationality is functional and analytic. It is functional in the sense of starting from a supposedly agreed objective, as a function of which the most effective and efficient means is worked out. It is analytic in the sense that problem solving is considered an intellectual or cognitive effort, best left to experts. A long time ago, Simon (1947) had already shown how this type of instrumental, bounded rationality can be systematically applied to create complex bureaucratic structures in which everyone expertly solves their partial problem within the decision premises or constraints imposed by the organisation's leadership. This means two things. First, through clever organisational design, humans can aspire to levels of rationality unachievable for the individual mind. Rationality, although bounded, may keep aspiring for comprehensiveness through social organisation. Second, the whole idea presupposes that problems come in a neatly packaged form; and if they do not, they can be made to come that way. 'Structure it!' is the hierarchist's primary orientation to the framing of problems.

How would a hierarchist policy maker or analyst deal with the manifold dimensions or aspects of real-life problematic situations as experienced by people, and turn these into a policy problem? Or, alternatively, what is a problem, so that it may be properly structured or defined for a hierarchist policy maker? (see Dery,

1984: 21-7; Hoppe, 1989: 23-4.) Three such rules for problem shaping and bringing closure on a problem definition appear to be typical. The first and foremost condition to structure a problem is decomposability[6] along lines pre-formatted by a paradigm in science, discipline, profession, political ideology, religion, or simply imposed by the organisational leadership and management. The problematic situation must be considered decomposable into relatively independent problem parts. This done, one may define the most important or salient variables or causes of these problem parts. Rastogi (1992: 120) puts it like this:

> Q. What are the most important elements of a phenomenon/problem? How may they be identified? A. Salient variables in the multi-cycle structure of a phenomenon/problem represent its most important elements. They are identified as variables associated with the largest number of input and output links.

The second condition is that the problem should be viewed from an interventionist perspective; the government or some other institution and its leadership must be presented as in control of the problematic situation, that is, in a position and endowed with resources to remedy it. In its turn, this means two things. First, the hierarchist policy maker/analyst should know precisely what the goal is, that is, knows how to specify what the solution to the problem looks like.

Our exemplary hierarchist analyst, Rastogi (1992: 56) speaks of determining the 'goal state' of the system by observing the 'viability' or effectiveness of variables in relation to 'a system's 'health':

> The solution of a problem refers to achieving a potential state of the problem situation wherein all the feedback cycles in the problem's multi-loop structure are operating in accordance with their intended regulatory roles of stability and/or growth. In each cycle, there is little or no discrepancy between the observed and desired values of the criterion variables. (Rastogi, 1992: 59)

Second, it means the identification of manipulable variables and major constraints from the regulator's or governmental perspective:

> Cybernetic methodology also provides additional insights toward policy identification. They are based on the identification of the most significant control, constraint, and change lever factors in a problem's multi-cycle structure. Control factors are those variables, which exercise a major controlling influence on the internal interactions within a problem's dynamic structure. Constraint factors are those variables, which constitute the major impediments in efforts to change the problem's behaviour. Change lever factors are those variables of

fundamental importance, which determine the strategy for long-term change in the problem's state and course. (Rastogi, 1992: 64-5)

The third condition is the translation of insights into control, constraint and leverage factors into detailed, custom-made action plans for a given organisation or set of organisations faced with a particular problem. In addition to a distinction between short- and long-term measures, this means developing an analytic capacity to differentiate between the relative importance of policy alternatives in relation to the relative urgency of problem dimensions:

> Differential relative importance of policy measures, and differing relative significance of problem dimensions, may be determined by a binary matrix analytic procedure, based on the concept of plural applicability of a solution/policy measure to more than one facet of the problem. (...) (This) is vitally necessary in the context of the optimal allocation of resources and efforts.... (Rastogi, 1992: 74-5)

The practical implication of this third rule is that, from the regulator's cognitive and evaluative perspective, some parts of the problem are not worth solving. Regarding all the rules for creating a structured problem, hierarchic policy makers effectively invert the common-sense logic of a one-to-one relation running from a problem to a solution. What counts as a 'problem' in fact depends on the chosen, elaborated 'solution' (Rittel and Webber, 1973: 161; Hoppe, 1989: 17).

An illustration is smoking regulation in the US (based on Nathanson, 1999). Until the 1950s, most people saw smoking, the smoker and cigarette smoke as emblems of power, autonomy, modernity and sexuality. Consequently, the smoking problem as a public issue was non-existent. This started to change slowly as a discourse coalition between the large health voluntaries, the federal public health service and policy entrepreneurs representing a well-educated, high middle-class non-smokers' rights movement, succeeded in structuring the problem. First, they successfully used a number of paradigmatic templates to change the meaning of smoking. On the relevant knowledge side, there was the paradigm of epidemiological research, enabling the American Cancer Association to use its huge volunteer constituency to establish beyond dispute the causal connection between smoking and lung cancer. Combined with a continued public communication campaign, in 1970, 70% of Americans (as compared to only 41% in 1954) were convinced of the truth of this causal link. Non-smokers gradually turned the tables against the smokers and the tobacco industry. On the values-at-stake side, in coining the idea of the 'right to breathe clean air' they successfully borrowed from constitutionally legitimated human rights discourse; and by imaging non-smokers as innocent victims of others' harmful habits, they managed to exploit the sympathy for those involuntarily exposed to external risk. Second, once structured, the problem lent itself relatively easily to identifying an interventionist perspective and realistic action plans. From the very beginning in 1971, the twin goals of the Group Against Smokers' Pollution (GASP) were to 'get non-smokers to protect themselves', and to 'make smoking so unpopular that smokers would quit'. Moreover, these were actionable goals. 'Bad behaviour' was clearly visible; and it was not difficult to blame a conspicuous source, the tobacco industry. In addition, government could be pressured to take action through legislative effort, monitoring and penalties, through public information campaigns like the Surgeon General's well-known warnings on cigarette packets, by making public and working spaces smoke free, by restricting access to tobacco for young people and, moreover, by holding the tobacco industry responsible through the courts.

In the case of smoking, US policy makers were eventually able to structure and deal with the public policy problem in a hierarchist way. However, where does this leave the hierarchist policy maker in dealing with the other three problem types? Evidently, they will consider every problem structured until proven otherwise. Consider the way conservatives resisting gun control in the US easily get away with framing the problem along the constitutional template of 'the right to bear arms'; and to discredit regulation as a form of failure-prone interference, not as a form of state protection, as the pro-gun control liberals would have it.[7] Or consider, at the opposite end of the political spectrum, the hopeless effort by Doctors Against Hand Gun Injury to impose structure on the issue through medicalisation and professionalisation; normatively, by categorising hand gun injuries as health risks; and empirically, by mobilising knowledge production and dissemination 'rooted in established principles of epidemiology and public health practice' (Seltzer, 2002: 19).

Consider also the way hierachically inclined policy makers and analysts in agencies for parliamentarian technology assessment in European countries structured the car mobility problem (Hoppe and Grin, 2000). Although there are many more ways of framing the car mobility problem[8] (to be discussed in later subsections), hierarchists wish to see car mobility as part of an orderly, reliable and manageable transportation system. In their view, congested roads and traffic jams are problematic because they create chaos and stagnation. This means that the system does not efficiently use available capacity to channel traffic streams through existing traffic infrastructure. Essentially, then, the congested roads or traffic jam problem is a systems capacity problem, solvable in principle by capacity expansion – unless it proves technically absolutely infeasible to meet the demand for mobility and transportation. Because hierarchists by definition choose a 'helicopter' or systems perspective, car mobility is reduced to a partial problem in an overall problem of transport mode selection and substitution. Because they can be implemented by experts, favourite hierarchist solutions have a large-scale and high technical-fix character – fast trains, underground transportation systems, 'mainports' and so on.

What others see as compelling evidence for the unstructured nature of the car mobility problem, hierarchist policy makers and analysts can easily define away as 'stupidity' or a self-interest-based, ill-considered opinion. Even if they fear that others may be correct in viewing a problem as 'wicked' or 'messy', they will still call it temporarily 'ill-defined', awaiting more extensive analysis before engaging in serious solution efforts. They may also belittle the problem's seriousness, and rationalise this by giving low weights to problem dimensions like urgency and estimated effectiveness of policy measures in their fancy alternative/criteria matrix analyses.

Because they can only deal comfortably with problems whose normative dimension is not openly contested, and they are used to impose their values and criteria on others, they are ill-disposed to deal with moderately structured problems/means. They will either ignore rival value/goal clusters – like the one that prioritises accessibility to different transportation modes over meeting an excessive demand for car mobility. Instead, they will implicitly impose their own values; or, if another hierarchy is too powerful, they will avoid dealing with such problems or problem parts. If the knowledge and technology base for problem solving is either insufficient or contested in their own eyes, hierarchists will only reluctantly deal with moderately structured problems/ends. Technology forcing, like in the state of California's zero emission mandates for cars, provides a good example. By imposing a zero emission target, California forces the car industry to speed up its R&D efforts for producing zero or extremely low emission vehicles. This corresponds to a hierarchist policy maker's preference for improving the problem's knowledge base. Simultaneously, it keeps open the possibility for wielding the hierarchist's preferred policy instrument – law enforcement.[9]

Isolates: 'surviving without resistance'

Isolates experience themselves as outcasts, subjected to a fate determined by dark forces or far-away ruling circles, both way beyond their influence. We all can easily think of the isolate as belonging to the contemporary underclass, that is, beggars, street people, the homeless, teenage prostitutes, drug pushers, addicts, alcoholics, compulsive gamblers, vandals, small-time crooks, educational drop-outs, poor single-parent families and all kinds of other groups who live a life of exclusion at the margins of modern society. It is a way of life not expected to be seen and heard in public life, let alone policy-making circles. This is why in many policy studies only the three 'active' voices – hierarchy, egalitarianism and individualism – are heard, and the 'passive' isolate appears to be absent.

'God is high, and the King is far' is a good expression of the isolates' state of mind. They perceive the institutional settings in which they find themselves in one of two ways. It is inherent in their world-making disposition to see the world as a lottery, and risk absorption as the most appropriate way of coping with this 'fact of life' (Thompson and Wildavsky, 1986: 280). Transferred to social, organisational and political relations, these worlds take on the qualities of unstable casinos. Dror (1986: 168) gives a dramatic description of these conditions:

> where not playing is itself a game with high odds against the player;
> where the rules of the game, their mixes of chance and skill, and the
> payoffs change in unpredictable ways...; where unforeseeable forms
> of external 'wild cards' may appear suddenly...; and where the health
> and life of oneself and one's loved ones may be at stake; sometimes
> without knowing it.

When isolates believe the unstable casino to be ruled by mere randomness, they may define the overall institutional environment as anarchy. For example, an isolate belongs to an anarchic organisation beset with garbage-can-like decision processes. His organisational function, competence, status, access to decision-making arenas and relationships to colleagues are continuously ambiguous, in flux and unpredictable; and so are the organisation's relations to its wider environment (March and Olsen, 1976). Alternatively, in a fatalist variation, he could define the institutional situation as a barracks, when he believes that the unstable casino is actually run by an all-powerful but unpredictable human despot or tyrant. He belongs to a highly rule-bound organisation; but the rules are changing, as are the conditions under which they apply, and the consequences of breaking them. Examples would be soldiers at the mercy of a whimsical drill officer, students dealing with stern but unpredictable teachers,[10] or bureaucrats serving an autocratic ruler, of a traditional monarchical, revolutionary religious or military 'caudillo' type (Heady, 1991: 310 ff).

The 'rationality' of the isolate and/or fatalist is a gaming or gambling one; it may also be characterised as inspirational and strategic. According to Dror (1986: 168-9), under conditions of adversity, policy makers resort to 'fuzzy gambling'. In its extreme, fatalist form, any decision making is senseless. Surprise dominates, better intelligence cannot improve ignorance, having goals and values is a luxury, and non-decisions or incremental decisions make no sense because experience and past performance have lost their anchoring functions in a highly volatile environment. In an effort to make the best of it, fatalist policy makers or analysts could try the policy principle of minmin avoidance, that is, choose a strategy that prevents the worst outcome, or at least minimises the damage (Dror, 1986: 10). Frequently, this means avoidance or procrastination of any decisive action. This fatalist attitude is epitomised in an observation by Chilean President Ramòn Barros Luco (1910-15), reputedly made in reference to labour unrest: 'There are only two kinds of problems: those that solve themselves and those that can't be solved' (Wikipedia, 2009). March and Olsen (1976: 12) describe anarchic organisations as plagued by numerous simultaneous and mutually reinforcing ambiguities:

> ... ambiguity of intention. Many organizations are characterized by
> inconsistent and ill-defined objectives. ... ambiguity of understanding.
> For many organizations the causal world in which they live is obscure.
> Technologies are unclear; environments difficult to interpret. ...
> ambiguity of history. ... What happened, why it happened, and whether

> it had to happen are all problematic. ... ambiguity of organization.
> At any point in time, individuals vary in the attention they provide
> to different questions ... the pattern of participation is uncertain and
> changing.

Given all this, the isolate, fatalistically inclined or more optimistic, will be predisposed to see any problem as unstructured. Believing that the world is a lottery and the social world an unstable casino, they will be unwilling or extremely reluctant to impose any definitive framing on a problematic situation. 'Survival' and 'resilience' are the isolate's watchwords (Schwarz and Thompson, 1990; Hood, 1998); they proscribe him/her to have any fixed ideas, let alone entire theories and explicit methods, about the nature of the problem and how to solve it. Instead, they must be totally flexible, keep options open in order to be maximally resourceful and alert at every opportunity to escape fate and grab the lucky number. It is recognised that this can lead to successful radical innovation. Schmutzer (1994) views the isolate as the latent source of most social and technological innovations. Expelled from one of the other ways of life but eager to leave this 'waiting room of history' behind, originality, creativity and true social innovation are the only way to return to the more established solidarities. March and Olsen (1976: 69ff) dwell on the possibility of a 'technology of foolishness' as a welcome addition to the standard repertoire, derivable from the unexpected and original ways in which ideas about problems and solutions get coupled and uncoupled in garbage-can decision making. Dror (1986: 174) speaks of 'throwing surprises at history' in the sense of adopting radically innovative and inventing quite unexpected options.

Given their primary disposition to see problems as unstructured, isolationists and/or fatalists tend to turn a blind eye to the occurrence of structured and moderately structured problems. Hence, they will rely on random search behaviour, inspiration, maxmax gambling or minmin avoidance[11] as problem–coping strategies. By imposing this frame on problematic situations, isolates produce self-fulfilling prophecies when confronted with problem definitions of the adherents from rival solidarities. The result is exclusion from or marginalisation in the halls of power and civility:

> It is at least uncivil and perhaps terminally so, to decline to take
> knowledge from authoritative sources.... Persistent distrust therefore
> has a moral terminus: expulsion from the community. If you will not
> know, and accept the adequate grounds for, what the community
> knows, you will not belong to it, and even your distrust will not be
> recognized as such. (Shapin, 1994: 20)

Issues of car mobility were mentioned above as typical examples of an unstructured problem; while in the previous subsection, on hierarchist problem-framing strategies, it was shown how policy makers nevertheless frame it as a structured problem of transportation infrastructure capacity. Senior policy makers in complex bureaucracies for obvious reasons resist the self-image of 'gambling professionals', let alone admit 'fatalist' problem-definition behaviour (Dror, 1986: 172). Only a small minority will articulate that economic, societal and technological developments have strong autonomous evolutionary force, by definition impervious to governmental steering. Yet, a decade ago, Dutch environmental policy makers came close for a short while. They declared, first, that the increasing number of traffic jams was beyond rational policy intervention; and, second, that allowing traffic jams to grow in number and length of time delay was their only hope of making the problem disappear by itself! After going on record with these surprising policy alternatives, politicians, not amused, and concerned about their public image, summoned them back to more hierarchist (see above) and individualist problem definitions (see below).

Another example is the fate of the third report on immigrant integration *The Netherlands as an immigration society* (2001) by the prestigious Scientific Council for Government Policy (WRR). In this analysis the WRR reframed the paradigm for Dutch immigrant integration policies (Scholten, 2008). It described past national policy as in fact strongly constrained by globalisation and Europeanisation as a trend beyond the scope of political influence. The Netherlands had become an immigration society; and hence, the WRR concluded, policies ought to be adapted to the externally imposed realities; instead of spending immense, but probably wasted energy in stemming the tide. By following and fuelling strong currents in public opinion, protagonists of an activist and assimilationist turn in immigrant integration policy quickly disposed of the WRR advice as too fatalist:

> Thought about immigration and asylum has been framed too much as 'out of control'. This self-declared impotence has wide-ranging consequences for our democratic culture. Who considers himself incompetent in such a vital issue, undermines the idea of national citizenship. (Scheffer, 2007: 146, translation RH)

A final example, a case of fatalist issue avoidance, is the American gun control issue. For the neutral observer, here is a clearly unstructured problem. Proponents and antagonists in the gun control issue have never enjoyed scientific and professional consensus on 'gun scholarship', reflected in a highly divided and divisive public opinion. On the values-at-stake side, there rages an incessant paradigm battle, in which the dangerous or protective quality of guns, and the role of government, remain as divisive an issue as ever, among gun scholars, advocacy groups and the public at large (Nathanson, 1999; Kahan and Braman, 2003a). In 1995, William J. Vizzard (1995), a long-time policy analyst and civil servant in federal gun control policy making, analysed it is a classical example of garbage-can-like processes. Only after focal events like presidential assassinations, 'cop killer bullets' or another high school massacre, for brief periods of time policy windows open up for government regulatory policy. And although there were numerous initiatives, almost none of them survived the stage of practical implementation. Vizzard (1995: 346) blames the policy stalemate on disinterestedness of legislators, and risk avoidance of bureaucratic staff:

> The crafting of effective public policy, absent great luck, requires significant grasp of ... such issues as the mechanics of the firearms market, the role of firearms in social behavior, and options for firearms control.... Legislative staffs have spent minimal time mastering such mundane issues, because legislators show little interest.... [The] bureaucracy has followed the safest course of action and avoided association with significant proposals for policy change.

Contrast the issue avoidance by US policy makers with the evidently well-prepared, swift and decisive policy action by the Conservative(!) Howard Government in exploiting the 1995 Port Arthur massacre in breaking a similar long-term gun control impasse in Australia (Van Ecker, 1997).

Enclavists: 'it's not fair!'

When one prefers a way of life permitting warm, personal relations with like-minded people and as little interference as possible from outsiders, one joins a clan, club or commune; even when this means to inhabit an enclave encircled by a hostile world. In grid-group cultural theory, such people are consequently called enclavists. The prototypical enclavist way of life manifests itself as a reactive, absolutist and comprehensive mode of anti-secular religious activism. Enclavism is not always a preferred way of life; in some cases the enclavist way of life is an imposed choice, like for Jews in 19th-century Eastern-European ghettos. The world-making disposition that creates and reproduces enclaves is best described as *groupthink enlarged*.

In public policy and corporate management studies, this phenomenon of combined inside moralism and outside criticism is well known as a threat to high-quality decision making in small groups at the top of the pyramid of hierarchist organisations (Janis, 1982). When groups consist of members with homogeneous social and ideological backgrounds, have no tradition of impartial leadership, and perceive their context as threatening or crisis-ridden, symptoms of groupthink may occur. They are described (Janis, 1982: 244) as an overestimation of the group through illusions of invulnerability and inherent morality, closed-mindedness manifest in collective rationalisations and outsider stereotypes, and strong pressures towards uniformity through self-censorship, illusions of unanimity, direct pressure on potential dissenters, and self-appointed mind-guards. What is frequently overlooked in social-psychological analyses of organisational behaviour is that an enclavist way of life sustains itself by systematically producing the groupthink cultural bias in society at large. Guarding the group boundaries by picturing the outside world as evil and mean is the principal way of keeping a group of enclavists together. This is exactly what the enlarged groupthink symptoms achieve. If they fail, expulsion, always disgraceful and sometimes violent, is the enclavist's means of last resort.

The world-making disposition of enlarged groupthink is imbued with a communicative form of value rationality. It is communicative because verbal means of persuasion, from public debate to speeches to sometimes vitriolic propaganda campaigns, are the only allowed means of creating consent in a community of equals. It is value rational in the sense that normative standards and goal-finding are the major focus of attention in problem-solving efforts, because the mix of inside moralism and outside criticism makes enclavists never miss an opportunity to point out the value conflicts between 'us' and 'them'. The major route to a solution is that 'they' give up their 'wrong' values and change their ways accordingly. Enclavists proselytise, and outsiders should convert to their values and lifestyle.

This assumption of ubiquitous value conflicts leads enclavist policy makers to structure problems as moderately structured/means. The normative problem dimension is stressed. This does not mean that enclavist policy makers and analysts scrupulously survey all relevant and appropriate values. The search is bounded by the 'us' versus 'them' dialectic. Opposing 'our' values to 'theirs' – frequently attributed on the basis of stereotypes – is sufficient. The same logic breeds close monitoring of differences between groups in society; particularly differences in treatment by government. Thus, frequently, the value conflict is shaped as an issue of distributive justice, equality or (broadly understood) fairness.[12] Since the 1980s, the environmental movement's and citizen protesters' major complaint in the Schiphol Airport expansion issue is that government weighs fragmented benefits to the population as a whole and concentrated benefits for the aviation-related business interests higher than the concentrated costs accruing to resident groups in the airport's vicinity. In doing so, the fairness problem frame spills over into a problem of trust in the sphere of interaction and institutional relations.

The enclavist policy maker's absorption in the value dimension of a problem is at the cost of its cognitive aspects. Poor information search, and incomplete search for alternatives and risks of a preferred choice, are typical defects triggered by groupthink symptoms (Janis, 1982: 243-5). Given the excessive attention to values, there is a distinct tendency to let ends justify means, irrespective of their effectiveness, efficiency and even counterproductive side effects. Criticising 'their' knowledge base and repertoire of policy instruments is frequently mistaken for a policy alternative of equal standing. A vivid illustration is Van Eeten's (1999: 39ff) policy 'tale of Riverland', about the paralysing controversy between experts of the Dutch Department of Traffic and Water Management and the environmentalist movement over the flooding problem and dike improvement plans:

> The dike improvement argument ... is a strong line of reasoning that in [a] ... deductive way derives the required dike designs from the choice of an acceptable level of dike failure.... [T]he most important cohesion in the anti-dike improvement protest is that the arguments are ... aimed against the practice of dike improvement. If one examines

the structure of the [environmentalist, RH] argument opposing dike improvement, it soon becomes clear that this is ... a 'critique' [or] an argument that is a point-by-point rebuttal of another policy argument that has the conventional structure. (Van Eeten, 1999: 54-5)

Enclavistically inclined environmentalists were implicitly accepting higher flood risks by opposing to the bitter end dike improvement designs by hierarchistically inclined water engineering experts. The example also shows that enclavists are prepared go to great lengths to reject problems of the fully structured type and obstruct its solutions.

How about the remaining two problem types? Regarding moderately structured/ends problems, one would predict that enclavists frame them as distributive justice or fairness issues of who gets what, when and how. Invoking Rawlsian rules like 'favour the most disadvantaged group' (see also Chapter Nine), enclavist negotiators may comfortably, but not very powerfully, participate in public policy making.[13] Given their inclination to 'critique', which brings with it a natural scepticism to non-shared value aspects and strong doubts about the validity of any knowledge base, enclavists easily join the isolate's or fatalist's attraction to unstructured problems. After all, cultural theory sees egalitarian enclavists as the natural allies or 'defenders' of fatalist isolates as 'victims'. They share positions on the negative power diagonal in the grid-group typology because both isolates and egalitarians have a negative attitude to power. Contrariwise, hierarchists and individualists have a positive attitude towards power, and happily use it to defend and strengthen their own ways of life against the others. An ambivalent attitude to the exercise of power in order to strengthen one's own way of life puts enclavists sometimes at a disadvantage in the struggle for power with its two activist rivals.

The way the car mobility problem was framed by several technology assessment agencies working for national Parliaments in Europe (Hoppe and Grin, 2000) offers an example of the enclavist's preferred problem-definition strategy. The enclavist-egalitarian perspective defines the real issue at stake as equal access to public space for all. Car mobility is a partial problem of excessive demand, over-expanded infrastructure, pollution of public space, and violation of health, ecological balance and quietude of residential areas. Ultimately, the problem is one of control and cutting back on demand for car mobility, and substitution with more 'friendly', low-tech and small-scale transport modes such as bicycles and light, zero-emission (electrical) vehicles.

A strong example of the moral overtones in an enclavist and egalitarian problem definition is the way some framed the AIDS problem, like South-African President Thamo Mbeki, or Jonathan Mann, former head of the World Health Organization's AIDS programme:

A sick society [can] not rid itself of disease.... Discrimination, marginalization, stigmatization: all heightened vulnerability to HIV.... The best-demonstrated cofactors were social inequalities.... One account earnestly claimed that, to prevent sexual transmission of HIV, universal peace had to be attained to end machismo and its attendant rape; global wealth had to be redistributed to make condoms available and obviate the need for prostitution; and religious leaders needed to support nonpenetrative and therefore nonprocreative sex.... Tackling AIDS ... required a new conception of social solidarity that redefined the boundaries between self and other and refused to separate the fate of few from the many. (Baldwin, 2005: 23)

Individualists: 'let's make things better!'[14]

In the low-group/low-grid cell of the typology one finds the individualist way of life. In terms of interaction patterns, adherents prefer freely chosen market-type exchange relations to other people. Except in the institutional domains of economic markets, they find and (re)create spontaneous exchange relations in social networks. In such networks, individuals easily and flexibly 'socialise' with partners in longstanding friendships or brief encounters, which results in a flurry of networking activity, with people continuously moving in and out of and between networks as they see fit. In networking, they live out their world-making disposition of seizing opportunities for individual, possibly but not necessarily mutual, benefit. 'Benefit' here may mean everything deemed meaningful, valuable or useful, for whatever reason, from an individual's point of view – 'from pushpin to poetry' in Bentham's winged words (Mill, 1974: 123).

The individualist type of rationality is functional and strategic. It is functional, in the sense that the individualist policy maker searches for usable knowledge, that is, data and information that help them maximise their utility, or at least satisfice at the self-selected aspiration levels (Simon, 1947). It is strategic, in the sense that individualists are adept in getting usable knowledge by exploiting their personal networks. It is 'the rationality of [a very busy, influential person, RH] ... for shifting the really vital discussions away from the formalised information-handling system and on to the informal old boy net. We characterize this strategy as individualist manipulative' (Thompson and Wildavsky, 1986: 280-1). In a sentence, the individualist's basic orientation to problems and problem solving is: 'let's make things better; let's get usable knowledge'.

Given all this, what is a policy problem, so that it may be properly defined for an individualist policy maker or analyst? Essentially, for a politician or policy analyst of an individualist bent, a 'problem' is an opportunity for improvement.[15] Defining a problem is framing it as a choice between two or more alternative means to seize that opportunity (Dery, 1984: 27). This approach to problem definition implies some very strict rules of closure. So strict, actually, that to the egalitarian-minded enclavists and the hierarchist experts, individualist policy makers frequently appear casual or outright indifferent about many bridgeable gaps between given and valued situations (Dery, 1984: 26). To begin with, as the above individualist framing of a problem as a choice between means implies, individualists stress means over goals. The individualist policy maker does not reason from goals to means; but from means to goals. Only those goals are worth considering for which effective means are available – organisationally, technically and financially. Feasibility as an overriding criterion in problem definition rules out many problems as unsolvable or not worth solving. The principal but negative task of the policy analyst is to point out constraints and determine (in)feasibility of a policy proposal (Majone, 1978).

Individualists do not care much for explicit value search and goal formulation anyway. They actually resist political rhetoric, slogans and rallying cries, because they do not express what actually moves people. In relation to the AIDS problem, for example, the individualist, voluntarist strategy proved to be an attractive option to many. Prevention and a technical fix was so appealing precisely because it sidestepped the need of passing moral judgement on AIDS-related behaviour and people or groups as carriers of the disease (Baldwin, 2005: 33, 259-60). Preferences develop with experiencing particular situations over time; therefore, they usually change and are hard to predict. Rather than 'deduce' unambiguous criteria from lofty but shaky ideals, individualist policy makers express 'concern' about 'threats', or 'ills from which to move away rather than goals towards which to move' (Braybrooke and Lindblom, 1963: 102). Partly, this ameliorative attitude to the normative dimension of problems depends on an individualist understanding of the nature of policy problems as

> problems ... which [encompass] a host of disparate but interlocked individual and group problems.... [F]ocusing on a synthetic problem is no longer a simple situation in which goal achievement is thwarted but an extremely complex adjustment-of-interests situation.... [A]ll that can at best be defended as a right 'solution' is that a series of conciliatory moves be made. (Braybrooke and Lindblom, 1963: 55)

Always taking present conditions as an evaluative baseline, individualists limit their preferences to comparisons of incremental change:

> He need not ask himself if liberty is precious and, if so, whether it is more precious than security; he need only consider whether an increment of one value is desirable and whether, when he must choose between the two, an increment of one is worth an increment of the other. (Braybrooke and Lindblom, 1963: 85)

In this way, the individualist believes that he can safely forgo the vicissitudes of goal formulation and priority setting. His continuous incremental comparisons have implicit, contextually shifting policy-preference rankings as a side product. This largely implicit, ameliorative way of treating values and goals fits the individualist networking style of political interactions hand-in-glove. Being casual about political ideology and explicit policy values allows individualist policy makers to see shared interests, concerns and threats easily – even with potential opponents (see Sabatier and Jenkins-Smith, 1993: 223-5). Likewise, preference aggregation among many individualist policy makers comes about as an epiphenomenon of the ongoing partisan mutual adjustment in policy networks (Braybrooke and Lindblom, 1963: 15; Lindblom, 1965).

On the cognitive side of problems, the individualist policy maker's instrumental outlook logically values know-how over know-that. They do not care that much for scientific or professional expert information and knowledge. They need usable knowledge (Lindblom and Cohen, 1979), irrespective of its source. Sometimes the source is scientific or professional inquiry. In the case of tackling AIDS, the individualist approach that defined liberty as resting on moderation of lustful behaviour, personal hygiene and latex, had as a necessary corollary fast progress in developing a preventative or curative vaccine; and made heavy funding of medical research a must. But more often they rely as much or more on common sense and practical knowledge of fellow policy makers, civil servants, consultants and analysts, or ordinary people. Here again, their interaction style helps them mobilise the usable knowledge or 'intelligence of democracy' (Lindblom, 1965) implicitly stored in their networks.

If a problem should be solvable and worth solving (Dery, 1984: 25-7) according to the above criteria and rules for closure on the scope and form of a problem, it follows that the individualist policy maker clearly prefers defining a problem as moderately structured/ends. But how do they deal with the other problem types? As soon as they are convinced that a problem is worth solving, and the knowledge base permits, they will not resist defining a problem as structured. As in cost-benefit and to a lesser degree in cost-effectiveness analysis, they may even be at pains to elaborate algorithms and standardised calculation methods that help them perform their incremental comparisons between means by determining their monetised costs and benefits to themselves (Weimer and Vining, 1999). But unstructured and moderately structured/means problems are clearly not worth the individualist's precious time. They tie the individualist up in unproductive value talk or equally unproductive debates about the misery of the human condition. The individualist would rather avoid both as obstacles to 'make things better' – if only a little bit. In the gun control controversy in the US, for example, individualist policy analysts typically resist an all-too-moralistic gun control advocacy and join hierarchist anti-gun control advocates in a call for more 'dispassionate', 'pragmatic' information, evidence, research and a consequentialist type of policy discourse on what works and at what costs (e.g. Cook and Ludwig, 2003).

The voluntarist-consensual public health approach used in tackling AIDS is a good example of the individualist's preferred problem definition strategy. Public health, in a multicultural society allergic to the slightest form of public moralising, was supposed to be a problem of self-control, voluntary compliance and individual responsibility: 'Every man may be his own quarantine officer' (John Snow, quoted in Baldwin, 2005: 129). But this clearly depended on every man's willingness and ability to digest every bit of usable knowledge provided by professional, public information and education campaigns, and advocated in behavioural change strategies.

Technology assessment studies of the car mobility problem also provide us with examples of typical individualist problem framing (Hoppe and Grin, 2000). They all define the car mobility problem as threatening free access to roads, and thus to the individual's right of freedom of movement. Thus, the car mobility problem is a lack of space, a shortage of passable roads, a lack of useful traffic information, a loss of valuable time. Given the total demand for car mobility, the problem ultimately is undersupply of transport possibilities per car or per car owner. As a choice of means problem, individualist policy analysts try to find out which alternative road pricing mechanisms and information systems will rebalance supply and demand under which conditions.

Conclusions

Cultural bias and problem structuring

Does grid–group cultural theory throw any additional light on questions like: Why do some political or policy makers prefer to define a problem as Type A rather than Type B? Can politicians or analysts caught up in the different ways of life be predicted to have differential affinities and skills in coping with different problem types? Does grid–group cultural theory somehow organise or synthesise the disparate and fragmented frameworks and attempts at theory construction in the emergent subfield of the politics and analysis of problem definition, especially translation and framing dynamics?

Figure 4.2 summarises the results achieved by bringing grid–group cultural theory to bear on the problem typology. It shows that there is a rather straightforward one-to-one match between cultural ideal-types and the policy problem types. More precisely, each solidarity corresponds closely to one *focal* problem-definition strategy. This focal or default strategy is part of a repertoire of problem-framing and problem-definition strategies. However, each solidarity also shows a differential set of affinities to *non-focal or secondary strategies*. For further theory construction and testing, the secondary strategies are as important as the focal ones. Remember that we deal with ideal-types and know that reality is replete with hybrids, and 'impurities' are the rule. Particularly, in politically and ideologically plural societies it is difficult to imagine that politicians and policy makers of just one cultural disposition hold a monopoly on a policy domain and its political arena or network. Rather, different coalitions will compete over the power and authority to define the policy problem, which is to direct and constrain further policy-making efforts. That is, in order to turn a static problem typology into a dynamic theory of the process of problem framings and definitions, the affinities to the secondary strategies in a problem-framing and problem-definition repertoire determine the possibilities and constraints on building credible advocacy coalitions (Sabatier and Jenkins-Smith, 1993) or productive discourse coalitions

(Hajer, 1995) with adherents of other ways of life. But this is yet another theoretical and analytical task in linking the problem typology to types of policy making (see Chapters Five and Six).

Figure 4.2: Cultural bias and problem framing

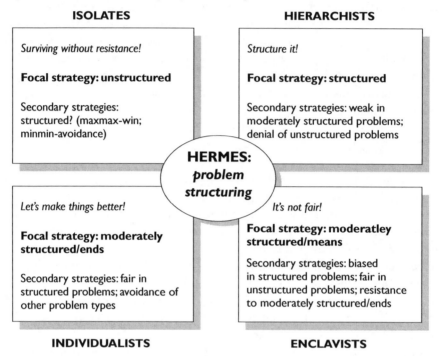

One way of summarising the results of this chapter is to return to Gusfield. His cultural analysis of public policy problems stresses the configuration of three elements that conjoin in the structure of each public policy problem: ownership, causality and accountability. The theoretical analysis and empirical illustrations allow the proposition that at least four types of such structures of public policy problems will be identifiable. Hierarchically inclined policy analysts will opt for the government or officials as problem owners; they will select the theory of causality with the highest academic credibility; and they will prefer an accountability that reflects the 'one-for-all' principle (Bovens, 1998). On the contrary, policy analysts predisposed in isolationist or fatalist ways, believing in 'survival without resistance', will consider everybody, but nobody in particular, as a problem owner, or rather, victim; every causal theory will be rejected as 'not of this world', and thus discarded in favour of stories and anecdotes about good and bad luck; and from both previous beliefs and attitudes it follows that when, fully according to expectations, things go awry, nobody can be held accountable.

Enclavistically predisposed policy makers will claim problem ownership for 'the people', 'the citizens' or those who demonstrably belong to a worthwhile target group, for those, in brief, with whom they can identify as a group ('ours', 'of our kind') or as a person ('mine', 'of my kind'). For them, a malfunctioning 'system' always is the root cause of the problem, and in support for this claim they will appeal to both cognitive authority (counter-expertise) and lay knowledge; self-evidently it is 'them' who are accountable, meaning either evil outsiders or neglectful superiors – that is, government officials or other authority figures who represent the collective (Bovens, 1998). For an individualistically programmed policy maker, the problem owner simply is someone who happens to have the highest stake, or who for other motives has become deeply involved in solving the problem; they prefer usable knowledge of whatever kind, which frequently means – *contra* Gusfield – that causal knowledge counts but for little; and those individuals – not groups or collectivities – are held accountable who were in a position to prevent bad results and damage but failed to do so (Bovens, 1998).

The reader should take note of the fact that cultural theory not just complements Gusfield's cultural analysis of policy problems by pointing out predictable differences between four types of problem structure. The theory also implies an amendment: it stresses that knowledge remains a vital element in a problem structure, but that causal knowledge is less important than Gusfield predicts After all, in three out of four types – individualist, enclavist and isolationist policy makers – detailed knowledge of causes and effects is unnecessary. Consequently, some even argue that cultural worldviews much better explain positions in policy translation and problem framing dynamics, and that these worldviews filter the kinds of information and information sources believed credible enough to influence one's position (compare Kahan and Braman, 2003a, 2003b; Braman et al, 2005).

Spin-offs for doable policy analysis

A logical next question is: do conclusions and findings in this chapter have spin-offs for doing policy analysis? Is the theory relevant for what-to-do and how-to-do-it questions of policy analysis? The brief answer is: yes. It teaches analysts precisely which four problem-definition strategies to expect. It also gives them clues about which types will confront each other in policy arenas, and which hybrid strategies are likely and less plausible. This is usable knowledge. Deliberate cognitive *problem structuring* by analysts and reasoned *problem choice* by democratically accountable public managers, high-level administrators and politicians are indispensable in avoiding policy controversies and breaking deadlocks (also in Hisschemöller and Hoppe, 1996; reprinted in Hisschemöller et al, 2001). It involves the confrontation, evaluation and integration of as much contradictory information as possible. It leads to what Hannah Arendt (1968: 241) called political judgement through representative thinking:

> The more people's standpoints I have present in my mind while I am pondering a given issue, and the better I can imagine how I would feel and think if I were in their place, the stronger will be my capacity

for representative thinking and the more valid my final conclusions, my opinion.

Apart from many social and political conditions, problem structuring requires policy analysts endowed with skills of problem reframing or 'the capacity to keep alive, in the midst of action, a multiplicity of views of the situation' (Schön, 1983: 281). Precisely at this point, grid–group cultural theory offers inspiration. Thompson et al (1990) have defended the thesis that at the intersection of grid and group on the socio–cultural map sits a fifth ideal-type. They call this ideal-type the 'hermit', because of their self-conscious withdrawal from commitment to and involvement in the other four ways of life. Schmutzer (1994) stresses free access and movement between the four cultural biases as another aspect of both aloofness from and prudent use of the four solidarities. He therefore interprets the fifth ideal-type as a Hermes, the fast-running messenger and clever translator, the god of commerce and traffic of the Greeks. Policy analysis needs Hermes-like practitioners for problem structuring to become an accepted tool of the trade (Hoppe, 2007).

Notes

[1] Some cultural theorists prefer to speak of 'solidarities', because by organising *preferred* social relations, they represent different types of solidarity between people. This is true even for 'isolates', who implicitly or explicitly choose this way of life, if only temporarily, like voluntary soldiers or students. It is perhaps less appropriate for the compulsory isolationism of the truly marginalised and outcasts, who are indeed condemned to the 'fatalist' ways of life. Nevertheless, I will use 'way of life' and 'solidarity' interchangeably as synonyms.

[2] These terms are intended to be as neutral and ahistorical as possible in order to facilitate dispassionate comparisons across regions and time. Unfortunately, it is logically impossible to jump over one's own constructivist shadow and find a terminology that is at once technically correct, easily understandable and not burdened (for some readers) by unintended historical, political or contextual connotations (compare Douglas, 1996b: 175).

[3] The army and police come to mind as the prototypical hierarchical public sector organisations. But, of course, there are numerous other hierarchical institutions outside of the public sphere. Lakoff (1996) anchors the conservative worldview in the US in the hierarchical prototype type of 'strict father', heading a traditional nuclear family 'with the father having primary responsibility for supporting and protecting the family as well as the authority to set overall policy, to set strict rules for the behaviour of children, and to enforce the rules. The mother has the day-to-day responsibility for the care of the house, raising the children, and upholding the father's authority.' Lakoff anchors the liberal, or in cultural theory terms, egalitarian worldview, in another, 'nurturant parent' type of family system.

[4] Kenneth Boulding (1956) linked knowledge to 'faith', instead of 'truth'. He argues that it is the scientist's or expert's faith in scientific method that is the kernel of knowledge, especially the belief that applying knowledge to political and/or organisational decision and action makes it 'rational' par excellence. On top of that, the 'faith'-character of knowledge leads to its use in the social formation of shared images and collective beliefs able to coordinate action.

[5] Of course, Rastogi is eccentric, but honest, in explicitly founding his normative position on religious inspiration. Policy analysts, consciously or not, usually take either a cognitivist or a non-cognitivist meta-ethical stance. Cognitivism in policy analysis is frequently identified with Arnold Brecht's Scientific Value Relativism (or Alternativism). Scientists cannot scientifically determine whether or not something is ultimately valuable; but 'given' an ultimate value, they can use their scientific methods to clarify all the implications and consequences of adhering to this 'given' value. But most policy analysts, for example cost-benefit analysts and pragmatic incrementalists, adhere to some form of emotive non-cognitivism, that is, they deny ethical statements any cognitive status beyond emotional expressions of ephemeral and temporary preferences. The only thing scientists may do is observe people's preferences as manifested in their behaviour, and adopt these 'observed' preferences as normative lodestars. Paradoxically, these more scientifically inspired and, therefore, more frequent meta-ethical positions, in practice, amount to the same hierarchical bias in favour of experts who claim the right to force-feed their interpretations and 'empirical' indicators for values to politicians, policy making officials and citizens (Van de Graaf and Hoppe, 1989: 141-57; Fischer, 1990).

[6] Decomposability is a general characteristic of professional problem solving. Decomposability pre-formatted by an undubitable, or in practice undoubted, paradigm distinguishes the hierarchist's way of problem definition and solving. Compare this to Don Schön's reflective practitioner whose hallmark is the ability to simultaneously entertain more than one alternative way of decomposing problems.

[7] Some might object to this argument that hierarchists by implication are supportive of state control. This overlooks that hierarchists see 'order' as overriding value orientation. Difficult as it may be for Europeans to understand, in the US, 'order' was created by ordinary people resisting French and English colonial powers and their imposed 'order'. More than in Europe, US conservatism blends a strong dosage of religiously and historically inspired hierarchy with a fair amount of 'state-free' individualism.

[8] For example, Coughlin (1994) analyses the traffic congestion problem in the US as a 'tragedy of the concrete commons' from a traditional economic growth and a green perspective.

[9] That is, if they are convinced that government intervention is the proper thing to do. The gun control issue proves that, in some cases, hierarchists prefer government to leave other hierarchically run institutions (like families, churches and certain types of schools) alone.

[10] Schmutzer (1994), an Austrian scholar, views schools and other educational institutions as the typical isolationist organisation. Interestingly, March and Olsen (1976) use US and Norwegian universities and faculties to illustrate their theory of anarchic organisations and garbage–can decision-making processes.

[11] Some might argue that maxmax gambling and minmin avoidance can be viewed as 'strategies' for 'structured' problems.

[12] So strong is this tendency that, in many versions of grid–group cultural theory, enclavists are called 'egalitarians'.

[13] This may be the reason why, at face value, interest groups are always drawn into using enclavist-like rhetoric in advancing their cause. Still, there is no necessary positive relationship between the enclavist frame and interest group behaviour. After all, interest groups may hold very different cultural biases. A labour union or an interest group representing the physically challenged may, indeed, espouse egalitarian beliefs. But a Chamber of Commerce or Rotary Club representative will more likely embrace individualist beliefs. The impression of a one-to-one connection between the politics of interest group representation and the enclavist problem frame actually derives from stolen rhetoric. The contemporary media demand strong policy statements, packaged as soundbites. This type of communication of group interests will always stress the group's cause at the expense of everything else; thereby lending such types of statements the semblance of pure enclavism.

[14] Any similarity with an advertisement slogan of a multinational company is wholly intentional.

[15] The Pareto optimum in cost-benefit analysis – choose the alternative(s) that make at least one person better off, and nobody else worse off – is the algorithmic form of the individualist position.

FIVE

Problem types and types of policy politics

[T]he identification of the nature of the policy subsystem in a given policy sector reveals a great deal about its propensity to respond to changes in ideas and interests. (Howlett, 2002: 237)

Introduction

The previous chapter looked at translation and framing dynamics from the perspective of the distribution of cultures in society. It inquired into congruencies of citizens' ways of life with policy makers' styles and strategies in problem framing and structuring. This chapter will deal with *policy politics* in policy networks. If policy making is intertwined cogitation and interaction (Wildavsky, 1980 [1979]), then policy politics is the combination of types of cognitive processes and styles of interaction, characteristic for problem processing in an issue domain. Policy politics is the specific mode or style of policy making among the set of political actors, proximate policy makers, stakeholders, civil society associations and citizens involved on a more or less continuous basis, and with more or less intensity, in processing a particular public issue or problem.

The idea of policy or issue domains means that, in a way, a political system at large becomes a 'federation of sectors' (Wildavsky, 1980 [1979]: 73). The incessant bombardment with demands facing a political system or polity is sorted or clustered in policy or issue domains. They are components of the political system organised around apparently similar or affiliated substantive political problems. These politico-administrative structures effectively couple decision makers to implementers and citizens, both top down and bottom up, in translation and framing dynamics of their own. Policy networks create de facto linkages between those controlling formal governance arrangements and those engaged in the sub-politics of running the normal, day-to-day social or socio-technical practices in less formal or completely informal arrangements on the ground.

Policy politics is to be distinguished from *macro politics* at national or international levels. At the macro-political level, the socialisation and politicisation of conflict is the essential political process in a democracy (Schattschneider, 1960 [1988]: 138). At the macro level, issues are processed serially, which is a severe restriction on the number of issues that can be handled simultaneously. The threat of system overload is omnipresent (Easton, 1965), but held in check by creating relatively autonomous policy domains. In these domains, many issues can be dealt with simultaneously, in parallel processing. 'Relative autonomy' of policy domains means that macro politics and policy politics penetrate each other, with macro–political constraints more likely to affect policy politics than the other way around.

To the extent that Lowi (1995) was right in claiming that properties of policies – as temporary, but authoritative problem/solution designs – correspond to properties of politics, one would hypothesise that different problem types normally correspond to certain modes of problem framing, information search and decision making. Thus, this chapter demonstrates to what extent the problem types create, so to speak 'behind the backs' of those involved, their own modes of governance, types of power arena and types of political process. The chapter pays special attention to the ways in which policy debate is closed down and opened up; to how problem types generate or inhibit access to the policy-making arena for proximate policy makers and other stakeholders, individual citizens among them; and to how problem types impose or lift constraints on them, for example through rules for entry into policy networks; and to the ways in which policy makers and stakeholders may disagree without being excluded from the policy game.

From a cogitative perspective, policy politics describes a particular governance space that coordinates the production, dissemination and acceptability of knowledges for political decisions. 'Knowledges' is used in the plural because normally political decisions have to align different types of knowledge from different actors: citizens, professionals, bureaucrats and experts. The policy politics of a certain domain acquires its special character precisely because it implicitly or explicitly constructs a particular public epistemology, that is, the taken-for-granted expectations about the legitimacy and validity of these knowledges. Thus, policy politics involves contests about the availability of knowledge, about powers and competencies to frame and define problems and about the legitimacy of knowledge claims.

In this chapter, a tentative taxonomy of policy politics is developed by briefly tracing the history of policy-making theories. It is shown how they have evolved from models of policy decisions by 'leaders' or top levels of organisations to models of inter-organisational policy networks. This history is then simplified in four ideal-typical styles of policy politics, each one fitting one type of problem structure: structured problems have regulatory politics (*rule*), moderately structured problems (goals) have a politics of advocacy coalitions and problem-driven search (*negotiation and search*), moderately structured problems (means) have a politics of conflict management and discourse coalition building (*accommodation*) and unstructured problems are characterised by either populist leadership politics and crisis management or serious efforts at learning through deliberation (*leadership and/or learning*).

From policy decision making in and between organisations, to networks

Historical overview

In Chapter Three, a problem typology based on two dimensions was introduced: the degree to which multiple policy makers agree on values at stake and the degree of certainty about relevant and available knowledge. These two dimensions were in fact inspired by a 50-year-old typology of organisational decision making devised by Thompson and Tuden (1959). In an effort in heuristic concept stretching, their typology will be used to create a loose and tentative taxonomy of types of policy politics. In a way, it will be shown why the Thompson and Tuden typology may still be regarded as a set of useful meta-types for theorising on the policy process.

But first, the intellectual history of modelling the policy-making process has to be briefly set out. During and after the Second World War, the social sciences experienced a turn to social relevance. To prove their value to society and politics, the social sciences had to address identifiable actors that disposed of the resources to finance research that was clearly relevant to their actor-specific purposes. Pragmatically, this meant turning to governmental-public and corporate-private bureaucracies; conceptually and from an institutional perspective, it meant establishing public and business administration, and policy and organisation studies as academic fields, or rather interdisciplinary movements in the social sciences (Wagner, 2001: 72). This, of course, could be done at several levels of analysis and from varying epistemological orientations, depending on the type of actor addressed.[1] Broadly speaking, the analytical drift in the history of models of the policy-making process from the 1950s to the present runs from models of individual policy makers (by Simon, 1947, 1957, Lasswell, 1930, 1986 and Dror, 1964), to models of organisational policy making (by Allison [1971], Steinbrunner [1974], Mintzberg et al 1976], March and Olsen [1976] and Kingdon [1984]), to the present models on policy making as networks, governance, discourse and deliberation (Parsons, 1995; and especially Howlett and Ramesh, 1998; Hall and O'Toole, 2004; Bogason, 2006; Klijn, 2008).

This history of policy-making theory may be conceptualised as a development along two axes. The first axis is the familiar Wildavskian polarity, well expressed in Wildavsky's (1980) aphorism 'speaking truth to power'. All policy making is an intricate intertwinement of cogitation and interaction. Cogitation implies thought processes, involving truth, logic, analysis, argumentation, creativity, design, ingenuity and prudence. Interaction is about processes of collective will formation, involving power, instigation, manipulation, support building for majority formation, rhetoric, heresthetics,[2] mutual adjustment, and vigilance or alertness. The second axis is about how the intricately intertwined, yet contrasting, processes of cogitation and interaction unfold (Bogason, 2006): as imposed top-down processes of organised order through coordination, or as bottom-up, muddled, epiphenomenal and emergent processes of coordination-without-acoordinator (Lindblom, 1965) or self-guidance (Lindblom, 1990). If one projects half a century of theorising on policy making in a property space defined by these two axes, the result is Figure 5.1.

Figure 5.1: From policy decisions to policy networks

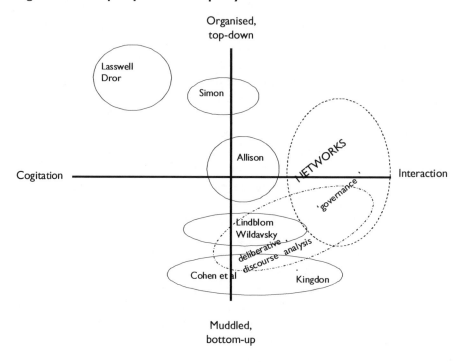

Striking in this depiction is the solid theoretical tradition of linking interactive to cogitative styles in policy making, all the way from Simon (satificing by administrative man) in the 1940s and 1950s, through the work of Lindblom/ Wildavsky (disjointed incrementalism) in the 1960s, Allison (organisational process and bureaucratic politics models), to Cohen, March and Olsen (decision making as garbage cans) in the 1970s. Equally striking, however, is that the more recent network and discourse or 'governance' approaches to policy making apparently have given up on the empirical and normative task of linking network interactions to cogitation styles or patterns. A governance-of-problems approach as advocated here aspires to rebalance, however tentatively, the cogitative and the interactive dimensions in network thinking.

Decision making by leaders, or rank and file

The first step to social relevance was to turn scholarly attention to decision makers at the top of political and corporate organisations. Setting up authority, and using expert knowledge in order to create orderly social and material production processes, was dealt with as a problem of rational leadership. Rationality was considered to be a sequence of logically ordered, transparent and self-conscious thought movements. This view of rationality resulted in the many sequential or stage theories of decision and policy making that until this very day dominate fields such as business administration, public administration, policy analysis and organisational, even psychological, decision making (see Chapter Two). In political science, public administration and policy analysis, the works of Lasswell (Lerner and Lasswel, 1951; Lasswell, 1971) and Dror (1971) are exemplary for efforts at rationalising policy making based on scientifically enlightened leadership.

But even in those early years there were dissenters and sceptics whose influence was to grow. They started modelling the decision making and design behaviour, not of leaders, but of the rank and file. Most famous among those, of course, is Herbert Simon, who coined and theoretically elaborated the concept of bounded rationality (see Chapter Three). In order to deal with sometimes quite complex problems, attention scarcity and limited time, people unavoidably develop simplifications in the representation of a problem, the number of alternative solutions considered and the consequences to be taken into account in evaluating alternatives. Simon himself developed the model of '*administrative man*'; a kind of middle manager in a large firm, or mid-level official in an administrative organisation. He finds the (cogitative) constraints on his problem–processing work closed by the (organisational and interactional) givens of his role and position in a hierarchical organisation. He follows a design and decision strategy called '*satisficing*'. Comprehensively rational decision making is impossible in principle; even optimising is very often impossible for pragmatic reasons. Thus, most frequently, only those solutions are considered that come up in sequential search processes, and that attain satisfactory levels of criterion variables (Simon, 1947; 1957). When a satisfactory alternative is found, the search process stops and the alternative is selected. If satisfactory alternatives come up easy and fast, the aspiration level for what counts as 'satisfactory' is raised. Only when no satisfactory alternative is found after a long search, more than one alternative at a lowered satisfactory threshold may be considered.

Thinking along the same lines, but applying them to the context of policy officials in politicised bureaucratic settings, Lindblom (Braybrooke and Lindblom, 1963; Lindblom, 1965) modelled policy-making practice as disjointed *incrementalism*. The shift in context is important. Lindblom tackles political problems, and officials in bureaucratic roles, but in thoroughly political settings. This complicates the task environment considerably, as 'the human capacity for heuristic reasoning creates conflict, as well as creating uncertainty, in that it creates new problems and objectives' (Grandori, 1984: 204). In these more complex political environments, policy-making bureaucrats apply a simple strategy of ameliorative incrementalism. This cognitive strategy may be applied only because the bureaucrats implicitly trust in the safety nets of normal political interaction: first, the 'invisible hand' of partisan mutual adjustment at work in interest-group pluralism; and second, the trial and error of the never-ending sequence of policy cycles. Through successive limited comparisons of alternatives against each other and the status quo as the bottom line, by agreement on limited actions as variations on existing policy, and by comparing such small moves with existing solutions at the margins, slow but solid progress can be made. According to Lindblom, in political and policy matters, step-by-step policy change is a wiser, more error-proof strategy than reaching for comprehensive rationality and radical change (Lindblom, 1959, 1965, 1979, 1999; Braybrooke and Lindblom, 1963). After all, even '[c]apitalism was only a series of patches on feudalism' (Dahl and Lindblom, 1953: 86).

It is stressed again that Simon and Lindblom were actually modelling the decision-making behaviour of *non-leaders* in different contexts. Maybe this is one of the reasons why it took so long for their ideas to become fully accepted. Many academics and politicians believed that leaders at the apex of organisations might well aspire to and maybe even achieve higher levels of rationality. And did not leaders exist to break through the complacency, sluggishness, inertia and conservatism of the rank and file, in order to strive for a more active, rationally ordered society (Dror, 1964; Etzioni, 1967, 1968)?

Towards contingency in decision strategies

In elaborating incrementalism, Lindblom actually restricted himself to one of four major strategic aids to 'rational calculation' set forth by himself and Robert Dahl a decade before (Dahl and Lindblom, 1953: 64ff). In addition to incrementalism, they saw science, calculated risk, and utopianism as alternative overall methods to deal in politics and governance with problems of information, communication, large numbers of variables and the complexity of interrelations between them. For the purpose of this analysis, the most interesting part of Dahl and Lindblom's argument is the development of a crude contingency theory of circumstances in which one design and decision strategy is to be preferred over the others:

> Incrementalism is not always satisfactory.… Calculated risks are often necessary because scientific methods have not yet produced tested knowledge about the probable consequences of large incremental changes, small changes will clearly not achieve desired goals, and existing reality is highly undesirable.… In such situations, the calculated risk is the most rational action one can undertake – for all alternatives, including the alternative of simply continuing existing policies, are calculated risks.… As models, utopias … help one focus on long-run goals; unaided by the imaginative impact of utopias, incrementalism might easily degenerate into petty change, fear of the future, a placid tolerance of existing distress, and an irrational unwillingness to take calculated risks.… The danger of utopias is not that man has utopias. It is his use of utopias to blind him to the art and science of rational calculation. (Dahl and Lindblom, 1953: 85–8)

But Lindblom and Dahl dropped the fledgling theory of conditions for success of different decision-making strategies in the daunting field of political and governance practice. Both opted for a narrower and more manageable focus on, respectively, incrementalism in pluralist democracies, and democracy in the framework of comparative political science. Thus, it fell to Thompson and Tuden (1959) to publish the first self-conscious *contingency theory* of decision strategies in the somewhat less complex field of organisation and administrative studies. They spelled out a theory, descriptive and normative at the same time, on different conditions or task environments, in which different forms of strategising by organisational leaders might be called 'rational'. That is, they tried to specify conditions under which, negatively, a particular decisional strategy, satisficing say, would be inapplicable, and, if applied, would render inferior results; and positively, conditions under which satisficing would be applicable and appropriate in the sense of generating favourable outcomes. In fact, using later terminology by Gigerenzer et al (1999), they were packing theories of (bounded) rationality into a meta-theory of ecological rationality.

In defining conditions or task environments, Thompson and Tuden (1959) considered the environment as a source of information on values and interests, and on descriptive and causal knowledge. They used degree of agreement on goals or ends, and degree of uncertainty about means to achieve ends, as two dichotomised dimensions to create a typology of four cells (see Figure 5.2). If goals are clear and there is no or only low uncertainty about the means to achieve them, they expect (and advise) leaders and their staff to use a *computational* approach to decide on the best course of action. If goals are agreed but there is considerable or a lot of uncertainty about means, they are supposed to use a *judgemental* approach to figure out what instruments to use. If, on the other hand, means are pretty certain but the goals cannot be agreed upon, *compromising* and *bargaining* are indicated to reach common ground for joint action. Finally, if both goals remain contested and means are uncertain, *inspirational* decision making and leadership are called for to move people into action.

It is now clear why the problem typology used throughout this book originates in the Thompson and Tuden typology. The four types of policy problems basically correspond to the four cells in their typology of organisational decision making.[3] The problem types remain rooted in the Thompson and Tuden typology, but the types of policy politics to be distinguished later are not derivable from their types of decision strategies. Computation, judgement, bargaining[4] and inspiration are concepts that suggest modes of cogitation possibly used by chief executive officers or leaders and their staffs to decide on implementation plans and operating procedures by their (business) organisations. Later developments have refined both the concepts of organisations and of their environments.

Yet, many scholars to this day have found it useful and inspirational to adapt and conceptually elaborate upon the Thompson and Tuden typology. Miller (1996) demonstrated its usefulness as a meta-theory for organising the literature on organisational learning; DeLeon (1998) argued the same for systems of public accountability; and Husted (2000, 2007) showed the same for measuring corporate social performance and dealing with moral problems in business. Empirically informed models of policy making in the single organisation saw many new developments (for overview, see Miller et al, 1996) that may similarly be ordered along the Thompson and Tuden meta-theoretical template. Much of this literature can be read as a sustained attack on the rational–computational mode. Quinn (1978) elaborated Lindblom's theory about public sector policy making and transformed it into logical incrementalism as a business strategy. Allison (1971) showed how the Cuban missile crisis could be explained from alternative perspectives like an organisational process model focusing on standard operating procedures (see also Steinbrunner, 1974), and a bureaucratic politics model focusing on the power tactics of agencies in the national political arena (see also Halperin, 1974). Cohen et al (1972) developed the witty-named garbage-can model, showing that organisations frequently make decisions in settings of ambiguous preferences, unclear technologies and fluid participation. A decade later, the idea was picked up, severed from organisational contexts, and applied by Kingdon (1984) to political agenda-setting and policy-formulation processes. Meanwhile, studies by Mintzberg et al (1976), Nutt (1984), the Bradbury group (Hickson et al, 1986) and Hoppe et al (1995) kept demonstrating empirically the enormous variety of types of decisional processes in private and public organisations. Efforts to synthesise this huge scientific output typically hark to the Thompson and Tuden scheme as meta-theoretical organiser (e.g. Choo, 1998: 171). Figure 5.3 is a reproduction of Stacey's (1996: 47) synthesis of the field (from Rooney et al, 2003: 79). In a Thompson and Tuden property space, Stacey groups 12 modes of decision making in five types of contexts.

Figure 5.2: Four types of decision rules

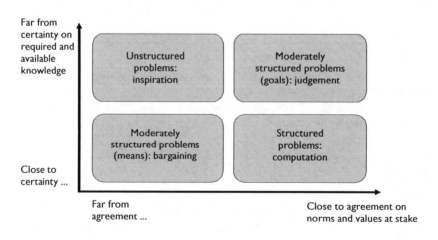

Source: Adapted from Thompson and Tuden (1959)

Figure 5.3: Stacey's use of Thompson and Tuden's typology as meta-theory for mapping theoretical developments in organisational decision making

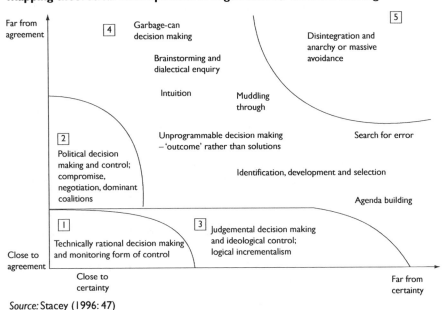

Source: Stacey (1996: 47)

Prescriptive implications

From a normative point of view and equally important for the purpose of this analysis, Grandori (1984) demonstrated how alternative decision strategies like satisficing, incrementalism, (cybernetic) feedback on day-to-day standard operating procedures, science, and random responses, each had their own place in the typology's logic. Dunn (1988) normatively reformulated the theory of contingent forms of rationality as a principle in policy analysis. He argued that too many policy analysts cope with the 'wilderness' of ill-structured problems through conventional methods of policy analysis suitable only for well-structured problems. Instead, analysts ought to acknowledge the *principle of methodological congruence*: the appropriateness of a particular type of method is a function of its congruence with the type of problem under investigation.

More recently, Paul Nutt (2002) showed the topicality of this prescription. Using a database of 367 cases drawn from strategic decision making in organisations in the public, private and third sectors, he found that leaders violated the congruence principle in six out of ten cases, thereby dramatically lowering their chances for success. Paparone and Crupi (2005/2006) wrote that the US Department of Defense violates the principle of methodological congruence. In their view, the global war on terror cannot be fought well as long as policy analysts are 'addicted' to methods of operations research and systems analysis, suitable only for well-structured problems. In addition, at the US Department of Agriculture's

Forest Service, adaptive management is advocated as the right way to deal with the uncertainties and ambiguities that the ecological challenge brings to forest management (Stankey et al, 2005).

Policy making in and through networks

Not only theories on intra-organisational decision making blossomed, so did theories on inter-organisational relationships. Thompson and Tuden, of course, also looked at an organisation's environment. However, they took the focal organisation as the unit of analysis and considered its exchange partners as sources of information. In contrast, the inter-organisational approach focused on more aggregate fields as the unit of analysis. For example, research zoomed in on the set of organisations engaged in some form of service delivery in a town or region, as they were considered to exhibit a societal trend towards 'functionally differentiated sectors whose structures are vertically [more than horizontally, RH] connected with lines stretching up to the central nation state' (Meyer and Scott, 1992: 139).

In public policy studies, this work on inter-organisational relationships was quickly integrated into research and theory on policy implementation (for an overview, see Hill and Hupe, 2002). The trend in social science theory and research (Börzel, 1998; Klijn, 2008) to conceptualise increasing social complexity as 'governance through networking' between organisations of all institutional domains (public, private, third sector) perfectly matched the holistic ideal in public policy studies (Nelson, 1996). In one of the first books to use the network concept to study collective action and decision processes, entitled *Interorganisational policy-making: Limits to central coordination and control*, Fritz Scharpf (1978: 346) expressed this tendency well:

> It is unlikely, if not impossible, that public policy of any significance could result from the choice process of any single unified actor. Policy formation and policy implementation are inevitably the result of interactions among a plurality of separate actors with separate interests, goals, and strategies.

Social scientists have been ambivalent about the almost unchecked growth of the network concept since the 1980s. Some consider it a particularly apt descriptive and analytical device for our late-modern type of society (Castells, 2000), while others criticise it as just another hollow metaphor (Dowding, 1995; Börzel, 1998). Although the jury is still out, policy network research and theory have delivered insights that are important for a perspective on the governance of problems and problem structuring (especially Howlett and Ramesh, 1998; Howlett, 2002; Bogason, 2006; Klijn, 2008). The most important one is that policy networks matter. Policy network theories specify properties such as network membership and mode of interaction that appear to affect the articulation of values, interests, goals, ideas and knowledge in public policy making. The theories also suggest propensities of different types of networks to be tuned to specific forms of collective 'puzzle work' leading to different types of policy change. In the following, these insights will be discussed with particular reference to problem structuring. They are listed in Table 5.1.

Closed, institutionalised networks, or policy communities

Empirical evidence from both the US and the UK focusing on who is actually involved in public policy making has suggested a simple dichotomy between closed and open policy networks (Börzel, 1998). It could be shown that, in technical policy areas such as chemical or toxic substance regulation, or in policy domains where the state tries to regulate particular branches of economic activity (industry, agriculture), there exist small policy 'communities', 'sub-governments' or 'iron triangles'. The last of these terms aptly characterises the closed nature of a continuous, triadic interaction in policy making between bureaucrats in state agencies, politicians in congressional or parliamentarian (sub)committees and lobbyists working for organised groups at federal or national level. Influential pressure groups with strong lobbies are Pattern A groups par excellence (Edelman, 1964), with vested interests and generally accepted expert knowledge.

Through their continuous interaction and mutual adjustment of political positions and perspectives on the world they jointly regulate, this small subset of authoritative and proximate policy makers develop a strong consensus on major policy beliefs, often resulting in one hegemonic belief system that informs day-to-day decisions. Closed membership of the policy network also means practical insulation from the dynamics of macro-political, electoral trends or media-generated issue hypes. Such insulation frequently is conditional, or mandated: for as long as they tolerate it, or during set periods, politicians invite bureaucrats and technocrats to 'run' the network for them. When statutes expire, or the bureaucratic, scientific or corporate network actors deem statutory powers and authority too weak, they may resort to national Parliaments for legislating stronger or longer-term mandates. However, under normal conditions this is 'not done' because 'political bickering drives out good policy'.

Frequently, such closed networks privilege the role of knowledge in policy, and suppress the political element inherent in policy making. Since problem structure is fixed for a long time, scientists can play their favourite role as problem solvers (Hisschemöller et al, 2001: 447-9). They are an epistemic community (Haas, 1990) of 'guardians' (Hisschemöller, 1993), who have specialist or professional knowledge about the technical and regulatory policy area. These scientists or professionals have roles such as process managers, engineers, model-designers and -constructors, or inspectors and monitors. They are either directly employed by state agencies, inspectorates or public R&D agencies; or indirectly employed by the state in quasi-autonomous, sometimes commercial, sometimes university-based laboratories and research institutes (Hisschemöller et al, 2001: 447-8; Ravetz, 2001: 488; Halffman and Hoppe, 2005).

Table 5.1: Properties of policy networks relevant to problem structuring

Network type	Closed, institutionalised	Open, emergent/ decaying	Oligopolistic competition, institutionalised	Designed, established/ terminated
Number of actors	Small	Large	Restricted, but open	Restricted
Actor configuration	Community, sub-government, 'iron triangle', Pattern A groups only	Issue network, coalitions of convenience, policy entrepreneurs, Pattern A and many Pattern B groups	Advocacy coalitions, pluralist or neocorporatist, Pattern A groups mainly	Discourse coalitions, principle issue networks, representatives of selected Pattern B groups
Relation to macropolitics	Mostly insulated	Exposed	Moderately insulated	Temporarily insulated
Type of knowledge actors	Epistemic community of inspectors, monitors, engineers, modellers	Citizens, critical, and sensitising scientists; advocacy scientists	Experts, advisers, lawyers, process managers, consultants, advocates	Crisis/process managers, mediators, specialists, critical scientists
Type of boundary arrangement for science–politics interaction	Knowledge privileged: technocracy and/ or bureaucracy	Politics privileged: advocacy or enlightenment	Pragmatic: engineering, advocacy, bureaucracy	Pragmatic: coping, discourse coalition formation
Number/ dominance of belief systems	Hegemonic	Many	Dominant, but disputed	Contested, but depoliticised
Type of policy making	Rational-analytic problem solving	Garbage-can-like problem and goal finding; and/ or dramaturgical incrementalist problem solving	Partisan mutual adjustment, and incremental analysis for goal setting and problem solving	Deliberative and procedural accommodation of conflicting goals, conflict/problem avoidance
Type of learning	Analysis/ instruction learning	Variety/selection learning; hoping for synthesis	Interactive and institutional learning	Interactive, organising for synthetic learning
Network management	Strong, hierarchical	Impossible to weak	Moderate	Strong, if possible
Type of policy	Information and rule-driven	Symbol-driven	Incentive-driven	Discourse-driven, deliberative, procedural
Potential policy change	Slow, incremental; rationalising breakthrough	Rapid, radical but symbolic; calculated risk; non-decision	Slow or fast, incremental	Slow, radical; symbolic; non-decision

The boundary between science/profession and politics is institutionally arranged as a mandate to bureaucratic government or 'invited' technocracy (Hoppe, 2005). Such arrangements result in a policy-making style that participants themselves consider a close approximation of rational–analytic problem solving. This shared conviction about the best way of making policy allows for strong, hierarchical types of network management. The when, how and why of participation by particular sets of professionals and experts in the decision- and policy-making process is not politically contested. It frequently takes the form of an allegedly unilinear process of knowledge transfer and use: from experts and analysts, to policy analysts who, in a mediating role, 'translate' scientific findings into policy arguments for those who formally take policy decisions but most of the time just follow advice.

Knowledge in the form of policy-oriented learning definitely precedes policy action. Policy-oriented learning is defined here like in Sabatier (1999: 123), as 'relatively enduring alterations of thought or behavioral intentions that result from experience and/or new information and that are concerned with the attainment or revision of policy objectives'. In closed policy networks run by experts, it frequently has the character of analysis/instruction learning. First, it is structural, that is, methodical through an agency's experience in standard operating procedures. Second, it is analytical, through systematic, intense, preferably experimental or quasi-experimental, sometimes simulated modes of information gathering and new knowledge production. Finally, it is instrumental, mostly concerned with more effective and efficient means for goal achievement.

The small set of network actors engaged in rational-analytic problem solving and analysis/instruction learning just 'knows' that its task environment is relatively stable, tends to equilibrium and thus is predictable. The policies they produce are rule driven, that is, they are of the type 'if x is the case, then do y', and so on. However, both the observation of 'x' and the implementation of 'y' may have a complex, very technical nature. Rules promulgated in official policy guidelines are likely to change only slowly, and in incremental ways. Long-term policy change is now generally believed to follow a punctuated equilibrium (PE) model of long periods of incremental change and short, sudden bursts of radical policy innovation, in the longer run tending to new incremental equilibrium (Baumgartner and Jones, 1993, 2002). The small, closed policy network described here creates and holds a monopoly over the problem definition. Because it successfully resists the entry of new proximate policy makers, the stable, small set of core policy makers can also resist learning about new images, framings and definitions of the policy problem and new ideas about its solution.

Thus, closed policy networks resemble 'communities', and thrive on stable, well-structured policy problems at the heart of their belief system. The closure on membership partly even depends on closure in the definition of the problem. Closed networks that resemble technical or professional 'communities', and engage in modes of regulatory policy, create and prolong the long periods of equilibrium, and resist the punctuations in the PE model of policy change. Of course, in theory, problem-solving technical communities may realise truly innovative policy breakthroughs in the long run. In reality, such non-incremental leaps are never realised by the 'same' policy community. They require strong, competing, expert-like communities, which are frequently part of other types of (non-policy) networks, before invading and taking over closed policy communities.

Here we see a first glimpse of an insight that will occupy us later at greater length: the types of policy networks coexist, overlap, impact on each other, and (co-)evolve over time. Therefore, strategically minded and entrepreneurial policy makers sometimes have a choice between them, or an opportunity to disorganise and dismantle one, and mobilise, organise or nurture another. As substantive policy does change, so does the policy network – and vice versa.

Open, agonistic, emerging or decaying issue networks

In the beginning stages of network theory development, closed policy networks had open issue networks as opposites. Such issue networks were open to many societal actors as candidate proximate policy makers next to the conventional bureaucratic and political players and representatives of vested interests. Although most of the time there is a longstanding core policy community, in open issue networks political access and membership are possible for typical Pattern B groups (Edelman, 1964), that is, groups of people with high anxiety levels and only stereotypic information about a policy issue. It is exactly because they feel they have a stake in the issue, but little information about it, that they can be mobilised, either through the media, or by clever policy entrepreneurs representing organised citizen associations (like the US Group Against Smokers' Pollution [GASP]), or social movements (like the Dutch *Stichting Milieu en Natuur* [SMN], or Foundation for the Benefit of the Environment and Nature), or public interest lobbying groups with letterhead, credit card membership and charity funds (like the Dutch *Vereniging voor Natuurmonumenten* [Association for Nature Monuments]).

Such associations or clubs frequently have or can mobilise counter-expertise to compete with the policy community's core policy makers. The easy in and out of sometimes not-so-proximate policy makers makes for rather accidental issue networks, and equally short-lived coalitions of convenience between stakeholders who find it in their interest to collaborate. Open issue networks are also much exposed to macro-political developments: frequent issue reframing for political mobilisation and creating a bandwagon effect. Parties with high stakes in the issue try to mobilise many others to enter the network as allies, even if the price is bending the original framing of the issue this way or that. Due to this political dynamics in issue networks, stable problem framings that pre-structure authoritative problem definition are almost out of the question. Each new participant is likely to bring to bear his own worldview, belief system, social myth, religious or ethnic perspective, or simply group interest to bear on the issue. The number of belief systems in the policy issue area is large, with multiple belief systems vying for dominance in rather chaotic processes.[5] Issue networks breathe an atmosphere of political strife, adversarial debate and agonistic participation. Strikes, sit-ins, demonstrations, inflammatory speeches and other forms of political agitation, propaganda and power struggle aimed at mobilising masses of people (rather than arguments or money) are normal. This may lead to situations where charismatic inspiration by leaders and populist politics are seen as the main vehicle to frame inherently unstable issues into structured problems.

Although open issue networks certainly privilege the political over the cognitive element in policy making, this is not to say that issue networks are devoid of players who try to bring knowledge to bear on the issue. In open issue networks around unstructured problems, scientists may play the role of problem finders and clarifiers (Hisschemöller et al, 2001: 253-4). Some scientists and scholars define themselves, not as guardians, but as public intellectuals, or as responsible citizens with a special kind of expertise for the public interest. Certainly, when an issue is not (yet) recognised by the politically interested as salient enough for public attention or public agenda status, sensitising scientists have a role to play. Perhaps the most well-known example is Rachel Carson, who wrote *Silent spring* in 1962, and is widely credited for launching environmentalism as a serious public issue all over the West. Local citizen groups that feel duped by government or corporate actions – like in the famous Love Canal or Seveso industrial toxicity scandals – are sometimes helped through scientific reports by citizen scientists to get their claims recognised by the authorities. In addition, sometimes critical intellectuals, through op-eds and other forms of debate in the media, may shock public opinion into awareness of a public issue.

In the US particularly (Rich, 2004), more recently followed by Germany (Strassheim, 2007: 281), numerous ideology- and issue-driven think tanks are continuously feeding public debates and political decision processes by taking an advocacy role to certain group interests. But issue networks do not have many institutionalised boundary arrangements between science or professions and the world of politics and policy. To the extent that they contribute to stepping up the political salience of an issue, this may be knowledge driven in a pure enlightenment attitude, where the scientist does not feel actively responsible for how their ideas are picked up by the public or by proximate policy makers. More frequently, the scientist's intention is to have an advocacy role; and provide interest groups with argumentative and intellectual ammunition in their political struggles (Weiss, 1980; Hoppe, 2005).

Thus, the policy-making style in issue networks is characterised by the fluid participation, ambiguous preferences or goals, and unclear 'technologies' in chaotic political processes, typical for garbage-can-like decision-making situations. Hence, any effort at process management is almost bound to fail; although clever policy entrepreneurs may, from time to time, succeed in forging more or less effective coalitions of convenience. In the case of truly agonistic and agitating populist politics, process management boils down to crisis management and political 'fire fighting'. To the extent that policy-oriented learning is discernable in issue networks, it is interactive and local-experimental. It is interactive in the sense of an emergent, spontaneous type of learning-through-debates between the leading personalities of issue network participants. It is experimental in an equally spontaneous, but atomistic and ad-hoc way. Experiments emerge as opportunistic, remedial actions to local problems. In contrast to the controlled, instruction/ analysis type of learning in policy communities, open issue networks display a variety/selection type of learning process, as in random–evolutionary processes.

Sometimes, clearinghouses or other forms of internet-assisted knowledge and learning centres may be organised between local stakeholders or chapters of social movements. Always, the intention is that emergent, interactive and local-experimental learning will somehow spark off the creative leap into *synthetic learning*. This is a type of learning that reframes an unstructured problem into a novel kind of structured problem, amenable to collective action through new sensible modes of problem decomposition and subsequent solving of partial problems. In other words, entry of new actors may be a *necessary* condition for interactive and experimental learning leading to non–incremental policy innovation. Only linked up to synthetic policy learning, *sufficient* conditions are present.

This insight brings to light the superficiality in much current theorising on the advantages of open as opposed to closed networks (Howlett and Ramesh, 1998: 474, table 5, following Baumgartner and Jones, 1993). Most authors posit rapid, radical or paradigmatic policy change as the probable result of access of new, highly motivated policy actors in issue networks. But open policy issue networks are far from guaranteed policy innovation machines: 'there is a large difference between bursts of attention to issues that previously lacked salience and genuinely non–incremental change' (Hayes, 2001: 96). For one thing, their character as garbage cans may as well predispose issue network policy making to *random decisions* that in the longer run just mean stalemate. For another, their capricious long–term developments often result in implicit or explicit *non-decisions*.[6] Another possible result of issue network politics and policy making is a policy of *calculated risk*. Policy makers may strongly disagree about desirable end states, and may also be lacking in certain knowledge about how to achieve them. They may still be agreed in their rejection of a continued current state of affairs. Welfare dependency, demographic change and the long–term tax burden brought politicians of both Right and Left to take the calculated risk of experimenting with individualising, more market–type welfare reforms, both in the US (Hayes, 2001: 123-47)[7] and in Europe (e.g. Visser and Hemerijck, 1997).

Yet another possibility is for issue network policy making to result in merely *symbolic reassurance*, or 'words that succeed and policies that fail' (Edelman, 1977). Citing evidence from the 1970 Clean Air Act and the Nuclear Freeze movement in the US, Hayes (2001: 72-98) demonstrates a front–and–back–office flip–flop of *'dramaturgical' incrementalism* as another possible outcome of issue network policy making. On the one hand, official policy makers give in to an alarmed public opinion and a majority of challenging groups. This they achieve through 'front-office' symbolic non–incremental policy change, which is the result of policy escalation leading to legislation beyond budgetary and/or technical capacity. Simultaneously, and on the other hand, elaboration and implementation of formal policy is steered into alternative venues of decentralised, state or local policy making. The waning of public arousal over time, and the dominance of the 'usual suspects' in such networks, makes for the partisan mutual adjustment that assures tapering down from the optimal to the feasible in processes of normal incremental policy making.

The occurrence of dramaturgical incrementalist policy making and its resulting symbolic outputs once more demonstrates that politicians and policy makers sometimes have a choice or an opportunity for combining or shifting between types of policy politics. Suffice it to say here that open issue networks more often than not cannot succeed in processing unstructured policy problems into successful, feasible forms of collective, organised action. They remain locked into a populist type of politics, with agonistic, highly adversarial modes of ad-hoc participation by sometime proximate policy makers. Often, crisis management is necessary to keep conflicts within non-violent bounds. The most that can, perhaps, be expected is some accumulation of variety/selection learning about unstructured problems in emerging policy networks. Only if such learning leads to a transformation of the policy network itself, and the emerging network turns out to have the staying power to get institutionalised, successful policy action is brought nearer. Contrary to many superficial interpretations of the punctuated equilibrium model of policy change, entry of new actors by itself is perhaps a necessary, but not a sufficient condition for non-incremental policy change.

Competitive advocacy coalitions in oligopolistic, institutionalised policy subsystems

A third type of policy network is not closed or open to new proximate policy makers, but is half-open, or oligopolistic. It is closed in the sense of restricting membership; it is open in that it does not exclude entrance for new, serious competitors. However, new players need to pass a kind of admission test. They need an indisputable stake in the issue; they ought to show sustained and willing attention to the policy issue; they need the skills of recognised expertise; and their contributions to policy debates should be (most of the time) sincere and honest (Fox and Miller, 1995: 118-27).[8] Under these or similar conditions, new stakeholders may get access to well-delineated, mature (Sabatier and Jenkins-Smith, 1993) or institutionalised policy subsystems. Examples are well-institutionalised policy domains concerned with socio-economic policy, educational policy, social welfare policy, environmental policy, or traffic and transportation policy.

Usually, stakeholders and other proximate policy makers are recruited into the two or three longer-standing advocacy coalitions in such a policy subsystem. Coalitions come about because policy actors are aware of basic congruencies in their policy belief systems; and on this basis decide to pool resources and coordinate strategic policy influence. Advocacy coalitions attempt to influence the goals, instruments, budgets and personnel for government policy making in their own direction. In pluralist (US) subsystems, advocacy coalitions come about because parties (sufficiently) agree on basic policy assumptions (Sabatier and Jenkins-Smith, 1993); in neo-corporatist ('European') subsystems, continued strategic coordination of policy action – for example between employers' associations and trade unions in socio-economic policy; or between school administrators' and teachers' associations in education policy – may be founded on the procedural belief that the benefits of compromise 'under the shadow' of state intervention structurally outweigh advantages of building strong and lasting counter-coalitions (Visser and Hemerijck, 1997; Börzel, 1998). Although institutionalised policy subsystems are relatively autonomous from macro politics, international and national political developments bear much more heavily on the constraints and opportunities of advocacy coalition behaviour than in closed, technical policy communities.

The functioning of institutionalised policy subsystems depends on processes of partisan mutual adjustment between members (Lindblom, 1965; Scharpf, 1997). These are political processes, where practitioners' information and knowledge count as much as or more than professional and academic expertise. More than previously, such processes are organised, moderated or managed by people inside and outside bureaucracy who describe themselves as process managers, facilitators, fixers or reticulists (Klijn, 2008). Policy subsystems often also have institutionalised boundary arrangements between knowledge and policy functions. Expert organisations usually are very applied or problem driven, but have a pragmatic, dialogue-stimulating function, meant to support consensus or compromise building in the partisan mutual adjustment stream.

Expertise may have the form of advocacy advice, like the study centres affiliated with employers' associations and trade unions (Hisschemöller et al, 2001: 449-51); of outsourcing studies to commercial consultants employing a (social) engineering type of academic researchers or advisers; or in-depth studies, annual reports and advice produced by quasi-autonomous advisory bodies affiliated to government (like the Dutch Bureau for Economic Policy Analysis; CPB) or Parliament (like the British Parliamentary Office of Science and Technology; POST). They are founded for the purpose of long-term policy-oriented learning and feedback. Not infrequently, national or subnational government agencies have their own look-out or knowledge centers, where knowledge brokers manage and disseminate the incoming stream of information from the other policy subsystem actors to relevant units. Boundary arrangements of the advocacy, engineering and learning types all eventually have the function of bolstering or undermining the dominant policy belief system of the advocacy coalition in power. Learning takes place interactively in the give-and-take of adversarial, but compromise-oriented debate. As convincingly argued by Sabatier and Jenkins-Smith, such learning is instrumental most of the time; second-order learning across belief systems of different coalitions about adjustments in policy goals, values or higher-order principles and assumptions is not excluded, but only occurs under the spur of exceptional circumstances (Sabatier and Jenkins-Smith, 1993: 48-55) .

Actor configurations of advocacy coalitions and boundary arrangements for instrumental learning generate a mode of policy making fit for moderately structured problems with a fair degree of goal consensus. Moderate degrees of goal consensus are likely because, in their mutual bargaining and adjustment, policy actors share a meliorative approach to goal finding: gradually moving away from a problematic situation or process (Braybrooke and Lindblom, 1963).

This 'negative' way of problem finding uncovers agreed constraints on ends, but is no incentive for truly consensual and committed 'positive' goal setting and formulation (Hoppe, 1983). Hence, there will remain some ambiguity and political distance around policy goals, which is typical for the cautious policy problem framing in this kind of policy subsystem. Incremental analysis proceeds through successive limited comparison of alternatives and the status quo to solutions that are considered marginal improvements. Policy design and formulation usually precede policy legitimation; proposal selection is a bargaining process of tapering down from the optimal to the feasible and politically acceptable (Hayes, 2001). The result commonly is (dis)incentive-driven policies that bring about slow or fast, but incremental change.

Summarising, institutionalised, oligopolistic policy subsystems are characterised by advocacy coalition politics, incremental analysis, problem–driven search and instrumental learning. This generates and maintains moderately structured problem frames; but in spite of vacillating goal preference, incremental analysis permits identification of politically acceptable, although marginally effective and efficient, policies. Institutionalised policy subsystems embody the narrow political margins of normal democracy.

Discourse coalition building in designed networks

The open issue and oligopolistic subsystem types of policy networks come about in processes of spontaneous evolution and institutionalisation. Like the closed policy community, the fourth type of policy network is clearly the conscious product of political architecture. It emerges when political and policy actors on both sides of an issue, usually after long stretches of bitter combat and controversy, come to realise that their predicament may end in serious, potentially harmful conflict. Both those in power and the challengers have a point, but the issue is really divisive in a conflictual way. For quite some time they may have hoped that a stroke of brilliant leadership would miraculously transform controversy and stalemate into a 'tamed' problem, back into normal policy-making procedures. But sooner or later it dawned on them that: 'The muddled middle is often muddled, not because it is composed of morons, lunatics, or unprincipled opportunists but because it is composed of people trying to reconcile conflicting principles and commitments that are all quite legitimate' (Mansbridge, 1986: 192).

Under such conditions, some policy actors may decide to bring together a new network of a selected, restricted number of proximate policy makers, some of them as representatives of groups outside normal venues of policy making. Contrary to issue networks' spontaneous processes of garbage cans, dramaturgical incrementalism and variety/selection learning, *institutional design* is the catchword here. The design is for building of discourse coalitions[9] between participants with different, sometimes diametrically opposed, belief systems. The design is for interactive learning aiming for synthesis, or some other means for turning divergent views and mutual criticism into opportunities for policy change (Roe,

1994;Van Eeten, 1999). In case synthesis and change are a 'bridge too far', design is for modest ways of deliberative and procedural accommodation of conflicting values, principles and goals, like finding means for credible conflict management and pacification, or gaining time to avoid solving the problem immediately, without losing trust and legitimacy of citizens. Clearly, designed networks for discourse coalition formation need strong network management, in both their creation and maintenance.

In order to build institutional crosswalks, such orchestrated networks have to be moved out of the political spotlight. At least for a while, policy actors have to be insulated from normal political processes and public scrutiny, where accountability is measured in terms of consistency with previous positions, not creativity and ingenuity in coming to new insights and agreement. The turn from political contestation to deliberation, and the gestation of new ideas in a learning exchange of views, needs periods of depoliticisation. Frequently, scientists are called upon to assist in discourse coalition building. They can play the role of crisis and process managers; as specialists or critical scientists they may clarify concepts and values due to their normally larger repertoire of factual knowledge, theories, assumptions and perspectives; and some scholars make excellent mediators (Hisschemöller et al, 2001: 451-3).

If successful, deliberative and procedural accommodation leads to policies that allow actors to cope with, not solve, the problem without damaging the network and public trust. Usually, policies have an information-driven, symbolic or procedural character. However, accommodation politics is a risky strategy. In the best of cases, potential policy change is quite radical or innovative, although perhaps slow in its realisation. In other cases, partial problems may really get processed for incremental solutions, while other problem parts will only get symbolic treatment (Hoppe, 1989). In the worst-case scenario, efforts at accommodation end in failure and non-decision, like in Dutch controversies over flooding and dike improvement, and over chlorine and sustainability in waste packaging (Van Eeten, 1999).

Because of the relative unfamiliarity of this type of policy making, let us take a closer look at the politics of accommodation in a restricted policy network, designed for coping with moderately structured problems with intransigent value conflicts and (sometimes manipulated) consensus on means. It is clear that, as a Dutch policy scholar, I am familiar with this policy-making style. For me, it is historically rooted in the Dutch political experience of forging peaceful co-existence in a 'pillarised' society. Members of the (four) pillars had their own religious beliefs or worldviews, and only managed to peacefully live together on a relatively small territory through separation of ordinary people in 'pillarised' organisations and day-to-day activities, and compromise among their political elites on unavoidable issues (Lijphart, 1967; Ravetz, 2001). Contemporary Dutch abortion and euthanasia policy, to name but a few well-known examples, are still based on the principle of accommodation politics and procedural solutions for individual cases. Yet, it would be wrong to conclude that this policy-making style is typically 'Dutch'.

In Chapter Four, the US gun control controversy was discussed as an issue condemned to the quagmire of unstructured policy problems by the fatalist attitude of policy makers at the federal level. Kahan and Braman (2003a, 2003b) have analysed how cultural orientations and political preferences dominate the US gun controversy to such an extent that evidence or knowledge appears to play no role at all. Rather, opponents and proponents of gun control effortlessly use identical information, or different aspects of the same pool of information, to bolster their preferred policy position. For example, in the April 2007 Virginia Tech massacre, proponents of gun control constructed the sad events as one more case that proves that ordinary citizens should not have weapons at all; opponents argued that, had fellow students not been barred by university regulations to carry guns, the death toll would have been far less.

In such controversies, Kahan and Braman (2003) argue, you need a breakthrough politics model to start moving again. It is a political strategy that comprises three more or less simultaneous processes. The first is devising a type of policy discourse or idiom they call 'expressive overdetermination'. Such a policy discourse ought to be sufficiently rich in social and political meanings that individuals of opposing views on a policy issue can see their convictions and behaviour as reflected in it. Only if policy discourse affirms the good sense and legitimacy of their original positions, will they open up to whatever 'objective' information and 'neutral' knowledge is available. A second step is what they call 'identity vouching'. Public figures, politicians or scientists associated with the diverging positions should step forward as advocates or protagonists of the new discourse, and derived policy proposals. A final process is called 'discourse sequencing'. The new policy discourse, popularised and disseminated by identity vouchers, creates a new standard for intelligent public discourse on enlightened public action. Those who stubbornly rejected parts of the information and knowledge on stalemated, unstructured issues due to alleged bias or strategic manipulation of its source, start to accept and use it as a basis for their own thinking and political action.

Kahan and Braman's analysis is perhaps too optimistic in the expectation that identity vouching triggers true policy learning on both sides of a controversial issue. But what they describe as a policy discourse of 'expressive overdetermination' is exactly what is meant in pushing an unstructured policy problem in the direction of a structured problem by transformation in a moderately structured problem (means). People may remain ambiguous in their policy preferences, but they open up again to information and knowledge. This might become a sound basis for finding more common ground for shared policy measures or instruments that serve a double, ambiguous purpose.

It remains telling that Kahan's and Braman's analysis is considered sufficiently innovative to be published in prestigious US law journals, while its political practice belongs to the tradition of Dutch politics. Perhaps two-party political regimes are less likely to develop and use a politics-of-accommodation style of policy making to deal with highly controversial and explosive political issues. Why take this tortuous political route when both parties may hope to push through their policy ideas simply by winning the next election? It suggests the hypothesis that not all political regimes or systems are equally likely or able to use all of the four policy styles identified in this chapter: rule, negotiation and search, accommodation, and learning. This hypothesis will be discussed later in this book.

In summary, in situations of prolonged deadlock and controversy, politicians and other policy makers sometimes resort to a politics of transformative discourse coalition construction, conflict management, and accommodation and pacification of conflicting values. This requires restricted, designed policy networks in which skilful mediation and value or concept clarification assists in generating learning processes.

Summary

The upshot of the argument so far is that, using network theory, four types of policy politics can be specified that tend to generate the four types of policy problems, and vice versa, in a kind of self-reinforcing process (see Figure 5.4).

Figure 5.4: Problem structure typology and types of policy politics

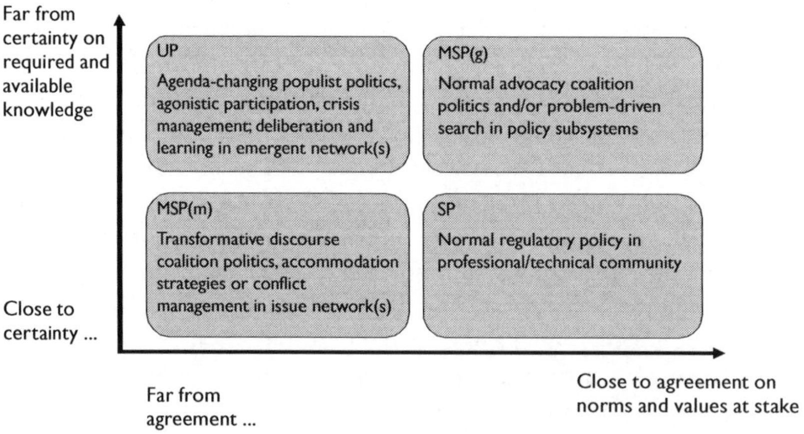

The closer the policy network under scrutiny resembles the properties listed above for the four types, the more likely one is to find a particular problem structure at the heart of the dominant groups' policy belief system. Stylised into a set of ideal types, we have: *rule* for professional communities and structured problems, *negotiation and search* for advocacy coalitions and moderately structured problems (goal consensus), *accommodation* for contrived networks and moderately structured problems (means consensus) and *leadership or learning* in open issue networks and unstructured problems.

To demonstrate the plausibility or empirical adequacy of the types of policy politics in different kinds of policy networks, and to put some flesh on the bones of the typology, each of the types will be illustrated by one or more examples in Chapter Six. On top of that, the opportunity will be seized to illuminate how, in the real world, the types coexist, overlap and (co-)evolve, giving politicians and policy makers opportunities for combinations and shifts in efforts to move away from unstructured problems, or to break up entrenched policy communities and structured problems.

Notes

[1] For policy studies, see Fischer (1980), Diesing (1982) and Bobrow and Dryzek (1987). For a more general argument on 'epistemic drift' in science, see Elzinga (1985).

[2] Heresthetics means to set up the situation in such a way that other people will want to join – or feel forced by circumstances to join – even without any persuasion at all; structuring the world so you can win (Riker, 1986).

[3] There are differences too. The dimension 'degree of certainty on relevant and available knowledge' as used in Chapter Two is broader than 'degree of certainty of means to achieve ends' as used by Thompson and Tuden.

[4] That Thompson and Tuden believe that one can/should bargain about seriously conflicting goals betrays their tacit assumption of a commercial, not a political organisation or environment.

[5] In Chapter Four, the US gun controversy was described as a typical case of an unstructured policy problem. After the April 2007 Virginia Tech massacre, in which a depressed and suicidal killer took the lives of 32 fellow students, New York City mayor Michael Bloomberg immediately stepped in to mobilise more support for the city mayors' law-and-order agenda in the gun debate (*Newsweek*, 30 April 2007: 33): 'The fact is, there's common ground on this issue for anyone who is willing to look at it honestly, not ideologically. This isn't about gun control. It's about crime control. The question is, can't we protect the rights of law-abiding gun owners while also doing more to keep guns out of the hands of criminals?.... One of our allies is the American Hunters and Shooters Association.... In 12 months, more than 200 mayors have signed on – and we're still growing. Our message is ... [i]t's about law enforcement. It's about getting data on guns used in crimes, one of the top tools our police have for cracking down on illegal weapons.'

[6] Dramatic shooting incidents in schools, and more occasionally highly visible murders of public figures, have caused numerous calls for action by local, state and federal government; they have led to legislative hearings and many public statements by leaders on both sides of the gun control issue; but net policy change from these policy dynamics has been marginal, at best (Spitzer, 1995: 14). The 60-year long struggle for an Equal Rights Amendment to

the US Constitution by feminist groups ended, three states short of ratification, in non-decision in 1982 (Mansbridge, 1986).

[7] Hayes (2001: 129, figure 7-2) places the 'calculated risk' type of policy in the cell of 'pure problems of knowledge base'. Given my views on the inescapable intertwinement of cogitation and interaction in policy making, '*pure* problems of knowledge base' do not exist in politics; certainly not in the Lindblomian world that Hayes also believes to be the most realistic one. In my typology of task environments facing policy networks, 'pure problems of knowledge base' correspond to moderately structured problems (goals); with normal incrementalism and problem-driven search as the most likely type of policy-making process. In view of the rest of Hayes' argument, it is a bit odd that in figure 7-2 normal incrementalism is saved for unstructured problems, where, by his own case examples, it is actually only one of several possible outcomes.

[8] In the late 1990s, a new bureau for economic research and advice, Nyfer, tried to get standing at the policy table of the Dutch socio-economic policy subsystem. To achieve this, it had to compete with the quasi-autonomous, but government-sponsored, Center for Economic Policy Analysis, which had a longstanding monopoly of expert advice in this field. Nyfer lost the battle because most institutionalised players felt that its contributions were tainted with too much 'advocacy' for preformed political positions.

[9] I use the term 'discourse coalition' in a much more restricted way than Hajer (1995), who characterises all policy making as discourse structuration and formation.

SIX

Problem-structuring dynamics and meta-governance

To be a man, then, is to be one who inhabits institutions in such a way that he preserves them even while transforming through his own initiative. (Dauenhauer, 1986: 135)

Introduction

This chapter explores a theory of problem-structuring dynamics. It follows the structuration logic proposed by Giddens (1979), showing how policy actors can influence the nature of institutionalised systems of interaction while at the same time being constrained by them. On the one hand, problem-frame shifts and the possibilities for policy change depend on the structure of policy networks. A closed, institutionalised policy network differs from an open, emergent or decaying network. Part of the difference is in shaping different types of policy-making processes, with different capacities for problem processing, and, therefore, speed, scope and direction of policy change and innovation. On the other hand, problem-frame shifts and policy change depend on the actions of players in the network. The policy players are constrained, but also exploit the opportunities offered by the network structures. Some policy players may come to see an existing policy network as insufficiently geared to the emergent new problem framing and the solutions it is generating. Hence, they may engage in interventions that gently nudge a policy network to change from one type to another, with concomitant changes in opportunities and possibilities for policy change. This reflects a sort of policy entrepreneurship, occasionally amounting to institutional and intellectual entrepreneurship, which may be called the *meta-governance* of problems. It operates on a higher level than 'ordinary' policy entrepreneurship.

This chapter serves a triple purpose. First, the types of policy politics introduced in the previous chapter are clarified and illustrated through four case examples. Second, it is shown how types of policy politics shift through time. Policy problem-network configurations are not static, but dynamic. Third, in the concluding section, attention is focused on this co-evolution of problem reframing and the shifts between types of policy politics. Transitions from one type to the next, whatever the other possible factors involved, apparently cannot be explained unless taking into account the meta-governance interventions of some policy-*cum*-institutional entrepreneurs.

Structuring the policy problem: prenatal screening in the Netherlands (1990-2007)[1]

Medical-technological possibilities for genetic screening and early warning for lethal diseases or diseases with severe negative impacts on quality of life have increased considerably. In 2007, the Dutch government put into force a screening programme for all pregnant women, which enables (but not forces) them to know whether they are carrying a foetus with an increased probability for Down's syndrome or neural tube defects (potentially leading to *spina bifida* or *anencephaly*). Deep-rooted ethical ambivalences and technological uncertainties around prenatal screening generated an unstructured, seemingly 'wicked' problem. It took 20 years of political and policy debate for it to be successfully structured or 'domesticated'.

Prenatal screening as an unstructured problem: non-decision making in an open issue network (1990s)

In the late 1970s, the Health Department introduced the opportunity of free (that is, reimbursed through public health insurance) voluntary prenatal testing to the limited category of women aged 36 years and over. But as late as 1989, the then deputy minister resisted pilot research into the possibilities for offering prenatal screening to all pregnant women irrespective of age. In making this non-decision, he rejected Health Council advice to seriously study the possibilities for population testing; in fact, he elevated a dissenting minority position to majority political judgement in the Cabinet and Parliament.

This political judgement rested on a web of ethical and technical arguments. Technically, prenatal testing technology showed many false positives and false negatives; and there were a considerable number of iatrogenic miscarriages. On the ethical side, one feared that these technical imperfections meant a disproportionate psychosocial burden on the women to be tested. Organisationally, the decentralised infrastructure of obstetric care made uniform medical standards and quality control almost infeasible. Furthermore, and more importantly, there being no further medical treatments for foetuses with neural tube defects, one doubted the relevance of testing as long as parents-to-be actually did not have options other than abortion. To consider abortion an ethically acceptable option to be facilitated by government became one of the major political battle lines in the policy debate. For children born with Down's syndrome, one feared stigmatisation of families as imposing an 'elected' physical-mental disability on the child. Generally, it was felt that prenatal screening for the entire population of pregnant women was 'medicalising' normal physical events like pregnancy and motherhood.

Overall, the Dutch government, especially the Christian-Democratic part of the Cabinet, considered the issue of further expanding prenatal testing an unstructured problem, not yet fit for authoritative decisions. All it had to do to justify its non-decisions was to assemble the doubts and objections raised by the players who happened to take part in the social and public debate on the issue (see Figure 6.1). As it could not stop medical–technological, organisational and communicative advances in certain academic medical research centres in the practice of testing women aged 36 and over, the government erected another barrier. In 1991, it ruled that if in the future prenatal screening was to be offered to all women, as of 1996 screening centres would need official permits under the Law on Medical Population Screening (*Wet Bevolkingsonderzoek*).This law formally intended to guarantee good quality of the testing methods and organisation of screening programmes.

In practice, the announced law had two impacts. First, it led to hot debates on whether or not pregnancy was an indication for necessary medical care; and whether or not *informing* pregnant women about prenatal screening was subject to a licence requirement, or just the actual *testing* itself. Second, the law was a spur to improve the sensitivity and specificity of tests in prenatal screening. It put a premium on intensified research for technological advance. Yet, due to successful political tactics of debate avoidance, it was not until 1998 that the Health Department formally requested new advice by the Health Council on this issue.

Both the distribution of substantive issue positions and the policy actor constellation show this period until 2000 to have the properties of an open issue network. Multiple actors, mainly professional associations, interest groups and some individual ethicists, participated in the debate; the positions diverged strongly; and although some alliances between players were visible, it was hard to discern any dominant voices in the debate.

Figure 6.1:The open issue network, until 2000

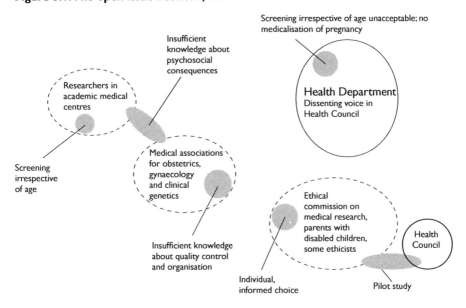

Source: Adapted and translated from Meijer (2008: 34)

Problem structuring in a designed network (2001-03)

Responding to the minister's 1998 request, in May 2001 the Health Council published its new advisory report. Acknowledging considerable technological advance in screening technology, the Council stated that:

> [U]nder provision that all preconditions can be met, probabilistic screening for Down syndrome and neural tube defects is so superior an alternative to the existing opportunities for women older than 36, that offering prenatal screening to all pregnant women should no longer be delayed. *Screening does offer actionable options (including abortion) to parents-to-be.* (emphasis added)

This advice, of course, caused a lot of upheaval and intense public and political debate by many participants. In October 2001, the Health Department organised a large-scale consultative meeting. The list of participants included two women interest groups, six parental and patient associations, seven medical-professional associations, two researchers and a representative of the major national research institute for public health (RIVM), two other advisory institutes and five government agencies. The department clearly structured the debate by focusing on the ethical and practical preconditions for the introduction of population screening:

- good counselling and psychosocial coaching for women and couples in order to guarantee free, autonomous and informed choice;
- development of new, improved documentation and information materials for women and couples;
- guaranteed societal acceptance and good care for all people who have physical and/or mental disabilities;
- centralised implementation and organisation of new procedures;
- putting in place a sound system for evaluation and monitoring of screening practices; and
- putting in place facilities for preparatory and retraining for future implementers.

During the consultative meeting and in ensuing debates, the participants were clearly split into two camps (see Figure 6.2): a larger one in favour of, the other against the introduction of, expanded screening opportunities.

Interestingly, both professional and parental and patient associations were to be found on both sides of the issue. More importantly, positions on the ethical issues clearly converged. Protagonists and antagonists mainly differed in their judgements of the practical constraints. With the benefit of hindsight, one may conclude that the Health Department transformed the policy problem in organising and structuring debate during the consultative meeting. It is apparent that the department aimed for discourse coalition building. It desired to strongly

Figure 6.2:The government-designed consultative network, 2001-03

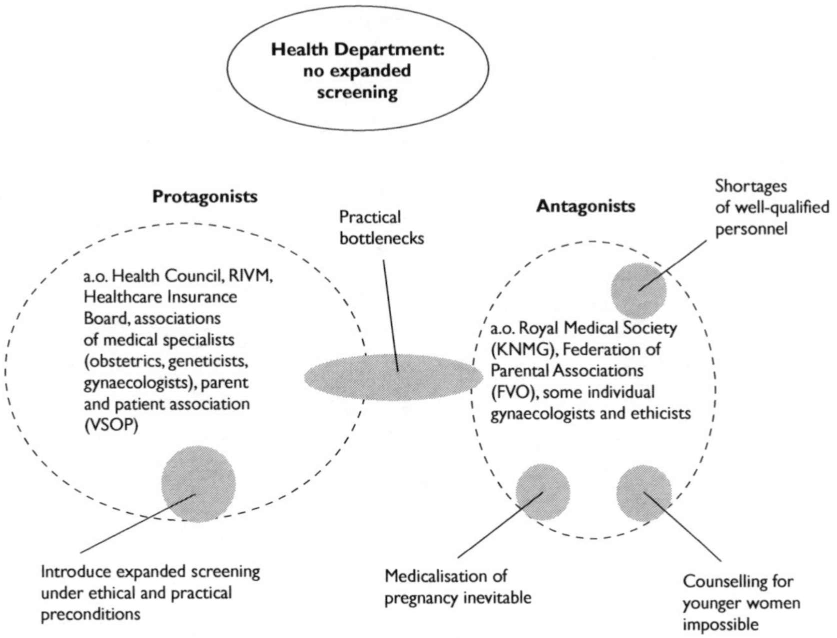

Health Department:
no expanded
screening

Protagonists

Practical
bottlenecks

Antagonists

Shortages
of well-qualified
personnel

a.o. Health Council, RIVM,
Healthcare Insurance
Board, associations
of medical specialists
(obstetrics, geneticists,
gynaecologists), parent
and patient association
(VSOP)

a.o. Royal Medical Society
(KNMG), Federation of
Parental Associations
(FVO), some individual
gynaecologists and ethicists

Introduce expanded screening
under ethical and practical
preconditions

Medicalisation of
pregnancy inevitable

Counselling for
younger women
impossible

Source: Adapted and translated from Meijer (2008: 34)

link the introduction of expanded screening possibilities to agreement on a series
of constraints, as a precondition for its approval of the new policy. It pushed for
ethical convergence in a convenient yet representative issue network of invited,
knowledgeable stakeholders. This indicates strong conflict management in a
designed policy network.Yet, although the Health Department's policy network
management was successful, macro-political developments caused the fall of two
Cabinets and prolonged the period of non-decisions by two more years.

Implementing prenatal screening in a closed professional community (2003-present)

In 2003, the deputy minister of health announced the introduction of the
programme for expanded screening.Yet, he did not completely follow the issue
network's apparent majority. Henceforth, all women aged under 36 would be
informed about the possibilities for prenatal screening, but, contrary to those
aged 36 and over, still had to pay out of their own pocket for the screening and
subsequent diagnostic procedures. This decision set in motion the final stage
of problem structuring: composing and putting to work a closed professional
implementation network around the by now fully structured problem (see Figure
6.3). Since 2006, this closed professional network is hierarchically coordinated
and managed by the RIVM's Centre for Population Research.

Figure 6.3: Contemporary closed professional network

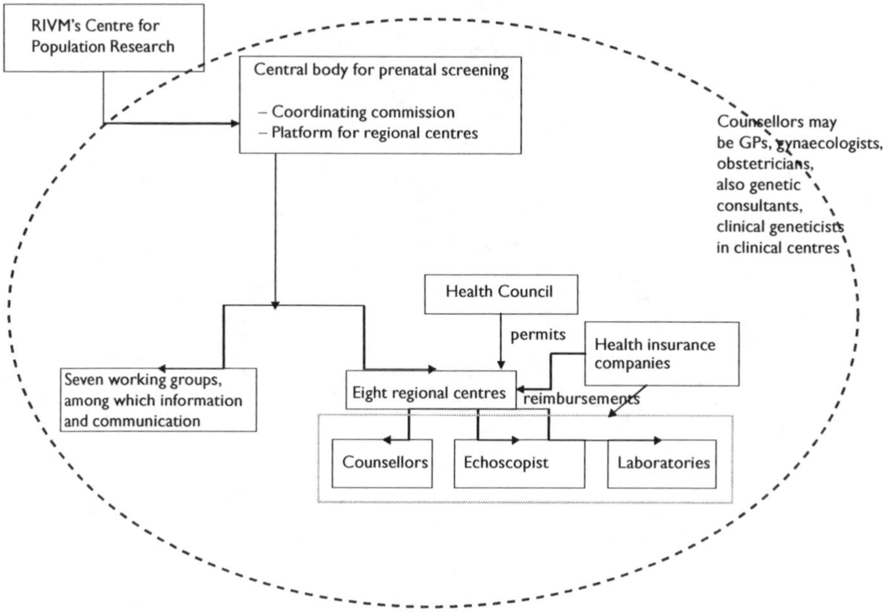

Source: Adapted and translated from Meijer (2008, appendix IV)

Up until now, monitoring and evaluation of the operation of the screening programme have shown satisfactory results – except for the counselling of younger women. Evaluations in 2003 and 2006 indicate that many women cannot adequately process the information on which they have to decide to have a test. Much the same applies to the communication with medical professionals in interpreting test results. Consequently, as much as one third of all women cannot be said to make autonomous, well-informed choices. Yet, excellent counselling in order to guarantee free, autonomous and well-informed patient choice was the single most important ethical precondition for implementing the expanded screening programme. Well-designed user-focused evaluation research and subsequent redesign of information materials and counselling practices may still remedy this problem. Yet, with the absence of tangible improvements on this score, the structured character of the prenatal screening issue may well be challenged in the future.

Breakdown of a structured problem: soil pollution in the Volgermeer Polder (1980-81)[2]

Citizens get an unpleasant surprise

In the early 1980s, people living in the surroundings of a rubbish dump in the Volgermeer Polder clashed with the city government of the nearby Dutch capital,

Amsterdam. The city government, facing a lack of sites to dump and process its city waste, badly needed the Volgermeer dump. In the spring of 1980, barrels with toxic substances were discovered there. A dragline driver mentioned his alarming find to an employee of the city government's Central Environmental Laboratory. By the end of April, the city government publicly mentioned the discovery of the toxic barrels in a press release. In May, a working group of expert civil servants was appointed to formally coordinate city government policy. Next to people from the Environmental Laboratory, colleagues from the city government Public Health Department were members of this expert group. Samples from the dump's mud and water were drawn and sent to the (at the time) National Institute for Public Health (RIV).

Inhabitants of the village adjacent to the dump – Broek-in-Waterland – were informed about the existence of a serious environmental problem by the press, not by the government. They became alarmed when one of them speculated that among the toxic substances there might be the highly toxic dioxin. Dioxin had been released in a 1963 explosion of the Philips Duphar production site at the North Sea Channel (close to the Amsterdam harbour area). The explosion had contaminated the entire building to such an extent that it had to be torn down and dumped in the ocean. Until that time, Philips Duphar was one of the users of the Volgermeer dump. Although city government officials denied the speculative assertion, anxiety among the inhabitants mounted. In August 1980, they founded the Citizen Committee Rubbish Dump Broek. The committee demanded full disclosure of research reports, participation in the city government's coordination working group, instant closure of the dump in order to prevent further leakage of toxic substances in the environment, and serious attention to medical and psychological consequences of the pollution. In agenda-building terms, the citizens of Broek-in-Waterland mobilised to transform needs and demands into an issue on the city government's political agenda.

The municipal government, decides, announces and ... loses

In the beginning, the city government responded negatively. Its strategy was based on the following vital policy-diagnostic assumptions. Pollution at the Volgermeer dumping site is a waste-dump *capacity problem* for Amsterdam and other surrounding local governments. The policy's major goal is safeguarding this *public interest*. People living in the dump's surroundings typically exhibit Not-In-My-Back-Yard behaviour, informed by pure self-interested needs and worries. In a political and administrative weighing of a public versus a private group interest, the public interest naturally prevails. The policy instrument to achieve the goal is, first, a problem survey, and second, a solution for the pollution problem. This is technically complex, so research and risk assessment ought to be delegated to technical experts with the right (toxicological, medical and legal) expertise to interpret research results and to translate them into policy measures. Therefore, citizen influence is undesirable, let alone participation in the coordination committee. Citizens lack expertise; they have panicked and, therefore, they are unable to appreciate well-reasoned judgements or have an unbiased eye for the public interest. Of course, inhabitants should be well informed by prudent communication policy. The communication policy's goal is to counteract anxiety; and the principal means is caution in releasing new information, which might nourish existing anxiety and worries. In summary, on these assumptions, the city government considered the policy problem *structured*, its solution a technical fix, and its overall political and administrative strategy one of *rule*. 'Decide-announce-defend' is a good characterisation.

This strategy started to crumble in the autumn of 1980, mainly because of blunders in the communication of research findings, subsequently exposed and skilfully exploited by the Citizen Committee. Late October 1980, the Central Environmental Laboratory's director, in a city council meeting, had to concede that small, but in his expert view not risky, amounts of dioxin had indeed been found in the barrels, as well as in the mud samples. In the same meeting, the Alderman for Environmental Affairs announced that the Citizen Committee would no longer be excluded from the policy-making process; henceforth it was invited to official meetings of the coordinating working group. During November–December 1980, the front-office semblance of governmental unity broke down irrevocably. There came different policy statements by councillors, and even by high-level officials in several city government departments. The Province of North Holland's Inspectorate for Environmental Hygiene publicly supported the Citizen Committee's demand for closure of the dump at short notice. Facing so much criticism from many sides, the Alderman for Public Works felt compelled to publicly defend the definition of the problem as a waste-dump capacity problem.

New players, and two advocacy coalitions

Paradoxically, the alderman's defence of the old, structured-problem definition disclosed that the taken-for-granted political strategy of the closed Amsterdam policy community was breaking down. The policy network expanded from city government experts and aldermen to include, next to the Citizen Committee, the other local governments involved in the issue; the office of the dike-reeve with high stakes in the issue; the Environmental Inspectorate of the Province of North Holland; and even the national Department for Public Health and Environmental Hygiene. Formally, the *Provinciale Waterstaat* (PWS), or North Holland division of the national Directorate General for Public Works and Water Management, became the new authority for policy formulation. The city government's coordinating working group, henceforth called the Working Group Volgermeer, became a subgroup of the PWS's working group on soil clean-up policy.

This new policy network was split into at least two advocacy coalitions. One advocacy coalition around the Amsterdam city government kept denying a causal connection between the pollution and still unproven *health* risks; and therefore advocated to keep the dump open as long as possible to meet capacity problems.

The challengers, led by the provincial Inspectorate for Environmental Hygiene and, of course, the Citizen Committee, considered a plausible causal connection between pollution and environmental damage more than sufficient reason to close down the dump and start a clean-up operation as soon as possible. When the representative of the national government expressed willingness to pay up to 90% of the clean-up costs, the policy network converged on the new goal of cleaning up the pollution. But the scope and thoroughness of the clean-up, largely depending on a more precise assessment of environmental and health risks of the amount of pollution, was to remain a bone of contention between the advocacy coalitions for quite some time. Insisting on research by experts, and respect for the findings among the non-scientists or non-experts in the network, the new policy subsystem acquired its definitive shape. In the end, the Citizen Committee had to accept the experts' considered judgement that no additional health risks existed.

Negotiating a solution in an expanded, but controlled policy network

Starting from December 1980, a new approach emerged that substituted governmental and technocratic guardianship for more political pluralism. The policy-making process opened up to public scrutiny; the small, closed policy community gradually gave way to a much more expanded policy network; actor-members of the network recognised that they had different interests, and were allowed to design and formulate their own policy positions, and could enter into negotiations with each other to form partnerships or alliances. Of course, all policy actors were committed to some form of majority rule. But in order to influence majority building, policy actors were allowed to use information strategically, in the sense of using the same, public information in bolstering one's own policy position. In doing so, however, one had to respect the legitimacy and expertise of other network members. After a while, the new policy network was institutionalised under the formal authority of provincial, and indirectly even national, government.

In this case it is interesting to observe how subtle intervention by national government, the Department for Public Health and Environmental Hygiene, in fact opened up the space for a new moderately structured problem with some goal consensus (soil clean-up) through making available financial resources. Yet, simultaneously, national intervention constrained the bargaining space for the other policy actors by making the scope (and thus, total costs) of the clean-up operation dependent on further risk assessment by experts. Next to making negotiation possible, problem-driven, scientific research was part of the constitution of the new policy network as a well-delineated subsystem. Higher-level government intervention thus both enabled and constrained the creation of the new policy subsystem. In this new policy subsystem, advocacy coalitions could work out a compromise on the means to solve a new, moderately structured problem. They could compete and negotiate but had to respect and use the results of problem-driven expert search.

From rule to learning, on to bargaining ... and back? Drug policy in Swiss cities (1980s-90s)[3]

Repression by a closed professional community

Like in so many other countries, in Switzerland the AIDS/HIV explosion of the mid-1980s had a far-reaching impact on policies towards drugs and drug users. Table 6.1 provides an overview of policy change before and after the 1980s. Policy network dynamics is the result of cognitive and political interaction between three advocacy coalitions.

Table 6.1: Advocacy coalitions and their belief systems in Swiss drug policy, 1980-2000

	Prohibition and abstinence coalition (hegemonic until around 1985)	Harm reduction coalition (dominant but disputed since late 1980s; forced into alliance with quality of life advocates in 1990s)	Neighbourhood quality of life coalition (somewhat successful coalition with abstinentists; since 1990s successful alliance with harm reductionists)
Policy subsystem membership	Policy community of public prosecutors, judges, police; most medical sector professionals; later, some right-wing, conservative politicians	Advocacy coalition of converted health professionals, social and youth workers, churches and charitable institutions, left-wing politicians and journalists	Advocacy coalition of shopkeepers' and parents' associations, neighbourhood associations, planning groups, ad hoc committees, landlords, real estate developers
Deep core	Citizens owe deep respect to dominant socio-cultural norms; repression is a legitimate instrument of state authority to correct 'deviants' – hierarchical bias	Individuals' integrity and autonomy more important than social order; individuals should be helped, but free to reject assistance – individualist, liberal bias	Social, cultural and economic prosperity for cities and neighbourhoods; minimise disturbances for normal urban policies; mix of egalitarian-communi-tarian and individualist biases
Policy core	Abstinence from psychoactive drugs; forced therapy	Treatment should be a drug addict's free choice; harm reduction facilities (especially needle exchange programmes) allow both individual physical integrity and avoidance of social harm	Public order and security; expressed as demand for 'Stadtverträglichkeit' (compatibility with normal city life) of harm reduction measures for drug addicts
Instrumental beliefs	Primary prevention; policy repression against drug users and dealers; offer efficient therapy; elimination of services that make drug users feel comfortable	Loosening policy protection; 'open scenes' for effective outreach for and access to harm reduction facilities; pioneer projects; managing harm reduction facilities in conformance with '*Stadtverträglichkeit*'	Experts in most instruments for urban policy; actively monitoring the management of harm reduction facilities

Source: Kübler (2001)

Prohibitionists or abstentionists represent the control–and–contain strategy (described in Chapter Three), typical for a hierarchical way of dealing with structured problems (in the cultural-theory terms of Chapter Four). It was the hegemonic, mono–paradigmatic belief system of relevant policy makers for most of the 20th century. Looking at the actor configuration it is clear that policy-making responsibility was in fact handed over to a closed policy community of medical and law–and–order experts. During the 1980s, the prohibitionist policy of repression, penalisation and (some) therapy started to have visible counterproductive effects. Drug users found themselves in poor health and difficult social conditions partly because of the stigmatising effects of a penalising approach. Where local concentrations of drug users occurred, needle sharing posed excessive risks of exposure to HIV-contaminated blood. Drug prostitution was an important link in the potential transmission of the disease to the population at large. Especially health professionals who worked in fields such as infectious diseases and public health warned about the social risks implied by the repressive policy.

These medical professional circles were the breeding ground for an alternative, harm reduction policy belief system; described in Chapter Three as voluntarist-consensual, and individualist in cultural orientation (Chapter Four). From about 1985, the public health professionals effectively challenged the hegemonic belief system and policy practice by criticising its counterproductive side effects. On the level of values and goals, law and order should be weighed against both individual freedom of drug users, and the social risk posed to the larger population by drug use. Instead of one overarching goal, there were three goals to consider. On the level of policy instruments, the official prohibition to distribute clean needles and syringes to drug users was criticised in particular. Health professionals were joined in their criticism by street and youth workers, who started illegal experiments such as 'stress-free zones', where drug users were safe against police repression and had easy access to harm reduction facilities and other forms of social assistance. This counter-coalition between a 'hard' and a 'soft' profession was ambivalent about policy preferences, but convinced that repression was no longer priority number one. It had many uncertainties about the best way to deal with AIDS/HIV, but the certainty that drug use was a dangerous disseminator of the disease. Therefore, it urged the federal government to initiate an innovative, experimental policy approach.

Thus, the political predicament became a highly unstructured policy problem. In the words of a former network manager: 'And they [the private organisations and associations, RH] finally understood that I (incarnating the state), given the complexity of the problem, had no idea as to who was right and who was wrong, and that indeed I would be a fool to choose' (Wälti and Kübler, 2003: 505).

Opening up to policy change

Fortunately, key federal policy makers and top-level bureaucrats realised that learning about a new approach was inevitable. They took the calculated risk to open up the policy-making process to new participants and trial-and-error learning. However, they had to act against a mounting stream of political opinion that 'less government' was called for, and that the then current economic recession did not economically allow new government tasks to be taken on. Nevertheless, they managed to free sufficient financial and other resources to help the harm reduction coalition to promote their policies of creating more, and more accessible harm reduction facilities.

They did so through a two-pronged strategy. On the one hand, they supported scientific research and evaluation on harm reduction measures through funding by the Federal Office for Public Health. On the other hand, through start-up subsidies they tempted local and cantonal governments, traditionally responsible for public health and the provision of help to drug users, into local experiments and pioneer projects. At the urban and local levels, this led to a significant diversification of the network of actors dealing with the problem. In all major Swiss cities, commissions or forums were formed with consultative functions. They were composed of representatives of both the public and the private sector; yet formally designated by government. These commissions and forums were linked up to special, new inter-agency coordination structures. They were complemented by other organisational mechanisms for involving neighbourhood and citizen groups in the learning-for-policy-making process.

In realising the harm reduction facilities policy, social, street-corner and youth workers succumbed to the predictable organisational efficiency-compulsion to make the facilities as large, user-friendly and accessible as possible. This meant that they were located as close as possible to the 'stress-free zones' or 'open drugs scenes', where the concentration of drugs users made it easier to reach as many clients as possible. By maximising target group reach and organisational feasibility, the harm reduction policy actors burdened many citizens with many social nuisances. Open drugs scenes just are not very compatible with nearby schools or shopping malls.

Among others, shopkeepers' and parental associations rather quickly formed a third advocacy coalition that comprised all sorts of people interested in neighbourhood quality of life. In terms of the cultural orientations in Chapter Four, the policy belief system of the neighbourhood quality of life coalition was communitarianism in a capitalist economic environment: a blend of egalitarian and individualist assumptions and preferences. In the beginning, the harm reduction people just accused the neighbourhood quality advocates of short-sighted and self-interested NIMBY-behaviour. Nevertheless, when local coalitions of convenience between abstentionists and neighbourhood security advocates proved successful in stopping local harm reduction facility building, harm reductionists sought a coalition with the neighbourhood security people. Since the latter were not really opposed to the principle of harm reduction, but mainly worried about negative side effects on their localities, across-coalition learning on the instrumental level of policy beliefs and practices turned out to be possible. Members from both advocacy coalitions gradually worked out the principles and practices of '*Stadtverträglichkeit*' or 'urban compatibility': a new local–evel balance between public order and public health policies on drug use. The harm reduction facilities were moved out of public sight and out of the vicinity of other indisputably public institutions for ordinary citizens. In addition, neighbourhood security people actively participated in monitoring the management of harm reduction facilities.

Return to a new 'subgovernment'?

This turned out to be a sustainable compromise. It was largely made possible, first, by the institutional crosswalk created by the 'new governance' and broader scope of 'associative pluralism' in the new drug policy network and implementation structure. Yet, second, the learning process was strongly facilitated by city government officials acting as network managers, who succeeded in setting up the forums in such a way that 'the right people talked to each other about the right issues' (Wälti and Kübler, 2003: 516).

However, the longer the 'new governance' type of policy network exists, the more learning tends to be substituted for negotiation among a smaller number of selected proximate policy makers. Learning and deliberation in emergent new issue networks with many new proximate policy makers appears to be a transition stage between rule by a policy community of experts, and negotiation between policy makers belonging to a new advocacy coalition. It may even evolve into another 'iron triangle' around a newly shaped hegemonic policy belief system. Wälti and Kübler (2003: 521) conclude their empirical analysis of Swiss drug policy by observing the development of a new type of 'subgovernment':

> The network of actors, which emerged in the beginning of the 1990s as a result of deliberate efforts to diversify the approach to drug related problems in the urban context, has subsequently been subjected to a concentration and centralisation around a number of privileged private partners dealing with state agencies.... [T]he joint aim of new governance structures to foster both coordination and competition leads to a certain 'cartel'-building among associations.... [T]he state's attempt to govern pluralistic networks seems to foster the emergence of new corporatist arrangements.... [T]his concentration is not only structural but also of 'ideational' nature, in that associations tend to be selectively excluded if they do not comply with the dominant policy paradigm.

From unstructured problem to accommodation: protecting the Wadden Sea area's ecological values (1965-80)[4]

Deconstructing a structured water management problem

The Wadden Sea is a shallow strip of sea extending along the northern Dutch North Sea coast and several small islands. Diking and land reclamation is part of the Dutch identity. Since the Middle Ages, dikes were built and land reclaimed also in the Wadden Sea landscape. Until the Second White Paper on Spatial Planning,[5] approved by both chambers of Dutch Parliament in 1966, diking and reclamation of the entire Wadden Sea area was an indubitable, official policy goal. Next to a century-long logic of flood prevention and water management, long-term demographic and (regional) economic prognoses justified reclamation of large stretches of the Wadden Sea area. Based on a confluence of safety issues and demands for more space in a taken-for-granted definition of the public interest, this policy logic was to be undermined in the 1970s and 1980s.

In a first stage, roughly from 1965 until 1974, the nature of the issue of the Wadden Sea area shifted from a self-evident problem of water management and economic development, to a problem of preservation of environmental and ecological values. The unstructuring of the traditional problem structure was initiated in 1965, when 16-year-old Kees Wevers took the initiative to establish the Association for the Preservation of the Wadden Sea, or the Wadden Association, for short. The established nature conservation associations, focusing on buying and preserving small, isolated nature patches, were considered unsuitable in finding and shaping a completely new political problem: the ecological interdependency of the entire Wadden Sea area. Only a short while later, the Royal Academy of Sciences established a multidisciplinary commission of independent experts, to study the spatial planning and ecological dimensions of the Wadden Sea area. In a later stage, civil servants from the National Spatial Planning Directorate (*Rijkplanologische Dienst*; RPD), the departments of Traffic and Water Management (*Verkeer en Waterstaat*; VandW) and Culture, Leisure and Social Work (*Cultuur, Recreatie en Maatschappelijk Werk*; CRM) were to participate in this committee's study. It was the first, feeble sign that the new problem framing had attracted the attention of those setting the political and policy agendas of the national government.

In 1968-69, it had become clear that, for the first time in Dutch political and administrative history, the Directorate General of Water Management (*Rijkswaterstaat*; RWS) no longer had a monopolistic competence in preparing land reclamation policy. For the Wadden Sea area, RWS had to share its competency with a broad interdepartmental commission, consisting of proponents and opponents of new land reclamation. In 1971, the official government agreement of the new Dutch coalition government mentioned the possibility of keeping the Wadden Sea untouched. When the interdepartmental commission published its policy recommendations by 1974, the result was a draw, to be interpreted as a moral victory for the opponents. The advice was to give up any plans for wholesale or partial diking and land reclamation. However, the commission refrained from any positive policy advice, stressing instead the inevitability of new political choices in a pioneering compromise between advantages and disadvantages of land reclamation and threats to ecological values.

An unstructured problem is born

What apparently happened in the interdepartmental commission was a learning process. Unstructured problems show uncertainty about available and required knowledge, and a re-evaluation of old and an introduction of new values at stake. Both uncertainty and value conflict and ambiguity were unmistakable in this case. The Royal Academy of Science's expert committee indicated that knowledge uncertainty was genuine. If such a prestigious scientific body shows concern, it means that opponents of the Wadden Association, or established policy makers and political organisations for that matter, could no longer ignore new information as biased or disingenuous evidence. In the interdepartmental committee, it became clear that the traditional confluence of military and economic interests with water management was disputed in the case of the Wadden Sea area. The department of Defence considered military purposes better served when the Wadden Sea was left alone; the oil companies, eager to explore gas reserves, feared interference from other economic interests in the area; and there were other regional economic interests to be considered, such as cockle fishery, tourism and shipping. Thus, the department of Economic Affairs could no longer unconditionally support the RWS interests.

Of course, uncertainty about traditional values was skilfully exploited by the proponents of new ecological value. However, most important, and contrary to the Volgermeer case discussed above, the existence of uncertainty was openly acknowledged by the authorities. Instead of a 'decide-announce-defend' strategy, in the Wadden Sea case the authorities opted for a 'let's-make-new-sense-together' strategy. Colliding and challenging visions were allowed on the policy table; and to the extent possible there was a serious effort to integrate old and new problem framings and visions. That explains why new information and insights penetrated the political agenda rather swiftly and smoothly, and was not only used strategically. That is why it is justified to typify the political and administrative process as learning. Of course, this does not mean that opposition all of a sudden completely vanished. It just means that ecological values had acquired standing among authoritative policy makers. Instead of being disregarded, they had to be taken into account as a legitimate normative and knowledge dimension in policy discussions.

Domesticating the 'wicked' problem by proceduralisation

The second stage of the policy-making process, between roughly 1974 and 1980, shows how policy makers transformed the unstructured problem of conflicting values around the Wadden Sea area into a moderately structured problem. Opponents and proponents of ecological values worked out compromises around an abstract and global, but consensual goal formulation in a fixed legal–administrative procedure. This second stage may be characterised as a process of constructing a discursive, as well as a procedural, crosswalk.

In fact, there were two parallel processes of institutional and discursive design – one governmental, the other nongovernmental and initiated by the Wadden Association. The latter established an expert commission of legal and administrative scholars to design the contours of an optimal administrative structure, which ought to ensure that '[the Wadden Sea area] is administered and managed in the only right way, that is such that its ecological value does not decline, and later generations cannot blame us for careless treatment of the relatively most unspoilt nature area in the Netherlands' (Commissie Staatsen, quoted in Hisschemöller and Van Koolwijk, 1982:45). The commission opted for a special Wadden Sea Law, because this vast area could only be protected, maintained and restored by the state if there was indubitable, visible support by a majority in Parliament. On top of that, the ambitious goal might only be achieved when its legal basis forced other government bodies to take it seriously, even if they referred to other laws. In legal appeal and redress procedures by lower governments, administrative judges ought to be able to use it as a legally based, overriding criterion for their rulings. Administrative and policy responsibility for policy preparation and implementation was to be vested in one department, for Culture, Leisure and Social Work, at the time the department accountable for nature conservation. In addition, a Wadden Council was to be set up as a political, public forum to initiate debates on the operationalisation of the abstract policy goal. In addition, the administrative structure was to feature an interdepartmental commission and an inspectorate for the Wadden Sea area.

The expert commission's proposal was a compromise between technocratic guardianship and normal democratic politics: ensuring a kind of 'special status' authority for well-integrated policy for the nature conservation goal on the one hand; and on the other, the requirement of a lasting democratic process of interest representation and trade-offs. In the governmental venue the trade-off between these opposed requirements was shaped differently. The formal policy goal was less ambitious, 'the protection, maintenance, and where necessary restoration of the Wadden Sea as a nature area' (quoted in Hisschemöller and Van Koolwijk, 1982: 47). Policy initiative and administrative discretion were vested in the department of Housing and Spatial Planning, particularly its Directorate General for Spatial planning (RPD). This is because, in the Netherlands, spatial planning is a policy domain that is largely procedural, not substantive; and oriented towards interdepartmental and intergovernmental interest mediation, with substantive policy making and policy implementation taking place at lower levels of government, with (partial) access for other national departments.

Furthermore, the emerging goals consensus was not to be anchored in law, but in a special legal-administrative procedure for key decisions on spatial planning, the so-called '*planologische kernbeslissing*' (PKB). This procedure starts with government announcing a fairly detailed policy intention, followed by official meetings in which organised or unorganised citizens can raise their voice ('*inspraak*'), and by required advisory procedures, the most important of which concerns the Advisory Council on Spatial Planning (*Raad van Advies voor de Ruimtelijke Ordening*; RARO). Based on citizen comments and official advice, government then formulates a final proposal for parliamentary approval. In this case, this PKB procedure lasted four years, from 1976 until 1980.

It is clear why the Wadden Association preferred its own design. A PKB procedure lacks the force of law; meaning that Wadden Sea ecological values and goals may loose out to sectoral policy intentions enshrined in law. Second, official policy intentions not only mentioned a Wadden Sea major goal, but also mentioned secondary goals that might conflict with the major goal. This implied that, for example, decision making on exploratory drilling for gas reserves on the island of Ameland, or on harbour facilities for the Eems Harbour near Delfzijl, would not find their basis in official Wadden Sea policy, but would be subjected to normal political struggles between the usual suspects of vested interests in local, provincial and national policy making. In terminology introduced above when discussing policy making in open issue networks, the Wadden Sea Association feared dramaturgical incrementalism.[6] Finally, although the PKB procedure offers formal opportunities for citizens and non-governmental organisations like the Wadden Association to make their voices heard, this is only after government formulated and argued its policy proposals. In this late stage of policy preparation, the government has an interest in sticking to its position, often an interdepartmental compromise, at the expense of public transparency. In other words, compared to the Wadden Association's discursive and institutional design, the PKB procedure was a typical, government-centred and -controlled proposal. Yet, the Association accepted it, but only as a first step towards its own preferences.

The choice for a PKB procedure is clearly a political one, rooted in a couple of agreed policy beliefs. The Wadden Sea area is an irreplaceable nature area under threat; so we deal with a vulnerable interest that, without special governmental attention, will lose out to stronger interests. This implies the setting of a major new policy goal: protection and, if necessary, restoration of environmental and ecological values. However, next to the major policy goal, there are other values and goals that clearly qualify as public interest, worthy of government attention; their disregard will most probably erode the consensus about the new major policy goal. Hence, an integrated policy for the new major goals cannot be achieved without global consensus among major stakeholders in society. Therefore, we need a decision-making procedure, in this case the PKB, which in fact ties multiple policy actors together in a global consensus on a rather abstract goal; which means that public participation and public transparency have to be tapered down considerably. Clinging to this procedure as if it were the policy goal itself creates practical certainty around the means for accommodating the value conflict around policy goals. It is a depoliticising strategy of accommodation, or pacification of conflicting, sometimes intransigent values. It is a strategy that is conflict avoiding, because any conflict that publicly articulates the implacable value positions, will nurture polarisation of views and exacerbate political compromise.

Problem structuring, change in policy politics, and meta-governance

Problem-structuring trajectories

The case examples allow two major conclusions. First, contrary perhaps to what they suggest, the problem type–policy politics type couplings are not necessarily stable configurations. Rather, both typologies should be considered as a kind of conceptual canvass for visualising and demonstrating the dynamics or drift in problem structuring in a policy domain. Clearly, problem-frame shifts do occur (Schön and Rein, 1994). More than that, and in addition to Rein and Schön's original analysis, provided the frame shifts imply a shift in problem type too, they bring shifts in policy network type or policy politics in their wake. Figure 6.4 summarises and captures the problem-structuring trends in the case examples for the periods observed. Note that analysis registers and focuses on a historical trajectory of changing hegemonic or dominant problem structurings in a policy domain.

The prenatal screening case shows how the Health Department, in close coordination with the Health Council, through non–decision making and clever political manoeuvring, manages to transform and 'domesticate' an unstructured

Figure 6.4: Problem-structuring trajectories in the four cases

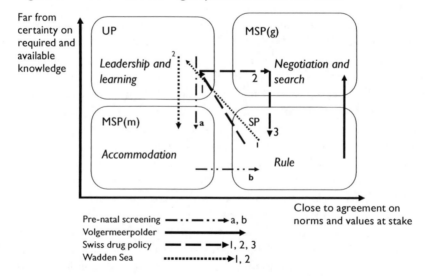

or 'wicked' problem. As such, the case clearly illustrates the tendency among politicians and civil servants to entrust policy implementation, under politically determined constraints, to a closed professional implementation network.

The Volgermeer case shows how, under pressure by an accidental find of toxic substances and an aroused public opinion, a closed local community of municipal policy makers and experts had to give up their preferred policy problem structure; and how it was transformed into a moderately structured problem with considerable normative consensus, as policy politics was reshaped into an oligopolistic policy subsystem with competing advocacy coalitions.

Swiss drugs policy saw the thorough unstructuring of a structured problem, a subsequent restructuring into a moderately structured problem with normative consensus, and later a relapse into a new hegemonic belief system with its own newly structured problem. At first, the closed policy community was opened up in local, but open issue networks to learn about more successful ways of dealing with drugs issues. These open issue networks quickly institutionalised into oligopolistic, clearly delineated policy subsystems with one dominating advocacy coalition. The lasting dominance and political legitimacy of this advocacy coalition entails a new period of rule by a hegemonic, expert-led group of policy makers.

The Wadden Sea case also is about the breaking up of the hegemonic belief system and problem structure of a small expert policy-making group of water managers by a challenging group of proto-ecologists. In the episodes analysed, the process indeed starts with a learning experience, which unstructures the old diking and land reclamation policy logic. However, it only adds ecological values and knowledge to the policy predicament, without a clear, politically legitimised, but innovative problem structuring. The threatening political impasse is averted by transforming the unstructured new problem into a moderately structured problem. This actually condemns a restricted group of policy makers to find procedural and/or substantive compromises in a long drawn-out process of accommodation and continued problem structuring.

The need for meta-governance

The second major conclusion is that the dynamics or drift in problem structuring needs some form of human agency. It is indeed a dialectical process of structure and agency, mutually constituting each other. In all cases, a longstanding, institutionalised policy type–network type structure was challenged by new agents. In the case of prenatal screening, the new agents were medical–professional innovators, backed up by members of the Health Council; in the Volgermeer case, it was public opinion and the citizen committee, backed up by the provincial Inspectorate for Environmental Hygiene; in the Swiss drugs case, it was public health specialists of the medical profession and youth workers, backed up by some politicians and civil servants at the federal level; and in the Wadden Sea case, it was the establishment of a new, ecologically inspired civic association, supported by scientists and some civil servants.

In all cases too, the '*gear shifts*' from one problem type to the next, from one type of policy politics to the next, were facilitated by some form of *interaction between macro politics and policy politics.* Although the spur for problem reframing and policy innovation came from inside the standing policy networks, the challenge was successful due to support from agents working at the interstices between the policy network and higher administrative and political governance levels. In the prenatal screening case, it was prudent political manoeuvring by the Health Department, which transformed the problem into a structured one. In the Volgermeer case, the provincial Inspectorate and national departmental policy makers gently nudged the Amsterdam policy makers towards a new problem framing by offering financial assistance in the clean-up operation. The learning in open issue networks around drugs problems in Switzerland, similarly, was made possible by start-up subsidies and seed money from policy makers at the federal level. In the Wadden Sea case, some enlightened national policy makers saw the cognitive relevance and political threat of an apparently regional development for national policy making. Hence, they were able to install interdepartmental committees with both protagonists and opponents of the new ecological problem frame, while simultaneously accommodating all parties in a new cognitive and political process design.

One might consider describing the roles of these agents as *policy entrepreneurs.* Roberts and King (1991) define policy entrepreneurs as policy players who manage to navigate an innovative idea through the agenda–setting, policy-adoption and implementation stages of the policy process. Kingdon (1984) sees policy entrepreneurs as patiently awaiting or bringing about a policy window or propitious timeframe to push through an innovative policy idea. They actively work to link the three more or less autonomous dynamics of problems (challenges), policy (solutions) and politics (political events). Pralle (2003) has broadened Kingdon's idea by speaking of policy entrepreneurs' role as venue shopping. This is finding a decision setting or a policy network that offers the best prospects for achieving desired policy change. For example, if Parliament is unwilling to adopt an innovative policy or Bill, maybe regional or municipal governments, or expert advisory bodies, offer a better venue (Timmermans and Scholten, 2006; Hoppe, 2008a). Pralle (2003) has stressed that policy entrepreneurship through venue shopping is sometimes less a deliberate than an experimental activity; that some venues are sought not for tactical reasons, but because they better fit the identity of the policy advocates; and, sometimes, venue shopping takes place not for tactical or identity reasons but because policy advocates have arrived at a new understanding of the nature of the policy problem.

None of these definitions of policy entrepreneurship quite captures what was going on in the above cases as indispensable for the desired policy change. Pralle's conception of venue choice due to problem reframing comes closest. However, the policy entrepreneurs observed above do not *shop*, but *shape* venues. As Baumgartner and Jones (1993) state, under conditions of rapid change and entrance of new policy players, old policy subsystems crumble (like the creative destruction that Schumpeter (1942) thought so characteristic for economic entrepreneurs) and new policy networks may emerge. In the above cases, policy entrepreneurs certainly contributed, quite consciously it seems, to the emergence of new policy networks. Moreover, these networks not only contained a new set of policy players in different advocacy coalitions. The structure of the policy network itself was consciously reformed; the policy network shifted from one type to another one.

In institutionalist theory, this kind of achievement is called '*institutional entrepreneurship*' (Garud et al, 2007). The concept was coined by DiMaggio (1988: 14), who held that 'new institutions arise when organised actors with sufficient resources see in them an opportunity to realise interests that they value highly'. Institutional entrepreneurs break down existing practices that reflect the rules, norms and beliefs of the institutionalised policy network. They pick up the new meanings of policy practices invented and negotiated in other contexts, sometimes not immediately policy-related environments. By reframing the policy problem and rethinking the conditions for this new frame to become legitimate, they translate the new contextualised meanings into rules, norms and beliefs that infuse and unite a wider field of action, which may eventually grow into the performance scripts of repeated activities in a new policy network. This translation work of institutional entrepreneurs depends on their locus at the margins or 'above' policy networks. Being familiar with more than one policy-framing and policy-political logic enables them to think more innovatively than the network 'insiders'. In addition, they can draw on financial and communicative resources outside the normal network structures to bolster their efforts. This type of policy-*cum*-institutional entrepreneurship can be designated the *meta-governance of problems*. Some creative and far-sighted policy entrepreneurs arrive at the considered judgement that the existing network structures no longer hold the promise of improved policy-making capacity through 'repair work'. Only by becoming institutional entrepreneurs too, through the translation work for the transition to a new type of policy frame and network structure, policy-making capacity might again be up to the new challenge.

Although in the cases above, this ambition and insight were conscious, it does not mean that these policy entrepreneurs were institutional leaders 'in control'. What they were doing, gently nudging the existing policy network in a more desired direction through translation work, was perhaps a necessary, but by no means a sufficient, condition for bringing about the desired policy innovation. Meta-governance constitutes the endeavour by politicians or some other policy entrepreneurs to influence the discourse, the composition and participation modes of actors, the rules of the game, and the interdependencies between actors in governance networks (Sørensen and Torfing, 2005: 202-5). But it would be difficult to draw the line between deliberate meta-governance and political tinkering or *bricolage*. The system is simply too complex and self-controlled to be amenable to meta-governance as top-down steering from a central control unit. In societies like ours, with complex, overlapping, partially contradictory governance systems, the only way to 'steer' is by using the forces and drivers already effective in it; to 'interpolate' small doses of change in such a way that the balance of forces is changed in the desired direction (Dunsire, 1986; Hood, 1986). This interpolable balancing style of policy-*cum*-institutional entrepreneurship is most valuable for political systems. It is an unobtrusive but essential ingredient of a political system in the responsive and creative governance of problems.

Notes

[1] This case study is based on Stemerding and Van Berkel (2001), Meijer (2008), Merkx (2008) and Hoppe (2008a).

[2] This case study is taken from Hisschemöller (1993: 128–44).

[3] This case study is based on Kübler (2001) and Wälti and Kübler (2003).

[4] This case study is based on accounts by Hisschemöller (1993: 145-61) and Turnhout (2003: 69–82).

[5] The Dutch stubbornly hold on to 'spatial planning' where the English mean 'town and country planning'. I am no exception.

[6] Later developments show that this fear was not unjustified, especially when, starting in 1982, Wadden Sea policy was internationalised in a Trilateral Wadden Sea cooperation with Germany and Denmark (Turnhout, 2003).

SEVEN

Making policy analysis doable and reflexive

> Scientific method is one important way to make sense of some bits of
> human experience, useful where applicable, potentially disastrous when
> it is used in an attempt to monopolize discourse. By recognizing the
> essentially political purpose of scientific method, we will be better able
> to evaluate its contributions and its limits in creating and sustaining
> communities of shared meaning. (Sederberg, 1984: 43)

Introduction

Chapters Three through Six dealt with the transition dynamics of the relation
between policy designs and the socio–political contexts of cultures and policy
networks. Now the focus moves to the realms of framing and design dynamics
in the knowledge context of designing policies (see Figure 2.4, Chapter Two).
This knowledge context is made up of three elements:

- citizens' and civic associations' *experiential constructions* of knowledge deemed
  relevant for interpreting what policies mean to them;
- the *knowledge constructions of practitioners* with active roles in policy networks; and
- the constructions of those who deal in a *scientific* way with problems and policies.

Of course, the knowledge context is a 'trialogue' between these three types
of constructions; they all mutually influence each other. The approach to this
intertwined system of knowledge constructions will start from the lens of the
scientific constructions; more particularly, with how academic and professional
policy analysts have proposed to deal with scientific knowledge constructions
methodically and systematically in designing and evaluating public policies.

Policy analysts first thought that they could legitimately limit themselves to
consideration of scientific constructions only. This original position is summarised
in Wildavsky's (1980 [1979]) aphorism for policy analysis as 'speaking truth to
power'. In later developments, this original position was thoroughly criticised.
Academic policy analysis acknowledged the poverty of its original position, and
the necessity of including practitioners' and experiential knowledge accounts into
the problem framings underlying the designs and evaluations of public policies.
This new position suggests that policy analysis is 'making sense together' all the
way down (Hoppe, 1999). Yet, the protagonists of 'making sense together' all too
often advocate different scientific theories and methodologies for its achievement.

To the extent that they are interested in research of how policy analysis is actually done, they select cases that may easily be interpreted in terms of their own methodological and conceptual preferences (Hajer and Wagenaar, 2003: 33–112). The empirical study of discovering different modes of making policy analysis doable in decision and action contexts has hardly begun (Colebatch et al, 2010: in press).

The first section in this chapter is about the changing scientific landscape in which policy analysts are supposed to keep speaking truth(s) to power(s) (Radin, 2000; Anderson, 2003). In the second section, epistemological developments that changed views on the nature of 'rationality' and 'being scientific' are reviewed. The third section demonstrates how these changes in epistemology have affected the academic conceptions of policy analysis. Briefly stated, it has moved away from a coherent but analycentrist position and taken an argumentative turn. Rather, under the unifying label of *the* argumentative turn, it has taken many different turns. The present situation of the field indeed is better described as a 'river delta' of policy orientations, arguing among each other about conceptual, theoretical and methodological pros and cons. The fourth section sketches a framework and research strategy for restoring some coherence and pragmatism to the field. Particularly, this section re-analyses the previous one from the perspective of making policy analysis doable. The result is a reflexive policy analysis, sensitive to context, especially to Dunn's rule of congruence between problem type and policy-analytic style.

Still speaking truth to power?

Knowledge in and of policy

According to Lasswell (1971), policy science is about the production and application of knowledge *of* and *in* policy. Policy makers who desire to successfully tackle problems on the political agenda, should be able to mobilise the best available knowledge. This requires high-quality knowledge *in* policy. Policy makers and, in a democracy, citizens, also need to know how policy processes really evolve. This demands precise knowledge *of* policy. There is an obvious link between the two: the more and better knowledge *of* policy, the easier it is to mobilise knowledge *in* policy. Lasswell expresses this interdependence by defining the policy scientist's operational task as eliciting the maximum rational judgement of all those involved in policy making.

For the applied policy scientist or policy analyst, this implies the development of two skills. Both derive from Lasswell's notion of policy science as a political idea; to mobilise (social) science to better solve political questions (Turnbull, 2005: 123). First, for the sake of mobilising the best available knowledge *in* policy, the policy scientist/analyst should be able to mediate between different scientific disciplines. Second, for the sake of optimising the interdependence between science *in* and *of* policy, they should be able to mediate between science and politics. Hence,

Dunn's (1994: 84) formal definition of policy analysis as an applied social science discipline that uses multiple research methods in a context of argumentation, public debate [and political struggle, RH] in order to create, critically evaluate, and communicate policy–relevant knowledge.

Scientisation of politics and politicisation of science

Historically, the differentiation and successful institutionalisation of policy science can be interpreted as the scientisation of the functions of knowledge organisation, storage, dissemination and application in the knowledge system (Dunn and Holzner, 1988). Moreover, this scientisation of hitherto 'un–scientised' functions, by expressly including science *of* policy, aimed to gear them to the political system. In that sense, Lerner and Lasswell's (1951) call for policy sciences anticipated, and probably helped bring about, the scientisation of politics.

Peter Weingart (1983) claims that the development of the science–policy nexus can be analysed as a dialectical process of the scientisation of politics/policy and the *politicisation of science*. Science Technology and Society (STS) studies can claim particular credit for showing the latter tendency (Cozzens and Woodhouse, 1995: 551). Applying critical sociology, symbolic interactionism and ethno-methodology to the innermost workings of the laboratories, STS scholars (Sismondo, 2004) have shown that the idealist image of science as producer of privileged, authoritative knowledge claims, supported by an ascetic practice of Mertonian norms for proper scientific conduct (Commonality or communism, Universalism, Disinterestedness, Organised scepticism – *CUDO* for short) is just the outside, legitimising veneer of scientific practices and successes.

Using interpretive frames from Marxist science studies, conflict theory, interest theory and social constructivism, a much more realistic perspective on science has been developed. Instead of Mertonian CUDO-norms, contemporary scientists de facto behave as if science were Proprietary, Local, Authoritarian, Commissioned and self-proclaimed Expert (Ziman, 1999 – *PLACE*). From Olympian heights of abstraction and curiosity-driven speculation, innovative but stringent experiments, and Humboldtian institutional autonomy, *small-s science* came down to earth as a social movement (Yearley, 1988: 44ff) driven by local and practical, sometimes openly political, interests. It had become entrepreneurial, fiercely competitive, speculative, with an 'anything goes' methodology, and selling itself to government and big business in the race for financial resources.

Changes in the 'covenant' between science and politics

Thus, the politics of science extended into the political domain. However, it would be wrong to attribute this just to science's institutional self-interest. To the extent that scientists were successful in producing authoritative cosmopolitan knowledge claims, and upholding them in their translation into successful large technological projects, they were invited by politicians and administrators as useful advisers. Thereby politics paradoxically contributed to its own scientisation.

At first, until the early 1970s, it looked like the science–politics nexus would be just mutually beneficial. The institutional 'covenant' between the two spheres, aptly named '*Science, the Endless Frontier*', meant a high degree of institutional autonomy, lots of resources, and privileged access to political decision making through advisory positions for science. Politics, impressed by and grateful for science's contribution to the war effort and to large infrastructural projects, rested content in expecting more of the same high pay-offs. As these promises turned out to be empty or merely disappointing, science's cognitive authority waned, and politics gradually revised the covenant by tightening its conditions for financial support and scientific autonomy.

The new inter-institutional contract has been relabelled '*Strategic Science*'. On the one hand, politics forces criteria of relevance on scientists, which clearly indicates the politicisation of science. On the other hand,

> [S]cientists have internalized the pressure for relevance, but at the same time have captured it for their own purposes by claiming a division of labor. Typical stories emphasize strategic research as the hero at the core of one or more 'innovation chains' where the switch from open-ended research to implementation would occur. (Rip, 1997: 631)

This, of course, points to the continued scientisation of politics.

Even though numerous studies of political controversies showed that science advisers behave pretty much like any other self-interested actor (Nelkin, 1995), science somehow managed to maintain its functional cognitive authority for politics. This may be due to its changing shape, which has been characterised as the diffusion of the authoritative allocation of values by the state, or the emergence of a *postparliamentary* and *postnational* network democracy (Andersen and Burns, 1996: 227-51). In such conditions, scientific debate provides a much-needed minimal amount of order and articulation of concepts, arguments and ideas. Although frequently more in rhetoric than in substance, reference to scientific validation does provide politicians, public officials and citizens alike with some sort of compass in an ideological universe in disarray.

For policy analysis to have any political impact under such conditions, it should be able to somehow continue 'speaking truth' to political elites who are ideologically uprooted, but cling to power; to the elites of administrators, managers, professionals and experts who vie for power in the jungle of organisations populating the functional policy domains of postparliamentary democracy; and to a broader audience of an ideologically disoriented and politically disenchanted citizenry. However, *what does it mean to 'speak truth to power' in contemporary society and politics?* To answer this question, first, some megatrends in epistemological debate will be highlighted. On that basis, second, its implications for the development of policy analysis will be delineated.

Epistemology: from instrumental to fallibilist-pragmatist rationality

Disenchantment of science

Once upon a time, social, political, managerial and administrative elites genuinely believed in scientific rationality as a key to solving collective (and personal) problems. Like scientists themselves, they were inheritors of the Enlightenment, who pictured unfettered growth of scientific knowledge as the driving force of social progress and individual 'pursuit of happiness'. However, after two World Wars, the *Shoah* and the *Gulag*, the nuclear race, the fall of 'scientific' communism, the ecological and, more recently, the financial–economic crisis, belief in scientific rationality is decaying. In all cases mentioned, science and scientists are, to a greater or lesser extent, accessory to human suffering and ecological degradation (Ravetz, 2005). For religious fundamentalists and modern neo-tribalists, this suffices to reject science in a 'rage against reason'.

Nevertheless, even moderate postmodernists reject claims to ground political and social ideas in scientific, rational, logical and consistent argument as potentially exclusive, imposing, suppressive, technocratic and ultimately undemocratic. Instead, they celebrate otherness, incompatibilities and ruptures between lifestyles, cultures, discourses, pluralism, the decentred ego, and the uniqueness, contingency and fragmentation of all social phenomena.

Towards interpretivism

Richard Bernstein (1991) has aptly characterised this new intellectual force field as the polarity of a 'both/and' situation: the modernist idea of the Enlightenment as 'unfinished project' and the postmodernist idea of the Enlightenment as 'historical error'. They are like opposites that can never be reconciled, yet are inextricably intertwined in that they mutually elicit and illuminate each other. Therefore, it is unnecessary to push matters to an extreme. It is more plausible to cast the modernism–postmodernism divide as different accents within a markedly revised concept of scientific rationality.

First, the conviction that empirical–analytic scientific procedure alone may lay claim to scientific rationality has become untenable (Diesing, 1991; Ziman, 2000). In this *(neo)positivist conception*, science is based on a strictly neutral, objective, carefully controlled sense observation of physical and social facts. Long observation is supposed to uncover regularities and patterns, which, constructed into abstract hypotheses, are amenable to further rigorous testing. Hypotheses surviving these further tests may be used in the formulation of deductive systems of law-like propositions, in which they enter as general premises in the covering-law model of truly scientific explanation and prediction.

Habermas (1971) has shown that this idea corresponds to just one knowledge interest constitutive of science, that is, the domain of labour, work and human control over a physical or social environment. However, humans know more action domains, and therefore knowledge interests. Interaction and mutual understanding of action motives and meanings is a second knowledge interest. It lends the *interpretive and hermeneutic* sciences their legitimate claim to scientific rationality.

Where meaningful interactions are suffocated by unconscious collective images or pre-understandings, which deserve articulation, reflection and critique, there is a legitimate task for *critical* science. Empirical analysis of data, skilful interpretation of socially constructed meanings, and social critique are equally important, vital elements of an enlarged concept of scientific rationality.

Towards fallibilism

Second, it is acknowledged by scientists that scientific knowledge is fallible. The Cartesian 'either/or' position has been left. Who likes to be considered scientifically rational can no longer appeal to rocklike cognitive certainties or axioms (be they God, the Cogito, or sense observation). Modern rationality rests on acknowledging that 'although we must begin any inquiry with prejudgments and can never call everything into question at once, nevertheless there is no belief or thesis – no matter how fundamental – that is not open to further interpretation and criticism' (Bernstein, 1991: 327).

Fallibility implies the expectation of being proven wrong, and therefore the willingness to revise one's insights. Rationality as openness to learning further presupposes the embeddedness of the scientist in a durable social context of dialogue and action. An action context, because only there the pragmatic alternation between thought and action exists which brings error to light. A context of critical dialogue, because this catalyses the learning process. It is not accidental, then, that Habermas, defender of the idea of the Enlightenment par excellence, has strongly argued the position that genuine cognitive-analytic rationality is unthinkable absent a rationality oriented towards mutual understanding; a rationality, which, thus, needs to be social, interactive and dialogical.

Postnormal science

Trying to save science from over-cynicism and attempting to preserve its functional authority to politics/policy, some practice-oriented epistemologists, building on the above-mentioned new constellation, have moved beyond the futile quest for clear a priori demarcation criteria to distinguish science from non-science. Instead, they try to delineate rules for 'good' scientific practice in the context of boundary work at the science–politics nexus (Gieryn, 1995; Jasanoff, 1990). Recognising the inadequacy of normal applied science and professional consultancy in political controversies under high uncertainty and high decision stakes over issues that show emergent complexity, epistemologists Funtowicz and Ravetz (1992) have proposed new rules for *postnormal science*. These rules apply when (based on Van der Sluys, 1997: 21):

- the research group is under external pressure due to the urgency, high stakes and disputed values in the decision to be taken;
- established boundaries between the politics/policy and science arenas become subject to continuous renegotiation (boundary work);
- research is issue driven; there is not one problem, but a tangled web of related problems; an unstructured problem, for short;
- a multitude of legitimate scientific and ethical perspectives on the issue web exists; conflicting certainties (appeals to so far fruitful paradigmatic canons, rules, standards, concepts) co-exist;
- research confronts many large, and partly irreducible, uncertainties; scientists are confronted with incomplete control and unpredictability of the analysed system.

Under such conditions, Funtowicz and Ravetz recommend application of a fine-grained system of types of uncertainty to painstakingly sift out the reducible from the irreducible uncertainties in order to set feasible research goals and priorities.[1] Another recommendation is to strengthen the quality control of scientific arguments through systems of extended peer review. In fact, following these proposals would mean to systematise intra-boundary work between scientific disciplines and groups (interdisciplinary research and *internally* extended peer communities) and extra-boundary work between scientists, policy makers and, sometimes, non-expert citizens (transdisciplinary research and *externally* extended peer communities). In the work of Funtowicz and Ravetz we see the implications of the paradox between the scientisation of politics and the politicisation of science at a high level of reflexivity. Yet what use is it to policy science and policy analysis?

Policy analysis: from analycentrism to the argumentative turn

Democratic aspirations in early policy science

Policy science is usually traced back to Harold Lasswell's intellectual underpinning of the endeavour to systematically and methodically gear the applied (social) sciences to the needs of long-term, strategic public policy making (Lerner and Lasswell, 1951; Lasswell, 1971). In Lasswell's designs the relationship between policy science and the practice of politics and administration was to be scientific, democratic and pragmatist. Yet, policy science was not to become a technocratic strategy in order to substitute politics with enlightened administration; nor was it a social technology, always at the service of politicians and administrators.

For Lasswell, policy science was a vital element in a political strategy to maintain democracy and human dignity in a post Second World War world. He follows in the footsteps of his pragmatist teachers, Dewey and Merriam. In the pragmatist view, politics is modelled after peer review in science: it is a dialogue between expert opinion and the opinions of a larger public, in a community united by the quest for answers to shared problems. Politics is seen as probing and honest debate, and not as conflict management that succeeds by cleverly exploiting the ignorance and incomplete knowledge of citizens. In a sense, political and policy science's goal is not to replace 'ordinary' political prudence and common sense with cognitively superior scientific knowledge, but to reinvigorate and systematise them (Van de Graaf and Hoppe, 1989: 61-3; Torgerson, 1995: 234, 238-9).

Lasswell's position is remarkable. He had read Freud and Marx, and had been exposed to war propaganda enough to be sensitive to the realities of ideological manipulation and the pathological sides of politics. He had even written books about it (Lasswell, 1927, 1930). He was also keenly aware of the impossibility of re-embedding political wisdom and prudence in the existing 'communities' of post-war America. Yet, Lasswell opted for a policy science in the service of democracy, and rational, active citizenship, unlike famous contemporaries like Lippmann, Schumpeter and Dror, who, convinced of the irremediable irrationality and lack of political common sense of ordinary people, chose the more 'realistic' strategy of developing an applied social science for an enlightened political and administrative elite.

Technocratic aspirations and instrumental rationality

Reality usually disappoints high aspirations. Nevertheless, it is ironic that policy science's breakthrough was intimately connected to a half-hearted post-behavioural turn in political science. Political scientists' call to recapture relevance in the face of exaggerated methodological rigour was translated into curriculum and research programme innovations focusing on the study of the content, processes, and impacts of public policy. But its purpose remained technocratic: replacing politicians' and citizens' ordinary and local knowledge of policy and policy making with a new, scientifically validated type of applied, general knowledge (Torgerson, 1995: 229-30). Better knowledge of causation and know-how about the application of scientific logic in decision making were the dominant claims on which the schools of public policy were erected in one after another US university and, later, in many European countries. Testimony to the dialectics between the scientisation of politics and the politicisation of science, the successful institutionalisation of policy science in US academia was partly due to favourable labour market prospects fuelled by a rising demand for policy analysis in the Kennedy and Johnson administrations (DeLeon, 1989). In Europe, similar influences were at work, especially in countries where social-democratic governments sought far-reaching social, economic and administrative reforms (Wagner et al, 1991).

From an epistemological point of view, when policy analysis was beginning, three cross-cutting and non-exclusive currents can be discerned: analycentrism, neo-positivism and critical rationalism (Dryzek, 1993: 217-22).

Analycentrism

Analycentric policy analysis claims cognitive superiority over practice based on the scientific logic and consistency built into analytic techniques like cost–effectiveness analysis, cost–benefit analysis, statistical decision theory, and planning–programming–budgeting. The analycentric policy analyst relies on algorithms, filled with data and insights from secondary sources, either scientific or practical. His value–added is merely to see to it that actual decision making follows rigorous scientific canons of procedural rationality (Behn and Vaupel, 1982). Analycentric policy analysis has been effectively criticised for its lack of political realism and, in spite of its alleged procedural neutrality, its introduction of politically biased assumptions in the guise of 'technicalities' (Tribe, 1972; Self, 1975; Wildavsky, 1980 [1979]; Fischer, 1980).

Neo-positivism

Neo–positivist policy analysis grounds its claim to cognitive superiority in its knowledge of causal links. The attractiveness of a neo–positivist concept of science is that knowledge of scientific laws, in technical–instrumental fashion, may be applied to the explanation of the emergence of policy problems and the prediction of impacts of certain policy interventions. After all, if a policy is a plan for achieving particular objectives with the help of certain means, certified causal knowledge is indispensable. For objectives are consequences preferred by policy makers; and means are their chosen and manipulated causes.

Although the grounding of policy analysis in causal knowledge lingers on, neo–positivist policy analysis has withered away. The above-mentioned Habermasean criticism certainly played a role here. However, applied to policy analysis, neo–positivism leads to obvious self-contradictions. If human behaviour generally is driven by laws governing the behaviour of ordinary people, why grant immunity of such laws to politicians and policy makers (Bobrow and Dryzek, 1987: 132)? In addition, neo-positivists overlook that causal knowledge may 'self-destruct' the causal laws on which a policy is based through humankind's capacity for learning.

Critical rationalism

Critical-rationalist policy analysis shares with neo–positivism its claim to superior causal knowledge. However, it strongly differs with regard to how to acquire it in the real world. In this respect, critical-rational policy analysis means an enormous step towards a fallibilist and learning concept of rationality. Building on Popper's falsificationism (Popper, 1963) and his political philosophy of piecemeal social engineering in an open society (Popper, 1945), Campbell and Stanley (1963) have developed critical-rational policy analysis into a sophisticated methodology of (quasi-)experimental impact evaluation. In their view, knowledge acquisition and progress is an evolutionary process of learning from trial and error in successive efforts to compare hypotheses of experimentally generated impacts. This is true for both ordinary and scientific knowledge. Science is the more efficient learning strategy due to stricter requirements for the conditions of learning and the interpretation of results.

Applied to policy making, a policy's content is seen as a hypothesis, and implementation is a social experiment. Braybrooke and Lindblom (1963) have observed such processes of serial policy adjustment in practice. However, unlike routine practice, in critical-rational policy analysis the controlled nature of the experiment is of prime importance. This means that policy analysts are responsible for keeping objectives and conditions for implementation stable during the process. Afterwards one may compare the impact of an intervention on the properties of an experimental group to those of a similarly composed control group. Any differences found may then be attributed to the policy intervention. Repeated experiments will gradually lead to better knowledge due to error elimination through criticism of the policy experiments. Ideally, true to the ideals of an open society, not just the experimenting and evaluating policy analysts, but also those subjected to the experiment can offer their views and criticisms.

Strengths and weaknesses

Critical-rational policy analysis has many strengths. By conceiving policy as hypothesis and implementation as experiment, it escapes from the neo-positivist illusion that delay of action may improve knowledge. The analogy between policy making and experimenting better fits a political reality of permanent time pressure and action imperatives. In addition, the doctrine of an open and experimenting society returns to pragmatist notions of the polity as a community of problem solvers. In principle, therefore, critical-rational policy analysis escapes the technocratic tendencies inherent in analycentric and neo-positivist approaches.

Nevertheless, there are several catches to critical-rationalist policy analysis. Some of the criticism focuses on the incremental or piecemeal nature of policy experiments and the slow progress of knowledge in implementing the critical-rational programme. It is argued that this does not fit a world of rapid change in which some policy experiments depend for their success on non-incremental increases in resources, and on enthusiasm rather than critique. Another type of criticism addresses the gap between the doctrine of the open, experimenting society and the practice of quasi-experimental impact evaluation. Stringent top-down implementation in different sites is a prerequisite for controlled social experiments. In practice, this justifies and leads to cosy relationships between reform-minded politicians, administrators and the scientific policy evaluators, who jointly treat citizens like objects not entitled to any criticism during or after the experiment (Dryzek, 1993: 220).

The most lethal criticism, however, concerns the analogy to scientific experiment underlying Popper's and Campbell's views. Especially Dunn (1993) has convincingly shown that the analogy runs into crippling objections if applied to social systems and policy problems. Even if reform-minded policy makers and evaluators go to great lengths in arranging the experiments in such a way that results that run counter to their expectations and preferences may occur, the social dynamics of human symbol internalisation and externalisation (Berger and Luckman, 1967) or structuration (Giddens, 1979) imply that:

> experimental [design and, RH] outcomes are unavoidably mediated by diverse standards of appraisal which are unevenly distributed among stakeholders in policy reforms.... Social theories, unlike physical ones, are difficult to falsify with experimental data because the interpretation of such data is mediated by the assumptions, frames of reference, and ideologies of social scientists and other stakeholders in reform. (Dunn, 1993: 259-60)

This poses no insurmountable problems in cases of well-structured, rather static and nearly decomposable policy issues. However, such issues are not the only type of policy problem, and decrease in frequency (Bobrow and Dryzek, 1987: 148) and urgency (Hoppe, 1989) in contemporary politics. Therefore, it may be concluded, as a fallibilist and error-eliminating method, critical-rationalism is only fit for avoiding first-order errors concerning the selection of the better of two or more causal hypotheses. It is of little significance and help in avoiding second-order errors of picking the more adequate of two or more problem definitions.

Although some critical-rationalists have embraced methodological multiplism as a remedy (Dunn, 1994: 8-10), on balance, when it comes to selection of problem definition and theoretical frames, critical-rationalism relies on 'qualitative, common-sense knowing of wholes and patterns' (Campbell, 1974: 3). Campbell has conceded that, where the results of a policy experiment frequently remain open to conflicting and ambiguous interpretations, 'an experiment is of itself no more than an argument' (Campbell, 1982: 330-1). Therefore, it is concluded that critical-rational policy analysis stopped on the verge of an argumentative turn (see below).

The post-positivist turn in policy analysis

Somewhere around 1980, policy science's original wave of success subsided. Lindblom and Cohen's (1979) *Usable knowledge* marks a period where policy scientists and analysts publicly doubted the value-added for ordinary knowledge of their professional social inquiry. From the disappointments with analycentric, neo-positivist and critical-rational policy analysis, Carol Weiss drew the conclusion that the field is in intellectual crisis:

> That social scientists shape the world they study by the way they define the problem has come to be accepted not only by social scientists but by sophisticated political actors as well. They are aware that researchers'

assumptions, theories, and choice of variables can have large effects on the answer they find. This new understanding throws into doubt the accommodation [with political and administrative practice, RH] that earlier generations of social scientists had negotiated. If they no longer claim to find 'truth' about 'reality', what is their role in the policy process? The time seems to have arrived for a new set of assumptions and arrangements. (Weiss, 1991: 321)

The new assumptions, hardly the new arrangements, had arrived in the shape of the post-positivist turn. This means that even policy analysts (in the social sciences a rearguard in leaving the positivist and pure critical-rationalist trenches) admitted interpretive, hermeneutic and critical approaches to their stock of knowledge and methods. Policy scholars had to admit that it was impossible to premise policy analysis on the analogy with science. Policy making could not fruitfully be studied as the monologic, methodological justification of the 'right' answer to a policy problem. Rather, it dawned on policy scholars that policy making is a continuous question-and-answer process; with policy analysis in the role of dialogical justification between people, of both questions and answers. Hence, in the post-positivist turn, issues of scientific methodology were superseded by questions of argumentation, dialogue and rhetoric (Turnbull, 2005: 132).

Within the post-positivist turn broadly perceived, four main currents may be discerned: relativistic, critical, forensic and participatory policy analysis.

Relativism

A relativistic policy analysis can be attributed to the 'early' Lindblom and Wildavsky. Lindblom's empirically grounded insights into the disjointed incrementalist practice of policy making (Braybrooke and Lindblom, 1963; Lindblom, 1965, 1968) have always held him back from any enchantment with the idea of the attainment in practice of a more comprehensive rationality suggested by a Lasswellian policy science. As a 'science of muddling through', the most that policy analysis could hope for was to provide policy practice with clever strategic shortcuts and simplifications (Lindblom, 1979). To escape from the dangers of oversimplification, one had to trust the practice of pluralist politics, its partisan mutual adjustment, and its trial-and-error learning in the successive limited comparisons of serial adjustments. Take note that Lindblom's theory harbours strong fallibilist and pragmatist convictions. In *Usable knowledge* (1979) he holds on to these vital insights. The impact of professional policy analysis is limited, and adds only modest increments to the ordinary knowledge of politicians and public officials. Policy analysts are condemned to provide argumentative ammunition for the rhetorical struggles of politicians (policy analysis as argument or data, Weiss, 1991); only occasionally they discover a nugget of enlightenment (policy analysis as idea).

Wildavsky's (1980 [1979]) views do not differ much from Lindblom's, but they are more optimistic about the 'art and craft of policy analysis'. After all, Wildavsky is the founding father of the University of California at Berkeley's policy analytic curriculum. Policy analysis Wildavskian style is depicted as a dialogical and prudential balancing act in which the policy analyst helps both politicians and citizens find a practical middle ground between the ever-present tensions of resources and constraints, cogitation and interaction, and dogma and scepticism. Like Lindblom in his widely acclaimed *Politics and markets* (1977), in the beginning of the 1980s, Wildavsky lost his trust in political pluralism as an error-correcting safety net for biased, incremental policies (Wildavsky, 1987, 1988: xv-xxi). Prophetically concerned about increasing ideological cleavages among the US political elite and their impotence to forge a new national consensus, he turned to grid-group cultural theory to better grasp their diverging political frames (Douglas and Wildavsky, 1983).

Until 1980, Lindblom and Wildavsky implicitly defended an interpretive-hermeneutic approach to policy analysis, in the sense that they, much like anthropologists among the tribes of policy experts, inquired into the policy practitioners' rules for problem definition, policy design, formulation and adoption, implementation and evaluation. This method accounts for the widespread acceptance of their empirical findings. Normatively speaking, however, their approach often meant unquestioned compliance with the rules of thumb and the supposed checks and balances of pluralist political practice. This is comparable to a hermeneutic approach to shared traditions and pre-understandings without any thought of the possibility of ideological, psychopathological or other reprehensible bias or prejudice (Torgerson, 1995; but see Lindblom, 1990; Lindblom and Woodhouse, 1993). Many have pointed out that such an uncritical interpretivist-hermeneutic approach to policy analysis can lead to a scientifically (Wittrock, 1991) or morally objectionable relativism (Dryzek, 1993).

Critical theory

The relativist approach has been attacked most by a critical-theoretical approach to policy analysis, advocated by Forester (1985, 1989) and Dryzek (1990, 1993; Bobrow and Dryzek, 1987). Their main accusation is that relativists disregard the conditions for consensus formation. Forester blames Wildavsky for failing to differentiate between political interaction (as a problem-processing strategy in its own right, in addition to cogitation or analysis) that does and does not elicit true learning among citizens (Forester, 1985: 265ff). Forester deems this distinction essential in a political system where common sense and shared meaning can no longer be presupposed, and groups with clashing political frames of reference have an interest in maintaining public deception and bias. In a similar criticism, Hisschemöller and Hoppe (2001: 54ff) point to bureaucratism, technocracy and econocracy (Self, 1975) as biases among policy makers that hamper learning processes. Habermas' communicative ethics, especially his thoughts on the ideal speech situation in which people communicate free from power relations, deception and self-deception, is used as a standard for judging the extent to which policy makers form a rational and genuine consensus. Policy analysts would have as their main task to monitor and foster means of authentic consensus formation.

To this end, Fox and Miller (1995: 118-120) have proposed criteria for legitimate contributions to public debate: sincerity, situation-regarding intentionality, willing attention, and unique and indispensable expertise. These criteria demonstrate that the critical policy analyst does not pursue public participation for its own sake. The analyst advocates discursive pluralism with an eye to the quality of decision making and the authenticity of consensus formation. Nonetheless, Fox and Miller admit that in the virtual reality and image-struggles of the contemporary news industry it is difficult to judge the extent to which political debate observes these four criteria. Forester (1989) has developed a typology of biased and distorted policy communication, and corresponding counterstrategies for restoring trust and authenticity. The implication is that policy analysts themselves ought to see to it that their own communicative and argumentative practices are in order (Forester, 1989: 148 ff). The art of listening, respectful treatment of target groups, avoidance of unnecessary 'officialese' and other expert discourse, and the craft of initiating and conducting mutually enlightening debate – such are the professional skills of the critical-*cum*-interpretive policy analyst.

Critical analysis is often criticised on two counts. Both regard the dangerous consequences of giving too much weight to the guiding ideal of the ideal speech situation (e.g. Pellizzoni, 2001). The first objection is that, however attractive from a theoretical perspective, these ideals are of limited validity in practice. Where is the borderline between deception and misunderstanding? Who is to determine what is the 'better' argument? To what lengths should we go in debate and communication, where we also know that human rationality is bounded and fragile and, eventually, we have to act? In other words, in all collective decision making we reach dead-ends, or situations where decisions cannot be made on cognitive grounds, where debate, reasoning and the force of the better argument are exhausted, and we have to shift to some form of collective will formation and legitimate power to bring the process to closure (Hoppe, 1983: 231-35; Bernstein, 1991: 221-22; Pellizzoni, 2001; see also Chapter Ten for a more extensive discussion). All political systems are in need of procedures of managing conflicts irresolvable by debate and reasoned argument. The critical approach to policy analysis turns a blind eye to this problem.

A second objection is that critical analysis often gets stuck in a form of counter-expertise disinclined to serious mutual reflection and learning. In such cases, the critical policy analyst just provides rhetorical ammunition for political fights, and just contributes to polarisation, zigzag policies, and stalemate (Schön, 1983: 349-50; Roe, 1994; Van Eeten, 1999). Torgerson (1995: 245) holds that:

> [C]ritique turns against both the domain of common understandings and the restricted nature of technocratic reason.... By ... setting

itself in judgment of common understandings, critique has an ironic potential to manifest itself as a mirror-image of technocracy.

In addition, a critical policy analyst, although a partisan of 'the people', easily overlooks or downplays divergent opinions among ordinary citizens.

Forensic analysis

For the forensic policy analyst this danger is non-existent (Fischer, 1980, 1995; Dunn, 1983, 1993; Paris and Reynolds, 1983; Schön, 1983; Jennings, 1987; Schön and Rein, 1994; Parsons, 1995: 440-4; Torgerson, 1995). To them, it is self-evident that, like in post-empiricist epistemology after Kuhn or the conditions for post-normal science specified by Funtowicz and Ravetz, policy practice is flooded by different thinking styles, diverging interpretive frames, competing policy belief systems, various ideologies, alternative professional paradigms, different worldviews, contrasting images of humankind and nature, multiple perspectives and so on. Such frames (Schön and Rein, 1994) are clusters of interlocking causal and normative beliefs, whose functions are at once cognitive, communicative, interest-driven, and expressive of one's identity. To infuse a polyvalent world with meaning, sense and purpose, and to make action and judgement possible at all, people need such frames as a sort of mental grappling hook. For instance, professional frames have been labelled the languages and cultures of 'tribes of experts' (Dryzek, 1993: 222), which create 'contradictory certainties' (Schwarz and Thompson, 1990). What people 'see', deem 'relevant', and judge 'persuasive evidence' on the basis of such frames, may indeed render them almost beyond comparison or translation.

The forensic policy analyst considers it their task to use the differences between frames to forge an innovative policy design from a combination of plausible and robust arguments (frame-reflective analysis), or to test and bolster some frames (frame-critical analysis, like in Mason and Mitroff, 1981; Paris and Reynolds, 1983). Ideally, following rules of hermeneutic policy evaluation for arriving at shared constructions with policy stakeholders (Guba and Lincoln, 1989), and acting on the precepts of reflective practitionership (Schön, 1983), analysts marry frame-reflection and frame-criticism in an optimal mix of hermeneutic and critical moments in policy analysis.

Forensic analysts do not unreflectively impose a particular professional or political frame on a problematic situation. Rather, they consider any problem as unstructured to begin with (see chapter Three). The challenge of good analysis is structuring problems in a simultaneous process of reflection, action and political strife (Hisschemöller and Hoppe, 1995/1996). Schön (1983) and Schön and Rein (1994) depict the forensic approach as an iterative itinerary among three force-fields: a continuous process of tinkering or *bricolage* between the policy analyst/designer, the policy design and its wider environment, in which the policy design ought to eventually function independently of the analyst/designer.

The process of analysis and design cannot be a straightforward one. Rather, the idea is to sustain creativity in one's response to empirical uncertainties and normative ambiguities in an ever-changing world. Neither goals nor means are fixed; they are transactionally constructed over and over again in intelligent deliberation and political argument, in a process of 'naming and framing' (Schön, 1983: 40-8, 68), which may repeatedly unsettle and attack apparently dominant concepts and frames of meaning.

It is obvious that the forensic approach, especially one that successfully combines frame-analysis, frame-reflection and frame-criticism, fully corresponds to the enlarged concept of rationality as learning. Yet, the approach faces serious hazards.

First, although some authors go to considerable lengths in describing and prescribing rules of thumb, adequate skills and examples of best practice (Schön, 1983; Schön and Rein, 1994; Grin et al, 1997; Hoppe and Peterse, 1998; Fischer, 2003; Loeber, 2004), the forensic approach remains relatively uncodified. This means that replication and error detection and elimination are weak. Partially, this is due to the nature of hermeneutics, critical theory and neo-pragmatism, which all believe that it is 'contexts all the way down'. This belief breeds scepticism, and sometimes downright rejection of codifying rules and formulating anything beyond the most general precepts of an approach to analysis.

Second, more than any other, the forensic approach is caught in a tension between the demands of good analysis and the daily practice of politics and public administration. The critical-rationalist and the relativist policy analyst uncritically adjust to common practice in the role of trusted adviser of the politico-administrative elite; and even the critical analyst easily slips into the role of a counter-expert. It is far more difficult to carve out an acceptable niche for a forensic analyst as 'counsellor' (Jennings, 1987) or 'participatory expert' (Fischer, 1993). Much more thought ought to be given to the institutional aspects of forensic policy analysis (George, 1980; Halffman, 2008). This is why, above, it was argued that the new post-positivist epistemological assumptions may be considered in place, but the new institutional arrangements for developing and implementing them in practice are slow in arriving. It is a question grappled with more extensively in Chapter Nine.

Participatory approach

A fourth, participatory current in post-positivist policy analysis should also be distinguished. Theoretically, this current is heterogeneous in that participatory analysts appeal to relativist, critical and forensic concepts and themes. What unites their paradigm is a principled selection of a fairly elaborate range of participatory analytic techniques, in which citizens *qua* citizens play important roles (Mayer, 1997).

Primarily those inspired by critical theory insist on the intrinsic merit of direct citizen participation in political decision making. They justify participatory analysis by claiming that it vitally contributes to participatory democracy as the only rational form of life for policy scientists and true democrats (Torgerson, 1986; Dryzek, 1990). These analysts systematically favour participatory techniques in which a somehow representative panel of citizens is at the heart of the analytic process, like methods for conducting consensus conferences (Klüver, 1995) or planning cells (Dienel, 1992). The policy analyst's role is to serve and bolster citizens' policy recommendations (Hoppe and Grin, 1995: 101-2).

Relativist, critical and forensic analysts value participatory analysis for instrumental and contextual reasons. They specify three situations in which the use of participatory techniques is indispensable:

* when a policy problem addresses citizens' actions upfront, and finding an acceptable solution depends on appealing to and mobilising citizens' knowledge of local or regional conditions;
* when policy issues have a strong ethical component (where experts have no privileged knowledge to bring to bear on the problem), or directly pertain to citizens' needs and wants;
* when experts are strongly divided over an issue.

Those who view participatory analysis more as an instrument than a goal per se, will prefer participatory techniques, which produce structured debate between citizens, politicians, officials, interest group representatives and experts, like scenario workshops (Mayer, 1997) and propositions debates (Hoppe and Grin, 1999). Here, the analyst remains in control of the analytic process; citizens' participation, in certain situations and under particular conditions, vitally contributes to the information base, validity or representativeness of the analyst's interpretation of public debate and their recommendations.

The advantages of participatory analysis are obvious. In the three conditions mentioned, citizens' input to analysis is equally, or even more important than the experts'. Methods of participatory analysis are excellent means of harnessing citizens' ordinary knowledge to analytic purposes. Participatory methods are hardly disputed as expansion of the toolkits of relativist, critical and forensic policy analysis. The most important criticism is that it is far from beyond doubt whether citizen participation actually improves and enriches the quality of policy debate. Formal evaluations document that citizens rate the quality of participatory debates systematically higher than policy makers and experts (Mayer, 1997: 138-40). In the absence of objective measurement and evaluation grounded in argumentation theory, it is difficult to judge the extent to which such ratings are based on self-interested prejudice by policy makers and experts.

More fundamental criticism remains focused on the aspirations for participatory democracy. In spite of the impressive possibilities of the interactive use of contemporary information and communications technology, the practical objections to participatory democracy are likely to stay. The results of participatory analytic exercises, even when the size of citizen panels runs to the hundreds or thousands (like in some recent applications), will never be able to claim the same representativeness as elections, referendums or even large-scale opinion surveys.

In that sense, policy science and analysis still face the dilemma between serving either participatory democracy and active citizenship, or an allegedly enlightened political and policy-making elite of the administrative state – a dilemma that is as urgent as ever, now that the political means for 'making sense together' look very fragile in the face of the fragmentation, incommensurabilities, ruptures and confusions between value systems and worldviews.

Towards pragmatic and reflexive policy analysis

Doable policy work

Policy analysis has moved from 'speaking truth to power' to a 'river delta' of different modes of 'making sense together' (Hoppe, 1999). Yet, somewhere during this journey, the coherence of the field was lost. Both recently published handbooks of public policy studies (Fischer et al, 2007; Moran et al, 2008) share the view that there is not one story to tell, and all different stories are irredeemably contestable. The idea of gradual progress towards more and better policy-analytic professionalism (like in Radin, 2000) is contested. Policy 'analysis' may be a far too lofty, rationalistic, over-intellectualised label for all kinds of hard and not-so-rational, down-to-earth 'work' that makes policy (Colebatch, 2006a; Colebatch et al, 2010: in press). Policy analysts ought to radically rethink the idea of one overarching and dominating type of rationality (Wagner, 2007:38). Instead of a history of *the* policy orientation of professionals, we have a story of the plurality and incommensurability between policy orientations (Torgerson, 2007: 25-6). Indeed, some students of public policy doubt the sustainability of policy analysis as a coherent academic field, and explore its viability as a 'diaspora' of policy scholars distributed over many interdisciplinary research groups (see the special issue of *Policy Sciences*, 2004; also Korsten and Hoppe, 2006). The least that can be observed is that the debate on policy analysis is conducted in a highly fragmented way (Mayer et al, 2004: 170). Another observation is that there is little effort to restore some kind of shared understanding of the field.

One promising move in this direction is a small article by Mayer et al (2004). It contains a number of fruitful ideas for what, through lack of a better term, might be called *pragmatic reflexive policy analysis*. It is pragmatic because it puts doability of policy analysis centre stage. It is reflexive, because it enables a questioning of the underlying ideals and methodologies in policy analysis. What follows is an interpretation of that article.

Core activities in policy analysis

Mayer et al (2004: 171-8) begin by identifying six major clusters of activities that can be observed to constitute the building blocks of most types of real-life policy analysis:

- research and analyse;
- design and recommend;
- advise strategically;
- clarify values and arguments;
- democratise;
- mediate.

These activities are elaborated below, illustrated by underlying political values, quality criteria, and images of the 'good' policy analyst and their audience. The attentive reader will easily recognise the theory- and methodology-informed positions sketched in the previous historical overview. Yet, because the organising principle is no longer paradigmatic watersheds in academic textbooks, but has shifted to observable core activities in real-life policy work, they will also detect some initial blurring of the battle lines.

Research and analyse

> Has the number of cases of driving under the influence of alcohol increased compared to previous years? Has privatisation of public utilities and services led to lower prices for consumers? Is our climate really changing? And if so, how is it likely to affect coastal regions? (Mayer et al, 2004: 174)

Policy analysts who research and analyse are objective researchers who care about the quality of knowledge. Good knowledge equals sound science, that is, it withstands scientific scrutiny as ordinarily understood: there is a clear distinction between subject and object in a realist ontology, empirical knowledge is variable-oriented, quantified, preferably codified information, and usable through validated models of causal relationships: 'Policy analysis will be judged by substantive (scientific) quality criteria such as validity and reliability, the use and integration of state-of-the-art knowledge, the quality of data gathering and the formal argumentation and validation of conclusions' (Mayer et al, 2004: 184). Policy making is a neatly ordered, logical sequence of thinking steps; each phase in the policy-making process builds on the previous one, and is duly supported by sound research and analysis.

Design and recommend

> What can the government do to improve the accessibility of large cities? What measures can municipalities take to improve local safety? How can the container storage capacity in harbor areas best be increased – by improving utilisation of existing capacity or by creating more capacity? (Mayer et al, 2004: 174)

Here, the good policy analyst is the impartial, expert adviser whose loyalty is to the professional or academic peer community, not to the client or principal (Hoppe and Jeliazkova, 2006: 41). Not quite a believer in sequentially ordered policy making, they nevertheless meticulously dissect the political arena through network analysis and stakeholder analysis, that is, the analysis of interests, belief systems, resource interdependencies, other power relations, and strategies of different stakeholders. Policy analysts who also recommend and advise believe that their work 'will be judged by instrumental criteria of policy relevance, such as usability and accessibility for policy makers, action orientation and utilisation, presentation and communication of advice, weighing up of alternatives, clear choices and so on' (Mayer et al, 2004: 185). In a political process-driven and design-oriented way, they use their knowledge to give advice that aligns good 'analysis' and good 'politics' (Prasser, 2006).

Clarify arguments and values

> Why, or more accurately about what, is there a clash of opinions between supporters and opponents of river dike enforcement or the expansion of a National Airport? What values and arguments come to the fore as regards approving or rejecting developments in the field of modern genetic technology, as in the case of pre-natal diagnosis and cloning? (Mayer et al, 2004: 175)

The good analyst is well trained in logic, ethics, philosophy and narrative analysis, and sensitive to metaphor, analogy, story lines and symbolism. Putting these skills to good use, the value conflicts and argumentation systems often tacitly driving policy debates are unearthed. This knowledge is fed into the policy-making process in order to enrich the quality of debate. Frequently, this means that the governmental policy-making process is no longer the central focus of analysis. In keeping with the expansion of the policy-making function to external players in expanded governance systems, public debate in civil society becomes pivotal:

> Policy analysis will be judged by quality of argumentation and debate criteria such as formal logic (consistency), informal logic (rhetoric and sophism) and quality of the debate in terms such as richness, layering, and openness of arguments. (Mayer et al, 2004: 185)

Provide strategic advice

> What should a government minister do to bring about acceptance of
> road pricing plans? What strategy can a government minister adopt
> to allocate radio frequencies? (Mayer et al, 2004: 176)

The analyst who defines himself as client/policy advocate (Hoppe and Jeliazkova,
2006: 40) continuously worries about the question 'What is best for my client,
or the problem-owner?'. Contrary to policy analysis as clarifying values and
arguments, strategic policy advice is narrowly focused on the players, circumstances,
power relations and causal drivers shaping a client's or principal's environment.
Whereas for the other types concepts like objectivity and neutrality are still a
source of professional identity, in the eyes of the advocates these 'old-fashioned'
views only create conflicts between politicians and civil servants. For this type of
analysis, the conflict between professionalism and loyalty is solved by the attitude:
our professionalism is completely in service of our commissioner or principal –
either due to loyalty, or motivated by monetary reward. Mayer et al (2004: 185)
state that, in policy analysis for strategic advice, success is judged

> by pragmatic and political effectiveness criteria such as the 'workability'
> of advice, political clearness and proactive thinking, greater insight
> (for the client) in the complex environments (political and strategic
> dynamics, forces and powers), targeting and achievement of goals.

Democratise

> How can citizens receive more and better information about how
> to have their say in decisions regarding important social issues like
> genetic technology or a new metro line? How can citizens make an
> informed choice when it comes to a tricky and difficult question like
> the reconstruction of a railway station area? (Mayer et al, 2004: 177)

The good policy analyst is preoccupied by the question 'How to improve
democracy in society and in politics?'. Therefore, he is a champion of democracy,
either more deliberation or more participation oriented. Ideals such as impartiality,
neutrality or value-free analysis have no place here. The political and governance
system's bias in favour of political, economic and scientific elites should be
corrected. Hence, the good analyst is an advocate for democratising expertise,
using scientific and professional knowledge for the empowerment of 'ordinary'
people as citizens: 'Policy analysis will be judged by democratic legitimacy criteria
such as openness and transparency of the policy making process, representation
and equality of participants and interests, absence of manipulation and so on'
(Mayer et al, 2004: 185).

Mediate

How can industry and government agree on the moderation of their dispute about the possible harm caused by zinc emissions to the environment and health? How can they deal with conflicting findings of scientific research on this matter? What is a good process for exploring the future of a municipality with all stakeholders such as citizens, businesses and so on? (Mayer et al, 2004: 177)

> The good analyst provides plausible answers to two interlinked questions, one substantive, the other procedural: 'What is good for mutual understanding between different stakeholders? What is good for the process of consensus building?' A policy analyst knows their way around in the worlds of negotiation, mediation, process facilitation and network management. They are well aware that their work will be judged 'by external acceptance and learning criteria such as the agreement that mutually independent actors reach on the process and/or content, support for and commitment to the negotiating process and solutions, learning about other problem perceptions and solutions' (Mayer et al, 2004: 185).

Styles of doing policy analysis

Having indicated core activities in real-life policy analysis, Mayer et al take a decisive further step: they propose to think in terms of *styles of doing policy analysis*. In their view, such styles should be thought of as combinations of two or more core activities:

- a rational style, or research and analysis combined with recommendation and advice;
- an argumentative style, or research and analysis while also clarifying values and argument systems;
- a client advice style, mixing recommendation and advice on a policy problem with strategic advice for a principal;
- a participatory style, attempting to introduce the critical clarification of values and arguments into the democratisation of expertise;
- a process management style, linking up mediation and strategic advice; and finally
- an interactive style, in which mediation for mutual understanding and consensus building is linked to democratisation efforts.

The underlying idea is, like in the social study of science and technology (e.g. Sismondo, 2004), but also in Colebatch's (2002a, 2006a, 2010) rethinking of policy analysis as policy work, that observers just register without scientific prejudice what the actors are actually doing. What they are doing usually can be described as making theoretically and methodologically highly complex sets of activities doable in a specific action context. This requires pragmatic alignments between the sometimes difficult-to-reconcile theoretical and methodological requirements of these activities; and, simultaneously, finding alignments with the practical constraints arising from the action context (Fujimura, 1987). It follows that in describing what is going on in 'policy analysis', observers have to treat scientific, professional, experiential and even lay knowledge symmetrically, that is, treat each knowledge type as equally important and informative for what is going on, both in 'analysis' and in the contextual setting.

Like laboratory scientists who engage in practices not necessarily reflecting the methodological precepts or textbooks of their discipline, policy analysts do not do exactly what they say or write they will do, or have done. Frequently, they find themselves unable to follow the precepts of their 'sacred' texts. Time is running out; data are unavailable; personnel are too unskilled or are too small numbers; money is in short supply; decision makers are too impatient and too interfering – and numerous other conditions that militate against methodology-and-theory maximising performance levels.

What actually happens is that analysts, in a very pragmatic and context-dependent way, and more or less successfully, make policy analysis doable as a mix of core activities (see Hoppe, 1983; Jasanoff, 1990; Noordegraaf, 2000; Colebatch, 2006a; DeVries, 2008).[2] In quantitative empirical research of types of policy analysts, the mixed core activities show up in the considerable number of professional norms and attitudes shared by all types; and in statistical intercorrelations or overlap between types (Durning and Osuna, 1994; Hoppe and Jeliazkova, 2006; Wolfe, 1997; Van Coppenolle, 2006). Confirming the importance of 'double vision' for reflective practitionership (Schön, 1983), Hoppe (2008b) found that especially the more experienced and academically articulate analysts designate themselves as adherents of more than one or two schools of thought; or practising more than one or two basic policy-analytic activities.

What Mayer et al have justifiably done is to distinguish between some typical, frequently observed combinations that jointly produce *styles* in doing policy analysis. In Figure 7.1 (page 190), these styles are depicted as pragmatic 'knots' between pairs of core activities. The styles are 'suspended' between the differential, sometimes quite antagonistic, requirements of the core activities; and each style is characterised by some kind of practical, context-dependent alignment of the resulting tensions. To bolster the plausibility of Mayer et al's theoretical construction, illustrations from empirical work are given.

The *rational style* is 'research and analyse' joined to 'design and recommend'. Analysts in the bureaucracy who can be designated as neo-Weberians (Hoppe and Jeliazkova, 2006: 40; Van Coppenolle, 2006) adhere to the rational style. If they are working for policy outside, but in service of governmental policy making, they are often called objective technicians, or issue specialists (Meltsner, 1976; Wolf, 1997; Hoppe, 2008b). Their professional self-image is to provide politicians, other civil servants, advisers and stakeholders with evidence-based intelligence, that is, information based on available and usable sound science.

Figure 7.1: Styles of doing policy analysis as 'knots' of two core policy-analytic activities

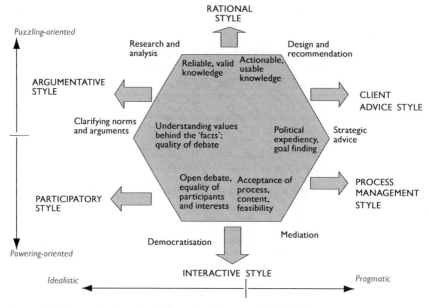

Source: Slightly amended version of figure 3 in Mayer et al (2004: 184)

Examples are economics-trained or –inspired analysts who see in cost-benefit, cost-effectiveness and multi-criteria decision analysis the exclusively valid policy-analytic methods; and who believe in (simulation) models as preferred way of encapsulating scientific knowledge and predicting policy effects. Another good example is the adherents of quantitative indicators for auditing in public management, quasi-experimental programme evaluation or, more generally, 'hard' evidence-based policy. It bears stressing that rational-style policy analysts differ from each other on their exact role in the political context, which influences their work. Some would dispose of any political influence in the name of objectivity and impartiality; others strongly believe that their expertness entitles them to some political authority and influence.

The *argumentative style* attempts to intertwine normative analysis through the clarification of norms and values with evidence-oriented research and analysis. This type of analyst may be considered to be a 'policy philosopher' (Hoppe and Jeliazkova, 2006). They consciously keep some distance from politics, in order to take a critical stance if necessary: 'You have to show that there is another reality out there next to the one of the policy decision-maker-politician.' A central part of the work of the policy philosopher is to become aware and to make others aware of other possible worldviews and their implications. Alternatively, this type of policy analyst may be designated as a 'mega-policy strategist'. Their professional catchphrase is 'Let's challenge government to think!' They claim a government-oriented think-tank function. They verify and critically examine strategic policy guidelines and assumptions, in light of the most recent sound science and arguments (Hoppe, 2008b). It is obvious that this role is anathema to most middle-ranking officials (Page and Jenkins, 2005; Van Coppenolle, 2006). Yet, high-ranking civil servants, experts in prestigious think tanks and even in commercial policy consultancies often claim this role.

The *client advice style* couples design and recommendation to strategic advice. This style is typical for analysts, generalists and specialists alike, who are also political and bureaucratic realists. They are called client advocates or client counsellors or policy advisers (Wolf, 1997; Hoppe and Jeliazkova, 2006; Van Coppenolle, 2006; Hoppe, 2008b). They consider it their main task to defend the interests of their commissioners. They keep their personal opinions to themselves, but have no trouble in shading analysis in their principals' interests by foregrounding certain facts and prioritising some arguments in such ways that, without actually biasing policy analytic reports, they bend conclusions and recommendations towards their principals' positions. The advocates justify their name because they strongly believe that the policy analyst is a producer of policy arguments, more similar to a lawyer than to an engineer or a scientist (Hoppe and Jeliazkova, 2006). Others would rather frame their roles as intermediaries or boundary spanners between expert advisers and their (political, bureaucratic) principals. In those cases, their advice is less politically shaded; instead, it stresses both political acceptability and organisational feasibility of policy proposals, incorporating usable, best available knowledge on 'what works' (Hoppe, 2008b). Yet, more than all other styles, the client advice style legitimises its role in the process of policy formation by appeal to the allocation of responsibility and authority in the regular political and bureaucratic system.

The *process management style* mixes the substantive task of providing strategic advice and the procedural challenge of good mediation. This style is engaged in by analysts who are called process director (Hoppe and Jeliazkova, 2006; Van Coppenolle, 2006), process facilitator, process manager or even network manager. Process directors face the same dilemma as most other types of policy analysts: to find a balance between their attitude towards the principal and their own convictions. They find involvement in the politics of policy making self-evident. The areas of their expertise are process management and process monitoring. The art of tactful steering and well-developed negotiating skills are fundamental parts of their craftsmanship. Mayer et al (2004: 181) describe the professional convictions of process managers as:

> based on the assumption that substantive aspects of the policy problem are, in fact, coordinate or perhaps even subordinate to the procedural aspects.... [He/she] creates 'loose coupling' of procedural ... and substantive aspects of a problem.... If the procedural sides ... have

been thought through properly, it will greatly increase the likelihood of substantive problems being resolved.

This policy–analytic style is observed in (Continental) European governance systems and appears conspicuously absent in the Anglo-Saxon world (but see accounts of US foreign policy making in Halperin, 1974; George, 1980).

The *interactive style* attempts to bridge the impartiality required in mediation and the partisanship needed for democratising policy analysis. Mayer et al (2004: 180-1) link this style to forensic policy analysis through continuous interaction and communication between analysts and stakeholders, leading to mutual learning processes. In a study on discourses on policy analysis in the boundary work between scientific expert advisers and analysts in the bureaucracy, Hoppe (2008b) found two types that fit the description in Mayer et al (2004) rather well. One type he called deliberative proceduralists, whose professional catchphrase is 'Organise frank debate between robust parties'. Analysts engaging in this style actively organise consultative and debating processes conforming to criteria for open and frank debate between robust parties, be they scientists, stakeholders, citizens, politicians or even dissidents.

The other style of policy analysis approaching the forensic ideal-type in practice was called postnormalist. Postnormal policy analysts insist on discussing the quality of all information and knowledge on the policy table, especially the uncertainties involved. Such discussions should not be limited to experts and officials; all involved stakeholders in interactive learning processes should open themselves up to 'extended peer review'. It would seem that postnormal analysts are influenced by and attracted to a conception of interdisciplinary, postnormal science (Funtowicz and Ravetz, 1992) emerging in fields like ecology and other domains affected by complexity science. In the US and Canada too, it has been found that ecology-inspired experts working in sustainability-related policy domains are open to views on science and policy analysis that are best described as 'postnormal' (Steel et al, 2004: 9).

The *participatory style*, finally, attempts to draw the analytical, argumentative clarification of values and argument lines into policy analysis as an effort to resist elitist bias and democratise expertise. It is concerned to turn democratised analysis into an asset in the service of citizens. Obviously, this style of doing policy analysis leads to difficult-to handle tensions between the facilitative and partisan roles of the analyst. These will be discussed at length in Chapter Nine.

Reflexivity in policy analysis

It is obvious that the list of six styles of doing policy analysis as 'knots' between analytic core activities is not meant to be exhaustive. The scientific literature mentions other types not listed here, such as issue advocate (Durning and Osuna, 1994; Wolfe, 1997), spin doctor, linking pin (Van Coppenolle, 2006), political realist (or 'politician') (Meltsner, 1976; Wolf, 1997) and knowledge broker (Hoppe,

2008b). In addition, Mayer et al have shrewdly positioned the different styles at the angles of their hexagonal model. They have only explored adjacent styles, which, in their view, are more easily combined than styles lying further apart. Systematic research along theoretical assumptions outlined in the frame work of Figure 7.1 will be needed to make the picture richer and more complete.

In spite of its shortcomings, Figure 7.1 opens up possibilities for reflexive policy analysis. First, and perhaps foremost, the helicopter view of modes of doing policy analysis and their potential interrelationships offered in the hexagon model counteracts the loss of an overall perspective on policy analysis as an academic field. Second, it manages to do so from the angle of making analysis doable in practical contexts – not from an apodictic theoretical or methodological point of view. This is important because the loss of an overall view and the highly conceptual and methodological 'dialogue of the deaf' between the different schools of thought endangered their relevance for policy-analytic practice.

Third, the framework makes it possible to design innovative policy analytic methods, and analyse and evaluate their use. For example, Stirling (2006) has designed a policy-analytic method – multi-criteria mapping – which cross-fertilises the rational style of multi-criteria decision analysis and the interactive style of stakeholder consultation and deliberation. It has been applied by the European Heart Network, commissioned by the European Commission, to design policy on the problem of preventing obesity among the young:

> The ... methodology [multi-criteria mapping, RH] involves scoring the options under different conditions, according to various criteria, and with the criteria weighted for their importance. An important feature of this approach is that the criteria used to judge the options can differ between the different participants, and can reflect each participant's judgments on what is important in policy development. Based on their scoring of the options, the options can be ranked, and the top-ranking options discussed as being commonly agreed by consensus as the most strongly supported, and the bottom-ranking options agreed as the least strongly supported. (Lobstein et al, 2006: 37)

As the rational and interactive styles of doing policy analysis are on opposite ends of the hexagonal model, it may be inferred that this is an original, but also risky policy-analytic design (e.g. Yearley, 2001; Tompkins, 2003). For example, multi-criteria decision analysis knows fairly transparent algorithms for aggregating single scores in an overall end-ranking of alternative options. What happens in the case where these scores are allowed to have different weights for different participants, but analysts still write up the 'final' score?

Finally, the framework may also help in applying Dunn's rule of methodological congruence, that is, in deciding which style of policy analysis, with its concomitant toolkit of methods and heuristics, is in principle appropriate given one's politico-administrative judgement on the type of policy problem at hand (see Figure 7.2).

Figure 7.2: Styles of doing policy analysis and problem types

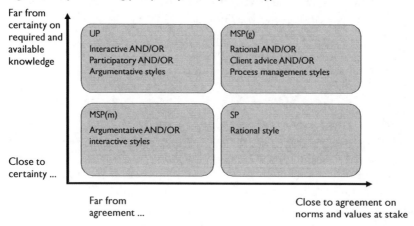

Neither personal inclination, nor methodological convictions, nor political context should determine which style of policy analysis will be applied. The typology of six styles of doing policy analysis, in the different ways just illustrated, invite practitioners to self-consciously reflect on the bases that underlie their reasoning in designing and applying a particular style. They may make doing policy analysis more reflexive.

Notes

[1] See Van der Sluys (1997: 173ff) for an application of this so-called *NUSAP procedure* to uncertainties in integrated assessment models of global climate change.

[2] Lindblom, in keeping with his own teachings, was not very specific in articulating the method through which he arrived at his formulation of the theory of incrementalism or the branch method of doing policy analysis. Yet, from the scarce references to his own practical experience (in Braybrooke and Lindblom, 1963), one may well believe that he used the method of observant participation and other techniques we would now describe as ethno-methodological.

EIGHT

The plural democracies of problems: a meta-theory

> The differentiation of the political ... follows from the fact that more and more modes of representation, types of supervision, procedures of monitoring, and manners of expression of preferences are becoming available.... (Rosanvallon, 2006: 221)

Introduction

Previous chapters have approached problem structuring in a policy- or programme-centred way. In the next two chapters, the focus is broadened to a polity-centred approach (Skocpol, 1992). If there are different types of public problems, the normative implication seems to be that political regimes should be able to equally well handle all four policy problem types. However, are polities robust against all problem types?

Representative and aggregative democracy frequently appears wedded to the metaphysics of a unified political will of 'we-the-people', to be uniformly imposed on a 'generalised' citizen. Therefore, democratic systems are adept in handling routine issues of large-scale interest articulation and negotiation, and issues that can be handed over for standardised treatment to professional groups, specialists and the legal system. But they look less well equipped to deal with the intractable controversies that frequently emerge around ethically divisive issues and 'wicked', or unstructured, problems (Schön and Rein, 1994; Hoppe, 2008a). The 'particularised' men in contemporary emancipated civil society need more appropriate, innovative institutional and process designs for more deliberative and integrative elements in democracy. The key is to unlearn to conceive of democracy in a singular way, and to learn to see it in a pluralist way.

Day-to-day practice of democracy requires different modes of democratic governance to successfully deal with different structures of problems. This argument will unfold in this chapter in several steps. The first section stresses and elaborates the findings of Chapter Six: policy change frequently comprises both substantive frame shifts and instrument choice, and *shifts in governance*, that is, shifts in network type. However, state-centred public administration, or managerialist theories of network management and procedural policy instrument choice, have the Machiavellistic shade of a central, not-so-rational-rule approach. Instead, the governance of problems will be discussed here from the perspective of democratic legitimacy. Democracy is not a troublesome normative add-on, but the core of practical thinking about intelligent governance. The governance of problems means optimal use of the intelligence of democracy (Lindblom, 1965, 1990).

From this perspective, it is useful to think of plural '*democracies of problems*' (Hisschemöller, 1993). The second section will demonstrate selective affinities between the politics of problem structuring or policy politics and political theories of democracy. Four different approaches to democratic governance correspond to the four problem types: technical, market, fairness and participation. In the third section, this leads to the formulation of a meta-theory of democracy as a method of decision making on problem structuring and solving that takes different views on problems into account. Structured problems need a technical-and-market approach, reflected in Schumpeter's (1942) procedural conception of democracy. Moderately structured problems with goal consensus need a market-and-participatory approach, consonant with standard liberal, pluralist democratic theories. Moderately structured problems with means consensus require a combined fairness-and-technical approach, to be found in accommodationist, elite-cartel concepts of democracy. Unstructured problems can be tackled through a fairness-and-participatory approach, best reflected in participatory and deliberative democratic theories and practices. The intelligence of day-to-day practice of democratic governance is continuous tinkering or *bricolage* with these different and contradictory notions and practices.

Democracy, frame shifts and network management

The role of network management

The conclusion in Chapter Six was that types of policy problems and analytical and political strategies of problem structuring co-evolve. According to Howlett (2000: 413, this means that policy makers, next to substantive policy instruments such as rules (sticks), incentive systems (carrots) and communicative tools (sermons), have developed a renewed interest in 'procedural tools designed to indirectly affect outcomes through the manipulation of policy processes'. Such network management or subsystem restructuring is done through manipulating the participation, nodes and links of the networks of policy actors (Kickert et al, 1997). Most authors on network management focus on more or less voluntary, collaborative governance arrangements crossing levels of government and transgressing the traditional boundaries between the institutional domains of public, private and civil society governance. Yet, Howlett correctly points out that procedural tools do not necessarily serve stakeholder collaboration or enrich policy-relevant knowledge. They may as well have negative impacts, giving network management and restructuring at least a shade of 'Machiavellianism':

> [F]or example, information-based procedural instruments include both provision of information, as well as its suppression, and the release of misleading as well as accurate information. Deception, obfuscation, and

other forms of administrative delay, similarly, are all forms of authority-based procedural instruments. (Howlett, 2000: 419)

On a more benign note, Howlett suggests a relationship between procedural policy instruments and legitimacy. More specifically, he hypothesises that levels of policy subsystem *de*-legitimation affect the extent of subsystem manipulation appropriate for the task of *re*-legitimation. If the capacity of governments to use existing networks for effective policy deliberations is threatened, it may become imperative to manipulating information production, to recognise new actors as legitimate 'players', to publicly fund interest groups and/or civic organisations or research institutes, or even to (re)design the institutional rules of the game themselves.

Howlett's hypothesis gets support from the cases reported in Chapter Six. The cases on prenatal screening, Volgermeer pollution and Swiss drugs policy all showed how central policy makers wielded procedural instruments. They used information provision, funding and recognition manipulation to nudge older networks that struggled with loss of output legitimacy into the direction of newer networks that hopefully would restore governability and legitimacy. Specific types of new research were ordered and financed; funding and recognition instruments were used to weaken the position of older, and strengthen the position of new, actors. They dismantled the older and created new networks of intergovernmental and inter-institutional governance. The Wadden Sea case involved recognition manipulation, as a new type of interest group and ecological expertise were officially given standing at national policy tables. The struggle between the two opposing institutional designs for accommodation politics were about the (re) definition of institutional rules of the game.

A democratic deficit in network management?

However enlightening the distinction between substantive and procedural policy instruments, the 'Realpolitik' of network management evokes uneasy questions about legitimacy and democracy. All forms of policy networks include some and exclude other actors; and this limited actor pluralism of all modes of governance may itself spawn conflict over participation in and design of the 'proper' democratic quality of the policy process. In the case of Swiss drugs policy, the new open issue network, a mix of local administrative and third sector regulation was approvingly dubbed 'associative democracy' by some (Hirst, 1994; Wälti and Kübler, 2003). Yet, it was criticised as depoliticising the issue by resisting normal democratic legitimation procedures by others:

> [T]he primary concern shared by local activists, social workers, the police and the medical sector was to achieve grassroots consensus supporting services and facilities intended for drug addicts, while attempting (not always successfully) to keep the issue off the

> parliamentary or referendum agenda, where 'moral' entrepreneurs can
> politicise the issue. (Papadopoulos, 2003: 481)

Generalising the argument from a representative democracy point of view, it could
be claimed that all forms of governance as collaborative policy making have an
inherent democratic deficit. Stakeholders and officials collaborating in policy
networks usually have no formal authority to take decisions. Yet, their influence
over policy options considered feasible and socially acceptable may become very
strong; so strong as to be unchallengeable by elected representatives in Parliaments.
Therefore, some scholars speak of network governance as 'post-parliamentary
governance ... of organizations, by organizations and for organizations' (Andersen
and Burns, 1996: 227). The conclusion is that it is imperative to think through the
relationship between cooperative procedures in policy networks and democracy.

Democracies of problems

Hisschemöller (1993) has posited the existence of plural democracies of problems.[1]
Under the semantic cloak of 'democracy', different democratic discourses and
practices are hidden. Democracy is a complex, multifaceted phenomenon, more
aligned to a complex society than is usually assumed. Drawing on standard
political theory accounts of desirable degrees of government intervention and
public participation, it can be shown that the four types of problem/network
configurations have selective affinities with different styles or modes of democracy.
For each type of problem structure, the key question is the amount and scope of
diversity or pluralism needed for responsible problem structuring and problem
solving. Schumpeterian-procedural, liberal-pluralist, elite-cartel accommodationist,
and participatory-*cum*-deliberative discourses and practices of democracy, allow
for different degrees of pluralism to become effective in policy making. Real-
life democracy is a permanent balancing act between these different styles of
democracy, with corresponding impacts on the problem-structuring and problem-
solving capacity of political systems.

A technical approach: guardians of the public interest and politically irrational citizens

Basic theoretical claims

For structured or easily structurable policy problems, problem solving is best dealt
with by handing over responsibility to a small, closed community of scientifically
and professionally trained and qualified policy makers. This is a *technical approach* to
problem solving; it would be outright technocracy, if not softened by democratic
accountability requirements, which turn it into invited or mandated technocracy.

The first claim of a technical approach is that the political mandate, in a
democracy anchored in the people, is handed over to a select group of specialists

or technocrats. Dahl (1985) calls them 'guardians'. Guardians are not aristocrats boasting an ascribed noble heritage, race or gender; they are meritocrats, claiming their privileged position based on education and training. By their own efforts they have acquired knowledge and virtues that make them more suitable for political and administrative leadership than ordinary citizens. In many elitist theories, guardians are pictured not only as virtuous experts, but also as natural members of a social vanguard in the progress to modernity. The guardian–vanguard idea, of course, is epitomised in communist theories about the leading role of the Communist Party. However, US progressivism is a moderate version of the same elitist thinking (Fischer, 1990).

The second important claim in a technical approach to problem solving is that citizens are uninformed, mostly uninterested, and if interested, ruled by their emotions. Therefore, it would be foolish to let them rule and decide. Understandably, after the follies of two World Wars, many political theorists around the 1950s strongly defended this claim on empirical grounds. Most famously, Joseph Schumpeter (1942: 262) concluded that, in political matters, the typical citizen drops down to an infantile level of mental performance. Even Robert Dahl (1963: 59, quoted by Hisschemöller, 1993: 93) wrote that 'man is not by instinct a reasonable, reasoning, civic minded being. Many of his most imperious desires and the source of his most powerful gratification can be traced to ancient and persistent biological and physiological drives, needs, and wants.'

Martin Lipset (1963), in his book *Political man*, concluded that in view of most citizens' irrationality, political apathy is best for a healthy democracy.

Strict theories of guardianship offer no scope at all for political pluralism. Every non–guardian is a dangerous dissident; especially former guardians who set themselves up as new leaders for 'outsiders'. Theories of irrational citizenship severely restrict political pluralism. For example, Schumpeter (1942) defines democracy as no more than a procedure or method for the election of members of political elites, in principle devoid of any relevance for policy making. The typical irrational citizen is contrasted to the politician–statesperson. As politicians, members of political elites should be able to mobilise votes in general elections. Once elected, they ought to act like statespeople, demonstrating their qualities as guardians, or trustees, of the public interest; if necessary, against the will of a majority of citizens. Democracy is a just a method for the peaceful circulation of elites. It has no function at all in signalling citizens' policy preferences. At most, it registers citizens' diffuse dissatisfaction with the policy performance of a political elite voted out of power.

Correspondence to democracy in practice

In late 20th and early 21st centuries, the idea of irrational citizenship was discredited on empirical grounds, at least as an across-the-board model (Carmines and Huckfeldt, 1996). However, it is still valid for a considerable segment of the citizenry. Research into styles of citizenship in the Netherlands revealed that up to 30% of the voting population could be labelled as 'outsiders' (Motivaction, 2001). They are described as disinterested, recalcitrant, passive, inactive and aloof, with a low degree of social involvement and negative attitudes about obligations and responsibilities; they distrust government and they are politically cynical non-voters or protest-voters. As far as lifestyles are concerned, they are found among 'modern citizens' and the 'comfort oriented'. The former are found to be conformist, status-sensitive citizens who balance traditional with modernist values like consume and enjoy. The latter are passive but impulsive consumers, primarily concerned with a carefree, pleasant and comfortable life. All in all, these 'outsiders' show a strong resemblance to what cultural theorists would call 'isolates' or 'fatalists', and what political theorists in the 1950s and 1960s would indeed see as irrational and irresponsible citizens.

In addition to these 'outsiders', the same research indicates that the 'deferential citizen' (Almond and Verba, 1963) is not an extinct species. Approximately 18% of Dutch voters can be labelled as dutiful, obedient citizens. Their attitude to politics is dependent, obedient to authority, with a need for leadership, but a huge experienced distance to national government. They are less informed about politics, and hard to communicate with. They are very locally oriented, and prepared to get involved only in issues concerning their immediate life world or environment. These dutiful citizens, or hierarchists in cultural theory terms, belong to the traditional citizenry, characterised as moralist, duty-bound, status-quo-oriented citizens, keen on keeping traditions and possessions.

Moreover, in policy problems predominantly considered as 'technical', the idea of restricting citizen influence is as seductive as ever. In a technologically advanced society, most educated and informed citizens consider themselves 'experts' in their own small field of expertise. As such, they claim their own professional discretion; and they are used to honouring the claims of fellow citizens to their restricted fields of 'expertise'. Thus, even modern citizens that may be considered informed and rational, usually recognise the validity of one-way flows of information and knowledge, and a 'give and take' of professional expertise in their own working lives. This alone would make them sensitive to political claims that certain issues – such as occupational health and safety risks, dealing with nuclear power and nuclear weapons, and so on – have such a high technical component that they should be delegated to the 'real' experts. It is only logical to expect that politicians be also inclined to give credence to such claims. After all, delegating problem-solving power to professionals and scientists relieves the political agenda. Political attention to technical issues is restricted to some monitoring – preferably by trusted peers of the delegated 'guardians' – and funding decisions. In certain cases, technical issues may be struck from the public, political agenda, and transferred to the private sphere, that is 'left to' market forces. However, when persistent and deeply felt dissent arises on the technical nature of the problem, political pluralism has been organised out of the political system; possibly to such an extent that a technical approach clashes with demands of contemporary democracy.

A market approach: a gap between general and individual interests

Basic theoretical claims

Moderately structured problems with considerable normative consensus but remaining uncertainties about available and relevant knowledge tend to be dealt with through the problem-solving efforts of temporarily dominating advocacy coalitions in rather stable policy subsystems. The core idea is that solving the problem means striking some sort of balance between risks, costs and benefits of a proposed solution to stakeholders.

This approach to problem structuring and solving may be called a *market approach*. Its first claim is that political involvement or engagement by citizens means that people recognise their personal, individual stakes in a political issue. Citizens are not infantile or irrational; they are considered quite capable of defining their own interests in matters of politics and public policy. Their political involvement increases with the potential stakes of policy decisions for their personal utility. It is their self-interest that drives citizens to discover consensus; and form collectives or interest groups.

Thus, this type of reasoning is typical for political theories that conceptualise political participation as an instrument for the protection of a citizen's self-interest. This is as true for Hobbes' Leviathan, as it is for later classical utilitarian theories. The political plurality of self-interested citizens is analogous to a market; and by the same analogy, democracy is a pluralist political process of bargaining about public policy among minorities, represented in political parties and/or different types of interest groups.[2] This view underlies many pluralist political theories of modern democracy or polyarchy (Dahl, 2000), from Westminster types with interest group pluralism to consensus types with interest group corporatism (Lijphart, 1999).

However, interest group theory is not identical to a market approach. After all, interest groups may be formed on other grounds than just individual utility maximisation. Exactly this is the vital claim in the strictest formulation of a market approach, i.e. the calculating citizen in rational choice theory. This theory rejects the notion that people with a shared interest will spontaneously and voluntarily unite to defend that interest once they become aware of group consensus. Olson's (1965) paradox of collective action is exactly that egoistic individuals will lack the individual incentives for group formation, because they will prefer a free ride: they will refuse to contribute to the provision of collective goods as long as they are uncertain about the contribution of others, and as long as there may be others who, acting alone or as a small group, have a sufficient interest in providing the collective good for themselves, irrespective of whether or not others contribute, and irrespective of their inability to exclude those others from also enjoying the collective good.

Rational choice theorists see many public choice situations in real-life politics as analogous to this paradox of collective action. The prisoner's dilemma and the 'tragedy of the commons' are only the most well-known *social dilemmas*. Rational choice theory thus explains why optimal collective outcomes can only be brought about through cooperation between plural citizens; but also why there is so often a gap between the realisation of collective goods or the general interest, and what actually happens. People have to decide in a situation of social uncertainty about other people's choices. Hence, they will decide in favour of their own self-interest, thereby foregoing the best possible outcome for themselves; but also the worst possible outcome of being merely exploited by others. Even if individuals for altruistic reasons would be inclined to bear costs for the provision of a collective good, they would realise that their contribution would be imperceptible, thus negligible. This is assumed to be true for many contemporary citizens who, as part of large, latent groups, do not know each other and do not experience their mutual interdependence; and thus have no incentive for exemplary moral action and solidarity.

The consequence is that, one way or another, citizens must be instigated to socially responsible behaviour. The paradox of the market approach is that a consistent application of its individualist utility-maximising principles requires the state as the only plausible source of required external intervention:

> As long as individuals are viewed as prisoners, policy prescriptions will address this metaphor rather than how to enhance the capabilities of those involved to change the constraining rules of the game to lead to outcomes other than remorseless tragedies. (Ostrom, 1990: 7)

The problem of governance is to fight free-ridership and design, and apply the right incentives for citizens to avoid the social dilemma. Such incentives may include both negative incentives, or penalties based on a legal system; and positive incentives, or rewards for responsible behaviour, for example where the state reinforces the outcomes of bargaining and negotiation between citizens and their interest groups by sharing in the collective costs, or by compensating weaker parties, through appropriate taxation and regulatory reforms. A strong but minimal state is compatible with both force and bargaining (Hisschemöller, 1993: 99-102).

The limits of the market approach become visible when pluralism is included to mean intrinsic values that are non-negotiable. This is not to say that one cannot jointly *deliberate* on the relative weight and priority of intrinsic values, like the value of breathing healthy clean air versus the value of car mobility, giving up smoking and building new infrastructure or housing. The point is that a market approach assumes that all values, policy preferences or interests can be *bargained* about; and thus, that a party losing out on one value may be compensated by gain on another value, usually money. In New Public Management lingo, this assumption is repeated ad nauseam in the injunction to policy makers and stakeholders to look for win-win situations. In spite of the penetration of economic rationality in many areas of life, there is not a market for all goods and values. The state itself cannot be created by market forces. Rules for well-functioning markets (like property rights, contract obligations and consumer sovereignty) belong to the class of non-market 'goods' themselves. On top of that, there is no consensus on which values are negotiable or not – that is, there is disagreement on the very distinction between collective and private goods (Lindblom, 2001: 85-107).

The rational choice theory of collective action underpinning pluralist theories of politics and democracy is about the provision or protection of collective goods – not about how to determine what they are. Neither does the theory deal with the important issue of which collective good to prefer in the case of more than one, potentially conflicting collective good – like employment and the environment. The theory assumes consensus on collective goods and their relative priorities (Olson, 1965: 60); and on that basis, rational choice theory posits the function of the state as that of manager of the public interest. However, managing based on consent on involved values is something quite different from constructing consent in a matter of public choice. The implication for pluralism is that the state cannot force consensus in cases of new insights regarding collective goods (*vide* the Wadden Sea case) or their definition, or serious conflict between different collective goods. The state cannot assume consensus when a consensus has to be achieved in the first place.

Correspondence to democracy in practice

A pluralist democracy where calculating citizens influence policy making through all sorts of interest articulation is nowadays the dominant view among politicians and policy makers. In 1990, and 2006 as well, more than 70% of Dutch parliamentarians believed that citizens follow their self-interests rather than the general interest (Andeweg and Thomassen, 2006: 25-6). The 'calculating citizen' has become much more than an ideal-typical construct in numerous government reports and policy papers. For many public servants it has become the dominant stereotype for citizen behaviour, informing their way of interacting with citizens in hearings, in interactive policy making and in street-level contacts.

Yet, research also indicates that properties of the calculating citizen apply to at most a quarter of the Dutch voters (Motivaction, 2001). Calculating citizens demonstrate a pragmatist and individualist attitude to politics, typified as informed but reactive, conformist, materialistic and self-interested; they are engaged, but at arm's length, with average social involvement, and have only modest trust in government. In terms of lifestyles, citizens with attitudes approaching the calculating citizen type are recruited either from the upwardly mobile (13%), who are career-oriented individualists, fascinated with status, new technology, risk and excitement; or from the group of postmodern hedonists (10%), who are pioneering the experience culture, where experimentation and deliberate breaking of moral and social conventions have become inherent goals of life.

A fairness approach: democracy, and the protection of most vulnerable interests

Basic theoretical claims

Moderately structured problems with deep and persistent value dissent require an approach to problem structuring and solving that defuses possible intolerance and doctrinaire stances. Policy deadlock and possible agonistic or even violent political struggle are to be avoided. Yet, parties to the conflict consider their values non-negotiable, and their differences of belief as unbridgeable. Only patient discourse coalition building and accommodation or pacification strategies appear viable modes of coping with such intransigent political problems.

The fairness or social justice view's central policy claim is that only the state can make and enforce policies on politically important, wide-ranging societal issues deriving from deep-seated, divisive value conflicts. Contrary to the market approach, which (re)allocates the policy-making task between politics, economics and civil society, in the fairness approach this is the state's exclusive burden and responsibility. Contrary to the guardian approach, the role of the state is not an implicit justification of the superior qualities or virtues of rulers, but of the state as social institution. Christensen and Laegreid (2002: 275-6) call this the institutional state model:

> The role of the state is to guarantee the moral and political order, and citizens have defined rights and obligations that protect the individual and minorities against the more powerful groups in society.... Political leaders are obliged to defend general standards of fairness and reasonableness with reference to what is best for society at large. The role of politicians is to protect *Rechtsstaat* values and rules, collective standards of appropriateness, and justice.

Although the technical and the fairness approach may be simultaneously used as complementary approaches, they are ultimately very different. The fairness approach is about public, political choice of values and problems; the technical approach is about a-political, non-public solutions to an unambiguous technical problem.

A second claim is that democracy implies value pluralism: not for technical choice, not for choice for private utility maximisation, but as a political choice from different, diverging, normatively founded values and goals that will guide public policy. A third and related claim is that the state needs to construct or create a sufficiently strong social support basis for its political choice. In guardianship theories, people will be glad to follow the experts. In the market approach, citizens and interest groups alone generate consensus, largely based on revealed preferences; or politicians tactically forge consensus between interest groups. In the fairness approach, the socially constructed nature of problems is acknowledged;

but citizen voices have to be reflected in the choice of values and in the course of action for solving problems.

Science plays an important role here, not only in fact-finding and knowledge production but also in evaluating the quality of policy proposals in light of the values defining the problem itself. Brecht's (1959) scientific value alternativism upholds the fact-value distinction, but claims that science may justifiably inquire into the precise meaning and consistency of value premises, and into the suitability, effectiveness, efficiency and side effects of alternative means for goal achievement. Ezrahi (1990) has pointed out that in doing so, science's function for politics is to legitimise and support an objective, neutral and depersonalised form of political authority.

The market and the fairness approaches (contrary to a participation approach, to be discussed later) both embrace democracy as rule of law and equality before the law. The market approach assumes – not realistically, according to many, for example Lindblom (1977) – that equality exists in the sense of a reasonable amount of equality in chances, or starting positions. In a fairness approach, this is not enough; active combat of inequalities is required. Equality is not just a fair starting position for everyone; fairness is a principle that extends to the race itself, and, to some extent, even to the results. Lack of equality destroys the feeling of belonging to and identification with a community, and in that sense is considered a threat to democracy.

Most characteristic for the fairness approach, however, is not that only the state can guarantee equality as fairness, but that this has to be done democratically. The most elaborate underpinning of this core element in a fairness approach is to be found in the work of political theorist and philosopher John Rawls (1971). His theory of justice as fairness was taken by many as the best justification of the post-War welfare states. Rawls sets out to justify a political regime that guarantees both a maximum of freedom and a maximum of equality. Assuming rational, moral people who have to choose a political order under conditions of a 'veil of ignorance', that is, without knowing their own social and economic position, Rawls (1971: 303) formulates as a basic rule for a just political order: 'All social primary goods – liberty and opportunity, income and wealth, and the bases for self-respect – are to be distributed equally unless an unequal distribution of any or all of these goods is to the advantage of the least favored.' As future generations may well belong to the 'least favored', the Rawlsian principle includes sustainability and careful use of non-renewable natural resources as public policy goals.

For a correct understanding of the fairness approach, two more points bear stressing. For moral people choosing rationally under a veil of ignorance, the idea of prioritising the most vulnerable interests has *in-principle* support. However, Rawls does not conclude that, in a democracy, it is up to fairness guardians to operationalise and implement this rule. Rather, the in-principle agreement on the fairness rule is interpreted to mean that most people realise that, in practice, they cannot combat inequalities on their own. They need a collective entity like the state to help them do this. In a democracy, the way this is done has to be tested and retested. This places upon politicians and policy makers the burden of creating a sufficiently strong social support basis for policy proposals. They need to construct the problem as a problem of social justice, and on a case-by-case basis get people to accept this problem construction.

The second important element is that Rawls posits a lexicographic ordering of values: freedom first and foremost; equality second, and always more important than effectiveness, efficiency and contribution to wealth creation. This helps in comparing inherent, non-negotiable values. Comparing all values on one utility curve, like in an ideal-typical market approach, is considered politically and socially unacceptable. The fairness approach, unlike all other approaches, holds that it is the government's responsibility to rethink or choose a new or revised lexicographic ordering of values for society. This is why the fairness approach appears the most suitable one for moderately structured problems with persistent dissent on values at stake.

Correspondence to democratic practice

The weakness of the fairness approach is that pragmatic, how-to-go-about-it issues are left largely untreated. How citizens would have to force governments to guarantee sufficient equality, and recognise the most vulnerable interests, is not very clear. Myrdal, Lasswell and many others hoped for a kind of scientifically guided society (Lindblom, 1990: 213-15), in which the (social) sciences would be of lasting support to governance actors as a kind of 'fairness guardian' under close democratic surveillance. It is this hope that in many democracies inspired the build-up of an extensive advisory 'infrastructure' around governments (Dror, 1971; see also Wagner, 2001, 2007). The governance actors themselves were supposed to act as political elites, capable both of morally steering public opinion in accordance with the fairness principle, and of accommodating or pacifying moral disagreements about its application among themselves.

Such an accommodationist and pacificatory style of democracy was first described and analysed by Lijphart (1967) for the Dutch political system in the early and mid-20th century. He acknowledged that under conditions of strong value dissensus, in a society fragmented along religious, cultural or ethnic lines, cooperation among minority groups would have to be very different from the usual electoral competition between political elites and bargaining among interest groups in culturally more homogeneous societies. Under such conditions, it would be wise to abstain from too much electoral competition, and to run the country as a kind of elite cartel between political elites. Voters would identify only with their 'own' elite; but in elections (under rules of proportional representation) the relative weight of the different groups and their elites would be accurately registered. For the rest, between elections, the business of governance would be left to the accommodationist and pacification practices of elites among each other.

Important among such practices was depoliticising problems and issues. One way of doing this was through the creation of collegial, independent bodies of a quasi-judicial character like Ombudsman bodies or administrative courts. Such venues of political influence and participation gave standing to many groups with less, or less powerful, political resources, and as such, contributed to the idea of justice as fairness (Christensen and Laegreid, 2002: 285). Another way was by 'parking' a politically hot issue in blue-ribbon advisory commissions of reputable politicians and academicians. Over the years, and behind closed doors, such commissions frequently were able to invent acceptable policy discourses about values and goals, and feasible procedures for dealing with the contingent, sometimes case-by-case, treatment of problems, usually under the guise of professional expertise. Under conditions of divisive value dissent, cultural fragmentation and threat of social intolerance and discrimination, some loss of democratic quality of governance is inevitable. However, the price paid is worth it because of the maintenance of a plurality of opinions and beliefs (to the extent of representation by political elites), the maintenance of the rule of law and avoidance of potentially violent conflicts.

It is clear that in neo-liberal, individualising and de-ideologising times, conditions for an accommodationist-democratic approach are less favourable. For a fairness approach to problem structuring and solving to be successful, citizens need to be deferential, resigned, but trusting in government and science. Citizens generally became less deferential, and thus less tolerant of being treated as mere laypersons in a science communication or public relations show; or less willing to be mere followers of one political elite. Moreover, it is exactly the seemingly boundless expansion of the welfare state and the more frequent, disappointing encounters between its bureaucracy and citizens, that have sparked the dependence-*cum*-distrust syndrome that was to undermine the belief in state intervention of the last decades.

A participation approach: deliberation as maximising equality and pluralism

Basic theoretical claims

At first sight, unstructured, messy or wicked problems are beyond structuring, let alone solving. They are left to social opinion formation, media or news industry hypes and cascading opinions, and Schattschneiderian political power tactics of socialising or privatising problems. There is a 'primeval soup' (Kingdon, 1984) of political and social efforts to mobilise support around issues and move them on and higher up the public and political agenda, or deny them agenda status. Dominant problem frames, like a 'deus ex machina', are supposed to emerge through chaotic and not well-understood variety-and-selection learning processes. Dominant problem frames resulting from such random political processes are supposed to offer politicians and policy makers handles for processing them into attractive policies. The question, then, is: to what extent is it possible to enrich the '*powering*' of usual agonistic agenda politics (of beating unstructured problems into the one-and-only favoured frame) with more '*probing*' (Lindblom, 1990), or better deliberation about possible problem framings before making a political choice among them?

Since the deliberative turn in democratic theory in the 1990s, many have endorsed the idea of more citizen engagement and participation not as a substitute, but as a complement to representative democracy. Proposals for putting more deliberation into normal democracy are many (about which later in this chapter), but its most important rationale is that participation beyond the pale of 'usual suspects' in a representative democracy increases decision quality through maximising pluralism. In other words, broader participation makes citizens not only more equal, it also mobilises their plural views, and thereby the collective *intelligence of democracy* (Lindblom, 1965).

Contrary to the market approach, where political participation is in the service of individual rationality as private utility maximisation, here participation is in the service of social rationality, what a person thinks is best for society and their fellow citizens. Moreover, in the mutual exchange of opinions and during debate, citizens discover, develop and refine ideas about their own goals and interests. Deliberation and interaction not only serve the expression of individual opinions and volitions; they also change them. Political participation is supposed to generate learning processes through which individuals become (more) aware of each other's problems. Sometimes this entails new insights in one's own position and preferences in social and political life.

In the market approach, the social contract justifies state force and citizen obedience in the citizens' individual interest. In the participation approach, the social contract is an obligation, not to the state but to one's fellow citizens. It is a promise of people to cooperate to mutual benefit: 'A promise is based on trust, keeping faith and responsibility, not the "natural morality" of possessive individuals, which is why it is promising, not contract, that is fundamental to social life itself' (Pateman, 1979: 170).

Therefore, according to these participation and social rationality theories, the state and its bureaucracy produce apathy and alienation. Gradually, the (welfare) state strips individuals of their personal responsibility towards themselves and the larger community. Whereas the market approach blames the state for destroying individualism and entrepreneurship, deliberationists blame the state for destroying social cohesion as manifested in family life, community life, social discipline, social obligations and responsibilities. Hence, there can be a strong communitarian element in the participation approach. After all, small-sized communities permit the face-to-face communication and deliberation required for participatory government and politics. Decentralising state powers and authority to local or community government levels is a favourite and readily available policy instrument.

Correspondence to democracy in practice

The claim that participation leads to more deliberation, and hence strengthens the intelligence of democracy, requires two complementary claims. First, people can judge rationally for themselves in issues they are involved or have a stake in. Second, people can let their judgement be guided by an awareness of social responsibility, not just self-interest. The former claim can hardly be said to be exclusive any more for a participatory democratic stance. Most voter studies now accept that ordinary citizens, while naturally concerned about containing the costs of acquiring and processing political information, are quite capable of acting purposefully based on available knowledge (Carmines and Huckfeldt, 1996: 248-50; Sniderman et al, 1991). The latter claim amounts to the denial of the major rationale for liberal democracy, namely the omnipresence of social dilemmas between egoistic and altruistic conduct, or self-interest- and general-interest-oriented behaviour. Yet, there exists considerable evidence for the contrary claim, both from field studies and controlled experiments in 'give'-problems of public goods and 'take'-problems of common pool resources. The findings for common resource pool problems were summarised as:

> [A] substantial number, but not all, of the individuals in these carefully controlled experiments are trustworthy and reciprocate trust if it has been extended. When behavior is discovered that is not consistent with reciprocity, individuals are willing to use retribution in a variety of forms. Individuals also rely on a battery of heuristics in response to complexity. Without communication and agreements on joint strategies, these heuristics lead to overuse. On the other hand, individuals are willing to discuss ways to increase their own and others' payoffs in a sequence of rounds. Many are willing to make contingent promises when others are assessed as trustworthy.... These conclusions are not consistent with predictions derived from classical game-theoretic models of participants focusing entirely on monetary returns in these situations. They are, however, consistent with evidence gathered from empirical research in the field. (Ostrom, 2005: 98)

These findings demonstrate the existence of situations where actors do not experience a dilemma between self-interest and a common, shared interest. They choose both rationally, and in a socially responsible way. It shows that a participatory-*cum*-deliberative approach to problem structuring and solving is a realistic option *under certain conditions*. Especially if opportunities for communication and deliberation are lacking, or if strong time pressure exists, feelings of social insecurity and uncertainty about others' behavioural strategies may bring people to resort to other, more self-directed strategies.

For adherents of participatory-*cum*-deliberative democracy it is therefore seductive to give in to the communitarian streak in their theories. More close-knit communities may strengthen feelings of social security and eliminate uncertainty about others' behaviour.[3] relocated endnote!Yet, this may easily lead to an over-idealisation of smaller communities as socially integrated and harmonious. Apart from possibly oppressing dissenting individuals, an alleged homogeneity or unity of opinion and belief in the community (Etzioni, 1996) runs counter to the primary goal of a participatory approach as maximising diversity or pluralism as a condition for high-quality collective decisions.

Another constraint on a participatory-*cum*-deliberative approach is that one cannot force people to participate. They may refuse to participate if they feel powerless, or not involved and not responsible, or totally lacking in knowledge about a public issue. Neither will deliberation and learning happen, if you force knowledgeable people to get involved and 'participate'. In an age of individualisation and de-ideologisation, the participatory attitude is undermined: A common interest is not necessarily assumed to exist, so why participate?; We dislike people speaking on behalf of others, or ourselves speaking on behalf of others, so what about social responsibility for each others' well-being? Let everybody speak for himself!

It is clear that for a participatory approach to problem structuring and solving to be successful, citizens need to feel socially and politically engaged and responsible. Their attitude to government and politics ought to be active, willing to participate and interact with politicians and government officials. They should be politically interested and, unlike pragmatist individualists, general-interest oriented. They should believe in well-functioning democracy and trust government, but in a critical and involved way.

Citizenship-style research estimates the category of such 'reliable' citizens at approximately 30% (Motivaction, 2001). In terms of lifestyles, they are to be found in roughly equal proportions among three categories of citizens:

- the new conservatives – liberal-conservative social upper-class, keen on technological innovation but resisting cultural and social innovation;
- cosmopolitans – open and critical citizens of the planet who integrate postmodern values such as self-development with modern values such as success, materialism and enjoying life;
- postmaterialists *avant la lettre* – idealists, critical about society, desiring self-development, supporting environmental goals, and actively opposing social injustice.

However, only the postmaterialists are true egalitarians and are fully supportive of a participatory approach. Given the relatively strong support for less dependence of government among new conservatives and cosmopolitans (Motivaction, 2001), there is an undercurrent among the majority of active and responsible citizens that is as likely to be individualist as communitarian. In both cases, the justification of the primacy of government has been eroded by doubt, alleged failure, and lack of self-confidence. This is equally true for the deliberationist belief in politics as the main mechanism through which moral dialogues among responsible citizens results in wise decisions. In conclusion, one may observe that even among active and trustful citizens as in principle sympathetic to a fairness or a participatory approach, active support is probably ambiguous and ambivalent.

A meta-theory of democratic practices

To what extent do the four ideal-typical approaches to problem structuring correspond to important arguments in political, especially democracy, theory? The conclusions underline the lasting importance of rejoining the separate fields of policy and political science in what Lasswell called the policy sciences of democracy (Lerner and Lasswell, 1951; more recently Dryzek, 1990; and Schneider and Ingram, 1997). Jointly, the conclusions may be stated as a meta-theory about the intelligence of democracy in the governance of problems (see Figure 8.1).

Figure 8.1: Problem types, political theories and types of democracy

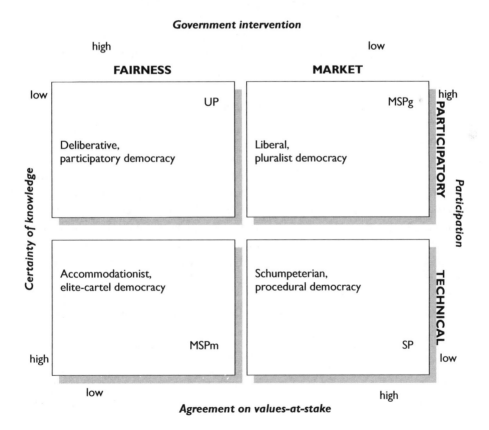

The point of departure was the typology of problem types, along the axes of (un) certainty on knowledge and (dis)agreement on values. The problem types appear to correspond to types of political arguments, along the axes of degree of government intervention (high: fairness; low: market) and degree of participation (high: participatory; low: technical). Thus, political discourse on structured problems (SP) is characterised by strong influences from both a technical and a market approach; on moderately structured problems with considerable goal agreement (MSPg), by a combination of arguments from a market and participatory approach; on moderately structured problems with considerable agreement on knowledge (MSPm), by a coalescence of the fairness and technical approach; and, finally, on unstructured problems (UP), by a synthesis of the participatory and fairness approach. Summarising, the four problem types correspond fairly well to standard distinctions in political theory on desirable degrees of government intervention and participation.

This convergence between policy and political approaches also extends to concepts of democracy. The rule approach to structured problems is compatible with a thin procedural interpretation of democracy as a mechanism for the peaceful circulation of elites under restricted popular influence. The negotiation–and–search approach to moderately structured problems with goal consensus is compatible with standard accounts of liberal, pluralist democracy, either in interest group theory or corporatist variations. The accommodation approach to moderately structured problems with knowledge certainty appeals to an elite–cartel democracy. The learning approach to unstructured problems calls for participatory-*cum*-deliberative modes of democracy.

There is no dearth of studies that spell out the contradictions between different modes of democracy. Such analyses usually discuss abstract criteria of input, throughput and output or outcome legitimacy for democratic decision making. Most of such analyses and assessments conclude that in practice these criteria conflict or rule each other out. The choice for a type of democratic method is thus constructed as dependent on the weight given to the different types of criteria. What is too easily overlooked in such theoretical exercises is that 'democracy', in political practice, is not a unified concept. In everyday political and administrative practice, 'democracy' is *bricolage* or tinkering with different and contradictory democratic notions and practices.

Not abstract legitimacy criteria, but the potential contribution to successful coping with social and political issues through politics and government, has been chosen in this study as the major legitimate goal of democratic decision making. Therefore, the connections of political and democracy theory to types of problems were discussed. From this perspective, it may be observed that the four different concepts of democracy, not separately but *jointly*, constitute an adequate description of the working of democracy in practice. Together they comprise inherently conflicting but constituent parts of the set of beliefs, rules and procedures that, with different degrees of success, are applied to the democratic governance of different types of policy problems. Depending on one's political judgement on a problematic situation, 'democracy' sometimes means simple majority decisions and mandated technocracy, sometimes stakeholder consultation, bargaining processes and applied research in stable policy networks, sometimes pacifying contradictory views, and in yet other times organising citizen participation in society-wide debates.

In other words, from the perspective of democratic governance as a contribution to problem structuring and solving, there exists an overarching norm that catches the different concepts of democracy in a meta-theory. That norm is expressed in the claim that different modes of democracy are justified on the basis of different insights about the nature of public problems and issues. What distinguishes democracy from all other types of politics is its respect for the dialogical character of human beings; hence, its willingness to foster the questioning of power by citizens and its suitability to allow the expression of dissenting views and voices in political decision making. Different types of public problems need expression of different, conflicting views in different degrees. On this basis, rule is justified as long as people agree on the technical nature of an issue; negotiation of interests is justified if people agree on the scope and nature of policy goals, or collective goods, or common pool resources; accommodation and pacification are justified when opposing parties, locked in sharp value conflict, threaten to exclude each other from meaningful political participation; and, finally, learning is justified as a strategy of democratic inquiry into the best ways of structuring unstructured problems. After all, authentic self-reflexivity and well-reasoned deliberation among involved stakeholders and citizens is the only way to do full justice to the socially and politically constructed nature of problems. It is in this sense that claims presented here jointly constitute a meta-theory about the maximisation of the intelligence of democracy in the governance of problems.

Notes

[1] The following sections are a digest of ideas and arguments much more fully elaborated in Hisschemöller's (1993) dissertation. For a much briefer version, focusing on the role of citizens in responding to science and technology, see Hisschemöller and Midden (1999).

[2] Compared to a Schumpeterian democracy, the market analogy is broadened from choosing among political leaders to bargaining about public policies.

[3] Other experiments have confirmed the Greed–Efficiency–Fairness (GEF) hypothesis by Wilke – that under conditions of deliberation and constrained social uncertainty, greed is considerably inhibited by considerations of efficiency and fairness (Eek and Biel, 2003).

NINE

Public engagement and deliberative designs

> Given its essentially intersubjective and dialectical character, political discourse and conduct are fundamentally to be measured ... against the standard of whether they acknowledge and sustain the interrogative dialectic. Only an unremitting interrogative dialectic allows men, if not to achieve fixed truths, at least to slough off errors. (Dauenhauer, 1986: 34)

Introduction

Applied to political regimes or systems as a whole, the meta-theory of plural democracies of problems has strong normative and prescriptive implications. Any policy-making system ought to be sufficiently robust and flexible to encompass in its political repertoire all four problem-structuring approaches, types of policy networks, styles of doable policy analysis, and democracy types. To the extent they have, moreover, they also ought to be able to rebalance the weight of these four modes in accordance with the development of dominant problem framings. That is, governance systems ought to be capable of flexible shifts from rule and analysis/ instruction learning, to negotiation, to accommodation and conflict management, to participatory and deliberative variety/selection learning. However, liberal democracies cannot handle all four different problem types equally well. In this chapter, the first section shows that especially unstructured problems tend to be neglected or approached the wrong way. The second section discusses whether and to what extent this type of democratic deficit may be remedied by gently nudging the political system and policy network to more deliberation-*cum*-participation by meta-governance or deliberate shifts in governance. Particularly, the third section discusses common problems in running deliberative-democratic experiments and the uptake of their outputs in normal, representative-democratic politics.

Wrong-problem problems

Type IIi errors

It was claimed in Chapter Eight that the meta-theory of democratic practice is descriptively adequate for democratic problem structuring and solving in many Western democracies. Nevertheless, this does not diminish its possibilities as a tool for assessment and potential improvements. This possibility is given with the concept of Type III errors, or wrong-problem problems (a concept introduced in Chapter Three), as structural or temporal mismatches between the effectively dominant governmental problem definition and alternative problem framings alive among other groups of citizens or stakeholders in society. In light of the previous discussion, such a mismatch may also be considered as allowing too little, or (in theory) too much, pluralism for successful problem coping.

The trouble with liberal democracies is that they are more solution than problem oriented. They are good at rapidly institutionalising sometimes complex routine issues in (quasi)professional networks that develop standards and systems of regulation and quality assessment. They are also good at institutionalising frequently recurring processes of interest articulation and aggregation in policy networks for negotiation. They even have available strategies for dealing with value conflicts like shifting the ethical burden to the legal system, or ethical commissions, or even, paradoxically, science. However, these readily available political institutions require for their effective functioning far-reaching degrees of problem structuring. Yet, liberal representative democracies turn over unstructured or wicked problems to unpredictable, chaotic and anarchistic processes of mass communication and opinion formation in a weakened civil society and a commercialised media system. For political parties and other traditional political channels of influencing public opinion, political agenda-building processes under current conditions of distrust of representation and authority are uncontrollable and erratic. Although traditional political intermediaries try hard to keep up with the new information technologies and the internet and use them as sources of information and influence, they appear to be marginalised more and more. At least, the traditional political intermediaries are no longer capable of providing citizens with the information and ideas that inspire citizens to positively identify with political parties, their platforms or other symbols capable of mobilising collective action based on shared systems of meaning and belief.[1]

Especially regarding unstructured or wicked problems, increasing in number and urgency in a risk society inhabited by monitorial citizens,[2] there is a need for more public spaces for somewhat more disciplined deliberation and serious debate. In such public spaces, traditional assumptions of representation and authority are bracketed. Deliberation between citizens should temporarily be freed from the socio-political constructions of a 'we-the-people' or 'we-the-community' (Catlaw, 2006). One should allow problematic situations to be radically deconstructed, as a starting point for developing new, potentially innovative, shared and collective meanings.

In solution-oriented democracy, citizens have insufficient incentives and spaces for this kind of collective exchange of views on societal problems. Citizens with diverging insights, experiences and interests are discouraged rather than encouraged to deliberate about their views. Political participation is allowed in the choice among a politically limited set of alternatives for problem solutions. However, the problem itself has been defined already, and policy-making officials and other experts fix the alternatives. Participation only serves the goal of determining who will be winners and losers. This is true for almost any form of current political participation, from varying procedures for hearings or voice, to referendums. The key question therefore appears to be: how to achieve a more problem-oriented democratic political practice? The problem may be illustrated by the situation in Dutch healthcare (Hoppe, 2008a).

Towards of primacy of problems in healthcare?

Have your own biological child, even though you are an infertile couple, or single parent. Bear your child irrespective of age. No more premature deaths due to shortages in donor organs. Celebrate your 100th anniversary in good health and excellent spirits. These are just some of the promises offered by innovations in medical science and technology. Biomedical technology, genetics, genomics, nano- and neuroscience will continue to generate wide-ranging medical-technological innovations. Because they are so tangible for most men and women as (potential) parents, this is especially true for technologies in human reproduction (Kirejzcyk et al, 2001), prenatal diagnostics and predictive medicine. Pre-implantation genetic diagnostics, therapeutic cloning (Swierstra, 2000) and preventive embryo selection are good examples. Figure 9.1 gives an overview of types of problems normally addressed in the healthcare policy network, with technologically not fully matured and ethically contested medical technologies as a growing segment of unstructured problems.

Figure 9.1: Problem types in healthcare

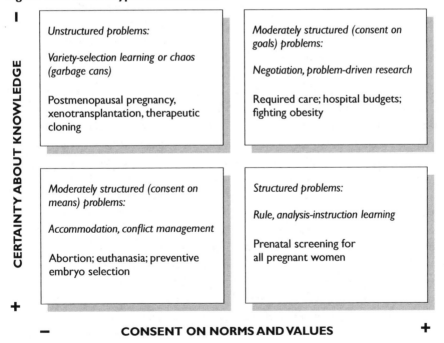

Source: Hoppe (2008a: 297)

In the Netherlands, the big issue facing players in the health policy subsystem for quite some time to come is whether or not, and to what extent, novel medical treatments using innovative but ethically contestable technologies ought to be included in the set of treatments routinely applied in clinics and reimbursed to patients with healthcare cost insurance, but partly also from the government budget. So far, government and health insurance companies rely on a system of provision on medical indication. Decision making seeks consent on the cost–effectiveness of the technology and derived treatment methods. This is the task of a rather closed, corporatist policy subsystem of stakeholders and medical professionals. On the one hand, there are the medical professional groups, like specialists, general practitioners, medical researchers, the many types of paramedical professionals, the pharmaceutical and biotechnology researchers and engineers in their industrial laboratory complexes. Their views count especially to establish sufficient certainty on the laboratory, clinical and real-life effectiveness of standardised treatments. On the other hand, there are stakeholders, like health insurance companies, hospital and other healthcare institution managers, representatives of the medical-pharmaceutical-biotechnological commercial complex, trade unions of healthcare workers and patient organisations. They are supposed to discuss matters of resource efficiency, implementation feasibility, patient acceptability and so on.

In fact, the policy-making system is a hybrid between professional self-regulation and corporatist interest articulation. The historical core of the system is shaped by defining the problem of medical technology and its impact on health policy as a moderately structured problem with knowledge certainty. Peer review took care of the knowledge dimension; the ethical dimension was left to politics. Politicians would have the role of linespeople: doctors should not mix up medical treatment with implicit, but constraining conditions that implicitly or explicitly reflect religious, ethical and political judgements on 'good parenting', or on the role of medical technology in a 'good society'.

Once new technologies were admitted, the system shifted to a rule-mode fit for structured problems, where everything was left to the medical profession. Owing to strong consensus on the goals for health policy – equal access to equal treatment for all Dutch citizens at reasonable costs – the health sector was allowed to grow and grow, seemingly under professional self-regulation. However, the ever-increasing macro-economic importance of health-related technological, industrial and service activities gradually led to more deliberate efforts at cost control. In essence, this took the shape of bargaining about healthcare costs in an 'iron triangle' between medical professionals, insurance companies and the state.

In the 1980s and 1990s, politicians facilitated the interests of patient groups as a kind of countervailing public power to curb the interests of the medical professionals. It is a clear case of policy subsystem restructuring. Politicians feared that the existing 'iron triangle' network, without a representative voice for the patient's perspective, threatened effective policy deliberation and the legitimacy of decisions on far-reaching reforms for managed competition in healthcare. In order to widen the deliberative capacity and save the legitimacy of political decision making, they recognised patient groups as legitimate 'players'; and used public funding of patient interest groups and organisations to expand the composition of the network. Hence, the problem definition shifted to moderately structured problems with considerable goal consent; and the policy subsystem acquired the corresponding traits of a neo-corporatist subsystem for stakeholder interest articulation – as an overlay on top, not as a substitute for the older institutional arrangements.

Moreover, next to the transition to managed competition, this hybrid, opaque and difficult-to-steer policy subsystem is also challenged by ethically contested new medical technologies. These innovations breed unstructured problems because frequently neither their cost-effectiveness nor their ethical dimensions have crystallised into clear, publicly defensible, and dominant policy views or beliefs. The contemporary policy system evolved from efforts to cope with both forms of moderately structured and fully structured problems. Yet, now it appears to have serious difficulties in dealing with the new type of unstructured problems. Thus, one may speak of a potential structural mismatch: a policy network, designed to cope with structured and moderately structured problems, is now 'bombarded' with 'unprocessable' unstructured problems because of rapid technological developments. The system was capable of relatively harmonious 'gear shifts' between accommodation, negotiation and rule as modes of problem coping. However, in spite of the presence of patient organisations and forums as a too modest shift to a more pluralist, participatory and deliberative style of policy making, the system shows strains to add a learning style of coping with unstructured problems to its repertoire.

In healthcare, the social, legal and ethical aspects of medical-technological innovations ought to be as intelligently and seriously debated as the more common scientific, technical and economic aspects. Based on the principle of the primacy or good governance of policy problems, the health policy system ought to be sufficiently robust and flexible to accommodate all policy-making styles for all types of problems. This is clearly not yet the case. What would be necessary, then, is to find institutional resources to inject more pluralism in more seriously and creatively dealing with unstructured problems through more public spaces for participation, deliberation and learning. How is this to be achieved?

The short answer to this question is: by gently nudging the policy politics of the health policy network to more deliberation and/or participation through meta-governance. As explained in Chapter Six, *meta-governance* constitutes the endeavour by politicians, policy intellectuals or some other policy entrepreneurs to influence the discourse, composition and participation modes of players, the rules of the game and the interdependencies between players in governance networks (Sørensen and Torfing, 2005: 202-5). Frankly speaking, it would be difficult to draw the line between meta-governance and political tinkering or *bricolage*. The health system is simply too complex and self-controlled to be amenable to meta-governance as top-down steering from a central control unit. The only way to 'steer' such complex systems is by using the forces and drivers already effective in it; to 'interpolate' small doses of change in such ways that the balance of forces is changed in the desired direction (Dunsire, 1986; Hood, 1986). One would have to fine-tune the relative weight of the different, partially opposing governance modes present in the overall constellation.

In healthcare, some developments are going in this direction already. Under managed competition, the role of (potential) patients as clients will gain in weight and influence in policy implementation as health service delivery. Patient self-management, case management, more choice in health service delivery, patient and user rankings of health service organisations – they will all become more important. Yet, bolder steps are required in dealing prudently with ethically contestable medical innovation. Under present conditions, patient organisations and platforms function as interest groups. Valuable as this may be, they have become part of the 'usual suspects'. The voices (in the plural) of ordinary people and citizens as *potential patients*, and as relatives, friends or caretakers of patients, are only faintly audible through the normal modes of political participation in representative democracy. To really inject more pluralism into creatively dealing with and collective learning about unstructured problems of medical-technological innovations, introducing more participatory and deliberative design elements in health technology assessments would be a good start.

Shifts in governance: meta-governance

Interpolable balancing as a quest for institutional alignments

Most policy domains are embedded in and constituted by multiple institutional orders. Healthcare is a telling example. If you get ill, you invoke the very different principles of multiple institutional orders to be cured. You rely partly on the spontaneous social solidarity of the household and civil society, that is, you count on your spouse, family, neighbours and friends to care for you. If your illness is bad enough, you invoke the expertise of medical doctors as members of their professional and scientific communities. If you need medicine or hospitalisation, the *quid-pro-quo* rules (prices) of health insurance companies, hospitals and the pharmaceutical corporations get you what you need. If this becomes too costly for an individual patient, many states have established compulsory health insurance systems, which somehow mix rules of solidarity and *quid-pro-quo* to guarantee equal access against acceptable costs to most citizens. This simple example of being ill and getting better shows that thinking in terms of separate institutional logics does not bring you far. Market interactions alone, or family care alone, or state authority alone, cannot cure you. It is not the institutions in isolation that matter to you as a patient; it is the institutional configuration or ensemble that matters.

This is equally true for policy analysts designing, for example, healthcare policy. In Chapter One, governance was defined as efforts to align or bring about concerted action across multiple modes of social coordination for public purpose. Interpolable balancing is the ongoing quest for new institutional alignments.

Accounts of policy change in grid–group cultural theory and institutionalist theory argue the same.

In cultural theory, it is stressed that the four cultural biases and corresponding institutional arrangements run into the limits of their own monistic logics, unless productive hybridity is established by means of apparently 'clumsy' institutions. This is called the requisite variety condition: 'each way of life, though it competes with the rest, ultimately needs them' (Thompson et al, 1990: 86). The freedom to contract in the market system can only be upheld through hierarchic state authority by way of rules and penalties applied by the judiciary. The solidarity of egalitarian groups needs correction by market-type efficiency tests. And so on. Applied to policy analysis, cultural theory supports interpolable balancing as social and policy-oriented learning. It offers easily applicable heuristics for anticipating side effects of too-dominant institutional logics, for finding overlooked options and for constructing productive culturally hybrid policy alternatives in policy brokerage and design (Hoppe, 2007: 295-8).

In institutionalist approaches, interpolable balancing is depicted as a quest for complementarity and hierarchy (Helderman, 2007: 98-121). Complementarity is a situation in which a particular institution works better because of the presence of some other forms of institution or organisation. For example, it may be argued that healthcare provision by professional medical associations works better because the state bureaucracy attributes monopoly competencies to, but also regulates, these professional communities; and because, through income redistribution and compulsory healthcare insurance, it regulates demand for healthcare. State hierarchy and professional association are symmetrical, complementary institutions, which co-produce a beneficial social effect.

Hierarchy means a situation in which one institutional order imposes its logic on the entire institutional configuration; one institution is dominating and constraining the functioning of alternative institutional orders, at least during a particular point or period in time. For example, by adding market-type incentives into a healthcare system characterised until the 1990s by supposedly complementary relations between bureaucratism and professionalism, many fear that in future the market will drive out professionalism. After all, the absolute quality standards adhered to by dedicated professionals will be subjected to the relative tests of price/quality standards dominating the market system. Hence, the market system will become hierarchic in healthcare.

Both in cultural theory and in institutionalist accounts, interpolable balancing is a never-ending activity because institutional ensembles are in a state of permanent dynamic imbalance. This may not be true for democratic political systems as a whole. Political and policy players will not (normally) waste their time discussing the constitution or other historically rooted and socio-politically well-embedded democratic governance practices. Nevertheless, in policy domains and networks policy players are keen on detecting strategic opportunities to advance the influence of their favourite institutions. In that precise sense, institutions need continuous maintenance, are never finished and are always in need of reform

(Dauenhauer, 1986:138). Shifts in the power balance of institutional orders directly influence stakeholders' resources, roles, responsibilities and tasks. Therefore, they will stand ready to form alliances with adherents of complementary institutions when it seems advantageous for furthering their own cause; and sever such alliances when they become disadvantageous. In the context of constantly changing opportunities and constraints, interpolable balancing takes shape as a gradual transformation of policies and institutional orders.

Following Streeck and Thelen (2005), there appear to exist some recognisable patterns of institutional transformation, depending on the relative strength of internal and external barriers to change: drift, conversion, layering and displacement/exhaustion (see Figure 9.2).

Figure 9.2: Four types of gradual institutional transformation

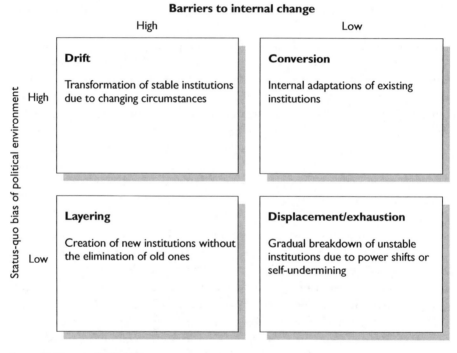

Source: Helderman (2007: 118)

Interpolable balancing as meta-governance would have to avoid the high–high and the low–low cells. Drift represents institutional transformation due to changing external conditions – either nature-made catastrophes or man-made crises – in the face of headstrong and persistent internal and external opposition to change. These deadlocked situations lead to uncontrollable changes in existing institutions. Sometimes they can turn into runaway institutional destruction through displacement and exhaustion. As meta-governance, interpolable balancing would rather aim at the layering and conversion types of institutional transformation. In cases of layering, new institutions are added to the older ones and they may grow in importance over time. In the healthcare system example, market-type institutional elements were introduced in a system governed so far by professionalism and buraucratism. Especially in such transformations, the notion of alignment and complementarity is essential. In the case of healthcare, the argument is that market-type incentives are needed to counteract both the tendencies of professionalism to infinite expansion, and the bureaucratic tendency for imposed inflexibility. In the case of conversion, institutions are adapted to serve the new goals and fit the interests of new policy players admitted to the policy network.

Nudging present systems of network governance to facilitate the structuring of unstructured or wicked problems, and to structurally accommodate the input of larger numbers of citizen, would appear to require exactly institutional changes in the sense of layering and conversion. They would require adding elements of deliberative and participatory democracy to the institutional repertoire, or changing existing non-deliberative democratic institutions into more deliberative directions.

Constraints on pluralism

However, first it makes sense to ask: what stands in the way of such institutional transformations? What, then, would be the constraints for more democratic pluralism and deliberation in our governance systems? Three come to mind immediately: network governance, the revival of the primacy of politics, and New Public Management.

Instead of constructing network governance as merely undermining representative democracy (Papadopoulos, 2003), some consider it a cradle of new forms of democracy. If most affected parties to a public problem join the network, the scope for discursive contestation is widened, because intermediate levels of sub-elites are mobilised. Vertically, they link central steering through representative democracy to forms of self-governing in communities and civil society associations. Horizontally, they link different policy or territorial (regional, local and neighbourhood) communities (Sørensen and Torfing, 2005: 200). In network governance, the trend is towards non-hierarchical, non-bureaucratic, cultural (Bang, 2004) or holistic governance (6 et al, 2002). Yet, one may be justifiably suspicious about the authentic quality of increasing public engagement with governance in these ways. Network governance, rather, uses backward mapping techniques (Elmore, 1985) and 'soft', communicative policy instruments to nourish the proper governmentality among target populations in order to keep the system running smoothly:

> [W]hen leaders and managers today increasingly choose to connect and empower, ... it is because they have come to recognize that in an increasingly 'glocalized' (global and local) world in which governing failure is inevitable, one must pay explicit attention to how to use

ethical–political communication strategically for involving civil society
and citizens in governing systems... Their survival and development
rely increasingly on their abilities to empower lay people and to
affect their identities in such a way that they act effectively and
self-responsibly and for the sake of the effectiveness, coherence and
integration as a whole....' (Bang, 2004: 165–6)

Bang (2004: 186) justifiably warns that cultural or holistic governance may
well develop into a 'pervasive form of systems colonizing of the life world'. If
politicians and administrators show the self-restraint and self-discipline expected
from democrats, these fears do not necessarily materialise. However, it requires
them to actually step outside their traditional roles of leader, man–of–reason and
expert. Instead, they would have to take on roles like facilitator, counsellor or
midwife (Catlaw, 2006). This might especially be true when formal changes of
representative democracy like people's initiatives in parliamentary agenda setting
and corrective referendums were to be put in place. Although most formal changes
in democratic rule are probably ineffective, these ones will probably foster more
citizen-regarding policy making as political leaders will 'govern under the shadow
of the referendum':

> [T]he optional referendum hangs like a sword of Damocles over the
> whole legislative process, potentially ruining entire bills. Consequently,
> institutional mechanisms have developed ... transforming Swiss
> democracy into a *negotiation democracy*.... [The aim of this is] ... to
> find a sufficiently strong compromise, allowing the future bill to be
> enacted as law without a popular vote. (Kriesi and Trechsel, 2008: 58)

Nevertheless, formidable constraints on fostering more difference and plurality in
public spaces of traditional representative and liberal democratic regimes remain.
One of its most conspicuous forms is the so-called restoration of the primacy of
politics. The intention is to restore the political authority of elected politicians
in representative institutions over bureaucracy and scientific or corporatist
consultation and advice. Yet, as an attempt to increase democratic legitimacy it
is a naïve and cramped effort to reinforce the political myths of 'we-the-people'
and popular sovereignty as vested in and represented by Parliament as the one-
and-only source of political authority. Even the most superficial reality check of
this endeavour reveals its emptiness. It locks the elite of front-bench politicians
inside the walls of Parliament, the cages of party politics and the negotiations
with powerful interest groups. In addition, it condemns them to rely on the
media industry and the craft of spin doctors to bring political messages and
intentions across to the public at large, or particular segments of the population.
As political talk in the media inevitably deviates from political decisions taken in
parliamentary, party and interest politics, politicians open themselves up to easy

attacks of lack of transparency and hypocrisy. This, of course, undermines their bid for primacy and authority.

Moreover, there is the pernicious combination of restoration of representative democracy in agenda building, policy formulation and adoption, and better implementation and service delivery through New Public Management. On the face of it, the formula that politicians have to 'steer', but leave the 'rowing' to public managers, is just another manifestation of the old politics/administration divide, putting politicians in the lead and constructing civil servants as neutral executors of political will. However, a second look at its practice under current conditions reveals its destructive impact on the primacy of politics. The practical translation of rowing/steering has frequently been that administrators and civil servants dominate the actual interaction between citizens and the state, where system meets life-world. Sometimes, they actively work to exclude politicians from interactive and participatory policy-making exercises. More frequently, elected politicians voluntarily back off (Bang, 2004: 172-3, 176-7; Monnikhof, 2006: 362; Cornips, 2008). The bulk of ordinary politicians thus find their jobs hollowed out; their political function of dialogue and cooperation with citizens usurped by administrators and public managers, especially where the latter practice cultural and holistic governance.

In this way, ordinary politicians are deprived of first-hand learning about the effects of administrative practices on the day-to-day lives of most citizens. Instead of direct reports of citizens' experiences, they have to rely on administrative and financial accounting documents. Only in the case of obvious scandals and fiascoes, they may decide to get immediate access to citizen experiences. Frequently this is too little, too late. Between steering and rowing there actually is a no-man's land, which cannot but destroy politicians' sources and antennae for political judgement as the art and skill to assess the meaning of context-bound events and situations in the light of more general principles and political values. Serious political judgement rests on the accessibility of the particular and the specific in concrete practices, in order to connect these practices to higher-order ethical beliefs and political convictions about the proper functioning of the larger system (Beiner, 1983: 150; Van de Graaf and Hoppe, 1989: 97-9; Hoppe, 1993).

In many cases, it is only the administrators and public managers who have the actual information to come to effective political judgements. However, mobilising pluralism for better political judgement is not their priority, since they are preoccupied to recruit the identities and skills of citizens in the service of their own system objectives. Summarising a decade of Dutch experience and a large number of in-depth analyses of interactive policy making, Monnikhof (2006: 372) reports 'a lack of open acknowledgement of diverging interests in favor of a "public interest" myth' and hardly any serious attention to analytical contributions of participants. Moreover, Hisschemöller et al (2009) claims that policy-analytical methods that are frequently used in supporting interactive and participatory policy making, such as brainstorming, focus groups, simulation and gaming, policy delphis and backcasting, actually prevent the articulation and assessment of conflicting knowledge claims. In other words, they in fact suppress, and not generate or mobilise, plurality. Time or financial constraints are sometimes used to put closure on plurality and debate. The famous Danish consensus conference model of citizen participation uses severe time pressure to force a consensus in the final, written reports to Parliament.[3] The citizen working groups in the Danish Integrated Urban Development Programme had to reach full consensus on its proposals as a non-negotiable condition for getting the financial resources for their implementation from the municipal government (Bang, 2004: 175).

Modes of participation and deliberation

Each of the four 'democracies of problems' has its own characteristic mode of political participation by citizens or stakeholders. Using the types of participation introduced in Chapter Six, problem-type–participation-type matches are summed up in Figure 9.3.

Figure 9.3: Types of problem structures and corresponding types of citizen participation

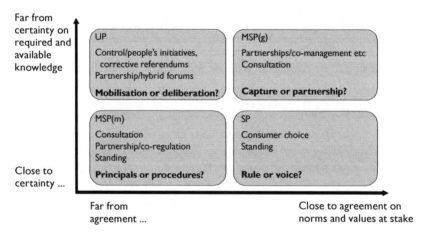

Dealing with structured problems (SP) in closed networks of professional experts most of the time is a matter of rule through autonomous professional-managerial decisions on solution alternatives. Occasionally, key stakeholders may be granted a voice by ad-hoc or structured contacts. Such contacts may be expanded to include selected segments of the citizenry. In both cases, the management decides alone in a manner that does or does not take stakeholders' or citizens' views seriously into account. Respecting this rule regime, there are two major ways of giving citizens more opportunities for voice. One is by traditional legal means, that is, by giving citizens legal standing and access to review procedures, tribunals or ombudsman-like arrangements. Legal standing is a weak influence restricted to individuals; expanded to open and third-party standing, it is stronger. In the shadow of representative democracy, legal standing and (administrative) review procedures are not just a mode of citizen participation, but also a potential source of information about detailed policy implementation for other political actors, like elected politicians.

New Public Management thinking also impinges on citizen and stakeholder participation in rules. On the one hand, maximising scope for management, less weight is given to judicial appeals and review procedures. The less formal rules, the better. On the other hand, New Public Management thinking is positive about a louder citizen voice through more possibilities for consumer choice in service delivery. Instruments explored and used include surveys and focus groups; client councils 'in the shadow of hierarchy' (Schillemans, 2007: 271-2); but also economic instruments like purchaser/provider splits, managed competition between providers/suppliers, case management, and vouchers for users.

Moderately structured problems with goal consensus (MSP-g), dealt with in stable policy networks through problem-driven research and negotiation, no doubt have the most developed opportunities for stakeholder participation. The variety of formal consultation and partnership arrangements is almost infinite; and they are flanked by informal variants. In capitalist societies, business stakeholders enjoy special privileges in public policy making (Lindblom, 1977; Flyvbjerg, 1998); even to the extent that partnership relations degenerate into a capture of regulatory and supervisory public agencies by the regulated and supervised interests. This danger looms especially large in corporatist co-regulation and co-management forms of partnership. In the Netherlands, longstanding co-regulation and co-management partnerships in labour reintegration and incapacity-for-work issues between the state, labour unions and employers' associations had to be abolished in the 1990s due to large-scale abuse by the private partners for their respective group interests. In fact, labour unions and employers' associations 'socialised' the costs of large-scale economic reforms by sending taxpayers the bill for the overgenerous treatment of laid-off workers (Visser and Hemerijck, 1997).

Another drawback of highly developed corporatist consultative and partnership arrangements is that they exclude less-organised interests, non-experts, communities and citizens from the regular policy-making arenas. This is especially true at national levels of governance. However, at subnational, regional, provincial and community levels, unorganised and organised ordinary citizens do have easier access to partnership arrangements such as co-production and community-based co-management, where government and interest groups and/or citizens cooperate in implementing a policy. Think of the many Neighbourhood Watch projects in public safety, or community clean-up and development plans in urban redevelopment, or involving farmers and communities in soil or nature conservation or waste treatment programmes, or fishermen in fisheries policy (Kooiman et al, 2005). Frequently in such programmes, joint fact-finding practices make all participants jointly responsible for establishing a shared 'database' accessible to all – instead of leaving this task entirely to experts. Joint fact-finding is the core of a growing literature on methods for (externally) extended peer review (Funtowicz and Ravetz, 1992;Van Asselt, 2000;Van Buuren and Edelenbos, 2004).

Coping with moderately structured problems with politically divisive value dissent (MSP-m) through strategies of discourse coalition building in designed networks, aiming at accommodation and pacification of open conflict, is an inherently somewhat elitist endeavour. Consultation practice will focus on participation by those who have a contribution to make to 'peace-keeping' policy ideas and a policy discourse of expressive overdetermination (see Chapter Four). This means recruitment of some immediate stakeholders, usually moderate, reasonable and realistic representatives of the conflicting parties. They are complemented by potential mediators, clarifiers, or other specialists in norm generation. Sometimes hybrid commissions of Wise Persons, consisting of reputed politicians, prudent scientists, representatives of contending parties, problem specialists and legal specialists prepare reports that may become the basis for parliamentary legislation. In other cases, permanent ethical commissions defuse and depoliticise issues, hoping to generate consensual norms, values and policy practices in the process.

Professional co-regulation and legal standing, usually in tandem, may be important elements in the participation repertoire for dealing with moderately structured problems (means). As demonstrated in Chapters Four and Six, an important way of taming 'wicked' ethical issues is to find some professional paradigm, which expressively overdetermines the conflicting principled positions of contenders on both sides of the issue. If such a paradigm can be found or constructed, it may be turned into the basis of formal legislation and policy; with delegation of day-to-day implementation and application to individual cases to the relevant professional community, which develops some kind of protocol for prudent and careful professional treatment. This is a mode of professional co-regulation. In order to guarantee transparency and public accountability, professional conduct is tied to particular legal sanctions, laid down in official legislation. In the Dutch abortion case, the conservative pro-life and feminist pro-choice positions were expressively overdetermined by some combination of a medical ('doctors may abort on medical indications') and a clinical-psychological ('abortion signals problematic parental relationships') paradigm. Lest these professional communities became too autonomous, they were tied to certain procedural rules, specified by law; and leading to prosecution in case of violation. From a problem-processing perspective, it should be stressed that the importance of the legal instrument and legal standing for citizens is not just the possibility for sanctions. A string of court reviews of concrete cases provides policy actors access to detailed information on implementation and application practice. In due time, this may lead to amended legislation, or adaptations in the protocols for proper professional conduct.

Intractable, 'wicked' or unstructured problems (UP) need learning processes to be organised somehow in open issue networks. Such learning processes, it has been argued, require maximising equality between citizens and pluralism of views for their success. Pluralism is necessary because dealing with unstructured problems requires 'prismatic' looking at an issue, from as many different positions or angles as is possible. Equality is required because only participation on an equal footing has a chance of maximising plurality and the mutual learning that is supposed to follow from being exposed to the views of other citizens. Catalysing mutual learning as dealing with unstructured or 'wicked' problems has a central place in the system of meta–governance as interpolable balancing. It acts as a kind of hothouse for political judgement and learning about problem decomposition and sorting (see Figure 9.4).

Figure 9.4: Political judgement as a decomposition and sorting device in learning about unstructured problems

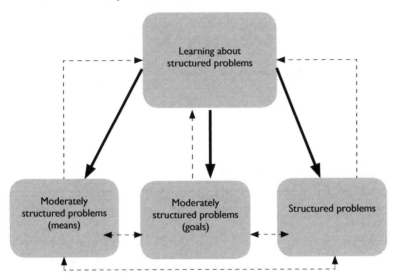

This is what was anticipated when it was argued, in Chapter Three, that, from a policy maker's perspective, it makes sense to deconstruct well-entrenched problem frames, and treat them as if they were unstructured. Apart from that, in real politics and policy making, some such traditional problem definitions do become unsettled and thus appropriate for reconsideration. In a sense, experiments in participatory-*cum*-deliberative democracy may be viewed as the 'gear box' enabling, as Connolly (1987: 141) puts it: 'Modern politics [to] simultaneously operate to unsettle dimensions that have assumed a fixed character and to achieve a temporary settlement in areas where a common decision is needed but the resources of knowledge or administrative procedure are insufficient to resolve the issue.'

In fact, a lot of institutional tinkering is currently going on in this field of injecting more deliberative quality[4] and direct citizen participation in representative democracies (Fung, 2003; Williamson and Fung, 2004; Van Stokkom, 2006). Any effort at generalisation, therefore, is premature and should be taken with considerable grains of salt. Nevertheless, it looks like four broad categories of participatory-*cum*-deliberative projects may be distinguished: formal control, participation as 'mini-people', participation and consultation as 'mini-public', and collaborative, hybrid forums and knowledge centres.

First, there are efforts to hand over *formal control* of an issue from Parliaments to the electorate. Examples are proposals for several types of referendums, for electronic voting, for participatory budgeting[5], or Dahl's (1989) proposal for a 'minipopulus', or Van Stokkom's (2006) idea of a 'citizen chamber'. Normal referendums and electronic voting by themselves are clearly unsuitable for dealing with unstructured problems. Yet, people's initiatives and corrective referendums would give citizens a means of signalling gross mismatches between dominant governmental problem frames and alternative framings alive in large segments of the public.[6] The same goes for proposals for a 'minipopulus' or a 'citizen chamber'. Their idea is to create a 'mini-*people*' through random selection of, say, 1,000 citizens. After deliberative processes supported by electronic means, expert, administrative and stakeholder hearings, and perhaps commissioned research, such a body could decide on an agenda of issues, which co-determines the parliamentary agenda. Each issue could be discussed and deliberated by some segment of the 'minipopulus'; the result would be a formal input to governmental decision making and the legislative process. This could take the shape of, for example, an obligation to publicly account for any substantial deviation from the citizen chamber's proposal.

The '*mini-people*' form of participation-*cum*-deliberation keeps alive the notion of representativeness through random selection of citizen participants. There are many forms of this *second method*, like participation as partnership that also aspires to weak forms of representation through random selection. They are commissioned by a public agency, and involve citizens in aspects of governmental policy formulation through advisory boards, citizens' advisory panels, public inquiries and so on. To be mentioned here are citizen juries, planning cells, consensus conferences and government-initiated public debates. Much more practiced is the *third method: creating a 'mini-public'* through stakeholder participation and consultation, for example in the much-practiced so-called 'hybrid forums' or 'platforms at national and regional government levels (Kern and Smith, 2008; Merkx, 2008). With no claim to representativeness, political and policy actors have more scope to tailor the composition of the mini-public to the (rather, their views of the) needs of the issue for deliberation. Most of the time, this entails possibilities for more structured processes of deliberative policy analysis, like future or scenario or backcasting workshops, strategic conferences, gaming exercises and decision conferencing (for an overview, see Mayer, 1997: 81ff). Both features probably make for the popularity among policy makers of this third participation method of creating mini-publics of stakeholders. Of course, there is a danger of over-designing stakeholder participation, thereby reducing its function as mobilising plurality for learning about unstructured policy issues.

Perhaps, one could discern a *fourth 'method'*. The word 'method' is bracketed because, in this form of participation, government commissioning and issue delineation are more or less absent. For developments in the US, Fung and

Williamson (2004: 11–12) speak of 'collaborative forums' as open citizen forums that create opportunities for gathering and discussing issues through presentation of information and 'working through' processes to arrive at responsible political judgements (Yankelovich, 1991). They are typically promoted by civic associations and organisations dedicated to improving the quality of citizen deliberation and public debate on important policy issues, like the National Issue Forums initiated by the Kettering Foundation.

Different from such grassroots initiatives is the development of 'knowledge centres' (Halffman and Hoppe, 2005: 144). They originate in bottom–up initiatives by policy experts and practitioners. They claim to make knowledge more available for policy use, either by integrating knowledge, simply accumulating knowledge or by performing a role as knowledge broker. Knowledge centres see themselves as facilitators of a collective and public learning process, targeted at non-governmental or governmental practitioners and citizens in general, rather than central government policy makers in particular. Their organisational form ranges from merely a portal website, run by a handful of people, to the research facilities of university research centres. Always, they operate chatrooms and offer other means for communication and deliberation between users. This means that knowledge centres, although sometimes originally formed around traditional disciplines or policy domains, can operate across well-delineated problem areas, research fields or professional jurisdictions. It is such cross-cutting potential between disciplines, between policy domains, and between government and civic society that makes for possible 'new combinations' (Van der Heijden, 2005).

Both collaborative hybrid forums or platforms and knowledge centres are potential 'hot houses' for innovative policy ideas on dealing with unstructured problems. In their hypothetical new problem decompositions they may hit on ideas for new problem structuring that move large chunks or smaller selected parts of unstructured problems to any of the other three problem types that are more amenable to policy-making routines in representative democracies. However, this is far easier said than done. Designing and running experiments in deliberative-*cum*-participatory policy making for unstructured problems is haunted by its character as an alien element in a representative democracy. Frequently, when political mobilisation for agenda status and decision making is in full swing, deliberation and learning have to be 'smuggled into' agonistic policy arenas. Sometimes, special forward-looking institutes on particular issue areas, like the Rathenau Institute in the Netherlands and the former Office of Technology Assessment in the US, attempt to initiate and ignite public debates on issues that in the (near) future will become politically salient but are as yet unknown to vested political interests, or declared anathema.

Goodin and Dryzek (2006: 219) speak of the problem of the 'macro-political uptake of minipublics'. Papadopoulos and Warin (2007: 460) strike at the heart of the problem when they state:

A crucial problem is that of the uneasy coupling of decisional arenas that operate under different principles of legitimation: deliberation and negotiation between (sometimes collective) stakeholders in participatory procedures versus competition for authorisation in the representative circuit.

To illustrate the problems in mini-public deliberative projects, some of the dilemmas and perplexities of democratic experiments in structuring unstructured problems will be discussed in the next section. The focus will be on the stakeholder variant of creating a mini-public, both because this mode is more practised; but also because it brings out the problems into sharper relief.

Perplexities of democratic experiments in problem structuring

As said, at present a lot of research is going on about the design, running, outputs and outcomes of democratic experiments (Mayer, 1997: 231ff; Fung, 2003; Loeber, 2004: 261ff; Papadopoulos and Warin, 2007; Hisschemöller et al, 2009). In bringing some order to the discussion of typical problems, Loeber's model of a mini-public deliberative project as research object will be used.[7] (see Figure 9.5) The model grasps the dynamics of such a project in depicting it as deliberative interactions among a variety of actors trying to come to joint political judgement, distributed over time and in space. This allows ordering the discussion in simple terms of input (t_0-t_1), throughput (t_1-t_2), output (t_2) and outcome (t_2-t_x). Input is the preparation stage of the project, before the actual deliberative process commences (t_1) and the frequently not so easily determinable moment when preparations seriously start (t_0). During the input stage, the project's aspirations, its problem framing(s) and the envisaged outputs are formulated. The end or output of the project (t_2) supposedly coincides with the formulation of some end-conclusion or advisory report, and its immediate 'selling' activities to key addressees. The impact or outcome of the project may be a multidimensional process continuing for quite some time, so that a clear endpoint usually cannot be given (t_x).

Input problems

In the input phase of a stakeholder variant of mini-public deliberative projects (M-PDPs), the same questions have to be answered as for any exercise in policy analysis, design and evaluation: who is to deliberate for whom on what, why, when and how (Van de Graaf and Hoppe, 1996: 385-92; Fung, 2003); or, whom to serve (Lindblom and Woodhouse, 1993)? As will be shown, these questions cohere and give rise to difficult choices when it comes to maximising plurality and ensuring some power balance or equality in view of learning about unstructured problems.

Institutional constraints of representative democracy usually mean that government itself, government agencies or Parliaments commission M-PDPs.

Figure 9.5: Simple timeframe model of a mini-public deliberative project

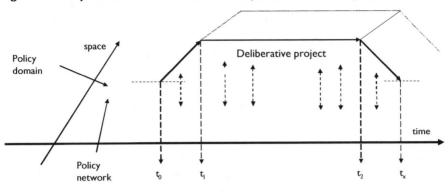

Exchange of information between project and political context

The Dutch Cabinet decided to conduct M–PDPs as part of its deliberations on whether or not to allow further expansion of Schiphol Airport and the Rotterdam Harbour. The Department of Transport and Water Management organised a number of M–PDP's under the label of 'future ateliers' in order to boost the creativity and out-of-the-box thinking of their own policy design on large-scale infrastructure. The Dutch Parliament decided that its own deliberations about GM food policy ought to be simultaneously flanked by a large-scale societal debate on the same issue.

The examples given already show why such M–PDPs are organised. Vested political bodies try to escape normal policy-making and decision-making routines and create a temporary niche for 'fresh' thinking and frank or open deliberation. This implies that the 'when' question is answered by looking at politically opportune moments, or fortuitous timing in the policy cycle, from the vantage point of normal policy players. This lends most of these exercises an ad-hoc, non-recurrent and non-formal character. The implications for the roles of both politicians and analysts/organisers in M–PDPs are profound. Politicians may have an interest in ordering a deliberative experiment, not in participating in it. Rather, they have an interest in just waiting for the results, and only then deciding on whether or not to use them. In other words, they are perhaps interested in M–PDPs for better quality of deliberations feeding them with fresh ideas, certainly not for more democratic decisions. At best, they pledge to take the outputs of an M–PDP seriously; but they almost never promise to follow it completely or even partially. In the interest of frank and open deliberation, they even find a rationale not to participate themselves. Partly there is merit in this argument. If the claims, concerns and issues of politicians come to dominate the deliberative process, freshness and openness may suffer. In addition, there are good reasons for scepticism about politicians' potential strategic and creative contributions to the debate (Bang, 2004: 172–3; Sørensen and Torfing, 2005: 215).

As for the policy analysts/organisers, their relation to the client commissioning the deliberative experiment is like professional civil servants or hired consultants.

Of course, this fact will be perceived by the participants and thus influence their attitudes and conduct towards them. In addition, most of the responsibility in answering the other questions on the design of the M–PDP falls to them. These questions are about the precise delineation of subject and scope of the deliberative process (what?), about participant recruitment and selection (who?, also why?), about prior alignment between commissioner, analyst (team) and participants about methodical aspects and closure of the deliberative process, including the analysts' role(s) itself (how?). Moreover, these questions are interrelated in many ways.

Substantive and participation closure in M–PDPs are highly interrelated. For instance, issue and scope determination is heavily influenced by balancing between two perspectives. One is substantive closure through loyalty to the claims, concerns and issues moving the commissioner in organising an M–PDP. The other is to let closure be more pragmatically arrived at through participant recruitment and selection, which requires responsive focusing (Loeber, 2004: 289) by taking seriously the claims, concerns and issues of the (prospective) participants themselves. Inviting certain stakeholders to participate means inclusion or exclusion, highlighting or de-emphasising certain aspects of the issue. Delimiting the scope of the issue, especially in time or institutionalised policy domain, includes, excludes or marginalises certain participants. This chicken-and-egg problem between issue delimitation and participant recruitment affects the entire deliberation process and its closure. In truly responsive focusing, participants influence the borders drawn around an issue. However, should new stakeholders be invited when the issue broadens, and some previously invited stakeholders leave the project if the issue becomes more narrowly circumscribed? Will commissioners still be interested in financing M–PDPs if they effectively have to fully respect the unstructured nature of issues by giving to participants every right to redefine and restructure the issue?

How are the 'stakeholders' constructed by the initiators; what are the 'stakes' and who are the 'holders', especially if the issue for deliberation is messy or wicked indeed? How to avoid the participation paradox, that is, that those most likely to have contributions to make are those who will make themselves heard anyway in the normal venues of policy making? How to deal with 'stakes' that are short term, but issues that are long range? How to find 'holders' if the 'stakes' are future generations of people, or nature? Should there be 'hot' deliberation between opinionated, maybe prejudiced participants with high stakes in the issue; or should one go for 'cold' deliberation between open-minded participants with lower stakes in the issue (Fung, 2003: 345)? Here 'who?' spills over into the 'how best to deliberate' question.

Meanwhile, deliberative policy analysts have developed a rather well-stocked toolkit of methods. However, key questions about the political biases of these methods, their propensities in eliciting or suppressing true pluralism of views, their catalytic functions for mutual learning and their impact on the quality of debate between participants, have hardly drawn sufficient attention (but see Hisschemöller,

2005, 2009). Given that M-PDPs cost time, money and personnel, concerning the 'how?' question there is a lot of implicit and unacknowledged influence by commissioners, who usually constrain all of the above. For example, although detailed studies show that 'ordinary' policy preparation processes on complex issues by civil servants from several departments take between two and four years (Hoppe et al, 1995), the time given for the completion of M-PDPs hardly ever surpasses six months to one year. In practice, this means that analysts/organisers have to pay more attention to project than to process management. This bears heavily on the issue of closure in deliberations. Novel ideas simply require time to emerge, participants need time to learn to understand each other's perspectives and ideas, and then to jointly elaborate new ideas into some state of 'joint construction' or maturity for serious political consideration. Given unrealistic time constraints, policy analysts/organisers have to use rather crude methods for bringing debates to closure (like the arbitrary time constraints mentioned above); or, alternatively, have to avoid the issue of closure and yet, somehow, write up some allegedly 'shared' conclusions. If stakeholders subsequently refrain from (publicly) endorsing them, politicians can hardly be expected to pay serious attention.

Another way in which the 'who?' and 'how?' questions interfere is in determining the purpose of the M-PDP. If only creativity and novelty of ideas matter, one would rather avoid participants with some relationship to the 'usual suspects' in the relevant policy network. However, when analysts are at all able to recruit truly visionary and creative participants from outside the well-known pools of expertise, 'outsider' participation will reduce the probability of uptake of the output of the deliberative exercise in normal policy making. The other way round, maximising chances for uptake by deliberate recruitment of participants with a clear reputation and stature with a 'constituency' of vested stakeholder groups may impair the quality and creativity of debate (Loeber, 2004: 226-7).

Throughput problems

In the actual process of deliberation, the 'how?' questions starts to loom large. There may be a well-stocked toolkit of methods for deliberative and frame-reflective, participatory policy analysts. Yet, this does not mean a well-developed, articulated consensus among analysts on the methodology for conducting M-PDPs. At best, one may speak of practitioners who discuss their experiences with peers in what may become an international community of practice. In spite of methodological indeterminacy, there are general ambitions and guidelines for sparking off responsible political judgement and learning in M-PDP's about unstructured problems. Inspired by Loeber (2004: 61-9), three maxims appear to orient such deliberative process:

- M-PDPs allow *both 'spectator' and 'actor' perspectives* on unstructured problems: 'Analysis that is intended to inform political judgment should adopt a hermeneutic approach to data collection which does not rule out the possibility or legitimacy of employing empirical–analytic methods to assess relevant facts, and which allows for a deliberative mode of exchanging information that results from such an assessment.'

- M-PDPs foster not just a meeting of horizons, but make a serious effort at a *fusion of horizons*: 'Analysis that is intended to inform political judgment should be organized as a participatory process, in which actors representing different perspectives on an issue participate in such a way that their "particularities" and viewpoints are sufficiently acknowledged in the deliberation to bear on the resulting problem definition.'

- M-PDPs are about *learning about action*: 'Analysis that is intended to inform political judgment should be organized in such a way that it may induce learning on the part of the participants as a result of an exchange of information (i) on the problem situation, (ii) on the way others define the problem, and (iii) on the particularities of the contexts in which these others operate, so as to make possible a reflection on their own interpretive frames, and to enable participants [to reflect on the conditions in the real world, under which they can, RH] act in line with the new insights.'

In practice, these guidelines or maxims pose challenges to three interrelated problem clusters: fostering conditions for real learning, maintaining some sort of power balance between participants with sometimes very unequal resources in the real world, and the role(s) of the analyst/organiser.

The spectator/actor split in deliberation requires accommodation of quantitative and qualitative research and findings in M-PDPs. As many stakeholders are used to, and scientific experts are trained in quantitative research methods and findings, dealing with qualitative approaches is considered problematic – even though qualitative approaches are intrinsically more suitable for deliberative exercises. In addition, scientists operate in disciplinary 'tribes' of peers. In M-PDPs on unstructured problems, they find themselves exposed to multidisciplinary contexts and highly unusual forms of peer review, extending even to non-scientists. For many scientists it is very hard to unlearn to think and act through disciplinary paradigms, and become truly open to interdisciplinary collaboration and transdisciplinary, extended peer review. Analysts/organisers should be careful to invite scientists with the requisite attitude and skills. More often than not, scientists have a role to play in M-PDPs as experts or expert advisers. To the extent that knowledge is power, their role vis-à-vis the non-scientific participants is ambivalent. On the one hand, it is argued that scientific information is unequally distributed; hence, for the sake of an equal power balance, information deficits should be counteracted through lectures, consultations and other means of making scientific information available. On the other hand, this invokes the deficit model in public understanding of science, which invites scientists to be teachers and all others to be students. Since deliberation, not education, is the purpose of an M-PDP, the teacher–student roles may insert the very power imbalances they were intended to remedy.

Regarding the effort to go beyond a mere exchange of perspectives and achieve some kind of fusion of horizons as closure in deliberation, analysts and participants suffer from ignorance and gaps in their knowledge. So far, insights into the impact of emotional dynamics, rhetoric, eloquence and charisma in M-PDPs on the power balance between participants and the quality of debate and deliberation is limited (Van Stokkom, 2005, 2006). Usually, it is doable to check for increases in instrumental or first-order learning among participants. But it is much harder to show second-order learning, that is, a certain method's effectiveness in inducing serious reflection on their own interpretive frames among participants; let alone increased skills in coming to shared insights in constructive political judgements, or learning to learn (third-order learning) itself. Consequently, it proves very difficult to establish the quality level of a debate, and therefore the value-added of deliberation in M-PDPs compared to, say, debates among experienced politicians in parliamentary subcommittees (Pellizoni, 2001; Steiner et al, 2004; Hisschemöller et al, 2009).

All this impinges on the so-called expertise and role of the deliberative analyst or organiser of M-PDPs. It was already pointed out above that the usual institutional setting of an M-PDP forces the analyst/organiser into the role of public servant or hired consultant. Hence, the other participants ascribe to them an inherent interest in consensus creation and producing knowledge usable for their commissioner or principal. Even when the analyst/organiser is prepared to take some action in guarding the power balance among participants, this role ascription will impair such efforts. But apart from that, even if both commissioner and analyst are committed to real change in standing policies and political judgements and framings of unstructured problems, what is the role of the analyst vis-à-vis the other participants? Facilitator, process manager, project manager, director of the show, counsellor to all parties, interpreter between all parties, change agent for the commissioner or servant for empowerment of the weaker parties?

Output and outcome problems

Path dependence theory suggests that the weight of the past may block serious policy change. Policy choices that are objects of deliberation in M-PDPs may be so locked in chains of past choices, that they are not easily unlocked. On top of that, the point with mini-public and stakeholder projects is that their output and outcome problems are quite comparable to those of non-routine, non-incremental administrative policy making. The problem is how to find a niche somewhere to think creatively, and engage in serious deliberation; and, returning from the niche with some fresh and productive ideas, how to insert them into normal political power games (Hoppe, 1983) and ongoing public-opinion-forming and social-learning processes. After the deliberate suspension of power differentials and lifting the constraints on deliberation and debate deriving from 'normal' political manoeuvring and strategising, all the institutional constraints return in full force to test the robustness of an M–PDP's results. Goodin and Dryzek (2006: 219) call this the problem of the 'macro–political up–take of mini–publics'.

Such uptake depends, first, on the dissemination strategies of the M–PDP's direct output. In fact, in many cases a carefully elaborated trajectory for follow–up care is considered an integral part an M–PDP. Potentially, there are many different types of addressees; and each one requires a different dissemination strategy. Igniting a large-scale public debate is very different from briefing department's policy-making officials who may be interested in using the M–PDP's ideas in their own policy proposals. In the former case, highly visible public figures may be recruited to present the major messages to influential media in popularised ways. In the latter case, picking a reputable analyst to give oral presentations and run a workshop or small conference is more effective. Which dissemination strategies are most effective for which audiences, or in influencing important policy-making and political decision-making processes, is an empirical matter. Another issue for more empirical research is the potential feed–forward between choice of methods during the deliberation process (the throughput phase) and dissemination strategy (output phase). There are cases where the commissioning party is willing to compromise the M–PDP's integrity as a deliberative-interpretive project in the wrapping up of its conclusions and activities, in order to facilitate its dissemination and boost its persuasive power to relevant non-participating audiences and interests (Loeber, 2004: 277-8, 292).

More generally, dissemination is a balancing act. On the one hand, one would want to safeguard the integrity of the deliberative project in outputs that convey, if only vicariously, the experience of intense deliberation and the efforts spent in getting to meaningful, valid closure. On the other hand, one is almost forced to give in to the pressure of the media, politicians and interest groups for soundbite-like summaries of the major message. Part of the dissemination efforts is for the sake of accountability of the commissioner and organiser to the public. Fung (2003: 346) writes that this is of particular relevance 'if we do not take it for granted (…) that deliberation and negotiation between stakeholders necessarily yield outputs that are beneficial to the public interest. If this is uncertain, then participatory procedures must be all the more subject to … *ex post* control.' In addition, the commissioner and organiser will desire to prevent others from selectively shopping or cherry picking from the proposals resulting from an M–PDP's total output.

However, much like authors cannot prevent readers from producing their own interpretation of a text, so the disseminators of M–PDPs' outputs cannot control the longer-term outcomes. Hopefully, there is the ripple effect of throwing a pebble in the pond, but this is uncertain. Goodin and Dryzek (2006: 225-37) list several potentially beneficial effects of M–PDPs.[8] Their outputs may in the near or longer future be taken up in normal policy-making and political decision-making processes. Media coverage of M–PDPs' outputs, if sufficiently extensive, may inform larger publics and help in sparking off public debates. M–PDPs may function somewhat like focus groups in marketing strategies. They 'market test' particular policy ideas for feasibility and acceptability for key stakeholders in society. Because participant recruitment for M–PDPs is considered a rather open procedure, they resist the co-optive politics of bringing in (alleged) opponents of proposed policies in standard consultation processes. M–PDPs can function as legitimatory devices for policies in whose production they are a part. The above-mentioned cases of expansion of Schiphol Airport and a second Rotterdam Harbour offer perfect examples.

Unfortunately, Goodin and Dryzek do not pay attention to other effects of M–PDPs, especially in relation to their embeddedness in an institutional setting of representative democracy. For example, following in the footsteps of Murray Edelman, one may as well consider the market-testing and legitimation effect of deliberative-*cum*-participatory exercises a mere symbolic ornament to the representative and corporatist modes of governance. The appearance of open participation in deliberative processes lends additional legitimacy to policies already considered, proposed and (almost) decided upon by elites. The ad-hoc character of many M–PDPs may even lead one to hypothesise that they channel away urgent political issues from genuine public debate in agonistic political settings of political mobilisation and agenda building. M–PDPs might be just one more instrument for depoliticisation and agenda control.

Many civic associations and non-governmental organisations are deeply involved in developing alternative problem framings and alternatives to dominant opinions about solutions. Yet, they frequently refuse to participate in M–PDPs on issues of their intense concern because they do not trust the intentions of the authorities that set them up. In the Dutch GM-food public debate, environmental groups and other associations walked out of the organised public debate because they felt cheated about their possibilities for influencing the agenda and focus of debate (Hage, 2002). More generally, they consider M–PDP's as public relations machines for manipulating public opinion. They see themselves as the legitimate problem owners; and much better representatives of a critical public opinion and a larger public than those invited by authorities to participate. In systems of representative democracy, authorities that initiate deliberative experiments on an ad-hoc basis, yet fail to institutionalise relations between deliberative procedures, representative bodies and their normal processes of decision making, do indeed deserve suspicion. By keeping open the option for themselves to not even respond to the outputs and recommendations of M–PDPs, they give the impression of not taking seriously procedures they have themselves set in motion (Joly and Marris, 2003).

In discussing the problems and perplexities of actually conducting deliberative-*cum*-participatory policy exercises in the context of representative democratic institutions and modes of governance, we have in fact hit upon an important gap in the meta-theory on democracies of problems as formulated in Chapter Eight. There, from a system's perspective, relationships between the four matches of problem structure type and democracy type were considered complementary. Hence, the possibility of thinking about meta-governance as shifting from one match to another; and, given the delays of path dependence and the hypercomplexity of capitalist and democratic governance systems, gently nudging the entire system to more deliberative modes through relatively unobtrusive strategies of interpolable balancing, like layering and conversion. Nevertheless, this picture may well be too rosy. A politics of deliberation will always meet its limits in a politics of vision and/or power (Dauenhauer, 1986). Therefore, in the concluding chapter, some blacks and greys will be mixed into the overall picture in order not to lose sight of the ironies of real power politics, and thereby safeguard reflexivity in meta-governance.

Notes

[1] Obama's campaign team allegedly heavily relied on the new media and internet to mobilise especially the younger segments of the electorate. Thus, one has to await a more definitive analysis of Barack Obama's successful presidential campaign to know whether this judgement can be upheld.

[2] Schudson (1998: 310-3111) discusses 'monitorial citizenship' as implying that 'the ... citizen engages in environmental surveillance more than information-gathering':'I would propose that the obligation of citizens to know enough to participate intelligently in governmental affairs be understood as a monitorial obligation. Monitorial citizens scan (rather than read) the informational environment in a way so that they may be alerted to a wide variety of issues for a wide variety of ends and may be mobilized around those issue in a large variety of ways.'

[3] Teknologi Radet (www.tekno.dk/subpage.php3?article=468andtoppic=kategori12an dlanguage=uk; emphasis added): 'The conference runs from Friday to Monday.... On the first day of the official conference programme, experts answer the questions posed in advance by the lay panel.... On the Saturday, the panel asks the expert panel to elaborate and clarify their presentations and the audience is also allowed to ask questions. Following the conclusion of the official part of the conference at noon on the Saturday, the citizens' panel begins discussing the expert presentations. *The goal is for the panel to achieve consensus and to subsequently write the final document with their assessments and recommendation.* On the Sunday, the citizens' panel continues discussing and formulating the content of the final document. *Typically, the work of the panel goes on throughout the night and is not concluded until consensus regarding the document has been reached.* The last day of the conference begins with the panel presenting their final document to the conference participants.'

[4] One could also mention efforts to make traditional, formal institutes in representative democracy, like Parliaments and expert advisory bodies, more deliberative and reflexive; examples for the Dutch situation are given by Halffman and Hoppe (2005: 145-6).

[5] A short description is given in Fung (2003: 360-2).

[6] Kriesi and Trechsel (2008: 115) state that, in Switzerland, all political actors capable of making a credible referendum threat – including major interest groups and even social movement organisations – have been integrated into the decision-making process by

way of elaborate pre-parliamentary consultation procedures. Obviously, then, the mere possibility of a referendum forces political elites to pay more attention to all kinds of people's representatives.

[7] Loeber's descriptive model has been successfully applied in detailed comparative descriptions, analyses and evaluations of three cases: the Phosphate Forum on clean laundry and clean water, the Novel Protein Foods project on sustainable technology development and the Gideon project on developing proposals on sustainable crop production for the Dutch Parliament.

[8] I have left out positive effects to be expected only from other than stakeholder-directed forms of deliberative projects, such as popular oversight, confidence building, and political mobilisation due to participation.

TEN

Responsible and hopeful governance of problems

We need to accept the impossibility of reasoning all the way to solutions, thus leaving generous room for power and arbitrariness. (Lindblom, 1999: 63)

Since ... in the density of social reality each decision brings unexpected consequences, and since, moreover, man responds to these surprises by inventions which transform the problem, there is no situation without hope.... (Maurice Merleau-Ponty, quoted in Dauenhauer, 1986: 246)

Introduction

This final chapter is devoted to reflecting on the answers to the questions formulated in Chapter Two. It looks back on the intellectual journey in this book, and asks how far we have come. Thus, the first section is a succinct list of answers to the questions raised about the governance of problems – about the meaning of the 'governance of problems' perspective itself, about the translation dynamics in *socio-political contexts*, about the framing and design dynamics or *policy-analytic aspects*, and about participation and democracy from an institutional or *polity-oriented perspective*. The second section picks up an implied question that has deliberately been sidestepped so far, that is, the dilemmatic relationship between puzzling and powering. It was argued that meta-governance as deliberate interpolable balancing is the only possibility of creating more space for deliberative-democratic policy making. However, one should be aware of the inevitable tension between powering and puzzling in policy problem structuring. Even though better deliberative-*cum*-participatory designs and more institutional spaces may lead to more successful avoidance of wrong-problem problems, the methods, rules and procedures of problem-sensitive and frame-reflective policy analysis may well be instrumentalised as one way of power politics, or fighting over policy. The last section grapples with the issue of how to respond to this inevitable tendency.

Propositions on the governance of problems

What does the 'governance of problems' mean?

The fundamental idea of the book was that it makes sense to see democratic politics as a question-and-answer game, and policy making as the governance of problems. The possibility of viewing politics as a question-and-answer game, and policy making as an interrogatory debate on collective problems, is rooted in an image of man as freedom-in-responsibility, as 'homo respondens'. The focus on problem processing derives from another image-of-man assumption, namely that man is unity-in-disharmony. The disharmony between man and his own self-image, between man and fellow human beings, and between 'is' and 'ought', turns the question-and-answer game into a contest between those who may pose which question, when, to whom; and those whose answers are to count, and why. The entire spectacle – the ensemble of institutions, beliefs, practices and rules in use by rulers and ruled to manage the question-and-answer game – was called the *governance of problems*. To get a rich picture, this governance of problems ought to be studied from three different, but interdependent angles – governance as puzzling, powering and participation.

A second key notion was that in the governance of problems, *problem finding* deserves at least equal, and perhaps more, attention than *problem solving*. In day-to-day politics and professional policy analysis, however, it is the other way round. Legitimation of answers through a mix of rules for political authority and scientific methodology is more important than posing the right questions. Hence, much policy analysis is the sophisticated answer to a wrong problem. The rest of the book is a sustained reflection on what better avoidance of wrong-problem problems means for policy analysis. In an important sense, it is a rethinking and updating of the Lasswellian idea, dating from the 1950s, of policy analysis as a problem-oriented intellectual endeavour. The later turn from government to governance, and the simultaneous scientisation of politics and politicisation of science (Weingart, 1983; Hoppe, 2005) make such a rethinking unavoidable for the viability of the field of policy analysis.

To get more grip on this broad *problématique,* three sets of questions about the governance of problems were distinguished (see Figure 2.4, Chapter Two):

- questions about *translation dynamics*, that is, how policy designs are attributed meaning in the socio-political contexts of cultures in society and policy networks;
- questions about *framing and design dynamics*, this is, about problem structuring as cognitive process, about how and why problem framings are socially and politically constructed and distributed by analysts and practitioners; and
- questions about *institutions* for the framing and design dynamics, and *modes of citizen participation* in these dynamics.

Answers to these questions developed in this book are listed below as propositions on the governance of problems.

Translation dynamics in the governance of problems

The *first question* in this set was: how to usefully conceptualise problem structuring and problem structures? The answer is given through a typology of policy problem structures and a number of related propositions:

1. *Image-of man-assumptions*: human beings act boundedly, ecologically and socially rational.
2. Proximate and authoritative policy makers are prone to using an *acceptability heuristic* in accounting for their preferences and choices in problem framing and problem definition.
3. Acting on an acceptability heuristic, they confront different potential situations, depending on *degree of consensus* on norms and values at stake, and *degree of certainty* about required and available knowledge (for solving the problem as framed or defined).
4. An authoritative public policy problem definition is *structured*, if the proximate and authoritative policy makers, as members of a dominant advocacy coalition or policy community, are closer to agreement on norms and values at stake, and closer to certainty on required and available knowledge.
5. A problem definition is *unstructured*, the more policy makers in an issue network disagree on norms and values at stake, and remain uncertain about required and available knowledge.
6. A problem definition is *moderately structured with normative agreement*, the more policy makers in a policy subsystem agree on norms and values at stake, and the more they remain uncertain about required and available knowledge; policy debates around the policy problem focus on effectiveness, efficiency and (the distribution of) risks and other side effects.
7. A problem definition is *moderately structured with knowledge certainty*, the more policy makers in the issue network disagree on the normative aspects and ethics of the problem, and the more certainty they have on required and available knowledge.
8. Working on public problems or *problem processing* involves *problem structuring* as a central socio-cognitive process to bridge problem finding, framing, definition and solving.
9. Problem structuring as a process depends on possible and plausible modes of problem decomposition and the history of constraint sequencing; path dependencies lead to the institutionalisation of problem definitions, or clusters of problem definitions in issue or policy domains.

The *second question* in this set was: do different social cultures alive among the citizenry align with different problem types and structures, and vice versa? It was affirmatively argued that:

10. Problem framings and definitions are used by proximate and authoritative policy makers to mobilise political support among the masses and in civil society through strategies of agenda setting and agenda denial for each other's favoured problem frames and definitions.
11. Policy makers with hierarchist cultural backgrounds exhibit the tendency to frame and define policy problems as structured (focal or default strategy); they will only have a weak tendency to frame and define problems as moderately structured (in either of the two variations; secondary or fallback strategy); and they will avoid framing and defining problems as unstructured.
12. Policy makers with isolationist or fatalist backgrounds will tend to frame and define policy problems as unstructured; if forced, they will approach problem framing and definition as maxmax-win or minmin-avoidance structured problems.
13. Policy makers with enclavistic or broadly egalitarian backgrounds will primarily frame or define policy problems as moderately structured problems with knowledge certainty; they will be sympathetic to problem framings or definitions as unstructured; if forced to structure them, they will be biased in favour of framing and defining policy problems as moderately structured with normative consensus on fair distribution of burdens and benefits.
14. Policy makers with individualist cultural backgrounds demonstrate strong tendencies to define and frame policy problems as moderately structured with normative agreement; they will be sympathetic to framing or defining problems as structured if at all possible; and they will avoid any other type of problem framings and definitions.

The *third question* was: do problem types or structures co-evolve with network types? Findings could be listed in the following propositions:

15. Using network theory, four types of policy politics can be specified that tend to generate the four types of policy problems, and vice versa, in a socially reproductive process.
16. Normal regulatory policy in professional or technical communities tends to reproduce structured problems; their policy politics may be characterised as rule.
17. Normal advocacy coalition politics in well-institutionalised, oligopolistic networks tend to reproduce moderately structured problems with normative consensus; their style of policy politics is negotiation and (problem-driven) search.
18. Transformative discourse coalition politics in designed and tightly managed networks tend to work on moderately structured problems with value ambiguity and antagonism, but knowledge certainty; their style of policy politics is accommodationist and directed at conflict management.

19. Open, emergent policy networks around unstructured, wicked problems have mostly agonistic politics, crisis management, and (charismatic) leadership, or a style of deliberation and learning.
20. In the real world, the types co-exist, overlap and co-evolve, giving politicians and policy makers opportunities for combinations and shifts in efforts to move away from unstructured problems, or to break up entrenched policy communities and structured problems.
21. This can be done in forms of meta-governance, taking the shape of interpolable balancing through venue creation, or policy and institutional entrepreneurship and leadership.

Framing and design dynamics in the governance of problems

The *first question* in this set about framing and design dynamics was: what epistemological changes or 'drift' may be observed in the development of policy analysis since the 1950s to the present? The answer to this question is summarised in the next propositions:

22. Generally, epistemological justification in policy analysis has moved from instrumental rationality to types of fallibilist-pragmatist rationality, from analycentrism to an argumentative turn – from 'speaking truth to power' to 'making sense together'.
23. Policy analysis was originally dominated by technocratic aspirations and instrumental rationality, expressing itself in analycentrism, neo-positivism and critical rationalism as dominant paradigms.
24. Since the 1990s, a post-positivist, or argumentative or interpretive turn has become equally strong, expressing itself in a 'river delta' of new paradigms: relativism, critical theory, forensic (argumentative, deliberative) analysis, and a participatory approach.

A *second question* was: is there a link, and if yes, to what extent, between styles of doable policy analysis in the practice of policy work and these epistemological debates in academic policy analysis? The answer found was:

25. There is evidence for the existence of a number of recurring *core activities* in policy analysis: research and analysis, design and recommendation, strategic advice, clarifications of values and arguments, democratisation, and mediation.
26 What actually happens is that analysts, in a pragmatic and context-dependent way, and more or less successfully, *make policy analysis doable as a mix of core activities*:
    - a rational style, or research and analysis combined with recommendation and advice;
    - an argumentative style, or research and analysis while also clarifying values and argument systems;

- a client advice style, mixing recommendation and advice on a policy problem with strategic advice for a principal;
- a participatory style, introducing the critical clarification of values and arguments into the democratisation of expertise;
- a process management style, linking up mediation and strategic advice; and finally
- an interactive style, in which mediation for mutual understanding and consensus building is linked to democratisation efforts.

27. Prescriptively, the styles of doable policy analysis may be turned into a reflective heuristics for applying Dunn's rule of methodological congruence, that is, decisions on which style of policy analysis and its toolkit of concomitant methods is appropriate given one's perception and definition of the politico-administrative environment and type of policy problem at hand.

Institutional questions for a governance of problems

The third and final set of questions pertained to polity-oriented, or institutional, dimensions in the democratic and participatory governance of problems. Two questions were posed. Is there a correspondence between problem structures and types or styles of democracy? How is it possible to deal better with wrong-problem problems, especially with unstructured problems? Regarding the former problem, three propositions were advanced:

28. The problem types appear to correspond to types of political arguments, along the axes of degree of government intervention (high: fairness; low: market) and degree of societal participation (high: participation; low: technical).
    - political discourse on structured problems is characterised by strong influences from both a technical and a market approach;
    - on moderately structured problems with considerable normative agreement, by a combination of arguments from a market and participatory approach;
    - on moderately structured problems with considerable agreement on knowledge and instruments, by a coalescence of the fairness and technical approach;
    - and, finally, on unstructured problems, by a synthesis of the participatory and fairness approach.
29. This convergence between policy and political approaches also extends to concepts of democracy:
    - The rule approach to structured problems is compatible with a thin procedural interpretation of democracy as a mechanism for the peaceful circulation of elites under restricted popular influence.
    - The negotiation-and-search approach to moderately structured problems with normative consensus is compatible with standard accounts of liberal,

pluralist democracy; either in interest group theories or corporatist variations.

- The accommodation approach to moderately structured problems with knowledge certainty appeals to an elite–cartel democracy.
- The learning approach to unstructured problems calls for participatory-*cum*-deliberative modes of democracy.

30. The four different concepts of democracy, not separately but *jointly*, constitute an adequate description of the working of democracy in practice; they comprise inherently contradictory but constituent parts of the set of beliefs, rules and procedures that are applied to the democratic governance of different types of policy problems; they jointly constitute a meta–theory about the *maximisation of the intelligence of democracy in the governance of problems*.

Regarding the question of how to deal better with the wrong-problem problem and especially unstructured problems, a last set of propositions was advanced:

31. In political systems dominated by representative democracy, politicians and proximate policy makers frame deliberative and participatory exercises as one set of possibilities for themselves in a list of venues for issue framing, agenda setting, policy formulation and policy evaluation.

32. Instead of a continuum from no to high citizen control, there appear to be five fundamentally different and discontinuous modes of citizen participation:
- participation as consultation: to encourage comments on policy proposals; participants' views may, but need not necessarily, influence subsequent formal policy formulation;
- participation as partnership: citizens, interest groups or civil society associations give policy advice through ad-hoc or formal advisory boards; sometimes followed by involvement in policy co-production, co-regulation and (community) co-management of implementation schemes;
- participation as standing influence: through formal legal hearing and administrative review procedures;
- participation as consumer choice: in service delivery citizens influence product specification or preferred provider choice, for example through client councils;
- participation as control: citizens make final decisions through referendums.

33. Different modes of participation are more compatible with different types of problem structures:
- a rule approach to structure problems is compatible with standing or consumer choice;
- a negotiation-and-search approach to moderately structured problems with normative consensus is compatible to partnerships and consultation;
- an accommodation approach to moderately structured problems with knowledge certainty is compatible with consultation, or partnership, or standing.

- a deliberative and/or participatory approach to unstructured problems is compatible with partnership, or, given sufficient spaces for deliberation, control.

34. In political systems with representative democracy, participatory and/or deliberative modes of doable policy analysis run into persistent problems in the input, throughput and output phase, largely because of motives and mechanisms to do with proposition # 31.

This list of 34 propositions can be read as a succinct overview of the argument so far. Yet, especially the last proposition, suggests that the three angles from which the governance of problems was analysed – powering, puzzling and participation – entail an important question not yet adequately dealt with. That question can be formulated as: what is the relation between powering and puzzling? Participation is either participation-in-puzzling or in powering; hence the question is limited to only the first two P's.

Asymmetry and polarity between puzzling and powering

Knowledge/puzzling and power/instigation

Ever since Francis Bacon, we suspect that knowledge is and generates power. Later, others like Nietzsche and Foucault argued the other way around: power defines knowledge, rather, defines what is to count as 'rational' knowledge of empirical or normative 'truth'. Given such widely diverging views, it is perhaps understandable that in theory and research on policy, planning, management and organisation the theme of their relationship is hardly addressed seriously. Yet, in view of some of the conclusions reached here, it is compelling to reflect on the relationship between knowledge or puzzling, and political interaction or powering in policy analysis as the governance of problems. The very distinction between 'policy' and 'politics' is rooted in somehow keeping 'puzzling' or analysis and 'powering' or politics apart in the governance of problems.

Like in the English language, the Dutch language has separate words for politics ('*politiek*') and policy ('*beleid*'). Somewhere in the beginning of the 20th century, '*beleid*' became a popular buzzword. Like the French playwright Molière's character who, to his own surprise, discovered he had been speaking prose all his life, so the Dutch started to fancy '*beleid*' or policy over '*politiek*' or politics. Politics acquired negative connotations like controversy, partisanship, manipulation and opportunism. Policy, on the contrary, was bestowed all the positive connotations of being businesslike, expert, objective and consensual (Van de Graaf and Hoppe, 1996: 15-18). The ascendancy of the concept of policy over politics is understandable from the double meaning of '*beleid*' in the Dutch language – on the one hand, leadership, and, on the other, prudence. These etymological roots strongly suggest that those engaged in policy work were statespeople and experts of a certain prudence and wisdom, rather than mere politicians concerned with the power games of sordid politics.

The result was that in everyday discourse politics came to be talked about more and more as policy making, or a contest over policies. This was reflected even in academic discourse, as in Wildavsky's (1980) notion of policy making as both intellectual cogitation and political interaction. Yet, this very notion reveals the implicit paradox in the double meaning of '*beleid*' or policy, namely the opposition between reason and power, and between reflection and decisive action in politics. In a short course on philosophy, German philosopher Karl Jaspers, mentor and friend of Hannah Arendt, points out that this paradox inheres in the very nature of politics (1974: 81): 'Politics is oriented in reference to two opposites: potential coercion and free association.... In their essential meaning, power politics and deliberative politics are mutually exclusive; yet, in their conjunction is the practice of politics, at least until this day and, as far as we can see, in the future.'

Truly reflexive governance is possible only in a well-articulated consciousness of this paradox between 'puzzling' or deliberative politics and 'powering' or collective will formation in power politics. This is even more necessary for a reflexive governance of problems in democratic politics; especially if such governance desires to create more opportunities and public spaces for deliberation and participation by citizens and stakeholders. After all, such governance seeks to rebalance democratic politics towards the pole of reason, deliberation and learning, and away from the pole of power backed up by authority and potential coercion. The feasibility of such an ambitious political project depends on one's insights and beliefs about the exact relationship between them. Therefore, it is imperative to dwell a bit longer on the exact relationship between the elements of the paradox.

'Knowledge' was already discussed in Chapter Two. There it was argued that it is a problematic and multifaceted concept. Knowledge is different from data and information. Data are loose 'bits' like numbers, words, sounds and pictures. When organised one way or another, they are the building blocks of information, for example as texts, statistics, tapes or movies. Knowledge comes about when intellects process, make sense of and give meaning to information. Rooney et al (2003a: 3) say 'we are better off not talking about knowledge (a noun) but about giving meaning and developing understandings in the act of knowing (a verb)'. Knowing is a complex, socially distributed activity that situates knowers in relation to larger interpretive contexts and other knowers. Puzzling actually is what knowers do when, in processing problems, they try to make sense of the particulars of their actions and contexts by relating them to larger interpretive contexts. Some may do this through religious faith in truthful life revealed to saints who wrote holy books; others through their faith in the methods of science to arrive at approximations of the truth as external, objective reality; and to organise bits of articulated knowledge in so-called 'universal', or at least more-than-contextual bodies of knowledge. The latter faith is more likely to be called rational. When speaking about 'puzzling', these more rational forms of sense making in problem processing are actually referred to. In puzzling, people communicate with each other through argumentation; they are persuaded to give up or advance positions on claims based on the force of the best argument. In that sense, most treatises on policy analysis are about rational puzzling on some collectivity's behalf.

'Powering' was introduced and discussed in general terms in Chapter One. Wrong (1979: 2) advanced a simple, yet effective definition of power as 'the capacity of some persons to produce intended and foreseen effects on others' (see also Giddens, 1984). This definition covers most modes of 'power' as distinguished by political scientists – control over manifest decision making, control over agenda-setting and non-decisions, and control over beliefs about needs and self-identity (Lukes, 1974). The definition is compatible with the idea of dispositional power, that is, people and organisations having more money, knowledge, personnel and technologies may in principle (not always in actuality) mobilise more power. The definition does not deny that the actual use of power is always structurally embedded and thus constrained in historically and socially constructed institutions and discourses. Yet, it stresses that people, even though in structurally 'given' situations and thus from starting positions that are not of their own making, always actively strive to change power relations – sometimes successfully. The definition also stresses both the enabling and constraining uses of power. As the example of technology as power makes clear, especially for problem processing, power is not a zero-sum game in which one person's or group's gain in power is another's loss. Although increases in power of some can weaken others, they need not necessarily do so. Power always poses a threat to freedom. Nevertheless, it is also necessary for freedom to assert and maintain itself. The ubiquitous character of coalition-building behaviour in policy making should have opened power analysts' eyes to the intransitive or non-zero-sum character of power (Arts and Van Tatenhove, 2004).

In problem processing, powering takes the form of mobilising the help of others, that is, *instigation*, or 'sparking off contributory actions in other persons' (De Jouvenel, 1963: 8). This can be done amicably; as happens each time an instigator approaches the *instigandus* as participant in a shared group to which the instigandus feels attached and which (co-)determines their political identity (for example, as member of the same political party, interest group, old-boys network or fellow countryman). In all such cases, 'powering' means an appeal to the instigandus's confidence in the instigator and loyalty to him and the collective he stands for; or 'that capital feature of the "political animal", the propensity to comply' (De Jouvenel, 1963: 73; there are excellent practical examples for the US in Halperin, 1974; and for the European Union in Eppink, 2007). In other cases, 'powering' or instigation rests on credible threats, occasionally the actual use of psychological or physical force. Only in a minority of cases, instigation rests on legitimate hierarchy, in which the power holder has a legal or otherwise socially acknowledged right to command, and the power subject an obligation to obey.

In powering, people communicate usually not through commands but by influencing each other's perception of the costs and benefits of commitment to a particular action. This may be a very discursive or argumentative process. Yet, in argumentation as puzzling the illocutionary speech act, the *internal* power of the argument (Pellizoni, 2001: 62), the 'what' of the argument is at stake, irrespective of who argues to whom. In powering it is the perlocutionary speech act, not the argument per se, but its *external* power (Pellizoni, 2001: 60), what one achieves by arguing something, that is at stake. Usually this is the relationship between the speaker and the listener, and the commitment of the listener to act upon the instigator's bidding. In more important cases, the inclusion or exclusion from the circle of competent and eligible speakers and listeners itself is at stake.

It is precisely because, contrary to many easy distinctions, arguing plays a role in both puzzling and powering that more reflection on their relationship is unavoidable. Such reflection may take the form of arguments in favour of some functional or principled primacy – of puzzling over powering, or the other way around.

Primacy for puzzling?

One author explicitly arguing in favour of a primacy for puzzling is the German political and policy scientist Thomas Saretzki. He examines and compares argumentation and negotiation as modes of communication in politics and policy making. His conclusion is that argumentation has a kind of communicative primacy because there can be no negotiation without argumentation; yet, there can be argumentation without negotiation (Saretzki, 1996: 36; also see Landwehr, 2009:110–128).

Stripping the concept from all thematic, contextual and actor role contingencies, Saretzki describes argumentation as the mode of communication for the vindication of claims of *validity* for empirical-theoretical and normative propositions. In case of doubt about the validity of empirical-theoretical claims, criteria of factual evidence and theoretical consistency are appealed to. In case of doubt about normative claims, criteria of consistency and impartiality are decisive. Negotiation is described as the mode of communication for the *credibility* of pragmatic, action-oriented claims or demands. In case of doubt, one has to establish the credibility of the negotiating parties. This may be done by examining the seriousness or flexibility in which they represent their demands; and by examining their preparedness and capability to really act on the promises, threats and exit options supporting their demands. Thus, in case of argumentation, the result is determined by argumentative power, or symbolic capital, or availability of good arguments; in negotiation, the result depends on bargaining power or the availability of material or financial resources and exit options (Saretzki, 1996: 33).

From a functional perspective, Saretzki argues, argumentation is a specialised mode of communication for solving cognitive problems; negotiations have this specialised function for distributive issues. The functional perspective has a corresponding structural aspect, that is, argumentation is triadic, negotiation is dyadic. In order to vindicate an empirical or normative validity claim, proponents and opponents have to appeal to an external, 'third' institution – like scientific methods in the case of empirical truth; or values, principles and norms laid down in constitutions, laws and treaties in the case of normative claims. In negotiation, ideally, there is no recourse to an outside agency or third party. The acceptability of practical claims is solely determined by the judgements of the negotiating parties involved in reaching an agreement. Finally, the functional and structural relations spill over to processual properties. Negotiation necessarily occurs sequentially, whereas argumentation has a kind of reflexivity characterised by simultaneity in the judgements about pattern or fit between parts and whole (Saretzki, 1996: 34).

On this basis, Saretzki observes a principled asymmetry between argumentation and negotiation. They have fundamentally different meanings for cognitive processes of problem finding and self-understanding, and they are not mutually substitutable. Cognitive problems cannot be solved by negotiation – there is no such thing as 'negotiated (empirical) truth', at least not in the end, and certainly not as an adequate way of problem processing. Eventually, negotiated truths will lead to the kind of structural mismatch between problems as experienced by problem owners directly involved in problematic situations, and the problem representations of the stronger parties in the negotiation. Vice versa, distributional issues may successfully be tackled without negotiation, as long as people get agreement on rules for distribution based on rationally legitimate principles of distribution and their scope of application. In other words, by argumentation one may successfully process both cognitive and distributional problems; yet, negotiation is functionally limited to processing distributional problems only. That is why Saretzki concludes that argumentation is elementary and multifunctional, whereas negotiations remain a derived, functionally restricted mode of communication.

Primacy for powering?

Saretzki is not politically naïve; he admits that processes of argumentation frequently, but not always, follow only after their scope and constraints have been determined in previous negotiations: 'Looked at from the beginning of the communication process (as well as from the use of their results) factual primacy lies with negotiation, not argumentation' (Saretzki, 1996: 37). Yet, others argue, not for a contingently historical, but for the law–like causal primacy of any type of power over argumentation. This argument comes in a structural, and in a constructivist or cognitive-psychological, version.

The first version is structural, that is, power and rationality mutually constitute each other. Power defines the constraints for what is accepted as rationality and truth, and accepted rationality and truth produce relations of power (Flyvbjerg, 1998: 225–36).[1] This statement should be understood to mean two things. Stable power relations generate a working consensus on rules that separate truth from untruth and reality from 'just storytelling'. Examples are to be found in political systems with coalition governments, which use formally established scientific advisory bodies or government-sponsored research and development institutes to depoliticise political issues. The scientific bodies both produce politically 'unassailable' facts for national governmental policy making, and simultaneously pass scientific judgements on the economic cost–benefit ratio and uncertainty of unwelcome political proposals launched by local governments, by the opposition, or by non-governmental players.[2] Thus, the maintenance of power also rests on a particular interpretation of reality; interpretation is not just commentary or judgement, but 'a means of becoming master of something' (Flyvbjerg, 1998: 117). In less stable power relations, any open confrontation will lead to rationality being trumped by power. 'Rationality' actors – like policy analysts, or advisers or alarmed scientists – are simply degraded by the 'power' actors – like politicians, high-level administrators and interest group leaders – from valued discussion partners to passive spectators and bystanders. This notion was particularly well expressed in a comment by an aide of the Bush government to journalist Ron Suskind (*New York Times Magazine*, 17 October 2004):

> The aide said that guys like me were 'in what we call the reality-based community, … [who] believe that solutions emerge from … judicious study of discernible reality.… That's not the way the world really works anymore.… We're an empire now, and when we act, we create our own reality. And while you're studying that reality – judiciously, as you will – we'll act again, creating other new realities, which you can study too, and that's how things will sort out. We're history's actors … and you, all of you, will be left to just study what we do.

A second type of argument for the law-like primacy of powering over puzzling is constructivist and rests on a radical interpretation of bounded rationality. It is succinctly and precisely stated by Karl Jaspers: our inability to (fully) know implies the unavoidability of our obligation to will. Lindblom (1968: 12) explicitly asked: 'How far can we go in reasoning out policy instead of fighting over it?' The brief answer is 'not very far'. Whether we see the boundedness of our rationality and hence deliberative skills in the neurophysiologic make-up of the individual's cognitive (Simon, 1957) and affective apparatus (e.g. Janis and Mann, 1977; Damasio, 2000); in the small group dynamics of group pressure or groupthink (Janis, 1982); in the mental 'cages' of a bureaucratic way of organising specialised knowledge and a division of labour (Forester, 1989); in the irresistible attraction of the preferred worlds of the cultures we live by (Thompson et al, 1990); or, as in philosophical anthropology and political philosophy, in the intersubjectivity, finitude and historicality given by the human condition (Merleau-Ponty, in Dauenhauer, 1986) – for us human beings reality is equally complex and overwhelming.

Even apparently simple (policy) problems become hypercomplex after some serious analysis and reflection. This not only pertains to 'facts' of the world. Bounded rationality spills over, so to speak, in the world of values, ideals and norms. As we tend to impute value to everything we observe and experience, bounded rationality also affects our ability to fathom and systematically deal with normative issues. Therefore, every plan or design, no matter how sophisticated the process of its production, is just a *latest fashion*; it may never pretend to be a *last word*. Logically, problems can be thought about, reasoned out and deliberated about without end or closure. For political decisions and collective actions the implication is that 'who may define a problem for deliberation, and when?' will become an issue of power struggle. Moreover, the same logic implies that the question of closure or 'does it make sense to deliberate longer?' similarly becomes a power issue. The nature of collective, political problems obviously is such that no self-evident 'rational' criteria can be formulated for starting up or closing down processes of reasoning and deliberation about them.

Thus, our bounded rationality and deliberative skills, sooner or later, force us to fall back on political instigations. On the way to collective actions, our mental efforts in thinking and the speech acts in our deliberations run into insurmountable complexities, normative ambivalences, dilemmas and inextricable 'knots'. If only because there are matters, especially in the public domain, that can be thought or openly said (like convincing a majority of the ingenious compromise between contradictory values in a bill) but not practically done (as any street-level bureaucrat can tell the lawmakers), and can be done (like being corrupt, or making a political deal) but not publicly said (Brunsson, 1993). The only way we know to deal with such 'knots' with a view to collective action, is to 'cut' them. The first step in moving from reason and deliberation to action, then, is to mobilise our will or volition and *decide* what to do – a word rooted in the Latin verb '*de-cidere*' which means to 'cut off' or 'cut through'. We have to cut off reason and deliberation and come to a decision. It appears that, far from a worn-out normative democratic cliché, the idea of a primacy of powering is a cognitive-affective and socio-political construct that is a necessary condition for bringing about collective action (see Williams, 1980: 5). Lindblom (1968) therefore called policy analysis not neutral, but partisan analysis; not a way of puzzling over policy, but an important method of fighting over it.

Note that in both the structural and cognitive-psychological versions of the primacy of powering, asymmetries are constructed. In the structural account, powering belongs to action and 'history makers'; puzzling is denigrated as a passive hindsight of spectators and jurors. In the cognitive-psychological account, powering is for those happily engaging in the competition of political will formation, and the political action in decision making; puzzling is for the speculative of mind and the deliberative of inclination. In both accounts, a sort of functional divide between practice versus theory, action versus spectatorship, willing versus thinking, future-looking decision versus backward-looking judgement is erected. Powering is for those who practice the art of politics and know how politics works; puzzling is for those who like to know (in advance, or after the fact) what politics is for, but not necessarily know how it works...

Not just asymmetry, but polarity

Next to asymmetry, there is another important aspect to the relationship between powering and puzzling not yet treated satisfactorily. One could say that judgement and instigation are condemned to each other. Most accurately, it is a *polarity*, that is, a relationship of mutually dependent, but contradictory forces that in their inextricable entwinement nevertheless should be seen and dealt with as one phenomenon, as a single object of analysis and unit of action (see Schmidt and Schischkoff, 1978: 529). Here, the focus is on the question of the mutual dependence part of the polarity. The contradictory aspects have been treated in the analysis of asymmetries; the entwinement aspect has been illuminated in the structural account of the relationship between puzzling and powering as mutually constituting a power/knowledge complex. This mutual dependency dimension can be brought out best by going into to the limits of powering or collective will formation in policy design.

Above, it was mentioned that Lindblom (1968) asked: how far could we go in reasoning out policy instead of fighting over it? Here, the counterpart question is asked: how far can we go in merely fighting over policy instead of reasoning it out? Maybe this question has drawn less scholarly attention because the answer is not flattering to scientists: 'quite far, much further at least than through reason and deliberation'. To investigate whether or not, and to what extent, instigation or collective will formation depends on reason and deliberation, it helps to take a more detailed look at what happens during instigation processes. Examining a simple two-person instigation process will bring out all elements necessary for answering the question (De Jouvenel, 1963: 69):

1. An instigator imagines a desirable future situation, and ways and means to achieve this desirable state at some future time; these also comprise which decisions and actions by other people will contribute to his goal achievement.[3]
2. The instigator communicates one other person (instigandus) what decision they desire them to take, or which action to perform.
3. The instigandus interprets the instigator's appeal; and subsequently complies (on to 4) or refuses (back to 1).
4. The instigandus decides or acts as the instigator wishes.

The first step immediately shows why and to what extent instigation depends on design, reason and deliberation. In the absence of any reasoning, the instigator would not know what to desire of others, let alone who these others could be. Availability of some rudimentary form of ratiocination is a necessary condition for instigation. This is Saretzki's argument of 'primacy' for puzzling or judgement, arguing from a communicative functionality. However, it is a far from sufficient condition. The dependence of instigation on some puzzling does not go beyond the mere existence of design – good or bad, sophisticated or simple. Examining steps 2 through 4 makes this abundantly clear.

De Jouvenel correctly emphasises that even if instigator and instigandus are completely equal in influence and status, the temporal sequence grants initiative to the instigator. This is a small, but potentially crucial advantage in exerting influence. It is at the root of the many political science theories that stress the importance of timing or 'windows of opportunity' in politics and policy making. The advantage is hidden in the instigator's possibility to bias the weight of motives for the instigandus in his own favour. Motives are considered 'substantive' if the instigandus' response is not significantly affected by the instigator's identity. As explained above, depending on his personality and the circumstances of the instigation, every instigandus will have to balance the 'what' and the 'by whom' of an instigation. This means that every instigator, by seizing the initiative, in principle, has an opportunity to frame or stage the instigation in ways that maximise the probability that 'by whom' motives prevail.

This largely explains why, in politics and policy making, instigation carries one further by a long shot than mere reason and deliberation. Although focused instigation requires one to have some plan or design in mind, its substance does not necessarily play a significant role in the instigation's success.

No policy comes about without reason and deliberation on the one hand, and instigation or power on the other; but the nature of their being necessary is very different. For their adoption and implementation, even high-quality policy designs remain vitally dependent on successful instigation and decision making. Nevertheless, designs soon hit upon insuperable limits to rationality, irrespective of whether they were reasoned out with or without much sophistication, and with or without extensive deliberation processes. On the way to collective action, these limits can only be overcome by falling back on instigations and decisions. Wishing powering away in advocacy of a power-free, deliberative politics is utopian (Pellizoni, 2001). Contrasting a scientific ideal of politics with the ideal of a self-regulating society, Lindblom (1990: 221–2) states:

> The science model frets about power and imposition…. The self-guiding society displays much less hostility to power … and probes how to distribute power or the capacity to impose in an appropriate way rather than entertain hopes, inevitably to be frustrated, of minimising its use.

Power, influence, sometimes coercion – these activities require some design; but after taking this relatively simple hurdle, there are no further limits that literally force them to revert to reasoning and deliberation. Having a plan – not: having a reasonably good, ethically acceptable plan – is just one necessary, possibly favourable, but my no means sufficient condition for successful instigations. Now, if one feels that politicians and policy makers get too far in merely fighting over and imposing policy instead of reasoning it out, one draws an ethical line. I believe that this boundary ought to be drawn where conscious, deliberate and transparent public transference of administrative and political competencies and responsibilities degenerates into (mass-)psychological, private and non-transparent, therefore democratically uncontrollable phenomena of social transference. These are situations where political leadership, instead of being constrained by legal rules and authority, becomes merely charismatic and totalising; or where political accountability is organised away in complex procedures and bureaucratic nightmares (Bauman, 1989). In these conditions, public morality withers away to such an extent that large numbers of politicians, administrators, civil servants and citizens too, manifest what Arendt (1979: 4) saw as typical for Eichmann: 'a manifest shallowness in the doer that made it impossible to trace the incontestable evil of his deeds to any deeper roots or motives.… [I]t was not stupidity, but thoughtlessness'.

Conditions for a responsible and hopeful governance of problems

If it is utopian to think of a power-free politics, if the hope to minimise the abuse of power and coercion is inevitably frustrated, how is it possible to realistically believe in the possibility of a policy analysis in the service of more deliberative spaces and designs in political systems with representative democracy? Why not be realistic and practise political satisficing about representative democracy in capitalist societies? Why not admit that representative democracy in its present functioning is the least bad system? Why not firmly believe that one has nothing to gain from an attempt to convert the increased veto and nuisance powers of civil society and ordinary citizens (see Chapter One) into positive contributions to deliberations for politically organised solidarity in shared projects and a common cause (see Chapter Nine)?

In the opening section of this book, it was argued that politics is intrinsically paradoxical. On the one hand, political organisation unifies a society's members in a common effort to bring about goods, services and performances that benefit all or most. On the other hand, the logics of power and division of labour divide society's members in groups at varying distances from the discretion and power of taking authoritative political decisions. Yet, if politics springs from humankind's nature as a responsible being in dialogue with others, then a responsible politics aims to subordinate the dividing feature to the unifying feature. Why not attempt to exploit the contextually distributed knowledges, discourses and action potentials for more intelligent, socially acceptable and contextually robust, shared plans and projects? The audacious attitude that best promotes a responsible practice of politics is one of a properly conceived hope, that is, not hope and pray, but hope as a deliberately adopted attitude towards acting in concert with others (Dauenhauer, 1986; Obama, 2006). It means that one cannot give up on constantly finding new ways to align productive puzzling to non-crippling ways of powering. In our complex societies, processes of division of labour and specialisation of knowledge will continue to produce divergent, contrasting rationalities and accompanying discourses, alienation, and huge power differentials. Still, one cannot give up on efforts to manage situations of domination and subordination in such ways that productive mutual recognition of roles between distant and more proximate policy makers is still possible:

> Exercises of power can and should aim to transform the relationship between power holders and power subjects from being a relationship of subordination into one of coordination, of reciprocal power sharing. Performances of the 'power holder' are legitimate only if they are compatible with the eliciting of genuine initiative from the 'power subject'.... Within the political domain, *practitioners of a politics of hope must constantly seek to bring new members into the ranks of political actors.'* (Dauenhauer, 1986: 144, emphasis added)

In a responsible and hopeful governance of problems, there appear to be at least three routes to achieve this aim. Public policy, like all human striving, is caught in the precarious position of both trying to understand society and simultaneously shape it. Therefore, the art and craft of policy analysis is about linking knowledge to action, through evidence and reason, in a context of political power. One way to avoid and actively resist a politics of resignation to power is to organise degrees of alternation or oscillation between powering and puzzling in clever process management of single projects or exercises in policy design and implementation (Hoppe, 1983; Van de Graaf and Hoppe, 1996; Hoppe et al, 1998). This is why it makes sense to keep studying the ways in which organisers of mini-public deliberative and participatory exercises in policy design handle the perplexities of such processes. However, it is of equal importance to study the balancing and oscillation between powering and puzzling in 'ordinary' policy making inside bureaucratic agencies and in the multilevel networks of 'normal' policy making.

The second route is to keep striving for institutional alignment through interpolable balancing in network governance (see Chapters Six, Eight and Nine): 'A responsible politics ... recognizes that no institution can be perfect, that every institution is finite and conditioned by historical circumstances – both material and cultural – in which it operates.... [A]ll institutions, political and otherwise, are always in need of reform' (Dauenhauer, 1986: 139). Reflexive network governance, however, requires a space where this reflexivity may be exercised. Preservation of such a space is at the heart of political democracy; and thus requires an autonomous political institutional domain. Particularly, this political domain will not allow political institutions to be dominated by other institutional spheres – neither religious theocracy, nor scientific technocracy, nor the market system's econocracy. During the last decades, most attention has been given to religious and technocratic threats to the autonomy of politics, with technocracy usually invoked against theocratic tendencies – and vice versa. After the recent financial and economic crisis it is high time to roll back the encroachment of market system rules and practices on politics (Lindblom, 2001). This is not a licence to politicise other institutional spheres of social and private life. A responsible politics will preserve the autonomy of the other spheres and remain permeable to their criticism and influence. A reflexive and responsible political governance of problems requires sufficient room for opposition – if necessary, facilitating such opposition.

A third way to keep the dilemmas, perplexities and ironies of puzzling versus powering within the bounds of the politically manageable, is to be alert to the conditions that indicate a responsible exercise of power and coercion. A responsible governance of problems foremost implies restraints of all participants. On the side of 'power holders', that is, authoritative decision makers and their staffs of policy workers and the circle of influential, proximate policy makers, restraint in the use of power and coercion means eliciting genuine initiatives by 'power subjects', and use of these inputs in the co-design of positive programmes for responding to citizens' needs, wants, and problems (Dauenhauer, 1986: 159-60). It means taking the first two routes, as indicated above, seriously. In addition, it means tangible efforts to lift impairments on citizen probing (Lindblom, 1990) by means of better citizen and science education; and, probably, fighting excessive misinformation in business reporting and advertising, and especially abuse of trust by business and private people in internet communication.

Restraints also apply to the side of the 'power subjects'. No responsible citizen can give unqualified priority to their own or their group's wants and needs. There is an obligation to listen to one another and to policy makers and political decision makers. Only if it is beyond reasonable doubt that mutual deliberation is impossible, or if proximate and authoritative policy makers cannot be convinced of tackling very serious wrong-problem problems, antagonistic politics that use all sorts of political protest and civil disobedience come into view. In a responsible governance of problems there is one very difficult-to-handle sort of constraint. On the one hand, a democratic governance of problems is rooted in a Socratic attitude to the question-and-answer game. Galvanising questions and awareness-raising answers nurture and direct the process of coming to prudential political judgements and action commitments. In the political question-and-answer game, citizens have the right and obligation to question power. On the other hand, uninhibited questioning or scepticism undermines the learning process. Although policies easily evolve into dogma for policy makers and decision makers, without considering certain issues fixed and taking certain practices temporarily for granted, serious debate and learning would come to a halt through overburdening the problem-processing capacities of individuals and the political system alike. Balancing dogma versus scepticism, then, is another important restraint in the responsible governance of problems (Wildavsky, 1980 [1979]: 16, 18-19).

The art and craft of policy analysis is about linking knowledge to action, through evidence and reason, in a context of political power. Under such conditions, policy analysts can adopt several basic attitudes to their own jobs. One attitude is succumbing to a politics of will, by developing ways and means for furthering plebiscitary and e-democracy. Modern information technology is harnessed to the revivification of the old myth of popular sovereignty. Another manifestation of bowing to political will formation is an absolute loyalty to political leaders. Policy analysts adopting this attitude become lawyers and advocates. Another basic attitude is to embrace a politics of vision, by giving more scope to autonomous bureaucratic agencies, independent oversight bodies, and expert advice. The volatility of the electoral cycle and political volition should be counterbalanced by locating power in people of vision – policy analysts among them.

In this book, a governance of problems is preferred that adopts responsible hope as its basic attitude. Power and coercion, rejection of mutual learning between rulers and ruled through deliberation and argumentation, sophisticated answers to wrong-problem problems – they all are certainly here to stay. A responsible governance of problems therefore allows and furthers policy analysis in the face of power. A hopeful governance of problems assumes and actively pursues that dedicated analysts and clever citizens always, sooner or later, find ways to inject solid puzzling in biased powering. Shrewd process management of policy projects, wise institutional alignment in network governance, and a restrained use of power and coercion lead to creative and collectively productive governance of problems.

Notes

[1] One is reminded here of the joke about the Indians and the meteorologists. Uncertain about whether or not to gather more wood for a long, harsh winter, the Indians' chief decides to telephone the meteorologist service for a scientific prediction. Convinced that Indian folk wisdom frequently is a better predictor than their data and scientific models, the meteorologists on their mountain top see the Indians downhill busily gathering wood, and thus tell their chief that winter will be harsh and long.

[2] Paradoxically, and testimony to the opportunism of contemporary mode-2 science, powerful corporations, such as in the tobacco, pharmaceutical and food industries, support and finance scientific research institutes that make it their business to exploit uncertainties in the research of their colleagues to help industry undermine political regulatory initiatives (Nestle, 2002; Michaels and Monforton, 2005; Michaels, 2008).

3. See Halperin, 1974, for many enlightening examples of bureau-political tactics in getting the president's ear from the US Departments of Defence and Foreign Affairs; and Eppink, 2007, for high-level bureaucrats working for the European Commission.

Bibliography

6, P., Leat, D., Seltzer, K., Stoker, G. (2002) *Towards holistic governance: The new reform agenda*. Basingstoke and New York, Palgrave.

6, P., Peck, E. (2004) 'New Labour's modernization in the public sector: a neo-durkheimian approach and the case of mental health services'. *Public Administration* 82(1): 83-108.

Abramson, J.B., Arterton, A.C., Orren, G.R. (1988) *The electronic commonwealth: The impact of new technologies upon democratic politics*. New York, Basic Books.

Ackoff, R.L. (1978) *The art of problem solving: Accompanied by Ackoff's fables*. New York, John Wiley & Sons.

Allison, G.T. (1971) *Essence of decision: Explaining the Cuban missile crisis*. Boston, MA, Little Brown.

Almond, G.A., Verba, S. (1963) *The civic culture*. Princeton, NJ, Princeton University Press.

Amenta, E. (2003) 'What we know about the development of social policy: comparative and historical research in comparative and historical perspective', in Mahoney, J., Rueschemeyer, D. (eds) *Comparative historical analysis in the social sciences* (pp 91-130). Cambridge, Cambridge University Press.

Andersen, S.S., Burns, T. (1996) 'The European Union and the erosion of parliamentary democracy: a study of post-parliamentary governance', in Andersen, S.S., Eliassen, K.A. (eds) *The European Union: How democratic is it?* (pp 227-51). London, Sage Publications.

Anderson, J.L. (1997) 'Governmental suasion: refocusing the Lowi typology'. *Policy Studies Journal* 25(2): 266-282.

Anderson, J.L. (2003) *Seeking truth, exercising power*. New York City, Columbia University Press.

Andeweg, R., Thomassen, J. (2006) *Binnenhof van binnenuit. Tweede Kamerleden over het functioneren van de Nederlandse democratie*, Den Haag, Raad voor het Openbaar Bestuu: 120 pp.

Arendt, H. (1958) *The human condition*. Chicago, IL and London, University of Chicago Press.

Arendt, H. (1968) *Between past and future: Eight exercises in political thought*. Harmondsworth, Penguin.

Arendt, H. (1979) *Eichmann in Jerusalem: A report on the banality of evil*. Harmondsworth, Penguin.

Arnstein, S. (1969) 'A ladder of citizen participation'. *Journal of the American Institute of Planners* 35(4): 216-24.

Arts, B., Van Tatenhove, J. (2004) 'Policy and power: a conceptual framework between "old" and "new" policy idioms'. *Policy Sciences* 37: 339-56.

Asard, A.W.L.B. (1997) *Democracy and the marketplace of ideas: Communication and government in Sweden and the United States*. Cambridge, Cambridge University Press.

Baldwin, P. (2005) *Disease and democracy: The industrialized world faces AIDS.* Berkeley, CA and New York, University of California Press – Milbank Memorial Fund.

Bang, H.P. (2003) 'Who will represent reflexive individuals?'. Paper presented to the workshop Political Representation, European Consortium for Political Research, University of Edinburgh.

Bang, H.P. (2004) 'Culture governance: governing self-reflexive modernity'. *Public Administration* 82(1): 157-90.

Barber, B. (1984 [1990]) *Strong democracy: Participatory politics for a new age.* Berkeley, CA, University of California Press.

Bardach, E. (1976) 'Policy termination as a political process'. *Policy Sciences* 7: 123-31.

Barzelay, M., Gallego Calderòn, R. (2005) 'From "new institutionalism" to "new processualism": advancing knowledge about public management policy change', Paper presented at the conference on Generation Reform in Brazil and Other Nations, organized by the International Public Management Network and the Escola Brasileira de Administração Pública e Empresa, Fundação Getulio Vargas, Rio de Janeiro, November 17-19, 2004.

Bauman, Z. (1989) *Modernity and the holocaust.* Cambridge, Polity Press.

Bauman, Z. (1992) *Intimations of postmodernity.* London and New York, Routledge.

Baumgartner, F.R., Jones, B.D. (1993) *Agendas and instability in American politics.* Chicago, IL and London, University of Chicago Press.

Baumgartner, F.R., Jones, B.D. (2002) *Policy dynamics.* Chicago, IL, University of Chicago Press.

Beck, U. (1992) *Risk society: Towards a new modernity.* London, Sage Publications.

Beck, U. (1997) *The reinvention of politics.* Thousand Oaks, CA, Sage Publications.

Becker, E. (1973) *The denial of death.* New York, Free Press.

Behn, R.D., Vaupel, J.W. (1982) *Quick analysis for busy decision makers.* New York, Basic Books.

Beiner, R. (1983) *Political judgment.* London, Methuen.

Berger, P.L., Luckmann, T. (1967) *The social construction of reality.* New York, Anchor Books.

Bernstein, R.J. (1991) *The new constellation: The ethical-political horizons of modernity/ postmodernity.* Cambridge, MA, MIT Press.

Bishop, P., Davis, G. (2002) 'Mapping public participation in policy choices'. *Australian Journal of Public Administration* 61(1): 14-29.

Blair, T. (1998) *The Third Way: New politics for a new century.* London, Fabian Society.

Blommaert, J. (2001) *Ik stel vast. Politiek taalgebruik, politieke vernieuwing en verrechtsing,* Berchem-Antwerpen, Uitgeverij EPO (accessed through http://www.flwi.ugent.be/cie/jblommaert/blommaert_bk_1.htm)

Blumer, H. (1971) 'Social problems as collective behavior'. *Social Problems* 18: 298-306.

Bobrow, D.B., Dryzek, J.S. (1987) *Policy analysis by design.* Pittsburgh, PA, University of Pittsburgh Press.

Bogason, P. (2000) *Public policy and local governance: Institutions in postmodern society*. Cheltenham, Edward Elgar.

Bogason, P. (2006) 'Networks and bargaining in policy analysis', in Peters, B.G., Pierre, J. (eds) *Handbook of public policy* (pp 97-113). London, Sage Publications.

Boom, H., Metze, M. (1997) *De slag om de Betuweroute: Het spel langs de lijn*. Amsterdam, Balans.

Börzel, T. (1998) 'Organizing Babylon - on the different conceptions of policy networks'. *Public Administration* 76(Summer): 253-73.

Bos, A.H. (1974) *Oordeelsvorming in groepen: Willens, wetens, wikken, en wegen: Polariteit en ritme als sleutel tot ontwikkeling van sociale organismen*. Wageningen, Veenman en Zonen.

Bosso, C.J. (1994) 'The contextual bases of problem definition', in Rochefort, D.A., Cobb, R.W. (eds) *The politics of problem definition: Shaping the political agenda* (pp 182-203). Lawrence, KS, Kansas University Press.

Boulding, K. (1956) *The image: Knowledge in life and society*. Ann Arbor, MI, University of Michigan Press.

Bourdieu, P. (1998) *Practical reason: On the theory of action*. Cambridge, Polity Press.

Bovens, M. (1998) *The quest for responsibility: Accountability and citizenship in complex organizations*. Cambridge, Cambridge University Press.

Bovens, M., Derksen, W., Witteveen, W., Becker, F., and P. Kalma (eds) (1995) *De verplaatsing van de politiek: Een agenda voor democratische vernieuwing*. Amsterdam, Wiardi Beckman Stichting.

Braman, D., Kahan, D.M., (2003a) 'More statistics, less persuasion: a cultural theory of gun-risk perceptions'. Public Law & Legal Theory Working Paper Series, Working Paper No. 05, 37 pp. (http://papers.ssrn.com/abstract=286205)

Braman, D., Kahan, D.M., Grimmelmann, J. (2005) 'Modelling facts, culture and cognition in the gun debate'. *Social Justice Research* 18(3): 283-304.

Braybrooke, D. (1974) *Traffic congestion goes through the issue-machine: A case-study in issue processing, illustrating a new approach*. London and Boston, MA, Routledge & Kegan Paul.

Braybrooke, D., Lindblom, C.E. (1963) *A strategy of decision: Evaluation as a social process*. New York, Free Press.

Brecht, A. (1959) *Political theory: The foundations of twentieth century political thought*. Princeton, NJ, Princeton University Press.

Brunsson, N. (1993) 'Ideas and actions: justification and hypocrisy as alternatives to control'. *Accounting, Organizations and Society* 18(6): 489-506.

Cabinet Office (1999) *Modernising government*. London, The Stationery Office.

Callahan, D. (2003) *What price better health? Hazards of the research imperative*. Berkeley, CA and New York, University of California Press and The Milbank Memorial Fund.

Campbell, D.T. (1974) 'Qualitative knowing in action research'. Kurt Lewin Award Address, presented to the Society for the Psychological Study of Social Issues, American Psychological Association, New Orleans, 1 September.

Campbell, D.T. (1982) 'Experiments as arguments'. *Knowledge: Creation, Diffusion, Utilization* 3: 327-37.

Campbell, D.T., Stanley, J.C. (1963) *Experimental and quasi-experimental designs for research.* Chicago, IL, Rand McNally.

Carmines, E.G., Huckfeldt, R. (1996) 'Political behavior: an overview', in Goodin, R.E., Klingemann, H.-D. (eds) *A new handbook of political science* (pp 223-54). Oxford, Oxford University Press.

Carson, R. (1962) *Silent Spring.* Boston, Houghton Mifflin

Castells, M. (1997) *The information age: Economy, society and culture: Volume II: The power of identity.* Oxford, Blackwell.

Castells, M. (2000) *The rise of the network society: Economy, society and culture.* Cambridge, Blackwell.

Catlaw, T.J. (2006) 'Authority, representation, and the contradictions of posttraditional governing'. *The American Review of Public Administration* 36(3): 261-87.

Chisholm, D. (1995) 'Problem solving and institutional design'. *Journal of Public Administration and Research and Theory* 5(4): 451-91.

Choo, C.W. (1998) *The knowing organization: How organizations use information to construct meaning, create knowledge, and make decisions.* New York, Oxford University Press.

Christensen, T., Laegreid, P. (2002) 'New Public Management: puzzles of democracy and the influence of citizens'. *The Journal of Political Philosophy* 10(3): 267-95.

Cobb, R.W., Elder, C.D. (1972) *Participation in American politics: The dynamics of agendabuilding.* Baltimore, MD, Johns Hopkins University Press.

Cobb, R.W., Ross, M.H. (eds) (1997a) *Cultural strategies of agenda denial: Avoidance, attack, and redefinition.* Lawrence, KS, Kansas University Press.

Cobb, R.W., Ross, M.H. (1997b) 'Denying agenda access: strategic considerations, in Cobb, R.W., Ross, M.W. (eds) *Cultural strategies of agenda denial: Avoidance, attack, redefinition* (pp 25-45). Lawrence, KS, Kansas University Press.

Coenen, F.J.H.M., Huitema, D., O'Toole, Jr., T. (eds) (1998) *Participation and the quality of environmental decision making.* Dordrecht/Boston/London, Kluwer Academic Publishers.

Cohen, M.D., March, J.G, Olsen, J.P. (1972) 'The garbage can model of organizational choice'. *Administrative Science Quarterly* 17: 1-25.

Colebatch, H.K. (2002a) *Policy.* Buckingham, Open University Press.

Colebatch, H.K. (2002b) 'Government and governmentality: using multiple approaches to the analysis of government'. *Australian Journal of Political Science* 37(4): 417-35.

Colebatch, H.K. (2005) 'Policy analysis, policy practice and political science'. *Australian Journal of Public Administration* 64(5): 14-23.

Colebatch, H.K. (ed) (2006a) *The work of policy: An international survey.* Lanham, MD, Lexington Books.

Colebatch, H.K. (2006b) 'What makes policy work?'. *Policy Sciences* 39: 309-21.

Colebatch, H.K., Hoppe, R., Noordegraaf, M. (eds) (2010: in press) *Working for policy*. Amsterdam, Amsterdam University Press.

Connolly, W.E. (1987) *Politics and ambiguity*. Madison, WI, University of Wisconsin Press.

Converse, P.E. (1964) 'The nature of belief systems in mass publics', in Apter, D. (ed) *Ideology and discontent*. New York, Free Press.

Cook, P.J., Ludwig, J. (2003) 'Commentaries: fact-free gun policy?'. *University of Pennsylvania Law Review* 151: 1329-40.

Cornips, J. (2008) 'Invloed en interactie: een onderzoek naar de relatie tussen instituties en invloed in lokale interactieve beleidsprocessen'. PhD thesis. Faculty of Management and Governance, University of Twente.

Coughlin, J.F. (1994) 'The tragedy of the concrete commons: defining traffic congestion as a public problem, in Rochefort, D.A., Cobb, R.W. (eds) *The politics of problem definition: Shaping the policy agenda* (pp 138-58). Lawrence, KS, Kansas University Press.

Coupal, L.V. (2004) 'Constructivist learning theory and human capital theory: shifting political and educational frameworks for teachers' ICT professional development'. *British Journal of Educational Technology* 35(5): 587-96.

Cowan, D.A. (1986) 'Developing a process model of problem recognition'. *Academy of Management Review* 11(4): 763-76.

Cozzens, S.E., Woodhouse, E.J. (1995) 'Science, government, and the politics of knowledge', in Jasanoff, S., Markle, G.E., Petersen, J.C., and T. Pinch (eds) *Handbook of science and technology studies* (pp 533-53). Thousand Oaks, CA, Sage Publications.

Crossan, M., Lane, H.W., Hildebrand, T. (1993) 'Organization learning: theory to practice', in J. Hendry, G. Johnson and G. Newton (eds) *Leadership and the management of change* (pp 229-65). New York, John Wiley & Sons.

Cuppen, E. (2009) Putting perspectives into participation. Constructive conflict methodology for problem structuring in stakeholder dialogues. Oisterwijk, BOXPress (PhD dissertation, Free University Amsterdam)

Dahl, R.A. (1963) *Modern political analysis*. Englewood Cliffs, NJ, Prentice-Hall.

Dahl, R.A. (1985) *Nuclear weapons, democracy versus guardianship*. Syracuse, NY, Syracuse University Press.

Dahl, R.A. (1989) *Democracy and its critics*. New Haven, Yale University Press

Dahl, R.A. (2000) *On democracy*. New Haven, CT and London, Yale University Press.

Dahl, R.A., Lindblom, C.E. (1953) *Politics, economics, and welfare: Planning and politico-economic systems resolved into basic social processes*. New York, Harper & Row.

Dalton, R.J. (2000) 'Citizen attitudes and political behavior'. *Comparative Political Studies* 33(6-7): 912-40.

Dalton, R.J. (2008) *Citizen politics: Public opinion and political parties in advanced industrial democracies* (5th edition). Washington, DC, CQ Press.

Damasio, A.R. (2000) *Descartes' Error. Emotion, Reason, and the Human Brain*, Quill

Dauenhauer, B.P. (1986) *The politics of hope*. New York and London, Routledge & Kegan Paul.

Davies, A.F. (1964) *Australian democracy*. Melbourne, Cheshire.

De Haas, W. (2000) *Formerly known as planning*. Delft, Eburon.

De Jouvenel, B. (1963) *The pure theory of politics*. Cambridge, Cambridge University Press.

De Vries, A. (2008) 'Towards do-ability: dealing with uncertainty in the science-policy interface'. PhD thesis. Science, Technology and Policy Studies. University of Twente.

De Vries, J., Van der Lubben, S. (2005) *Een onderbroken evenwicht in de Nederlandse politiek: Paars II en de revolte van Fortuyn*. Amsterdam, Van Gennep.

DeLeon, P. (1987) 'Policy termination as a political phenomenon', in Palumbo, D. (ed) *The politics of program evaluation*. Newbury Park, CA, Sage Publications.

DeLeon, P. (1989) *Advice and consent: The development of the policy sciences*. New York, Russell Sage Foundation.

Denhardt, R. (1981) *In the shadow of organization*. Lawrence, KS, Regents Press of Kansas.

Dery, D. (1984) *Problem definition in policy analysis,* Lawrence, KS, Kansas University Press.

Dery, D. (2000) 'Agenda Setting and Problem Definition'. *Policy Studies* 21 1: 37–47

Dienel, P.C. (1992) *Die Planungszelle: Der Bürger plant seine Umwelt: Eine Alternative zur Establishment-Demokratie*. Opladen, Westdeutscher Verlag.

Diesing, P. (1962) *Reason in society: Five types of decisions in their social contexts*. Urbana, IL, University of Illinois Press.

Diesing, P. (1982) *Science and ideology in the policy sciences*. New York, Aldine.

Diesing, P. (1991) *How does social science work? Reflections on practice*. Pittsburgh, PA, Pittsburgh University Press.

DiMaggio, P. (1988) 'Interest and agency in institutional theory', in Zucker, L. (ed) *Institutional patterns and culture* (pp 3–22). Cambridge, MA, Ballinger Publishing.

Dorst, K. (2004) 'On the problem of design problems – problem solving and design expertise'. *The Journal of Design Research* 4(3).

Douglas, M. (1978) *Cultural bias*. Occasional Paper No 35. London, Royal Anthropological Institute.

Douglas, M. (1986) *How institutions think*. Syracuse, NY, Syracuse University Press.

Douglas, M. (1996a) 'The choice between gross and spiritual; some medical preferences, in Douglas, M. *Thought styles: Critical essays on good taste* (pp 21–49). London, Sage Publications.

Douglas, M. (1996b) 'Prospects for Asceticism', in Douglas, M., *Thought styles: Critical essays on good taste*. London, Sage Publications.

Douglas, M. (1998) gridgroup.listserv, accessed 10 March.

Douglas, M., Ney, S. (1998) *Missing persons: A critique of personhood in the social sciences*. Berkeley, CA, University of California Press.

Douglas, M., Wildavsky, A. (1983) *Risk and culture*. Berkeley, CA, University of California Press.

Dowding, K. (1995) 'Model or metaphor? A critical review of the policy network approach'. *Political Studies* 43: 136-58.

Downs, A. (1967) *Inside bureaucracy*. Boston, MA, Little Brown.

Dror, Y. (1964) 'Muddling through – "science" or inertia'. *Public Administration Review* 24: 153-7.

Dror, Y. (1971) *Design for policy sciences*. New York, Elsevier.

Dror, Y. (1986) *Policymaking under adversity*. New Brunswick, NJ, Transaction Publishers.

Dryzek, J.S., Ripley, B. (1988) 'The ambitions of policy design'. *Policy Studies Review* 7(4): 705-19.

Dryzek, J.S. (1990) *Discursive democracy: Politics, policy, and political science*. Cambridge, Cambridge University Press.

Dryzek, J.S. (1993) 'Policy analysis and planning: from science to argument', in Fischer, F., Forester, J. (eds) *The argumentative turn in policy analysis and planning* (pp 213-32). Durham, Duke University Press.

Dunn, W.N. (1983) 'Values, ethics, and standards in policy analysis', in Nagel, S.S. (eds) *Encyclopaedia of policy studies* (pp 831-66). New York and Basel, Marcel Dekker.

Dunn, W.N. (1988) 'Methods of the second type: coping with the wilderness of conventional policy analysis'. *Policy Studies Review* 7: 720-37.

Dunn, W.N. (1993) 'Policy reforms as arguments', in Fischer, F., Forester, J. (eds) *The argumentative turn in policy analysis and planning* (pp 254-290). Durham, Duke University Press.

Dunn, W.N. (1994) *Public policy analysis: An introduction* (2nd edition). Upper Saddle River, NJ, Pearson Prentice Hall.

Dunn, W.N. (2004) *Public policy analysis: An introduction* (3rd edition). Upper Saddle River, NJ, Pearson Prentice Hall.

Dunn, W.N. (2007) *Public policy analysis: An introduction* (4th edition). Upper Saddle River, NJ, Pearson Prentice Hall.

Dunn, W.N., Holzner, B. (1988) 'Knowledge in society: anatomy of an emergent field'. *Knowledge in Society: The International Journal of Knowledge Transfer* 1(1): 1-26.

Dunsire, A. (1986) 'A cybernetic view of guidance, control and evaluation in the public sector', in Kaufmann, F.X., Majone, G., Ostrom, V. (eds) *Guidance, control, and evaluation in the public sector* (pp 327-48). Berlin and New York, Walter de Gruyter.

Durning, D., Osuna, W. (1994) 'Policy analysts' role and value orientations: an empirical investigation using Q methodology'. *Journal of Policy Analysis and Management* 13(4): 629-57.

Easton, D. (1965) *A systems analysis of political life*. New York, Wiley.

Eckstein, H. (1988) 'A culturalist theory of political change', *American Political Science Review* 82/3: 789-804.

Eckstein, H. (1997) 'Social Science as Cultural Science, Rational Choice as Metaphysics',. Ellis, R., Thompson, M. (eds.) *Culture Matters*, Boulder, CO, Westview Press

Edelman, M. (1964) *The symbolic uses of politics*. Urbana, IL, University of Illinois Press.

Edelman, M. (1977) *Political language: Words that succeed and policies that fail*. New York, Institute for the Study of Poverty.

Edelman, M. (1988) *Constructing the political spectacle*. Chicago, IL and London, Chicago University Press.

Edwards, A. (2002) 'The moderator as an emerging democratic intermediary: the role of the moderator in internet discussions about public issues'. *Information Polity* 7: 3–20.

Edwards, A. (2003) *De gefaciliteerde democratie: Internet, de burger en zijn intermediairen*. Utrecht, Lemma.

Edwards, A. (2006) 'ICT strategies of democratic intermediaries: a view on the political system in the digital age'. *Information Polity* 1(1): 163–76.

Eek, D., Biel, A. (2003) 'The interplay between greed, efficiency and fairness in public-good dilemmas'. *Social Justice Research* 16(3): 195–215.

Elder, C.D., Cobb R.W. (1983) *The political uses of symbols*. New York, Longman Publishing Group.

Elias, N. (1991) *The society of individuals*. Oxford, Blackwell.

Elmore, R.F. (1985) 'Forward and backward mapping: reversible logic in the analysis of public policy'. Hanf, K., Toonen, Th. (eds) *Policy Implementation in Federal and Unitary Systems*. Dordrecht, Kluwer, 33–70

Elzinga, A. (1985) 'Research bureaucracy and the drift of epistemic criteria', Wittrock, B., Elzinga, A. (eds) *The university research system. Public policies of the home of scientists*. Stockholm, Almqvist and Wiksell, 191–220

Eppink, D.-J. (2007) *Life of a European mandarin: Inside the commission*. Tielt, Lannoo.

Esping-Andersen, G. (1990) *The three worlds of welfare capitalism*, Princeton, NJ, Princeton University Press.

Etzioni, A. (1967) 'Mixed scanning: a "third" approach to decision making'. *Public Administration Review* 27: 385–92.

Etzioni, A. (1968) *The active society: A theory of societal and political processes*. New York, Free Press.

Etzioni, A. (1996) *The new golden rule: Community and morality in a democratic society*. New York, Basic Books.

Etzkowitz, H., Leydesdorff, L. (eds) (1997) *Universities and the global knowledge economy: A triple helix of university-industry-government relations*. London and Washington, DC, Pinter.

European Union (2001) *European governance: A White Paper: COM(2001) 328 final*. Brussels, Commission of the European Communities.

Ezrahi, Y. (1980) 'Utopian and pragmatic rationalism: the political context of scientific advice'. *Minerva* 18: 111–31.

Ezrahi, Y. (1990) *The descent of Icarus: Science and the transformation of contemporary democracy*. Cambridge, MA, Harvard University Press.

Finer, S.E. (1999) *The history of government: Volume III: Empires, monarchies and the modern state*. Oxford, Oxford University Press.

Fischer, F. (1980) *Politics, values, and public policy: The problem of methodology*. Boulder, CO, Westview Press.

Fischer, F. (1990) *Technocracy and the politics of expertise*. Newbury Park, CA, Sage Publications.

Fischer, F. (1993) 'Citizen participation and the democratization of policy expertise: from theoretical inquiry to practical cases'. *Policy Sciences* 26: 165–87.

Fischer, F. (1995) *Evaluating public policy*. Chicago, IL, Nelson-Hall.

Fischer, F. (2003) *Reframing public policy: Discursive politics and deliberative practices*. Oxford, Oxford University Press.

Fischer, F., Forester, J. (eds) (1993) *The argumentative turn in policy analysis and planning*. Durham, Duke University Press.

Fischer, F., Miller, G.J., Sidney, M.S. (eds) (2007) *Handbook of public policy analysis: Theory, politics, and methods*. Public Administration and Public Policy/125. Boca Raton, CRC Press, Taylor & Francis Group.

Flyvbjerg, B. (1998) *Rationality and power: Democracy in practice*. Chicago, IL, University of Chicago Press.

Forester, J. (eds) (1985) *Critical theory and public life*. Cambridge, MA, MIT Press.

Forester, J. (1989) *Planning in the face of power*. Berkeley, CA, University of California Press.

Fortuyn, P. (2002) *De puinhopen van acht jaar paars*. Rotterdam, Karakter Uitgevers, Uithoorn & Speakers Academy Uitgeverij.

Foucault, M. (2006) 'Interview: polemics, politics and problematizations'. http://www.scribd.com/doc/20244408/Foucault-and-Rabinow-Polemics-Politics-and-Problematizations-Michel-Foucault-Interview Retrieved 14 March 2006.

Fox, C.J., Miller, H.T. (1995) *Postmodern public administration: Toward discourse*. Thousand Oaks, CA, Sage Publications.

Frankena, W.K. (1973) *Ethics*. Englewood Cliffs, NJ, Prentice-Hall.

Fujimura, J.H. (1987) 'Constructing "do-able" problems in cancer research: articulating alignment'. *Social Studies of Science* 17(2): 256–93.

Fung, A. (2003) 'Recipes for public spheres: eight institutional design choices and their consequences'. *Journal of Political Philosophy* 11(3): 338–67.

Funtowicz, S.O., Ravetz, J.R. (1992) 'Three types of risk assessment and the emergence of post-normal science', in Krimsky, S., Golding, D. (eds) *Social theories of risk* (pp 251–73). Westport, CT, Praeger.

Gale, T. (2003) 'Realising policy: the how and who of policy production'. *Discourse: Studies in the Cultural Politics of Education* 24(1): 51–65.

Gallo, R.C., Montagnier, L. (1988) 'AIDS in 1988'. *Scientific American* 259(4): 25–32.

Garland, D. (2001) *The culture of control: Crime and social order in contemporary society*. Oxford, Oxford University Press.

Garud, R., Hardy, C., Maguire, S. (2007) 'Institutional entrepreneurship as embedded agency: an introduction to the special issue'. *Organization Studies* 28(7): 957–69.

George, A.L. (1980) *Presidential decisionmaking in foreign policy: The effective use of information and advice*. Boulder, CO, Westview Press.

Gezondheidsraad (2001). *Prenatale screening. Downsyndroom, neuralebuisdefecten en routine-echoscopie.* Nummer 2001/11. Den Haag: Gezondheidsraad.

Giddens, A. (1979) *Central problems in social theory: Action, structure, and contradiction in social analysis.* Berkeley, CA, University of California Press.

Giddens, A. (1984) *The constitution of society: Outline of a theory of structuration.* Cambridge, Polity Press.

Giddens, A. (1985) *The nation-state and violence.* Cambridge, Cambridge University Press.

Giddens, A. (1991) *Modernity and self-identity: Self and society in the late modern age.* Cambridge, Polity Press.

Giddens, A. (1994) *Beyond Left and Right: The future of radical politics.* Cambridge, Polity Press.

Gieryn, T. (1999) *Cultural boundaries of science: Credibility on the line.* Chicago, IL, Chicago University Press.

Gieryn, T.F. (1995) 'Boundaries of science', in Jasanoff, S., Markle, G.E., Petersen, J.C, Pinch, T. (eds) *Handbook of science and technology studies* (pp 393–434). Thousand Oaks, CA, Sage Publications.

Gigerenzer, G., Todd, P.M., ABC Group (1999) *Simple heuristics that make us smart.* Oxford, Oxford University Press.

Glick, H.R., Hutchison, A. (1999) 'The rising agenda of physician–assisted suicide: explaining the growth and content of morality policy'. *Policy Studies Journal* 27(4): 750–65.

Goldstein, W.M., Hogarth, R.M. (1997) 'Judgment and decision research: some historical context', in Goldstein, W.M., Hogarth, R.M. (eds) *Research on judgment and decision making* (pp 3–65). Cambridge, Cambridge University Press.

Goodin, R.E., Dryzek, J.S. (2006) 'Deliberative Impacts: The Macro-Political Uptake of Mini-Publics'. *Politics & Society,* 34(2): 219–44.

Grandori, A. (1984) 'A prescriptive contingency view of organizational decision making'. *Administrative Science Quarterly* 29(2): 192–209.

Greenberg, G.D., Miller, J.A., Mohr, L.B., Vladeck, B.C. (1977) 'Developing public policy theory: perspectives from empirical research'. *American Political Science Review* 71(4): 1532–43.

Grendstad, G., Selle, P. (1999) 'The formation and transformation of preferences: cultural theory and postmaterialism compared', in Thompson, M., Grendstad, G., Selle, P. (eds) *Cultural theory as political science.* London and New York, Routledge.

Grin, J., and H. van de Graaf, 'Implementation as Communicative Action. An Interpretive Understanding of Interactions between Policy Actors and Target Groups'. *Policy Sciences,* 29(4): 291–319.

Grin, J., van de Graaf, H., Hoppe R. (1997) *Technology assessment through interaction: A guide.* Den Haag, SDU.

Guba, E.G., Lincoln, Y.S. (1989) *Fourth generation evaluation.* Newbury Park, CA, Sage Publications.

Gusfield, J. (1981) *The culture of public problems: Drinking-driving and the symbolic order.* Chicago, IL, University of Chicago Press.

Guston, D.H. (2001) 'Boundary organization in environmental policy and science: an introduction'. *Science, Technology and Human Values* 26(4): 399-408.

Haas, E.B. (1990) *When knowledge is power: Three models of change in international organisations.* Berkeley, CA, University of California Press.

Habermas, J. (1971) *Theorie und Praxis.* Frankfurt am Main, Suhrkamp.

Habermas, J. (1981) *Theorie des kommunikativen Handelns* (Bd. 1: Handlungsrationalität und gesellschaftliche Rationalisierung, Bd. 2: Zur Kritik der funktionalistischen Vernunft), Frankfurt am Main, Suhrkamp

Hage, M. (2002) 'De maatschappelijke omgang met nieuwe risico's. Het publiek debat "Eten en Genen" als voorbeeld'. MA thesis. Catholic University Nijmegen: 136.

Hajer, M., Wagenaar, H. (eds) (2003) *Deliberative policy analysis: Understanding governance in the network society.* Cambridge, Cambridge University Press.

Hajer, M.A. (1995) *The politics of environmental discourse: Ecological modernization and the policy process.* Oxford, Clarendon Press.

Hajer, M.A. (2003) A frame in the fields: policymaking and the reinvention of politics. Hajer, M., and H. Wagenaar, *Deliberative Policy Analysis*, 88-111

Halffman, W. (2003) 'Boundaries of regulatory science'. Dissertation. University of Amsterdam.

Halffman, W., in cooperation with Bal, R. (2008) 'After Impact: success of scientific advice to public policy', in Halffman, W. (ed) *States of nature: Nature and fish stock reports for policy* (Preliminary Study V. 13, pp 29-44). The Hague, RMNO.

Halffman, W., Hoppe, R. (2005) 'Science/policy boundaries: a changing division of labour in Dutch scientific policy advice', in Maassen, S., Weingart, P. (eds) *Democratization of expertise? Exploring novel forms of scientific advice in political decision-making: Sociology of Sciences Yearbook XXIV* (pp 135-52). Dordrecht, Springer.

Hall, T.A., O'Toole, Jr., L.J. (2004) 'Shaping formal networks through the regulatory process'. *Administration & Society* 36(2): 186-207.

Halperin, M.A. (1974) *Bureaucratic politics and foreign policy.* Washington, DC, Brookings Institute.

Hammond, K.R. (1996) *Human judgment and social policy: Irreducible uncertainty, inevitable error, unavoidable injustice.* Oxford, Oxford University Press.

Hanf, K., Scharpf, F.W. (eds) (1978) *Interorganisational policy making: Limits to coordination and central control.* London, Sage Publications.

Hayes, M.T. (2001) *The limits of policy change: Incrementalism, worldview, and the rule of law.* Washington, DC, Georgetown University Press.

Heady, F. (1991) *Public administration. A comparative perspective* (5th edition). New York, Marcel Dekker.

Heclo, H. (1974) *Social policy in Britain and Sweden.* New Haven, CT, Yale University Press.

Heclo, H. (1978) 'Issue networks and the executive establishment', in King, A. (ed) *The new American political system.* Washington, DC, American Enterprise Institute.

Helderman, J.K. (2007) 'Bringing the market back in? Institutional complexity and hierarchy in Dutch housing and healthcare'. Dissertation. Erasmus University, Rotterdam.

Hendriks, F. (1999) *Public policy and political institutions: The role of culture in traffic policy*. Cheltenham, Edward Elgar.

Hickson, D.J., Butler, R.J., Cray, D., Mallory, G.R., Wilson, D.C. (1986) *Top decisions: Strategic decision-making in organizations*. Oxford, Basil Blackwell.

Hilgartner, S., Bosk, C.L. (1988) 'The rise and fall of social problems: a public arenas model'. *American Journal of Sociology* 94: 53-78.

Hill, M., Hupe, P. (2002) *Implementing public policy: Governance in theory and in practice*. London, Sage Publications

Hirst, P. (1994) *Associative democracy*. Cambridge, Polity Press.

Hisschemöller, M., Van Koolwijk Th.(1982) De Waddenzee, University of Amsterdam (unpublished research report)

Hisschemöller, M. (1993) *De democratie van problemen: De relatie tussen de inhoud van beleidsproblemen en methoden van politieke besluitvorming*. Amsterdam, Free University Press.

Hisschemöller, M. (2005) 'Participation as Knowledge Production and the limits of democracy', in Maassen, S., Weingart, P. (eds) *Democratization of expertise? Exploring novel forms of scientific advice in political decision-making* (pp 189-208). Dordrecht, Springer.

Hisschemöller, M., Cuppen, E., Dunn, W.N. (2009) 'Stakeholder dialogues as social experiment', ESF Workshop 'Mapping interfaces: the future of knowledge'. Reykjavik, Iceland.

Hisschemöller, M., Hoppe, R. (1996) 'Coping with intractable controversies: the case for problem structuring in policy design and analysis'. *Knowledge for Policy* 4(8): 40-60.

Hisschemöller, M., Hoppe, R. (2001) 'Coping with intractable controversies: the case for problem structuring in policy design and analysis', in Hisschemöller, M., Hoppe, R., Dunn, W.N, Ravetz, J. (eds) *Knowledge, power, and participation in environmental policy analysis* (pp 47-72). New Brunswick, NJ, Transaction Publishers.

Hisschemöller, M., Hoppe, R., Groenewegen, P., Midden, C. (2001) 'Knowledge use and political choice in dutch environmental policy: a problem structuring perspective on real life experiments in extended peer review', in Hisschemöller, M., Hoppe, R., Dunn, W.N, Ravetz, J. (eds) *Knowledge, power, and participation in environmental policy* (pp 437-70). New Brunswick, NJ, Transaction Publishers.

Hisschemöller, M., Midden, C.J.H. (1999) 'Improving the usability of research on the public perception of science and technology for policy-making'. *Public Understanding of Science* 8: 17-33.

Hodgkinson, C. (1983) *Towards a philosophy of administration*. Oxford, Basil Blackwell.

Hogwood, B.W., Lewis, L.A. (1986) *Policy analysis for the real world*. Oxford, Oxford University Press.

Hood, C. (1986) 'Concepts of control over bureaucracies: "comptrol" and "interpolable balance"', in Kaufmann, F.X. (ed) *Guidance, control, and evaluation in the public sector* (pp 765-86). Berlin and New York, Walter de Gruyter.

Hood, C. (1991) 'A public management for all seasons?'. *Public Administration* 69(1): 3-19.

Hood, C. (1998) *The art of the state: Culture, rhetoric, and public management.* Oxford, Clarendon Press.

Hoppe, R. (1983) 'Economische Zaken schrijft een nota: een onderzoek naar beleidsontwikkeling en besluitvorming bij nonincrementeel beleid'. Dissertation. Amsterdam, VU Boekhandel/Uitgeverij.

Hoppe, R. (1989) *Het beleidsprobleem geproblematiseerd: Over beleid ontwerpen en probleemvorming.* Muiderberg, Coutinho.

Hoppe, R. (1993) 'Political judgment and the policy cycle: the case of ethnicity policy arguments in the Netherlands', in Fischer, F., Forester, J. (eds) *The argumentative turn in policy analysis and planning* (pp 77-100). Durham, Duke University Press.

Hoppe, R. (1999) 'Policy analysis, science, and politics: from "speaking truth to power" to "making sense together"'. *Science and Public Policy* 26(3): 201-10.

Hoppe, R. (2002) 'Cultures of problem definition'. *Journal of Comparative Policy Analysis: Research and Practice* 4(3): 305-26.

Hoppe, R. (2005) 'Rethinking the science-policy nexus: from knowledge utilization and science technology studies to types of boundary arrangements'. *Poièsis and Praxis* 3(3): 199-215.

Hoppe, R. (2007) 'Applied cultural theory: tool in policy analysis', in Fischer, F., Miller, G., Sidney, M. (eds) *Handbook of public policy analysis* (pp 289-308). Boca Raton, London, New York, CRC Press Francis and Taylor Group.

Hoppe, R. (2008a) 'Public policy subsystems dealing with ethically contested medical-technological issues'. *Creativity and Innovation Management* 17(4): 293-303.

Hoppe, R. (2008b) 'Scientific advice and public policy: expert advisers' and policymakers' discourses on boundary work'. *Poièsis and Praxis* 6(3-4): 235-63.

Hoppe, R., Grin J. (1995) "Toward a comparative framework for learning from experiences with interactive technology". *Organization & Environment* 9: 99-120

Hoppe, R., Grin. J. (2000) 'Traffic problems go through the technology assessment machine', in Vig, N.J. and Paschen, H. (eds) *Parliaments and technology: The development of technology assessment in Europe.* Albany, NY, State University of New York Press (pp 273-324).

Hoppe, R., Huijs, S. (2003) *Grenzenwerk tussen wetenschap en beleid: Dilemma's en paradoxen.* Den Haag, Raad voor Ruimtelijke Ordening, Milieu en Natuur Onderzoek (RMNO).

Hoppe, R., Jeliazkova, M.I. (2006) 'How policy workers define their job: a Netherlands case study', in Colebatch, H.K. (ed) *The work of policy: An international survey* (pp 35-60). Lanham, MD, Lexington.

Hoppe, R., Peterse, A. (1993) *Handling frozen fire: Political culture and risk management.* Boulder, CO, Westview Press.

Hoppe, R., Peterse, A. (eds) (1998) *Bouwstenen voor argumentatieve beleidsanalyse.* 's-Gravenhage, Elsevier.

Hoppe, R., Van de Graaf, H., Besseling, E. (1995) 'Successful policy formulation processes: lessons from fifteen case experiences in five Dutch departments'. *Acta Politica* (2): 153–88.

Horowitz, I.L. (1988) 'The limits of policy: the case of AIDS'. *Knowledge in Society* 1(1): 54–65.

Howlett, M. (2000) ' Managing the hollow state: procedural policy instruments and modern governance'. *Canadian Public Administration* 43(4): 412–31.

Howlett, M. (2002) 'Do networks matter? Linking policy network structure to policy outcomes: evidence from four Canadian policy sectors 1990–2000'. *Canadian Journal of Political Science* 35(2): 235–67.

Howlett, M. (2004) 'Beyond good and evil in policy implementation: instrument mixes, implementation styles, and second generation theories of policy instrument choice'. *Policy and Society* 23(2): 1–17.

Howlett, M., Ramesh, M. (1998) 'Policy subsystem configurations and policy change: operationalizing the postpositivist analysis of the politics of the policy process'. *Policy Studies Journal* 26(3): 466–81.

Husted, B. (2000) 'A contingency theory of corporate social performance'. *Business and Society* 39(1): 24–48.

Husted, B. (2007) 'Agency, information, and the structure of moral problems in business'. *Organization Studies* 28(2): 177–95.

Inglehart, R. (1977) *The silent revolution.* Princeton, NJ, Princeton University Press.

Inglehart, R. (1990) *Culture shift in advanced industrial society.* Princeton, NJ, Princeton University Press.

Inglehart, R. (1999) 'Postmodernization erodes respect for authority, but increases support for democracy', in Norris, P. (ed) *Critical citizens* (pp 236–56). Oxford, Oxford University Press.

Janis, I.L. (1982) *Groupthink: Psychological studies of policy decisions and fiascos* (2nd edition). New York, The Free Press.

Janis, I.L., Mann, L. (1977) *Decision making: A psychological analysis of conflict, choice and commitment.* New York, The Free Press.

Jasanoff, S. (1990) *The fifth branch: Science advisers as policy makers.* Cambridge, MA, Harvard University Press.

Jasanoff, S., Markle, G.E., Petersen, J.C., Pinch, T. (eds) (1995) *Handbook of science and technology studies.* Thousand Oaks, CA, Sage Publications.

Jaspers, K. (1960) *Die geistige Situation der Zeit*, Berlin, Walter de Gruyter

Jaspers, K. (1974) *Kleine Schule des philosophischen Denkens.* München, Piper.

Jaspers, K. (1981) *Der philosophische Glaube*, München, Piper

Jennings, B. (1987) 'Policy analysis: science, advocacy, or counsel?', in Nagel, S.S. (ed) *Research in public policy analysis and management, vol. 4.* (pp 121–34). Greenwich, JAI Press.

John, P. (1998, 2nd ed. 2000) *Analyzing public policy.* London, Continuum.

Joly, P.-B., Marris, C. (2003) 'La participation contre la mobilisation? Une analyse comparée du débat sur les OGM en France et au Royaume-Uni'. *Revue Internationale de Politique Comparée* 10(2): 195–206.

Jones, B.D., Baumgartner, F.R. (2005) *The politics of attention: How government prioritizes problems*. Chicago, IL and London, Chicago University Press.

Joss, S., Bellucci, S. (eds) (2002) *Participatory technology assessment: European perspectives*, University of Westminster, London, Centre for the Study of Democracy.

Joss, S., Durant, J. (eds) (1995) *Public participation in science: The role of consensus conferences in Europe*. London, Science Museum and EC DG XII.

Kahan, D.M., Braman, D. (2003) 'Response: caught in the cross-fire: a defense of the cultural theory of gun–risk perceptions'. *University of Pennsylvania Law Review* 151: 1395-416.

Kahan, D.M., Braman, D., Gastil, J. (2005) 'A cultural critique of gun litigation', in T. Lytton (ed) *Suing the gun industry*, University of Michigan Press, pp 105-29.

Kaufman, H. (1976) *Are government organizations immortal?* Washington, DC, Brookings Institution.

Keman, H. (2008) 'Introduction: politics in the Netherlands after 1989: a final farewell to consociationalism?'. *Acta Politica* 43(2-3): 149-53.

Kern, F., Smith, A. (2008) 'Restructuring energy systems for sustainability? Energy transition policy in the Netherlands'. *Energy Policy* 36: 4093- 103.

Kickert, W., Klijn, E.-H., Koppenjan, J. (eds) (1997) *Managing complex networks: Strategies for the public sector*. London, Sage Publications.

Kingdon, J.W. (1984) *Agendas, alternatives, and public policies*. Glenview, IL, Scott, Foresman and Company.

Kirejczyk, M., Van Berkel, D., Swierstra, T. (2001) *Nieuwe Voortplanting: Afscheid van de Ooievaar*. The Hague, Rathenau Instituut.

Kleindorfer, P.R., Kunreuther, H.C., Schoemaker, P.J.H. (1993) *Decision sciences: An integrative perspective*. Cambridge, Cambridge University Press.

Klijn, E.-H. (2008) 'Policy and implementation networks: managing complex interactions', in Cropper, S., Ebers, M., Ring, P. (eds) *Handbook of inter-organisational relations* (pp 118-46). Oxford, Oxford University Press.

Klinkers, L. (2002) *Vakvereisten voor politiek en beleid*. Meise, Klinkers Public Policy Consultants BVBA.

Klok, P.-J., Denters, B. (2005) 'Urban leadership and community involvement', in Haus, M., Heinelt, H., Stewart, M. *Urban governance and democracy: Leadership and community involvement* (pp 40-64). London and New York, Routledge.

Klüver, L. (1995) 'Consensus conferences at the Danish Board of Technology', in Durant, J., Joss, S. (eds) *Public participation in science* (pp 41-9), Science Museum, London (with financial support from the European Commission Directorate General XII)

Knorr-Cetina, K. (1995) 'Laboratory studies: the cultural approach to the study of science', in Jasanoff, S., Markle, G.E., Petersen, J.C., Pinch, T. (eds) *Handbook of science and technology studies* (pp 140-66). Thousand Oaks, CA, Sage Publications.

Kooiman, J. (1988) *Besturen: Maatschappij en overheid in wisselwerking*. Assen/Maastricht, Van Gorcum.

Kooiman, J. (eds) (1993) *Modern governance: New government–society interactions*. London, Sage Publications.

Kooiman, J., Jentoft, S., Pullin, R., Bavinck, M. (eds) (2005) *Fish for life: Interactive governance for fisheries.* Amsterdam, Amsterdam University Press.

Korsten, A, Hoppe, R..(2006) 'Van beleidswetenschap naar kennissamenleving: voortgang, vooruitgang en achteruitgang in de beleidswetenschap', *Beleidswetenschap,* 20, 4, pp. 34–72

Krieger, M.H. (1981) *Advice and planning.* Philadelphia, PA, Temple University Press.

Kriesi, H., Trechsel, A.H. (2008) *The politics of Switzerland: Continuity and change in a consensus democracy.* Cambridge, Cambridge University Press.

Krimsky, S., Golding, D. (eds) (1992) *Social theories of risk.* Westport, CT, Praeger.

Kübler, D. (2001) 'Understanding policy change with the advocacy coalition framework: an application to Swiss drug policy'. *Journal of European Public Policy* 8(4): 623–41.

Laes, E., Meskens, G., D'Haeseleer, D., Weiler, R. (2004) 'The Belgian nuclear phase-out as a strategy for sustainable development: unstructured problems, unstructured answers?, in Biermann, F., Campe, S., Jacob, K. (eds) *Proceedings of the 2002 Berlin Conference on the Human Dimensions of Global Environmental Change 'Knowledge for the Sustainability Transition: The Challenge for Social Science'* (pp 271–84). Amsterdam, Berlin, Potsdam, Oldenburg, Global Governance Project.

Lakoff, G. (1996) *Moral politics: How liberals and conservatives think.* Chicago, IL, University of Chicago Press.

Landry, R., Lamari, M., Amara, N. (2003) 'The extent and determinants of utilization of university research in government agencies'. *Public Administration Review* 63(2): 192–205.

Landwehr, C. (2009) *Political conflict and political preferences. Communicative interaction between facts, norms and interests.* University of Essex, Colchester, ECPR Press

Lasswell, H.D. (1927, MIT Press Edition 1971) *Propaganda technique in the world war,* Cambridge, Mass., MIT Press.

Lasswell, H.D. (1930, Midway Reprint Edition 1986) *Psychopathology and politics,* University of Chicago Press, London

Lasswell, H.D. (1951) 'The policy orientation', in Lerner, D., Lasswell, H.D. (eds) *The policy sciences.* Stanford, CA, Stanford University Press.

Lasswell, H.D. (1971) *Pre-view of policy sciences.* New York, Elsevier.

Latour, B. (1994 [1st ed. 1987]) *Science in action: How to follow scientists and engineers through society.* Harvard, MA, Harvard University Press.

Lauman, E.O., Knoke, D. (1987) *The organizational state: Social choice in national policy domains.* Madison, WI, University of Wisconsin Press.

Lerner, D., Lasswell, H.D. (1951) *The policy sciences: Recent developments in scope and methods.* Stanford, CA, Stanford University Press.

Lijphart, A. (1967) *The politics of accommodation.* Berkeley, CA, University of California Press.

Lijphart, A. (1999) *Patterns of democracy: Government forms and performance in thirty-six countries.* New Haven, CT and London, Yale University Press.

Lindblom, C.E. (1959) 'The science of muddling through'. *Public Administration Review* 19: 78–88.

Lindblom, C.E. (1965) *The intelligence of democracy*. New York, Free Press.

Lindblom, C.E. (1968) *The policymaking process*. Englewood Cliffs, NJ, Prentice-Hall.

Lindblom, C.E. (1977) *Politics and markets: The world's political-economic systems*. New York, Basic Books.

Lindblom, C.E. (1979) 'Still muddling, not yet through'. *Public Administration Review* 39(6): 517–26.

Lindblom, C.E., Cohen, D.K. (1979) *Usable knowledge*. New Haven, CT, Yale University Press.

Lindblom, C.E. (1990) *Inquiry and change: The troubled attempt to understand and shape society*. New Haven, CT, Yale University Press.

Lindblom, C.E., Woodhouse, E.J. (1993 [1st ed. 1968]) *The policy-making process* (3rd edition). Englewood Cliffs, NJ, Prentice-Hall.

Lindblom, C.E. (1999) 'A century of planning', in Meadowcroft, J., Kenny, M. (eds) *Planning sustainability* (pp 39–65). London and New York, Routledge.

Lindblom, C.E. (2001) *The market system: What it is, how it works, and what to make of it*. New Haven, CT and London, Yale University Press.

Lipset, S.M. (1963) *Political man*. New York, Doubleday.

Lipset, S.M., Rokkan, S. (eds) (1967) *Party systems and voter alignments*. New York, Free Press.

Lobstein, T., Kestens, M., Loegstrup, S. (2006) Policy options to prevent child obesity. Stakeholder consultations carried out in the context of the project on 'Children, obesity and associated avoidable chronic diseases', European Heart Network.

Loeber, A. (2004) 'Practical wisdom in the risk society: methods and practice of interpretive analysis on questions of sustainable development'. PhD thesis. University of Amsterdam.

Lowi, T.J. (1995 [1972]) 'Four systems of policy, politics, and choice', in McCool, D.C. (ed) *Public policy theories, models, and concepts: An anthology* (pp 181–201). Upper Saddle River, NJ, Prentice Hall.

Lowi, T.J. (1997) 'Comments on Anderson'. *Policy Studies Journal* 25(2): 283–85.

Lukes, S. (1974) *Power: A radical view*. London, Macmillan.

Lyotard, J.-F. (1984) *The postmodern condition: A report on knowledge*. Minneapolis, MN, University of Minnesota Press.

Maassen, S., Weingart, P. (eds) (2005) *Democratization of expertise? Exploring novel forms of scientific advice in political decision-making*. Dordrecht, Springer.

MacRae, Jr., D. (1985) *Policy indicators: Links between social science and public debate*. Chapel Hill, NC, University of North Carolina Press.

MacRae, Jr., D., Whittington, D. (1997). *Expert Advice for Policy Choice. Analysis and Discourse*. Washington D.C., Georgetown University Press

Mahoney, J., Rueschemeyer, D. (2003) *Comparative historical analysis in the social sciences*. Cambridge, Cambridge University Press.

Majone, G. (1978 [1980]) 'The uses of policy analysis', in *The future and the past: Essays on programs* (pp 201-20). New York, Russell Sage Foundation. Reference to first publication, taken from: G. Majone (1980)'The uses of policy analysis', B. H. Raven (ed.), *Policy Studies Review Annual, Volume 4*, Sage, Beverly Hills and London, pp. 161-180

Majone, G. (1989) *Evidence, argument and persuasion in the policy process*. New Haven, CT, Yale University Press.

Majone, G., Wildavsky, A. (1979, expanded edition) 'Implementation as evolution', in Pressman, J.L., Wildavsky, A. (eds) *Implementation* (pp 177-95). Berkeley, CA, University of California Press.

Mamadouh, V. (1999) 'Grid-group cultural theory'. *GeoJournal* 46(3): 385-500.

Mansbridge, J.J. (1986) *Why we lost the ERA*. Chicago, IL and London, Chicago University Press.

March, J.G., Olsen, J.P. (eds) (1976) *Ambiguity and choice in organizations*. Bergen, Universitetsforlaget.

March, J.G., Simon, H.A. (1993 [1958]) *Organizations*. Oxford, Blackwell.

Mason, R.O., Mitroff, I.I. (1981) *Challenging Strategic Planning Assumptions. Theory, Cases, and Techniques*. New York etc., John Wiley & Sons

Matheson, P.E. (translation) (1916) *Epictetus: The discourses and manual*. Oxford, Clarendon Press.

Matthews, T.J., Bolognesi, D.P. (1988) 'AIDS vaccines'. *Scientific American* 259(4): 98-105.

Mayer, I. (1997) *Debating technologies: A methodological contribution to the design and evaluation of participatory policy analysis*. Tilburg, Tilburg University Press.

Mayer, I.S., Van Daalen, C.E., Bots, P.W.G. (2004) 'Perspectives on policy analysis: a framework for understanding and design'. *International Journal of Technology, Policy and Management* 4(2): 169-91.

McCool, D.C. (eds) (1995) *Public policy theories, models and concepts: An anthology*. Upper Saddle River, NJ, Prentice Hall.

Meier, K.J. (1999) 'Drugs, sex, rock, and roll: a theory of morality politics'. *Policy Studies Journal* 27(4): 681- 95.

Meltsner, A. (1976) *Policy Analysts in the Bureaucracy*. Berkeley, University of California Press

Meijer, S. (2008) 'Discussie en aanpak van het beleidsvraagstuk rondom prenatale screening op Downsyndroom en neuralebuisdefecten'. BA thesis. University of Twente.

Merkx, F. (2008) 'Organizing responsibilities for novelties in medical genetics', Enschede, University of Twente.

Meyer, J.W., Scott, W.R. (1992) *Organizational environments: Ritual and rationality*. Newbury Park, CA, Sage Publications.

Michaels, D. (2008) *Doubt is their product: How industry's assault on science threatens your health*. Oxford, Oxford University Press.

Michaels, D., Monforton, C. (2005) 'Manufacturing uncertainty: contested science and the protection of the public's health and environment'. *American Journal of Public Health, Supplement 1*, 95(S1): S39–S48.

Midgley, G. (2000) *Systemic intervention: Philosophy, methodology, and practice.* New York, Kluwer.

Mierlo, v., J.G.A. (1988) *Pressiegroepen in de Nederlandse politiek,* Den Haag, Stichting Maatschappij en Onderneming.

Mill, J.S. (1974) "Bentham," in *John Stuart Mill: Utilitarianism, On Liberty, and Essay on Bentham.* Ed. M. Warnock. [New American Library, 1974] 123.

Miller, A. (1996) 'A preliminary typology of organizational learning: synthesizing the literature'. *Journal of Management* 22(3): 485–505.

Miller, S.J., Hickson, D.J., Wilson, D.C. (1996) 'Decision-Making in Organizations', in Hardy, C., Clegg, S.R., Nord, W.R. (eds) *Handbook of organization studies* (pp 293-312). London, Sage Publications.

Mintrom, M. (2003) 'Market organizations and deliberative democracy: choice and voice in public service delivery'. *Administration & Society* 35(1): 52–81.

Mintzberg, H., Raisanghani, D., Theoret, A. (1976) 'The structure of "unstructured" decision processes'. *Administrative Science Quarterly* 21: 246-75.

Moe, T. (1980) *The organization of interests.* Chicago, IL, Chicago University Press.

Monnikhof, R.A.H. (2006) 'Policy analysis for participatory policy making'. PhD dissertation. Department of Technical Public Administration, Technical University Delft.

Moon, J.D. (1975) 'The logic of political inquiry: a synthesis of opposed perspectives', in Greenstein, F.I. Polsby, N.W. (eds) *Handbook of political science: Volume I* (pp 131-238). Reading, MA, Addison-Wesley.

Mooney, C.Z. (1999) 'The politics of morality policy: symposium editor's introduction'. *Policy Studies Journal* 27(4): 675-80.

Moran, M., Rein, M., Goodin, R.E. (eds) (2008) *The Oxford handbook of public policy.* The Oxford Handbooks of Political Science. Oxford, Oxford University Press.

Motivaction (2001) *Burgerschapstijlen en overheidscommunicatie.* Amsterdam, Motivaction.

Myrdal, G. (1996 [1st ed. 1944]) *An American dilemma: The negro problem and modern democracy.* New Brunswick, NJ and London, Transaction Books.

Nathanson, C. (1999) 'Social movements as catalysts for policy change: the case of smoking and guns'. *Journal of Health Politics, Policy, and Law* 24(3): 421-88.

Nelkin, D. (1995) 'Science controversies: the dynamics of public disputes in the United States', in Jasanoff, S., Markle, G.E., Petersen, J.C., Pinch, T. (eds) *Handbook of science and technology studies* (pp 444-56). Thousand Oaks, CA: Sage Publications.

Nelson, B.J. (1996) 'Public policy and administration: an overview', in Goodin, R.E., Klingemann, H.-D. (eds) *A new handbook of political science* (pp 551-92). Oxford and New York, Oxford University Press.

Nestle, M. (2002) *Food politics: How the food industry influences nutrition and health* (revised and expanded edition). Berkeley, CA, University of California Press.

Niskanen, W.A. (1971) *Bureaucracy and representative government*. Chicago, IL, Aldine-Atherton.

Noordegraaf, M. (2000) 'Professional sense-makers: managerial competencies amidst ambiguity'. *International Journal of Public Sector Management* 13(4): 319-32.

Nowotny, H., Scott, P., Gibbons, M. (2001) *Re-thinking science: Knowledge and the public in an age of uncertainty*. Cambridge, Polity.

Nutley, S.M., Walter, I., Davies, H.T.O. (2007) *Using evidence: How research can inform public services*. Bristol, The Policy Press.

Nutt, P. (1984) 'Types of organizational decision processes'. *Administrative Science Quarterly* 29(2): 230-61.

Nutt, P.N. (2002) 'Selecting decision rules for crucial choices'. *The Journal of Applied Behavioral Science* 38(1): 99-131.

Obama, B. (2006) *The Audacity of Hope. Thoughts on Reclaiming the American Dream*. New York, Three Rivers Press

Olsen, J.P. (1988) 'Administrative reform and theories of organization', in Campbell, C., Peters, B.G. (eds) *Organizing governance: Governing organizations*. Pittsburgh, PA, University of Pittsburgh Press.

Olson, M. (1965) *The logic of collective action*. Cambridge, MA, Harvard University Press.

Osborne, D., and T. Gaebler (1992) *Reinventing Government: How the Entrepreneurial Spirit Is Transforming the Public Sector*. Reading, Mass., Addison-Wesley

Ostrom, E. (1990) *Governing the commons*. Cambridge, Cambridge University Press.

Ostrom, E. (2005) *Understanding institutional diversity*. Princeton, NJ and Oxford, Princeton University Press.

O'Toole, L.J. (2000) 'Research and policy implementation: assessments and prospects'. *Journal of Public Administration Research and Theory* 10: 263-88.

Outshoorn, J.V. (1986) *De politieke strijd rond de abortuswetgeving in Nederland, 1964-1984*. Leiden, DSWO Press.

Outshoorn, J.V. (1989) *Een irriterend onderwerp: Verschuivende conceptualisering van het sekseverschil*. Nijmegen, SUN.

Page, E.C., Jenkins, B. (2005) *Policy bureaucracy: Government with a cast of thousands*. Oxford, Oxford University Press.

Palumbo, D. (eds) (1987) *The politics of program evaluation*. Newbury Park, CA, Sage Publications.

Papadopoulos, Y. (2003) 'Cooperative forms of governance: problems of democratic accountability in complex environments'. *European Journal of Political Research* 42: 473-501.

Papadopoulos, Y., Warin, P. (2007) 'Are innovative, participatory and deliberative procedures of policymaking effective and legitimate?'. *European Journal of Political Research* 46: 445-72.

Paparone, C.R., Crupi, J.A. (2005/2006) 'Rubrics cubed: are we prisoners of ORSA-style decision-making'. *Defense Acquisition Review Journal* 2005 - March 2006: 420-35.

Paris, D.C., Reynolds, J.F. (1983) *The logic of policy inquiry*. New York, Longman.

Parsons, W. (1995) *Public policy: An introduction to the theory and practice of policy analysis.* Aldershot and Brookfield, Edward Elgar.

Pateman, C. (1970) *Participation and democratic theory.* Cambridge, Cambridge University Press.

Pateman, C. (1979) *The problem of political obligation: A critical analysis of liberal theory.* Chichester, Wiley.

Pellizzoni, L. (2001) 'The myth of the best argument: power, deliberation and reason'. *British Journal of Sociology* 52(1): 59-86.

Peters, B.G. (1996) *The policy capacity of government.* Research Report No 18. Ottawa, Ontario, Canadian Centre for Management Development.

Peterse, A. (2006) *Simulating nature. A philosophical study of computer-simulation uncertainties and their role in climate science and policy advice.* Utrecht, University of Utrecht.

Pierre, J. (2000) *Debating governance.* Oxford, Oxford University Press.

Popper, K.R. (1945) *The open society and its enemies.* London, Routledge.

Popper, K.R. (1963) *Conjectures and refutations.* London, Routledge.

Pralle, S.B. (2003) 'Venue shopping, political strategy, and policy change: the internationalization of Canadian forest advocacy'. *Journal of Public Policy* 23(3): 233-60.

Prasser, S. (2006) Aligning "good policy" with "good politics"', in Colebatch, H.K. (ed) *Beyond the policy cycle: The policy process in Australia* (pp 266-92). St. Leonards, Allen and Unwin.

Putnam, R.D. (2000) *Bowling alone: The collapse and revival of American community.* New York, Simon & Schuster.

Quinn, J.B. (1978) 'Strategic change: "logical incrementalism"'. *Sloan Management Review* 20(1): 7-21.

RMNO (Council for Spatial, Environmental and Nature Research) (2009) Duurzame ontwikkeling en Schiphol. A.14. Den Haag

Radin, B. (2000) *Beyond Machiavelli: policy analysis comes of age.* Washington, DC, Georgetown University Press.

Raiffa, H. (1968) *Decision analysis.* Reading, MA, Addison-Wesley.

Rastogi, P.N. (1992) *Policy analysis and problem solving for social systems: Toward understanding, monitoring and managing complex real world problems.* New Delhi, Sage Publications.

Ravetz, J. (1999) 'What is post-normal science?'. *Futures* 31: 647-54.

Ravetz, J. (2001) 'Models of risk: an exploration', in Hisschemöller, M., Hoppe, R., Dunn, W.N. and Ravetz, J.R. (eds) *Knowledge, power and participation in environmental policy analysis. Policy Studies Review Annual, Volume 12.* (Transaction, New Brunswick and London, 2001): 471-92.

Ravetz, J. (2005) *The no-nonsense guide to science.* Oxford, New Internationalist.

Rawls, J. (1971) *A theory of justice.* Cambridge, MA, Harvard University Press.

Renn, O. (1992) 'The social arena concept of risk debates', in Krimsky, S., Golding, D. (eds) *Social theories of risk* (pp 179-96). Westport, CT, Praeger.

Renn, O., Webler, T., Wiedemann, P. (eds) (1995) *Fairness and competence in citizen participation: Evaluating models for environmental discourse.* Dordrecht/Boston, MA/London, Kluwer Academic Publishers.

Rescher, N. (1980) *Induction: An essay on the justification of inductive reasoning.* Pittsburgh, PA, University of Pittsburgh Press.

Restivo, S. (1995) 'The theory landscape in science studies: sociological traditions', in Jasanoff, S., Markle, G.E., Petersen, J.C., Pinch, T. (eds) *Handbook of science and technology studies* (pp 95–110). Thousand Oaks, CA, Sage Publications.

Rhodes, R.A.W. (2000) Governance and Public Administration. J. Pierre (ed.), *Debating Governance. Authority, Steering, and Democracy,* Oxford, Oxford University Press, 54–90

Rich, A. (2004) *Think tanks, public policy, and the politics of expertise.* Cambridge, Cambridge University Press.

Riker, W. (1986) The Art of Political Manipulation. New Haven: Yale UP

Rip, A. (1997) 'A cognitive approach to relevance of science'. *Social Science Information* 36(4): 615–40.

Rittel, H.W.J., Webber, M.D. (1973) 'Dilemmas in a general theory of planning'. *Policy Sciences* 4: 155–69.

Roberts, N.C., King, P.J. (1991) 'Policy entrepreneurs: their activity structure and function in the policy process'. *J-PART* 1(2): 147–75.

Rochefort, D.A., Cobb, R.W. (eds) (1994) *The politics of problem definition: Shaping the policy agenda.* Lawrence, KS, Kansas University Press.

Roe, E. (1994) *Narrative policy analysis: Theory and practice.* Durham and London, Duke University Press.

Rokeach, M. (1973) *The nature of human values.* New York, Free Press.

Rooney, D., Hearn, G., Mandeville, T., Joseph, R. (2003a) *Public policy in the knowledge-based economies: Foundations and frameworks.* Cheltenham and Northampton, Edward Elgar.

Rooney, D., Hearn, G., Mandeville, T., Joseph, R. (2003b) 'What is knowledge?', in Rooney, D., Hearn, G., Mandeville, T., Joseph, R. *Public policy in knowledge-based economies: Foundations and frameworks* (pp 1–15). Cheltenham and Northampton, Edward Elgar.

Rooney, D., Schneider, U. (2005) 'The material, mental, historical and social character of knowledge', in Rooney, D., Hearn, G., Ninan, A. (eds) *Handbook of the knowledge economy* (pp 19–36). Cheltenham and Northampton, Edward Elgar.

Rosanvallon, P. (2006) *Democracy past and future.* New York, Columbia University Press.

Rose, R. (1990) 'Inheritance before choice in public policy'. *Journal of Theoretical Politics* 2: 263–91.

Rose, R. (1993) *Lesson-drawing in public policy: A guide to learning across time and space.* Chatham, Chatham House Publishers.

Sabatier, P. (1991) 'Toward better theories of the policy process'. *PS: Political Science and Politics* 24: 147–56.

Sabatier, P., Jenkins-Smith, H. (1993) *Policy change and learning: An advocacy coalition approach*. Boulder, CO, Westview Press.

Sabatier, P. (ed) (1999) *Theories of the Policy Process.* Boulder, CO: Westview Press.

Sabel, C., O'Donnell, R. (2001) *Democratic experimentalism: What to do about wicked problems after Whitehall*. Paris, OECD.

Safranski, R. (2005 [1999]) *Das Böse oder Das Drama der Freiheit*. Frankfurt am Main, Fischer. (in Dutch: *Het kwaad*, Olympus, 2005)

Saretzki, T. (1996) 'Wie unterscheiden sich Argumentieren und Verhandeln? Definitionsprobleme, funktionale Bezüge und strukturelle Differenzen von zwei verschiedenen Kommunikationsmodi', in Von Prittwitz, V. (ed) *Verhandeln und Argumentieren: Dialog, Interessen und Macht in der Umweltpolitik* (pp 20-39). Opladen, Leske and Budrich.

Scharpf, F.W. (1978) 'Interorganisational Policy Studies: Issues, Concepts and Perspectives' (345-370). Hanf, K., Schaprf, F. (eds.), Interorganizational Policy-Making. Limits to Central Coordination and Control, London, Sage

Scharpf, F.W. (1997) *Games real actors play: Actor-centered institutionalism in policy research*. Boulder, CO, Westview Press.

Schattschneider, E.E. (1960 [1988]) *The semi-sovereign people: A realist's view of democracy in America*, Belmont, CA, Wadsworth Thomson Learning.

Scheffer, P. (2007) *Het land van aankomst.* Amsterdam, De Bezige Bij.

Schillemans, T. (2007) *Verantwoording in de schaduw van de macht: Horizontale verantwoording bij zelfstandige uitvoeringsorganisaties*, Utrecht, Lemma.

Schmidt, H., Schischkoff, G. (1978) *Philosophisches Wörterbuch*. Stuttgart, Alfred Kröner Verlag.

Schmutzer, M.A.E. (1994) *Ingenium und Individuum: Eine sozialwissenschaftliche Theorie von Wissenschaft und Technik*. Wien/New York, Springer.

Schneider, A.L., Ingram, H. (1997) *Policy design for democracy*. Lawrence, KS, Kansas University Press.

Scholten, P. (2008) 'Constructing immigrant policies: research–policy relations and immigrant integration in The Netherlands (1970-2004)'. PhD thesis. University of Twente.

Schön, D.A. (1983) *The reflective practitioner*. New York, Basic Books.

Schön, D.A., Rein, M. (1994) *Frame reflection: Towards the resolution of intractable policy controversies*. New York, Basic Books.

Scientific Council of Government Policy (WRR) (2001) The Netherlands as an immigration society, The Hague

Schudson, M. (1998) *The good citizen: A history of American civic life*. New York, Free Press.

Schumpeter, J. (1942) *Capitalism, socialism, and democracy*. London, Routledge.

Schwandt, T.A. (1994) 'Constructivist, interpretivist approaches to human inquiry', in Denzin, N.K., Lincoln, Y.S. (eds) *Handbook of qualitative research* (pp 105-17). Thousand Oaks, CA, Sage Publications.

Schwarz, M., Thompson, M. (1990) *Divided we stand: Redefining politics, technology, and social choice*. New York, Harvester & Wheatsheaf.

Sclove, R.E. (1995) *Democracy and technology*. New York and London, Guilford Press.

Scott, J.C. (1998) *Seeing like a state: How certain schemes to improve the human condition have failed*. New Haven, CT, Yale University Press.

Sederberg, P.C. (1984) *The politics of meaning: Power and explanation in the construction of social reality*. Tucson, AZ, University of Arizona Press.

Self, P. (1975) *Econocrats and the policy process: The politics and philosophy of cost-benefit analysis*. London, Macmillan.

Seltzer, R. (2002) 'Science and politics, or on the irony of the term political science'. *Journal of Urban Health: Bulletin of the New York Academy of Medicine. Special Feature: Firearms and Violence* 79(1): 19-25.

Shapin, S. (1994) *A social history of truth: Civility and science in seventeenth-century England*. Chicago, IL, Chicago University Press.

Sheridan, A. (1981) *Michel Foucault: The will to truth*. London, Tavistock Publications.

Shore, C., Wright, S. (1997) 'Policy: a new field of anthropology', in Shore, C., Wright, S. (eds) *Anthropology of policy: Critical perspectives on governance and power* (pp 3-39). London, Routledge.

Simon, H.A. (1947) *Administrative behavior*. New York, Macmillan.

Simon, H.A. (1957) *Models of man: Social and rational*. New York, Wiley.

Simon, H.A. (1973) 'The structure of ill structured problems'. *Artificial Intelligence* 4: 181-201.

Simon, H.A. (1992 [1st ed. 1969]) *Sciences of the artificial*. Cambridge, MA, MIT Press.

Sismondo, S. (2004) *An introduction to science and technology studies*. Oxford, Blackwell Publishing.

Sivan, E. (1995) 'The enclave culture', in Marty, M.M. (ed) *Fundamentalism comprehended*. Chicago, IL, Chicago University Press.

Skocpol, T. (1992) *Protecting soldiers and mothers: The political origins of social policy in the United States*. Cambridge, MA, Harvard University Press.

Smith, K.B. (2002) 'Typologies, taxonomies, and the benefits of policy classification'. *Policy Studies Journal* 30(3): 379-95.

Sniderman, P.M., Brody, R.A., Tetlock, P.E. (eds) (1991) *Reasoning and choice: Explorations in political psychology*. Cambridge, Cambridge University Press.

Sørensen, E., Torfing, J. (2005) 'The democratic anchorage of governance networks'. *Scandinavian Political Studies* 28(3): 195-218.

Spaargaren, G., Mol, A.P.J. (2008) 'Greening global consumption: redefining politics and authority'. *Global Environmental Change* 18: 350-59.

Spector, M., Kitsuse, J.I. (1977) *Constructing social problems*. Menlo Park, Cummings.

Spitzer, R.J. (1995) *The politics of gun control*. Chatham, NJ, Chatham House.

Stacey, R.D. (1996) *Strategic management and organizational dynamics*. London, Financial Times Pitman.

Stankey, G.H., Clark, R.N., Bormann, B.J. (2005) *Adaptive management of natural resources: Theories, methods, concepts, and management institutions*. Portland. USDA, Forest Service Pacific Northwest Research Station.

Steel, B., List, P., Lach, D., Shindler, B. (2004) 'The role of scientists in the environmental policy process: a case study from the American west'. *Environmental Science Policy* 7: 1–13.

Steinberger, P.J. (1995 [1980]) 'Typologies of public policy: meaning construction and the policy process', in McCool, D.C. (ed) *Public policy theories, models, and concepts: An anthology* (pp 220–33). Upper Saddle River, NJ, Prentice Hall.

Steinbrunner, J.D. (1974) *The cybernetic theory of decision: New dimensions of political analysis.* Princeton, NJ, Princeton University Press.

Steiner, J., Bächtiger, A., Spörndli, M., Steenbergen, M.R. (2004) *Deliberative politics in action: Analysing parliamentary discourse.* Cambridge, Cambridge University Press.

Stemerding, D., Van Berkel, D. (2001) 'Maternal serum screening, political decision-making and social learning'. *Health Policy* 56: 111–15.

Stirling, A. (2006) 'Analysis, power and participation: justification and closure in participatory multi-criteria analysis'. *Land Use Policy* 23: 95–107.

Stolle, D., Hooghe, M. (2004) 'Review article: inaccurate, exceptional, one-sided or irrelevant? The debate about the alleged decline of social capital and civic engagement in Western societies'. *British Journal of Political Science* 35: 149–67.

Stone, D. (1997 [1st ed. 1988]) *Policy paradox: the art of political decision making.* New York and London, W.W. Norton & Company.

Strassheim, H. (2007) 'Kulturen der Expertise und politischen Wissenproduktion im Wandel: vergleichende Beobachtungen', in Gosewinkel, D., Schuppert, G.F. (eds) *Politische Kultur im Wandel von Staatlichkeit* (pp 281–301). Berlin, edition sigma.

Streeck, W., Thelen, K. (2005) *Beyond continuity: Institutional change in advanced political economies.* Oxford, Oxford University Press.

Swierstra, T. (2000) *Kloneren in de Polder.* The Hague, Rathenau Instituut.

't Hart, P., Wille, A.C. F.M. van der Meer, R.A. Boin, G.S.A. Dijkstra, W.J. van Noort en M. Zannoni et al (eds) (2002) *Politiek-ambtelijke verhoudingen in beweging.* Amsterdam, Boom.

Tetlock, P.E. (1997) 'An alternative metaphor in the study of judgment and choice: people as politicians', in Goldstein, W.M., Hogarth, R.M. (eds) *Research on judgment and decision making: Currents, connections, and controversies* (pp 657–80). Cambridge, Cambridge University Press.

Thelen, K. (2003) 'How institutions evolve: insights from comparative historical analysis', Mahoney, J., Rueschemeyer, D. (eds) *Comparative historical analysis in the social sciences* (pp 208–40). Cambridge, Cambridge University Press.

Thomas, J.C. (1990) 'Public involvement in public management: adapting and testing a borrowed theory'. *Public Administration Review* 50(4): 435–45.

Thomassen, J.A.A. (eds) (1991) *Hedendaagse democratie.* Alphen aan den Rijn, Samsom H.D. Tjeenk Willink.

Thompson, M., Ellis, R., Wildavsky, A. (1990) *Cultural theory.* Boulder, CO, Westview Press.

Thompson, M., Wildavsky, A. (1986) 'A cultural theory of information bias in organizations'. *Journal of Management Studies* 23(3): 273–86.

Thompson, M. (1996) Inherent Relationality. An Anti–Dualist Approach to Institutions. LOS Report 9608, Bergen

Thompson, M., Grendstad, G., and Selle, P. (eds.) (1999) *Cultural Theory as Political Science*. London: Routledge

Thompson, T.J., Tuden, A. (1959) 'Strategies, structures and processes of organizational decisions', in Thompson, J. D., and J. Woodward (eds.) *Comparative studies in administration*. Pittsburgh, PA, University of Pittsburgh Press.

Throgmorton, J.A. (1991) 'The rhetorics of policy analysis'. *Policy Sciences* 24: 153-79.

Timmermans, A., Scholten, P. (2006) 'The political flow of wisdom: science institutions as policy venues in the Netherlands'. *Journal of European Public Policy* 13(7): 1104-18.

TNLI (1997) Toekomst Nationale Luchthaven Integrale Beleidsvisie. Perspectievennota 'Hoeveel ruimte geeft Nederland aan de luchtvaart. Integrale beleidsvisie'. Den Haag, SDU.

Tompkins, E.L. (2003) *Using stakeholder preferences in multi-attribute decision-making: Elicitation and aggregation issues*. Working Paper ECM-03-13. University of EastAnglia, Norwich, Centre for Social and Economic Research on the Global Environment (CSERGE) 20.

Torgerson, D. (1986) 'Between knowledge and politics: three faces of policy analysis'. *Policy Sciences* 19: 33-59.

Torgerson, D. (1995) 'Policy analysis and public life: the restoration of phronesis?', in Farr, J., Dryzek, J.S., Leonard, S.T. (eds) *Political science in history: Research programs and political traditions* (pp 225-52). Cambridge, Cambridge University Press.

Torgerson, D.J. (2007) 'Promoting the policy orientation: Lasswell in context', in Fischer, F., Miller, G.J., Sidney, M.S. (eds) *Handbook of public policy analysis* (pp 15-28). Boca Raton, CFC Press Francis & Taylor Group.

Trappenburg, M. (2005) *Gezondheidszorg en democratie*. Rotterdam, Oratiereeks Erasmus MC.

Tribe, L.H. (1972) 'Policy science: analysis or ideology?'. *Philosophy and Public Affairs* 2(1): 66-110.

Turnbull, N. (2005) 'Policy in question: From problem solving to problematology' PhD thesis. Sydney, University of New South Wales.

Turnhout, E. (2003) *Ecological indicators in Dutch nature conservation: Science and nature intertwined in the classification and evaluation of nature*. Amsterdam, Aksant.

Unger, R.M. (1987) *Social theory: Its situation and its task*. Cambridge, Cambridge University Press.

Van Asselt, M. (2000) *Perspectives on uncertainty and risk: The PRIMA approach to decision support*. Dordrecht, Kluwer Academic Publishers.

Van Buuren, M.W., Edelenbos, J. (2004) 'Conflicting knowledge: why is knowledge production such a problem'. *Science and Public Policy* 31(4): 289-99.

Van Coppenolle, D. (2006) 'De ambtelijke beleidsvormingsrol verkend en getoetst in meervoudig vergelijkend perspectief: een two-level analyse van de rol van Vlaamse ambtenaren in Vlaamse beleidsvorming'. PhD thesis. Instituut voor de Overheid, Faculteit Sociale Wetenschappen, Catholic University Leuven.

Van de Donk, W., Snellen, I.T.M., Tops, P.W. (eds) (1995) *Orwell in Athens: A perspective on informatization and democracy*. Amsterdam, IOS Press.

Van de Graaf, H., Hoppe, R. (1989 [1992, 1996]) *Beleid en Politiek: Een Inleiding tot de Beleidswetenschap en de Beleidskunde*. Muiderberg, Coutinho.

Van de Graaf, H., Hoppe, R. (1996, 3rd edition) *Beleid en Politiek*. Bussum, Coutinho.

Van der Heijden, J. (ed.) (2005) *Recombinatie van Overheid en Samenleving. Denken over Innovatie in Beleidsvorming*. Delft, Eburon

Van der Sluys, J.P. (1997) 'Anchoring amid uncertainty: on the management of uncertainties in risk assessment of anthropogenic climate change'. PhD Thesis. University of Leiden).

J. van der Sluijs, J. R., P. Kloprogge, J. Ravetz, S. Funtowicz, S. Corral Quintana, A.G. Pereira, B. de Marchi, A. Petersen, P. Janssen, R. Hoppe, S. Huijs (2003). *A leidraad for uncertainty scanning and assessment at RIVM*. Utrecht, Copernicus Institute for Sustainable Development and Innovation, Universiteit Utrech.

Van Ecker, E. (1997) 'New gun laws', in Prasser, S., Starr, G. (eds) *Policy and change: The Howard mandate* (pp 182-91). Sydney, Hale and Iremonger.

Van Eeten, M. (1999) *Dialogues of the deaf: Defining new agendas for environmental deadlocks*. Delft, Eburon.

Van Eeten, M.J.G. (2001) 'Recasting intractable policy issues: the wider implications of the Netherlands civil aviation controversy'. *Journal of Policy Analysis and Management* 20(3): 391-414.

Van Gunsteren, H. (nd) *Regimes and cultures*. Leiden, University of Leiden: 14 pages. (unpublished research paper)

Van Stokkom, B. (2005) 'Deliberative group dynamics: power, status, and affect in interactive policy making'. *Policy & Politics* 33(3): 387-409.

Van Stokkom, B. (2006) *Rituelen van beraadslaging: Reflecties over burgerberaad en burgerbestuur*. Amsterdam, Amsterdam University Press.

Vergragt, P.J. (1988) 'The social shaping of technological innovations'. *Social Study of Sciences* 18(3): 483-513.

Vig, N.J., Paschen, H. (eds) (2000) *Parliaments and technology: The development of technology assessment in Europe*. Albany, NY, State University of New York Press.

Visser, J., Hemerijck, A. (1997) *'A Dutch miracle': Job growth, welfare, and corporatism in The Netherlands*. Amsterdam, Amsterdam University Press.

Vizzard, W.J. (1995) 'The impact of agenda conflict on policy formulation and implementation: the case of gun control'. *Public Administration Review* 55(4): 341-7.

Wagner, P. (1994) *A sociology of modernity: Liberty and discipline*. London, Routledge.

Wagner, P. (2001) *A history and theory of the social sciences*. London, Sage Publications.

Wagner, P. (2007) 'Public policy, social science, and the state: a historical perspective', in Fischer, F., Miller, G., Sidney, M. (eds) *Handbook of public policy analysis: Theory, politics and methods* (pp 29-40). Boca Raton, London, New York, CRC Press Taylor & Francis Group.

Wagner, P., Weiss, C., Wittrock, B., Wollmann, H. (eds) (1991) *Social science and modern states: National experiences and theoretical crossroads*. Cambridge, Cambridge University Press.

Wälti, S., Kübler. D. (2003) '"New governance" and associative pluralism: the case of drug policy in Swiss cities'. *Policy Studies Journal* 31(4): 499-525.

Watzlawick, P., Weakland, J.H., Fisch, R. (1974) *Change: Principles of problem formation and problem resolution*. New York, W.W. Norton.

Webber, D.J. (1992) 'The distribution and use of knowledge in the policy process', in Dunn, W.N., Kelly, R.M. (eds) *Advances in policy studies since 1950* (pp 383-418). New Brunswick, NJ and London, Transaction Publishers.

Weimer, D.L., Vining, A.R. (1999) *Policy analysis: Concepts and practice* (3rd edition). Englewood Cliffs, NJ, Prentice-Hall.

Weinberg, A.M. (1972) 'Science and trans-science'. *Minerva* 10: 209-22.

Weingart, P. (1983) 'Verwissenschaftlichung der Gesellschaft - Politisierung der Wissenschaft'. *Zeitschrift fur Soziologie* 12(3): 225-41.

Weiss, C.H. (1980) 'Knowledge creep and decision accretion'. *Knowledge* 1(3): 381-404.

Weiss, C.H. (1991) 'Policy research: data, ideas, or arguments?', in Wagner, P.A. et al (eds) *Social sciences and modern states: National experiments and theoretical crossroads* (pp 307-32). Cambridge, Cambridge University Press.

West, W.F. (1988) 'The growth of internal conflict in administrative regulation'. *Public Administration Review* 48(4): 773-82.

West, W.F. (2005) 'The institutionalization of regulatory review: organizational stability and responsive competence at OIRA'. *Presidential Studies Quarterly* 31(1): 76-93.

Wikipedia (2009) Ramòn Barros Luco (accessed July 2009, http://en.wikipedia.org/wiki/Ram%C3%B3n_Barros_Luco)

Wildavsky, A. (1980 [1979]) *The art and craft of policy analysis*. London and Basingstoke, Macmillan Press.

Wildavsky, A. (1987) 'Choosing preferences by constructing institutions: a cultural theory of preference formation', *American Political Science Review*, 81, 1, 3-21

Wildavsky, A. (1988) *The new politics of the budgetary process*. Glenview, Scott, Foresman.

Williams, B. (1980) 'Review of J. Elster's *Logic and society* (1978), and *Ulysses and the Sirens* (1979)'. *London Review of Books* 2(8).

Williams, W. (1998) *Honest numbers and democracy: Social policy analysis in the White House, Congress, and the federal agencies*. Washington, DC, Georgetown University Press.

Williamson, A., Fung, A. (2004) 'Public deliberation: where we are and where can we go?'. *National Civic Review* (winter): 3-15.

Wilson, J.Q. (1989) *Bureaucracy: What government agencies do and why they do it.* London, Basic Books.

Wittrock, B. (1991) 'Social knowledge and public policy: eight models of interaction', in Wagner, P., Weiss, C., Wittrock, B., Wollmann, H. (eds) *Social science and modern states: National experiences and theoretical crossroads* (pp 333-53). Cambridge, Cambridge University Press.

Wolf, A. (1997) The Roles and Value Orientations of Policy Professionals in New Zealand, School of Business and Public Management, Victoria University of Wellington: 15pp. (unpublished research report)

Wrong, D. (1979) *Power.* New York, Harper & Row

WRR (Wetenschappelijke Raad voor het Regeringsbeleid) (2006) *Lerende overheid: Een pleidooi voor probleemgerichte politiek.* Den Haag/Amsterdam, WRR/Amsterdam University Press.

Yankelovich, D. (1991) *Coming to public judgment: making democracy work in a complex world.* Syracuse, NY, Syracuse University Press.

Yanow, D. (1996) *How does a policy mean? Interpreting policy and organizational actions.* Washington DC, Georgetown University Press.

Yanow, D. (1999) *Conducting interpretive policy analysis.* Thousand Oaks, CA, Sage Publications

Yearley, S. (1988) *Science, technology, and social change.* London, Unwin Hyman.

Yearley, S. (2001) 'Mapping and interpeting societal responses to genetically modified crops and food'. *Social Studies of Science* 31 (1): 151-60.

Zahariadis, N. (2003) *Ambiguity & choice in public policy: Political decision making in modern democracies.* Washington, DC, Georgetown University Press.

Ziman, J. (2000) *Real science: What it is, and what it means.* Cambridge, Cambridge University Press.

Ziman, J.M. (1999) 'What is happening to science?', in Cozzens, S.E., Healy, P., Rip, A., Ziman, J.M. (eds) *The research system in transition* (pp 23-33). Dordrecht, Kluwer Academic.

Index

Page references for notes are followed by n